Can Nations Agree?

Studies in International Economics

TITLES PUBLISHED

Can Nations Agree?

Issues in International Economic Cooperation

RICHARD N. COOPER

BARRY EICHENGREEN

C. RANDALL HENNING

GERALD HOLTHAM

ROBERT D. PUTNAM

The Brookings Institution
Washington, D.C.

Copyright © 1989 by

THE BROOKINGS INSTITUTION

1775 Massachusetts Avenue, N.W., Washington, D.C. 20036

Library of Congress Cataloging-in-Publication Data

Can nations agree? : issues in international economic cooperation
  Richard N. Cooper . . . [et al.].
      p.   cm.—(Studies in international economics)
    Includes index.
  ISBN 0-8157-1178-6 (alk. paper).
    1. International economic relations.   I. Cooper, Richard N.
II. Series: Studies in international economics (Washington, D.C.)
HF1359.C36   1989
337—dc20   89-32702
                                                            CIP

9 8 7 6 5 4 3 2 1

The paper used in this publication meets the minimum requirements of the American National Standard for Information Sciences—Permanence of Paper
for Printed Library Materials, ANSI Z39.48-1984.

Set in Linotype Walbaum
Composition by Graphic Composition, Inc.
  Athens, Georgia
Printing by R. R. Donnelley and Sons, Co.
  Harrisonburg, Virginia
Book design by Ken Sabol
Cover design by Richard Hendel

ℬ THE BROOKINGS INSTITUTION

The Brookings Institution is an independent organization devoted to nonpartisan research, education, and publication in economics, government, foreign policy, and the social sciences generally. Its principal purposes are to aid in the development of sound public policies and to promote public understanding of issues of national importance.

The Institution was founded on December 8, 1927, to merge the activities of the Institute for Government Research, founded in 1916, the Institute of Economics, founded in 1922, and the Robert Brookings Graduate School of Economics and Government, founded in 1924.

The Board of Trustees is responsible for the general administration of the Institution, while the immediate direction of the policies, program, and staff is vested in the President, assisted by an advisory committee of the officers and staff. The by-laws of the Institution state: "It is the function of the Trustees to make possible the conduct of scientific research, and publication, under the most favorable conditions, and to safeguard the independence of the research staff in the pursuit of their studies and in the publication of the results of such studies. It is not a part of their function to determine, control, or influence the conduct of particular investigations or the conclusions reached."

The President bears final responsibility for the decision to publish a manuscript as a Brookings book. In reaching his judgment on the competence, accuracy, and objectivity of each study, the President is advised by the director of the appropriate research program and weighs the views of a panel of expert outside readers who report to him in confidence on the quality of the work. Publication of a work signifies that it is deemed a competent treatment worthy of public consideration but does not imply endorsement of conclusions or recommendations.

The Institution maintains its position of neutrality on issues of public policy in order to safeguard the intellectual freedom of the staff. Hence interpretations or conclusions in Brookings publications should be understood to be solely those of the authors and should not be attributed to the Institution, to its trustees, officers, or other staff members, or to the organizations that support its research.

Foreword

Economic and political theorists have argued for cooperation among governments in the framing of their individual national policies. Yet history and theory have shown that the obstacles to cooperation are formidable. Examples of effective cooperation seem to be greatly outnumbered by instances in which governments failed to cooperate to foster mutual interest.

The research programs in Economic Studies and Foreign Policy Studies at the Brookings Institution have for many years encouraged analysis of the potential gains from international cooperation and the obstacles that impede it. All four of the essays in this book reflect this long-standing Brookings research interest. Two of the studies—one by Robert Putnam and Randall Henning and one by Gerald Holtham—focus on the economic summit meeting held in July 1978 in Bonn, Germany, which is widely regarded as the most important recent example of international economic cooperation. The essay by Richard Cooper examines the history of international efforts to control the spread of contagious diseases as a means of gaining insights into how modern efforts toward economic cooperation can be made more effective. Barry Eichengreen's study evaluates several episodes in the history of the international monetary system to analyze how differing conditions and institutional structures can influence the prospects for monetary cooperation.

These essays were originally commissioned as separate studies. The four are published here together because of the similar themes they address and the interrelated insights they offer. An introduction by Ralph Bryant and Edith Hodgkinson emphasizes the complementary nature of the problems and issues discussed in the four essays.

Ralph C. Bryant is a senior fellow in the Economic Studies program at Brookings. Richard N. Cooper is Maurits C. Boas Professor of International Economics at Harvard University. Barry Eichengreen is professor of economics at the University of California, Berkeley. Edith

Hodgkinson is a consultant and editor based in London, England. Gerald Holtham is senior economist with Shearson Lehman Hutton Securities in London. Robert D. Putnam is dean of the John F. Kennedy School of Government at Harvard University. C. Randall Henning is a research associate at the Institute for International Economics.

In addition to the assistance the individual authors acknowledge in their essays, several people contributed to the overall project. Evelyn Taylor assisted with administrative aspects of the studies. Nancy Davidson edited the manuscripts. Victor M. Alfaro and Anna M. Nekoranec verified the factual content, and Diana Regenthal prepared the index.

The studies received generous financial support from the National Science Foundation and the Ford Foundation.

The views expressed in the essays are those of the authors and should be not attributed to the authors' institutions or to the officers, trustees, or other staff members of the Brookings Institution.

BRUCE K. MAC LAURY
President

April 1989
Washington, D.C.

Contents

Can Nations Agree?

Problems of International Cooperation

RALPH C. BRYANT & EDITH HODGKINSON

INTERDEPENDENCE between nation states is not new. Transactions of many forms have taken place across borders throughout recorded history, and national governments of whatever kind have always had to bear in mind the cross-border effects of their own, and other's, policies and actions. Cooperation with other governments could more rapidly and easily achieve desired objectives—for example, the containment of piracy—than could unilateral action. In some areas cooperation was essential—for example, the suppression of smuggling and other illegal trade. Nations have therefore long recognized the value of cooperation in an interdependent world. This book examines the conditions that promote, and inhibit, such cooperation in the economic sphere.

In recent decades—since the end of World War II—interdependence has become more intense and the need to cooperate more urgent. Cross-border economic transactions have grown much more rapidly than overall economic activity, as advances in transport and communications technology have extended the scope for integrating economic activity and reduced its difficulty and relative cost. At the same time, economic expansion and technological development have opened new areas of interdependence—for example, and preeminently, pollution of the global environment. In the age of Three Mile Island and Chernobyl, of a new international trade in industrial and human waste, of the depletion of the ozone layer and the emergence of the greenhouse effect, the fact of interdependence and the urgency of international cooperation are supremely evident. There has been an increase in both the number and the significance of the problems that can be solved only through international agreement. This is also true in the more narrowly economic sphere, where the problems include speculative instability in financial and primary-commodities markets, competition in tax regimes, and greatly enhanced scope for tax evasion.

Recent decades have also been characterized by a rapid rise in the number of decisionmaking units, as the breakup of the European colonial empires has brought onto the scene many new nation-states jealous of their newly won independence. Thus on the one hand there is increased pressure to strengthen intergovernmental cooperation and international institutions so that national governments can identify their common goals and the means to achieve them; but, on the other, increased political pluralism and national self-awareness mean that there are more units to bring together and more, and sometimes stronger, national interests to reconcile. At the same time, the political and economic hegemony of the United States, which was at its height at the end of World War II, has gradually declined as its share of world economic activity has fallen from a third or more just after the war to just under a quarter in the 1980s. The dominance of the United States remains, but its economic power is now smaller relative to other successful capitalist countries like Japan and West Germany.

Can nations agree in such a world? What are the conditions that foster cooperation toward goals that are held in common? How can the friction arising from conflicting goals best be handled? Do certain structures work better than others to promote cooperation? Each of the four essays in this book addresses one or more aspects of these basic questions.

The 1978 Bonn Economic Summit

The economic summit held in Bonn, Germany, in July 1978 was heralded as a paradigmatic case of international economic cooperation. It is still regarded by many observers as the one summit meeting (of the series that began in 1978) that produced genuine changes in the policies of the participating countries. Because of its presumed qualitative differences from other economic summits, the 1978 Bonn summit is a particularly interesting case study of international economic cooperation; many would even regard it as the most important example in recent decades of international economic policy "coordination."[1] Two of the four essays in this book analyze that historical episode.

Robert D. Putnam and C. Randall Henning provide a detailed account of the events leading up to the 1978 summit and the bargaining that produced the eventual agreement. Their essay, "The Bonn Summit of 1978: A Case Study in Coordination," is based on extensive interviews with the summit participants and careful combing of the documentary evidence.[2] In an earlier book, Putnam and Nicholas Bayne had studied the entire process of economic summit meetings.[3] This new essay amplifies and deepens the earlier analysis.

The Putnam-Henning essay makes two different types of contributions to the understanding of international cooperation. First, it provides a careful account of what happened at the Bonn 1978 summit and why. For example, the authors explain how the summit accord came to include commitments on energy and trade policies as well as macroeconomics (what they term a "synergistic" linkage across issues). The raw material of the history has been ordered and interpreted, but many significant details have also been included in the account. Even readers with a different conceptual frame of reference from that of the authors can use the study to extract their own lessons from this episode.

Second, and at least equally important, Putnam and Henning use their case study of the 1978 summit to develop more general views about the conditions that foster—and those that inhibit—intergovernmental cooperation. In doing so, the authors, who are thoughtful readers of the economics literature but not economists themselves, challenge some of the recent theoretical preoccupations of economists trying to analyze intergovernmental consultations and negotiations. Putnam and Henning forcefully argue that economists have devoted too much attention to such problems as possible "cheating" in international economic diplomacy and have paid too little attention to the pluralism of authority and responsibility within individual national governments.

One of the provocative conclusions in Putnam and Henning's essay is that the 1978 summit accord was possible only because each of the major governments was internally divided. They show that international pressures were effective in catalyzing an agreement because those pressures were exploited by influential *minority* factions within each government. In Putnam and Henning's view, an analysis of the pattern of domestic and transnational alignments and of domestic decisionmaking processes is not merely a subsidiary filling-in of the details about international negotiations, but rather is a crucial element in understanding whether and when international agreements are possible.

Many observers believe that the 1978 summit was a constructive effort by the major governments to adopt a coordinated package of policy adjustments that would be mutually beneficial. Other observers, however, notably many critics in Germany, believe that the decisions reached at the 1978 summit were mistaken. Numerous German commentators, for example, have blamed Germany's inflation in 1979–80 on the expansionary fiscal actions agreed on at the 1978 summit.

This is the issue taken up in the second essay in this book, "German Macroeconomic Policy and the 1978 Bonn Summit," by Gerald Holtham. The essay focuses on the fiscal and monetary measures adopted by Germany following the Bonn summit and their effect on the German economy. It argues that the tax changes were broadly consistent with German fiscal policies pursued during the 1970s, and it was their scale and timing that was affected by the summit, rather than whether they were introduced. Holtham concludes that the fiscal measures agreed on at Bonn had little effect on inflation or the current payments balance, and that it was the second oil shock, in 1979, that was responsible for the "crisis" of 1980–81. Subsequent negative assessments of the Bonn summit have not been based on careful analysis of the consequences. In any case, the criticisms are not, strictly speaking, an attack on economic policy coordination. Rather they are directed at a whole era of German macroeconomic policies that have now fallen out of favor and that the Bonn measures typified. At the time, the agreement was regarded by all parties as mutually beneficial. Changes that were unforeseeable ex ante—in oil prices and in economic priorities—do not invalidate the effort to coordinate economic policy.

International Cooperation in Public Health

Putnam and Henning and Holtham study one recent, specific agreement among the major industrial nations and extract from that episode some general insights about intergovernmental cooperation in macroeconomic management. But can one also draw lessons from efforts at cooperation outside the economic sphere? The third essay in the book, "International Cooperation in Public Health as a Prologue to Macroeconomic Cooperation," by Richard N. Cooper, broadens the scope of inquiry by examining what is, to date, one of the most successful cases of international cooperation—so successful that it is now taken for granted. His essay examines international efforts during the nineteenth and early twentieth centuries to control the spread of contagious diseases.[4] A problem that transcended national borders was tackled, and in the case of smallpox resolved, through international cooperation. Yet an objective that seems to contemporary observers uncontroversial—clearly in the interests of all nations, and hence easily attainable—was not achieved easily or rapidly. Cooper's essay traces the evolution from the first call for international cooperation in controlling disease to the first steps taken in that direction more than half a century later, to the development of an organizational structure another half century on. He shows the interplay between events (epidemics), government responses to them, the evolution of professional opinion, and the various interests affected, political and economic, and draws a conclusion that is of relevance to international economic policy coordination in the late twentieth century. In his view, governments are likely to forge an agreement for dealing with a problem only after they—or the community of relevant professional analysts—have reached consensus in diagnosing the problem and identifying measures that will alleviate it. Consensus on an appropriate analytical framework, as well as on the objective to be pursued, is a necessary (although not sufficient) condition for successful negotiations.

Hegemony and Stability

What other conditions promote international economic cooperation? Barry Eichengreen, in the final essay, "Hegemonic Stability Theories of the International Monetary System," explores the view, put forward by specialists in international relations, that dominance by a single country—a hegemonic power—is most conducive to the smooth functioning of an international regime.[5] According to this view, the hegemon will act to ensure compliance with the rules of a system that embodies its dominance, either through positive incentives (for example, by serving as lender of last resort) or through deterrence (the threat of retaliation through its economic policies). In this way the system is kept stable.

Eichengreen looks at three incarnations of the modern international monetary system—the classical gold standard, the interwar gold exchange standard, and the Bretton Woods system. These offer two examples of hegemony (the United Kingdom in the first, the United States in the third) and one in which there is no hegemon (the interwar period). The author argues that, although one cannot reject the hypothesis that concentration of economic power contributes to the stability and smooth functioning of the international monetary system, a system predicated on the existence of a hegemon may be dynamically unstable. The three episodes in the history of the international monetary system would suggest that the hegemon's willingness to act to stabilize the system during one period tends to undermine its continued capacity to do so over time.

The Likely Future: Further Ferment and Controversy

In the 1980s, national governments have often publicly acknowledged, sometimes in ringing declarations, that their own economies are interdependent with those of other nations. They have also acknowledged that, this being the case, international cooperation is desirable when it enables them to identify and implement policies that further their objectives. The rhetoric favoring international cooperation has been impressive. Nonetheless, genuine progress—especially toward explicit coordination—remains highly uncertain.

International cooperation, and even coordination, are not synonyms for amity or altruism. Cooperation and coordination do not require that national governments have common goals, that all their goals are compatible, or that some governments must sacrifice their own goals in deference to the goals of others. With some exceptions, goals are not identical among nations. Inevitably, each government gives primacy to the welfare of its own citizens. Cooperation and coordination merely imply the self-interested mutual adjustment of behavior. The potential for large gains from cooperation in all its forms may well be greatest when goals are inconsistent and discord is high.

Notwithstanding the preceding truism, the achievement of international cooperation, and even more its sustainability, is more difficult when certain national goals are directly incompatible. For example, an effort by each nation to attain a surplus in the current account of its balance of payments would inevitably fail for some nations. In an environment of worldwide inflation, all nations could not simultaneously encourage disinflation by fostering appreciation of the national currency. Attempts to do individually what is impossible collectively are bound to lead to frustration and, possibly, outcomes for some or all nations that are inferior to those attainable through collective action. The channels of communication between national governments, both bilateral and multilateral, must be such as to identify direct incompatibilities in objectives and to facilitate their reconciliation. For successful cooperation, moreover, there must also be agreement on how reconciled objectives can be achieved.

The consensus that exists in, for example, the area of epidemic control is very far from being achieved in macroeconomics. Moreover, there are influential strains of thinking that are critical of economic cooperation in itself. Thoughtful economists have argued that efforts to cooperate, especially in the ambitious form of coordination, can divert national governments' attention away from concerns with higher priority—sometimes even providing a smokescreen, enabling a government to blame foreigners for inaction rather than taking responsible action itself.[6] Some adherents of a "public choice" view emphasize that governments are organizations with interests of their own that are different from, and potentially inimical to, those of general populations. Consequently the desirability of national governments' "colluding" comes into question, and a degree of intergovernmental competition, rather than coordination, can be seen as more likely to serve the interests of general populations. For example, the alleged inflationist tendencies of elected politicians may be kept in check, it is argued, by the threat of a spiraling depreciation of the currency if other governments are pursuing sound money policies—whereas coordination could remove this discipline.[7]

In practice a judgment has to be made about which is the greater danger: that, in the absence of cooperation between governments, international interaction will work to the detriment of public policy (with public policy representing the public purpose, albeit imperfectly); or, alternatively, that collusion between governments will work against the public interest. The underlying premise of the essays in this book, and of many other recent contributions to the economics literature, is that, on the whole, cooperation between governments, particularly democratic governments, can be plausibly expected to further the collective interests of their people.[8]

Even those individuals who regard it as desirable that national governments try to cooperate and coordinate acknowledge that such efforts may not be feasible. As suggested in Richard Cooper's essay, governments may be unable to reach agreements without further convergence of analytical views about the cross-border effects of national policies. Without more analytical consensus, furthermore, any agreement reached might rest on an inadequate technical base and therefore prove fragile and unsustainable. Uncertainty about how the world economy functions (sometimes referred to as "model uncertainty") may well pose the single greatest challenge to the feasibility of international cooperation.

Because of this uncertainty, disagreements arise even among proponents of international cooperation. For example, one view is that cooperating governments should not aspire to coordination per se. Uncertainty about the appropriate analytical framework could, despite their good intentions, cause them to make mistakes.[9] Moreover, attempts to achieve one-of-a-kind agreements in response to specific shocks to the world economy (the Bonn summit of 1978 may be viewed as an extended example of such coordination agreements) entail considerable transaction costs in time and effort and, perhaps, political credit. Such costs can make one-time agreements unattractively expensive, especially in a world where conditions and policy priorities are volatile. A more cost-effective and durable form of agreement, it is contended, is likely to be one that sets the framework for cooperation or establishes "rules of the game," which can substitute for coordination proper on specific, detailed targets.[10]

A second view acknowledges the difficulties of reaching and sustaining agreements on coordination per se but nonetheless tends to perceive better chances for a successful evolution of international cooperation along those lines than in trying to establish simplified rules of the game. Such rules, it is argued, tend to focus attention on only one or a few variables, presuming that such variables can be reliable surrogates for the true, ultimate objectives of policy. In practice, the surrogate targets can fail to serve as reliable guides for effective cooperation. Some noneconomists express skepticism about rules on political grounds. In their view, economists who advocate rules implicitly contrast rules drafted by angels (economists?) with discretionary, one-of-a-kind agreements forged by mortals (politicians?). A more balanced view, in their judgment, would acknowledge the dominant role of fallible politicians in all types of international negotiations and would doubt that transactions costs, obstacles, and expenditures of political credit are greater for one-time agreements than for (necessarily more far-reaching) rules. Finally, analysts inclined toward this second perspective tend not to regard the lack of consensus about the appropriate analytical framework as a valid justification for eschewing co-ordination and instead preferring simplified rules of the game. Even in the absence of a convergence of analytical views toward a consensus, they tend to favor discretionary efforts to achieve, and periodically to revise, coordination agreements—albeit with a cautious, evolutionary approach.[11]

On these issues about the feasibility of international cooperation, as about its fundamental desirability, intellectual ferment and disagreement are likely to continue. The venerable debate about rules versus discretion, which has so far been conducted essentially in domestic contexts, may gain a new lease on life from being extended into the international sphere. The essays in this volume can play a helpful role, we hope, in catalyzing this developing international debate.

Notes

1. "Cooperation" is best used to refer to the entire range of activities through which national governments might collaborate. "Coordination" refers to the more ambitious forms of cooperation in which governments mutually adjust their behavior after bargaining consultations. For discussion, see Ralph C. Bryant, "Intergovernmental Coordination of Economic Policies: An Interim Stocktaking," in *International Monetary Cooperation: Essays in Honor of Henry C. Wallich*, Princeton Essays in International Finance no. 169 (Princeton University, Department of Economics, December 1987), pp. 4–15; and Jocelyn Horne and Paul R. Masson, "Scope and Limits of International Economic Cooperation and Policy Coordination," *IMF Staff Papers*, vol. 35 (June 1988), pp. 259–96.

2. A first version of this essay was presented at a Brookings workshop on Intergovernmental Consultations and Cooperation about Macroeconomic Policies in April 1985. A subsequent revision, "The Bonn Summit of 1978: How Does International Economic Policy Coordination Actually Work?," was circulated in working paper form as Brookings Discussion Paper in International Economics no. 53 (October 1986).

3. Robert D. Putnam and Nicholas Bayne, *Hanging Together: Cooperation and Conflict in the Seven-Power Summits*, rev. ed. (Harvard University Press, 1987).

4. An earlier version of Cooper's essay was circulated in working paper form as Brookings Discussion Paper in International Economics no. 44 (March 1986).

5. This paper was first circulated in working paper form as Brookings Discussion Paper in International Economics no. 54 (February 1987).

6. For example, see Herbert Stein, "International Coordination of Economic Policy," *AEI Economist*, August 1987, pp. 1–7; W. Max Corden, "Fiscal

Policies, Current Accounts and Real Exchange Rates: In Search of a Logic of International Policy Coordination," *Weltwirtschaftliches Archiv*, Band 122, Heft 3 (1986), pp. 423–38; and Martin S. Feldstein, "Thinking about International Economic Coordination," *Journal of Economic Perspectives*, vol. 2 (Spring 1988), pp. 3–13.

7. James Buchanan is a noted expositor of the public choice view; see, for example, Geoffrey L. Brennan and James M. Buchanan, *The Power to Tax: Analytical Foundations of a Fiscal Constitution* (Cambridge University Press, 1980). Kenneth Rogoff, "Can International Monetary Policy Coordination Be Counterproductive?" *Journal of International Economics*, vol. 18 (May 1985), pp. 199–217, presents a theoretical model in which coordination among governments adversely influences economic welfare. See also Guido Tabellini, "Domestic Politics and the International Coordination of Fiscal Policies," working paper no. 226 (London: Centre for Economic Policy Research, January 1988).

8. For examples of other recent contributions that have regarded efforts at international economic cooperation as (on balance) desirable, see Jacob A. Frenkel, Morris Goldstein, and Paul R. Masson, "International Economic Policy Coordination: Rationale, Mechanisms, and Effects," in William Branson and others, eds., *International Policy Coordination and Exchange Rate Fluctuations* (University of Chicago Press for the National Bureau of Economic Research, forthcoming); Michael Artis and Sylvia Ostry, *International Economic Policy Coordination* (London: Routledge and Kegan Paul for the Royal Institute of International Affairs, 1986); and Bryant, "Intergovernmental Coordination of Economic Policies."

9. This possibility has been stressed by Jeffrey A. Frankel and Katharine E. Rockett, "International Macroeconomic Policy Coordination When Policymakers Do Not Agree on the True Model," *American Economic Review*, vol. 78 (June 1988), pp. 318–40; and Jeffrey A. Frankel, "Obstacles to International Macroeconomic Policy Coordination," *Princeton Studies in International Finance*, no. 64 (Princeton University, Department of Economics, December 1988).

10. Proposals for target zones for exchange rates emanate from this type of view. See John Williamson and Marcus H. Miller, *Targets and Indicators: A Blueprint for the International Coordination of Economic Policy*, Policy Analyses in International Economics no. 22 (Washington: Institute for International Economics, September 1987); and David Currie, Gerald Holtham, and Andrew Hughes Hallett, "The Theory and Practice of International Economic Policy Coordination: Does Coordination Pay?" paper prepared for a conference on Macroeconomic Policies in an Interdependent World, December 1988.

11. On the implications of uncertainty about the appropriate analytical framework, see Atish R. Ghosh and Paul R. Masson, "International Policy Coordination in a World with Model Uncertainty," *IMF Staff Papers*, vol. 35 (June 1988), pp. 230–58. The contrast between the two points of view about the feasibility of coordination is illustrated by Frankel's advocacy of internationally agreed target rates of growth for nominal domestic demand and

Bryant's sketch of a "first best" evolutionary approach emphasizing discretionary coordination: Jeffrey A. Frankel, "An Analysis of the Proposal for International Nominal Targeting (INT)," and Ralph C. Bryant, "Comment," in Branson and others, eds. *International Policy Coordination and Exchange Rate Fluctuations*.

The Bonn Summit of 1978:
A Case Study in Coordination

ROBERT D. PUTNAM & C. RANDALL HENNING

THE CONTOURS OF Western economic diplomacy during 1976–79 are strikingly parallel to those in the middle and late 1980s. In both cases a strong American recovery served for several years as a powerful locomotive for global growth but then began to show serious signs of strain. In both cases record U.S. trade deficits fueled demands for protection, despite a plummeting dollar. In both cases severe international monetary instability caused growing concern, first abroad and then in America. In both cases talks for a new round of trade liberalization under the General Agreement on Tariffs and Trade had begun but showed no signs of early progress. In both cases the U.S. administration faced severe criticism at home and abroad for economic indiscipline, and the administration replied that the primary obstacle was congressional obstructionism. Believing in both cases that an important part of the solution to American difficulties lay in faster growth abroad, particularly in Germany and Japan, the American administration mounted a vocal campaign to pressure those two countries to reduce their trade surpluses by stimulating additional growth in domestic demand. In both cases Tokyo and Bonn initially feared the effects of the declining U.S. dollar on their trade and monetary positions and resisted risking more rapid growth on their own.

In our research on the history of Western economic diplomacy between 1976 and 1979 we have benefited from the assistance and counsel of many generous individuals and institutions. To list them risks inadvertent omission, but we would be remiss not to mention Nicholas Bayne, Benjamin J. Cohen, Richard N. Cooper, Stuart Eizenstat, Edith Hodgkinson, Robert O. Keohane, Horst Schulmann, Margot Singer; the Atlantic Institute for International Affairs, Harvard's Center for International Affairs, the Institute for International Economics, the Deutsche Gesellschaft für Auswaertige Politik, the Social Science Research Council; the several dozen thoughtful scholar-critics who took part in the Brookings Institution Workshop on Intergovernmental Consultations and Cooperation about Macroeconomic Policies, April 16, 1985; the hundreds of participants in, and close observers of, Western economic diplomacy who have spoken generously and candidly with us about these events; and, above all, Ralph Bryant, whose idea this book was.

Of course there are some significant economic and political differences between the 1970s and 1980s. In the 1980s worries about developing country debt have replaced concerns about energy prices and supply on the global agenda. In the 1980s the American domestic impasse has concerned the fiscal deficit rather than energy. Finally, in the 1980s the trade and fiscal imbalances and the protectionist pressures in America have been considerably worse. The most important difference between the 1970s and the 1980s is that in the earlier case—but *not* in the more recent one—the major Western nations achieved a substantial degree of multilateral policy coordination.[1] To be sure, controlled experiments are impossible in the international political economy, for history never precisely repeats itself. Yet the parallels between the 1970s and the 1980s are significant. Thus understanding how agreement was achieved in the earlier period may contribute to an understanding of contemporary policy dilemmas as well.

In a landmark article on international economic policy coordination, Koichi Hamada has noted that "the strategic approach to macroeconomic coordination naturally leads us to the interdisciplinary realm of politics and economics."[2] We seek, perhaps imprudently, to explore that realm here. As political scientists, we are primarily interested in the political consequences (domestic and international) of economic interdependence. In this chapter, however, we reverse that focus, examining the effects of politics on economics. In the first section the groundwork for this interdisciplinary exercise is established through a review, from the point of view of political science, of basic issues in the theory of international economic policy coordination.

Some recent work in political science, like much recent work in economics, has drawn on game theory to explain international political economy.[3] Traditionally, however, the main comparative advantage of political science has been not so much theoretical formalization as sensitivity to institutions and contexts—in short, story telling. The primary aim in this chapter is to tell a story about the clearest instance yet of discretionary international economic policy coordination—the agreement announced at the Bonn summit conference of 1978.[4] In the course of this story we offer evidence that the Bonn accord was an instance of genuine international policy coordination, in that governments adopted policies different from those that they would have pursued in the absence of international negotiations. In the second section of this chapter, we present the story of Western economic diplomacy in detail.

In the third section, the theoretical core of this chapter, we ask what light the Bonn episode casts on current theories of policy coordination. One contribution that storytellers can make is to suggest which theoretical simplifications are empirically innocuous and which are seriously misleading. Thus, in this concluding section we suggest that in certain important respects the energies of theorists have been misallocated—directed at times toward issues that (however interesting theoretically they may be) have little empirical resonance in the story about the Bonn summit, and at times away from other issues that were crucial to the 1978 outcome.

Approaches to Policy Coordination

The central dilemma of contemporary international political economy is familiar: markets are increasingly internationalized, but policies are still set nationally. In principle, it can be shown, economic policy can sometimes be more effective if it is coordinated among independent national authorities. Such international coordination, however, is rare. What conditions, then, foster or inhibit international economic policy coordination? In other words, under what circumstances are international consultations likely to produce or facilitate national economic policies that are different from those that would otherwise have been pursued within a given period? Obviously, a single case history cannot sustain general analytic conclusions, given the need to rely on counterfactual conjectures, but this chapter uses the history of the Bonn summit of 1978 to address this basic question.

What Is "International Economic Policy Coordination"?

Much of the current debate about international economic policy coordination focuses on the distinction between rule-based and discretionary coordination.[5] Rule-based or "automatic" policy coordination is very important theoretically and seems to have been important in practice—for example, under fixed exchange rate regimes. Rule-based coordination, however, raises questions, not only economic but also political, that are beyond the scope of our inquiry. Hence we disregard it entirely, using "international economic policy coordination" to refer only to policy adjustments that are discretionary—the process by which national policies are adjusted to reduce the adverse consequences (or reinforce the positive consequences) that the policies of one or more states have on the welfare of other states, so that national policies differ from those that would have been expected from purely national or autarkic policymaking.[6] Discretionary policy coordination thus encompasses various types of cooperation, which can be arrayed along a rough continuum of increasing intensity:

—*Unilateral adjustment.* In this simplest case of cooperation, national policies are set unilaterally, but in light of information about the actual or intended policies of other nations. International exchange of information about policy targets and instrument settings is likely to improve policy efficiency, even in the absence of international agreement, although governments may have some strategic incentives not to provide full or accurate information to their foreign counterparts.[7] This type of policy cooperation is especially characteristic of small open economies, which are likely to be "policy takers" rather than "policy makers."[8]

—*Consultation.* In this type of cooperation national policies are set unilaterally, but after international consultation that has not merely exchanged information about the countries' respective policies, but also has modified national analytic models or perhaps even "clarified" national preferences. This sort of analytic convergence may be a key intermediate objective of international economic policy coordination. Although analytic agreement is, strictly speaking, neither a necessary nor a sufficient condition for policy adjustment, in practice much of what actually happens in international economic discussions falls under the rubric of consultation, as officials try to persuade one another that their respective analyses or preference schedules are confused or mistaken. Talk of "peer pressure" in the context of the current Group of Seven (G-7) arrangements for international economic policy discussions seems to refer to this type of cooperation.

—*Reinforcement.* This category refers to national policies that are determined unilaterally but whose implementation is facilitated by international agreement. In this case the policy chosen by national authorities is no different from the policy they would have preferred in the absence of international discussions, but the international deliberations increase the national government's "political will" at home. Domestic support for the policy in question might be bolstered by a preference for some offsetting foreign concession or by a preference for international cooperation in itself. Even if autonomous domestic processes would have led eventually to the same policy outcome, the *timing* of the policy change might be affected by the international reinforcement. Although not discussed in the economic literature on international economic policy coordination, this type may be common empirically.[9]

—*Package deal.* In this circumstance, national policies are determined as a part of a (conditional) international agreement involving mutual commitments, either within a given sector (macroeconomics, energy, or whatever) or across sectors. This is the full-blooded type that is most often analyzed in formal theories of international economic policy coordination. Some analysts reserve the term "coordination" for this form, using the label "cooperation" for the less intense types previously discussed.

—*Supranational integration.* In this case, policies are no longer determined nationally but rather are set through some supranational process, which may include voting by national governments, but whose outcome is binding on all participants. Obviously, this ambitious type of coordination is rare in today's world, although it is approached by the European Community (EC) in some policy domains. In effect, this sort of coordination seems implicit in McKinnon's well-known proposal for joint monetary policymaking by the American, German, and Japanese authorities.[10]

Why Coordination Should Occur but Rarely Does

Why do national governments, acting independently in an interdependent world, produce suboptimal policies? The universal dilemma of policymakers is that they have fewer policy instruments than policy targets. Trade-offs among these targets (for example, among growth, inflation, and external accounts) can often be improved through international policy coordination. In an interdependent world, national authorities are condemned to play a mixed-motive game involving both shared and conflicting interests. Without cooperation, the outcomes of these games may be collectively inefficient; that is, alternative policy combinations exist that could in principle make all parties better off. The earliest game-theoretic analyses of international policy coordination assumed a fixed exchange rate regime, but recent analyses have extended the general conclusion to flexible-rate regimes.[11] The global inflation of 1971–72 and the global recession of 1981–82 are sometimes cited as empirical instances of costly failures to coordinate policies internationally.

Yet the obstacles to successful international policy coordination are multiple. In the first place, coordination is complicated by different national starting points, including the following:

—*Differences in national objectives or utility functions.* Some countries give higher priority to price stability, for instance, or to social equality, than others.[12]

—*Differences in national economic structure.* Some countries are more trade dependent, for instance, or more inflation prone, than others.

—*Differences in economic analysis.* Some decisionmakers may be more convinced Keynesians, for instance, or more committed monetarists, than others.[13]

—*Differences in national institutions.* Some countries have weaker trade unions, for instance, or a stronger legislature, than others.

—*Differences in national political climate.* The party pendulums in different countries, for example, swing with different amplitudes and periods.

To be sure, not all such national differences would preclude mutually beneficial agreements. Several fundamental features of the international negotiating situation, however, impede policy coordination. These include the following:

—*Game-theoretic dilemmas of collective action.* This obstacle has, of course, received extensive attention in the recent literature. The specific obstacles under this rubric depend on the particular payoff matrix that is assumed, but fundamentally they derive from the condition of international "anarchy"—that is, the inability to enforce international agreements. Sovereign policymakers, it is said, often have an incentive to "cheat" on any cooperative agreement.[14] If verifiable, binding contracts among the parties are assumed to be impossible, international cooperation is a kind of public good that will be undersupplied because of the unavoidable temptation to "free-ride" that each party faces.

—*Uncertainty.* Uncertainty is intense, pervasive, and manifold in international economic policy coordination. It encompasses the (changing) structural features of the national and world economies, the preferences and trade-offs among the preferences of the national authorities, the policy choices of the foreign authorities, and various nonpolicy exogenous variables, such as crop failures or (to cite an example relevant to the 1977–78 case) the fall of the shah of Iran. The general effect of uncertainty is to reduce incentives for policy activism, including international economic policy coordination.[15]

—*Conflicts over the distribution of any joint gains.* Cooperation in any real-world game is likely to be a *range* of possible solutions, each implying a different distribution of the gains among the parties to the agreement. In practice, much of the bargaining turns on this point, rather than on the question of whether and how to reach Pareto optimality. In the real world of politics, tough distributive bargaining may impede any cooperation at all.[16]

—*Transaction costs.* The transaction costs in policy games rise sharply as the number of players increases, and (as evident from the case study below) the number of relevant players, both domestic and international, is quite high in any real-world case of international policy coordination. Economic analysis and political entrepreneurship of a very high order are necessary for success.

—*Limited prospective gains.* Although the theoretical advantages of coordination have been fairly clearly established, attempts to quantify the potential gains are rare. At least one pioneering study, however, suggests that the gains, measured in terms of the revealed preferences of the national authorities, may be much smaller than is often suggested.[17] That the odds of successful coordination are closely correlated with the potential gains is a plausible, if unproven, hypothesis.

Why the 1978 Bonn Summit Agreement Is a Crucial Case

Given the obstacles to successful international economic policy coordination just enumerated, it is not surprising that empirical examples of such coordination are uncommon. It is widely believed that the 1978 Bonn summit accord represented a rare, perhaps even unique, case of comprehensive policy coordination among the industrial democracies. For example, Oudiz and Sachs observed that "advocacy of international coordination has been far more plentiful than actual implementation. The 1978 Bonn summit is the principal example of a macroeconomic policy package adopted by the major economies."[18]

The linchpin of the Bonn accord was an agreement by the Germans and Japanese to add a dose of fiscal stimulus to their economies in exchange for a commitment by the Americans to raise U.S. domestic oil prices to world levels. A secondary element was acquiescence by reluctant Europeans to a successful conclusion of the Multilateral Trade Negotiations (MTN) within the General Agreement on Tariffs and Trade (GATT). Anthony Solomon, who helped prepare the Bonn summit, has argued that

> it was the only summit where the final agreement clearly represented a coordinated package, in which actions were pledged by each country in return for specific undertakings by others—all of which were capable of being implemented. In that sense, it was unique because it meant that countries were willing to make commitments that they hadn't necessarily planned to make on purely domestic grounds, but they were willing to undertake as a part of an overall deal.[19]

We do not address here the question that has preoccupied most of the relevant economic literature—that is, when are there potential welfare gains from international policy coordination, and how large might they be? Although we recognize that the potential benefits from coordination might often be outweighed by the costs,[20] we assume that at least some opportunities for welfare-improving international coordination are not exploited. However, we make no effort to estimate the actual welfare gains from the Bonn accord, nor even to show that there were such gains *ex post.*

The Bonn agreement is now widely believed to have been a failure in substantive terms. The trade deal and American oil price decontrol are in general regarded favorably, but many observers and policymakers claim that the stimulus measures ratified at Bonn contributed to subsequent budget deficits and inflation. This retrospective judgment may be justified, but it does not rest on much systematic econometric investigation. It is possible to argue that additional stimulus was the right medicine in July 1978, and that the subsequent troubles were due instead to the unforeseen Iranian revolution and the second oil crisis.[21] Given the currently almost-unchallenged condemnation of the Bonn summit's results, efforts to assess those results in a comprehensive and measured way should have high priority, but we do not address that task here. Our objective is to understand how and why the leading Western nations were able in 1977–78 to achieve this rare instance of international economic policy coordination.

Domestic and International Politics Intertwined

The narrative of economic relations among the advanced capitalist states during 1977–78 is a story of the divergence and reconvergence of macroeconomic and energy policies. Although the economic wisdom of policies implemented by the United States, Europe, and Japan in late 1978 and early 1979 is an unsettled issue, we argue that the resolution of the conflict was politically harmonious: that is, national policies hindered the attainment of reachable economic goals of partner states less sharply at the conclusion than at the outbreak of conflict, and the revised policies attracted commanding, although not unanimous, domestic support. The 1978 Bonn summit agreement to decontrol American oil prices and to stimulate the German economy was the core of economic coordination among these states. But contributions from Japan, France, the United Kingdom, Italy, and the EC were also integral parts of the macroeconomic agreement. Further, international trade and monetary issues were important in the process of coordination.

Prelude to Conflict, 1974–76

Contrasting responses to economic shocks. The 1977–78 economic conflict was rooted in the different responses by the summit countries to unprecedented shocks to the world economy in the early 1970s. Between 1971 and 1974 the Bretton Woods system of fixed exchange rates was replaced by one of "managed floating"; an "inflation scare" spread among the advanced Western countries and Japan; the Organization of Petroleum Exporting Countries (OPEC) raised oil prices fourfold; and the world economy entered the deepest recession since the Great Depression. Each development had implications for international economic coordination. Floating exchange rates held the prospect of conferring macroeconomic independence on the advanced capitalist countries; but that prospect was far from certain and, in the event, greatly exaggerated. The acceleration of inflation in 1972–73, widely attributed to the collectively excessive reflation of the Organization for Economic Cooperation and Development (OECD) economies, sensitized some governments to the need to consider the policies of others when setting their own.

The first oil shock presented the most formidable challenge to cooperation, in both macroeconomics and energy. Coming on the heels of accelerated inflation, the surge in oil prices caught the OECD economies in a dangerously exposed position. All realized that the oil price hikes would tend to inflate world prices further and that the terms-of-trade losses would reduce the real incomes of the oil-consuming countries. Indeed, the current account position of the OECD countries shifted from a surplus of $10.3 billion in 1973 to a deficit of $26.0 billion in 1974. As expected, the OECD economies went into a steep recession during 1974, while average inflation reached 13.5 percent, three times the normal level for the previous decade. In the first half of 1975, GNP in the OECD area shrank at an annual rate of 4.0 percent, and unemployment leapt to 15 million by 1975, against 9 million two years before.

The initial reaction of all the summit countries, except the United Kingdom, was to act against the inflationary pressure of the oil price increase. Most tightened monetary and fiscal policy during 1974; Germany had started doing so early in the year before. But these actions made the downward slope of the recession even steeper. In the first half of 1975, governments switched to stimulating growth, even though inflation still seemed dangerously high. Germany and the United States eased fiscal policy in early 1975, and expansionary public spending programs followed in Japan, France, and Italy later in the year. The French and Italian fiscal stimuli were premature, however, given the current account deficits of these countries. Serious international payments imbalances thus developed over 1974–76 among the summit and smaller OECD countries. The large countries found themselves in much more favorable current account positions than the smaller summit countries. Despite the terms-of-trade losses, Germany's current surplus soared to record levels during 1975 and remained in surplus in 1976 as well. The American current account peaked at an $18.8 billion surplus in 1976. Japan, after suffering an initial deterioration in 1974, quickly recouped the loss in 1975 and was in substantial surplus in 1976. In contrast, France, the United Kingdom, Italy, and Canada labored under recurring deficits during 1974–76. Their international financial positions precarious, these high-inflation deficit countries were forced to abandon or defer expansionary programs, in some cases under the supervision of the International Monetary Fund (IMF). Against this background, the recovery of late 1975 and early 1976 proved short-lived. The summit countries confronted a dilemma of collective action in reflating their economies: although some expansion seemed collectively desirable, any single country that tried to expand would find that the costs exceeded the benefits unless its trading partners joined in.

The summit countries also faced a dilemma of collective action in their policies toward OPEC: all would be better off if they could reduce their collective demand for oil, but each individually would be better off by not restraining its own demand. The United States had its own substantial oil production, which provided about two-thirds of its needs. The Americans advocated firm resistance to the OPEC cartel and collective action by OECD countries to conserve energy, develop new resources, and deal with emergencies. But the European countries and Japan were far more dependent on oil imports. France, in particular, argued against confrontation with OPEC and in favor of seeking an accommodation. The other Europeans leaned first one way and then the other. Eventually, a compromise of sorts was reached whereby the French acceded to the establishment of the International Energy Agency (IEA), and the Americans agreed to meet with OPEC, OECD, and developing countries in Paris at the Conference for International Economic Cooperation.

More important for present purposes, the domestic energy policy responses of the United States, Europe, and Japan differed markedly. Importing a smaller portion of its needs, the United States sought to insulate consumers from drastically increased world oil prices by a complicated system of crude oil price controls and entitlements to domestic oil refiners—in effect subsidizing consumption and encouraging imports. In contrast, after flirtation with short-term or symbolic attempts to limit the effect of the price increases, the European governments and Japan allowed their domestic oil prices to rise to the world level. Instead of subsidizing consumption, moreover, the European and Japanese governments taxed gasoline sales heavily.[22] Once the economic recovery got under way, the different levels of oil prices had their predictable effect on consumer demand, and American oil imports threatened to recreate the general scarcity under which prices had been raised initially by OPEC.

During 1974–76, the summit countries did not effectively meet the challenges of collective action presented in these macroeconomic and energy areas. In international trade and monetary affairs, however, significant deterioration in relations was successfully avoided. Despite predictions that the oil price increases and recession would create irresistible protectionist pressures, the summit countries and their non-communist industrial trading partners launched a new MTN round. That round, initiated at a GATT meeting in Tokyo, was given the green light by the U.S. Congress with the passage of the Trade and Tariff Act of 1974, which granted the president negotiating authority. But trade bargaining proceeded only very slowly during 1975 and 1976, hung up on the thorny agricultural issue and the prospect of elections in several important countries in 1976. On monetary issues, despite deep differences between the United States and the Europeans (the French, in particular) over what rules should replace the Bretton Woods regime, agreement was reached on amendments to the IMF's Articles of Agreement during the first economic summit meeting at Rambouillet in 1975. The kernel of that international monetary agreement was the French accession to flexible exchange rates and the American acceptance of responsibility to intervene when foreign exchange markets became "disorderly," an admittedly loose trip wire. Thus, although serious conflict on these issues was averted during 1974–76, it remained to be seen how the new floating exchange rate system would work in practice, and progress toward a successful conclusion to the new MTN round was far from certain.

Macroeconomic diplomacy. International economic diplomacy during 1974–76 set the stage for the controversy about reflation in 1976–78. By late 1976, pressure by some governments on others for changes in macroeconomic policy had become commonplace among the advanced capitalist countries. Further, the forums in which this pressure was brought to bear had become institutionalized in bilateral and multilateral organizations and procedures, foremost among which were the G-7 annual economic summit meetings.[23] Within those forums, governments exchanged views about the global economic crisis and bargained over the allocation of the costs of adjusting their economic policies. U.S.-Japanese economic relations during 1974–76 were tranquil, at least by comparison with the rest of the 1970s and 1980s, so macroeconomic bargaining during this period was primarily transatlantic and intra-European.

Compared with the later controversy about reflation in 1977–78, the German and American positions in 1974–76 were reversed. In the earlier period German Chancellor Helmut Schmidt was a vocal advocate of macroeconomic coordination programs of various sorts, whereas President Gerald Ford, unlike his successor, was at best lukewarm toward international coordination. (The British Labour governments were in the vanguard of international reflation throughout this period.) Schmidt recognized that, with demand within Germany remaining stagnant throughout 1974, it was important to ensure that demand be kept robust abroad. But when he succeeded Willy Brandt as chancellor in May 1974, with the economy contracting and unemployment rising, export orders began a rapid decline. At that point Schmidt mounted a two-pronged offensive: urging others to maintain demand, while expanding domestic demand just in case his international efforts proved unsuccessful. Shortly before the first of a series of post–oil shock expansionary programs was instituted in September 1974, Schmidt advised the United States to take a similar course. In doing so, he departed from his previous public statements, which had primarily stressed the need to contain inflation:

> There is a danger if in this late phase of [the recession] the United States should embark really, not only verbally but actually, on a strong deflationary economic policy. . . . It [would] mean less demand from the U.S. on the world market, and it [would] mean that we [could] sell less than we sold last year or last month. . . . You have to fight inflation, but please don't enter into deflation policy, because you might incur too much unemployment, too much deflation in the world economy.[24]

During autumn 1974, Schmidt continued to work both for American expansion and for anti-inflationary programs in other European countries. In November he proposed an agreement that envisioned additional expansionary measures in Germany in exchange for restrictive programs elsewhere in Europe, but his European partners turned this offer down.[25] Shortly thereafter, the chancellor traveled to Washington to meet with President Ford. Ford told Schmidt that he expected the U.S. recession to bottom out in the summer of 1975. Cognizant that his second expansionary program was being developed, Schmidt responded that it would be better if Ford would turn the American economy around sooner.[26] The chancellor returned to Bonn and supervised the passage through the Bundestag of a tax cut and spending package, the very measures that he had conditionally offered the Europeans in mid-November.[27] Schmidt's third macroeconomic stimulus, administered in August 1975 after he was told that the U.S. economy would recover very soon, was promoted as part of a joint reflationary package with the French. Aware that German exports to the

United States had fallen to approximately half of what they had been a year earlier, Schmidt restated that "it would be hard to imagine an economic recovery here without one in the United States."[28]

By the first summit meeting at Rambouillet in November 1975, economic growth had resumed within the OECD. The heads of government of the United States, Japan, Germany, and France reassured British Prime Minister Harold Wilson that they would not "allow the recovery to falter," while expressing equal concern to avoid "another outburst of inflation." The leaders declared their confidence that existing policies were compatible and adequate to produce recovery, but there was no coordination of policy and no echo of the differentiated approach favored by the OECD secretariat (whereby expansion would be pursued by some countries, restraint by others). The Rambouillet monetary agreements that obligated governments to pursue policies conducive to monetary stability and to intervene to modulate "erratic fluctuations" in the foreign exchange markets proved too weak to serve as a guide to (decentralized) collective policymaking.

Between Rambouillet and the second summit meeting in Puerto Rico in June 1976, Ford, Schmidt, and Japanese Prime Minister Takeo Miki were preoccupied with the potential problem of inflation. As the recovery progressed during the first half of 1976, the United States and Germany argued strongly that the summit countries should beware of collective overstimulation of the industrial economies, as had occurred in 1972–73. At Puerto Rico, the summiteers endorsed the conservative fiscal policies then being applied by the United States and Germany, which reversed the measures of stimulus introduced the year before. The United Kingdom and Italy argued for a less restrictive approach, with Prime Minister James Callaghan pointing to the dangers of prolonged high unemployment, but these views found little sympathy. Both countries were in a weak bargaining position, dependent on the goodwill of their more prosperous partners. Chancellor Schmidt, although warmly commending the U.K. incomes policy, was unyielding. The British were urged to make cuts in public spending and began to realize that, without such cuts, they could no longer count on U.S. and German help.

Financial support, both bilateral and multilateral, provided a specific lever by which the Germans and Americans could oblige the British and Italians to conform. In the months after the Puerto Rico meeting, Bonn and Washington used this leverage. When the pound dropped precipitously in September–October 1976, the British were forced to turn to the IMF for help. During the negotiations over conditionality for this lending, the U.S. Treasury insisted that the terms be severe and the loan short term. When Callaghan appealed to Schmidt to lobby the IMF on his behalf, the German chancellor, despite sympathetic ideological ties to the Labour government, took a hard line, advising the British prime minister to undertake decisive restrictive measures. Moreover, he dispatched Karl-Otto Pöhl, his closest financial adviser, to Washington with the message that the IMF negotiator should not back down from his stringent stance. Then, during the critical concluding negotiations in late November, U.S. Treasury Secretary William Simon intervened personally to support the stern IMF position.[29] Concurrently, in part out of concern for inflation, the Germans threatened the Italians—who had also turned to the IMF for help— with financial sanctions to block inclusion of the Communists in the Italian governmental coalition.[30] By mid-January 1977, Schmidt was praising Giulio Andreotti and Callaghan publicly for having put anti-inflationary programs in place and was advising them to continue that course. Both leaders had been successful—so far, at least—at fending off trade protectionism, the leftist solution to their countries' international payments problems.

Although President Ford had said at Puerto Rico that countries with large surpluses should allow their foreign balances to deteriorate, that position was not the main thrust of U.S. international economic policy. Even though it was apparent in autumn 1976 that the current account surpluses of Germany and Japan were growing rather than shrinking, the Ford administration refused to press either government to expand for the benefit of deficit countries, and the outgoing administration did not endorse what later came to be called the "locomotive" theory of world growth. In its last annual economic report, released in January 1977, Ford's Council of Economic Advisers argued:

> As the recoveries in Germany and Japan—as well as in the United States—proceed, demand for imports is likely to rise concurrently. But the total effect on world trade in 1977 exerted by about 1 or 2 percent faster growth in each of the big countries— which would imply rates of growth that are at the upper limit of what authorities currently judge to be compatible with noninflationary growth—might raise the currently projected 8 percent rate of growth of the volume of world trade to 9½ percent. This increase could not be enough to make a crucial difference to

those countries which still find themselves in payments difficulties despite the large growth in aggregate foreign demand registered in the past year.[31]

In large part because of the convergence of their economic views, Chancellor Schmidt publicly endorsed the reelection of President Ford in autumn 1976. This stance was not lost on the incoming Carter administration; nor was the chancellor's earlier advice to the Americans to reflate.

Thus by autumn 1976 macroeconomic policy coordination had become a standard item on the international economic agenda of the summit and the OECD countries. Although no comprehensive transatlantic macroeconomic program had been agreed, international coordination had earned a place among the range of instruments from which Western governments might choose in managing their economies. By the time Jimmy Carter assumed the presidency, the machinery had been put in place for negotiating over the allocation of the political costs of policy adjustment.

Macroeconomic and political developments at the time generated incentives to use that machinery. First, the dilemma of collective macroeconomic action that confronted the OECD economies was sharpened by a pause in the recovery in late 1976. Second, because elections in the United States, Japan, and Germany were held almost simultaneously during the autumn, each of these governments was sure to remain in power for several years: for better or worse, these governments knew that they would confront one another for some time. Further, the leaders who emerged from the elections in the three largest summit countries, as well as many of those who remained in government in the smaller summit countries, were confirmed proponents of greater international cooperation and were predisposed to use the machinery of international coordination.

The Outbreak of Conflict, 1976–77

Domestic politics and economics in Germany. The November 1976 national election was something of a setback for the coalition of Social Democrats (SPD) and Free Democrats (FDP), whose margin in the Bundestag fell from forty-six to ten seats.[32] Although the vote share of both coalition parties declined, the SPD lost the most seats. The FDP polled 8 percent of the national vote, safely above the constitutionally established 5 percent level necessary for representation in the Bundestag. However, the FDP was precariously close to losing representation in several *Land* parliaments. The Christian Democratic and Christian Socialist opposition (CDU-CSU) once again became the largest party in the Bundestag. Nevertheless, the SPD-FDP coalition emerged with a sufficient majority to govern effectively. Despite acrimonious exchanges between the SPD and CDU-CSU, macroeconomic policy had not been a prominent issue during the campaign.

Changes within the ruling coalition, both during and after the election campaign, had important ramifications for the future course of macroeconomic policy. The diverse views and interests encompassed by the government, ranging from the SPD left wing to the FDP liberals, had already shown their divergent tendencies during 1976, complicating the management of the coalition. In February the FDP split from the SPD in Lower Saxony and formed a ruling coalition with the CDU. Shortly thereafter, another FDP-CDU coalition was formed in Saarland. (These were the first of a string of FDP defections over the following years that presaged the change of government at the federal level in 1982.) After the FDP-SPD coalition suffered considerable losses in Baden-Württemberg in the spring, the FDP decided on a change of electoral strategy at the federal level. During the autumn campaign, the party emphasized its "individuality and independence" and promoted itself as the "intra-governmental opposition," checking the excesses of the left-wing elements of the SPD.[33]

During 1976 the government became increasingly estranged from the trade unions. Union leaders argued that wage moderation in recent years had resulted in labor-saving investment rather than any significant reduction in unemployment. They were frustrated by FDP blockage of profit-sharing and codetermination legislation, and they felt diminished influence with the chancellor himself. At the end of 1976, the president of the German Trade Union Association (*Deutsche Gewerkschaftsbund,* or DGB), Heinz-Oskar Vetter, declared that the honeymoon between the unions and the government was over and that the "possibilities for cooperation between the government and trade unions [had] been exhausted."[34] These strains jeopardized labor cooperation during the wage negotiations in the winter of 1977.

The German economy had surged strongly (7.5 percent on an annual basis) in the first half of 1976—convenient for a government heading into an autumn election. However, foreign observers questioned the government's optimism that growth would continue at that pace. The OECD secretariat argued that the upswing was because of temporary replenishment of inventories and short-lived policy stimuli. It recommended that the government develop and hold in reserve a set of measures to expand domestic demand in the event that a relapse should occur.[35] Foreign doubts about the sanguine official economic forecasts for 1976 proved prescient, and growth dropped sharply to 2.4 percent and 2.8 percent in the third and fourth quarters. The slowdown was welcomed in late summer by the FDP-dominated Economics Ministry as "fully in harmony with the growth strategy of the ministry, which aims at avoiding an early overheating." The ministry added, "We can therefore expect a recovery that gains in width, depth, and solidity," and the government maintained that growth would be vigorous in 1977.[36] Inflation remained under control, with consumer prices rising about 4 percent over the course of the year. But unemployment stopped declining and began a sustained increase in the fourth quarter.

After the 1976 election, government coalition leaders quickly agreed on their economic program for the following year, in part to preempt intracoalition squabbles over unsettled economic policy issues. Then Chancellor Schmidt presented the program to the Bundestag in mid-December. Although he mentioned a small employment-creation package and possible investment-incentive measures, the basic thrust of his program was continued budget "consolidation" (deficit reduction), founded on the assumption that growth in 1977 would be between 5 and 6 percent. That forecast was corroborated by a broad range of German expert opinion, although the Council of Economic Experts warned that growth might slow to 4.0–4.5 percent unless a small expansionary package were adopted.[37] Cognizant of this warning, aware of criticism that consumption expenditures were taking up too large a share of the budget, and, perhaps most important, concerned about trade union agitation, Schmidt announced that a medium-term public investment program (ZIP, by its German acronym) would be developed over the coming months, although he left its size and timing unspecified. The government also announced its intention to raise the value-added tax (VAT) by 2 percent, effective January 1978, and to reduce other taxes simultaneously, leaving no change in 1978 tax revenue. As of the beginning of 1977, a tax reform program eliminating double taxation and raising excise taxes became effective. Also at this time, the Bundesbank announced that its target rate for money growth would again be 8 percent in 1977. With these policies in place, the government forecast that unemployment and inflation would both remain at less than 4 percent over the course of the coming year.[38] The OECD secretariat again disputed the government forecast, projecting 3.5 percent growth, at the November meeting of the OECD's Economic Policy Committee (EPC).[39]

In late 1976, Chancellor Schmidt therefore had reason to be content but not complacent. With the help of a nicely timed economic recovery, he had successfully campaigned as the self-assured manager of *Modell Deutschland*. He had surmounted difficulties within his coalition to put together a widely accepted macroeconomic program. Prospects for macroeconomic performance appeared to him to be good for the coming year. On the international scene, inflation fighting had gained the upper hand in Europe, with the most inflation-prone countries having instituted serious stabilization programs within the last few months. American politics, however, posed several difficulties for the chancellor. Jimmy Carter's victory over Gerald Ford in the November election threatened to reverse Schmidt's gains—by offering hope to the inflation-prone deficit countries that reflationary help was on the way, and by complicating the management of Schmidt's coalition, within which differences between the more expansionary SPD left and the unions, on the one hand, and the more restrictive FDP, on the other, had only just been muffled.

Domestic politics and economics in the United States. During the 1976 U.S. presidential campaign, American inflation hovered around 6.0 percent, with unemployment around 7.5 percent, and growth slowed to 3.0 percent in the fourth quarter. Economic performance thus placed Carter in a good position to argue that the Ford administration had not properly managed the economy and that the government should adopt a more aggressive role in stimulating a self-sustaining recovery. Carter made macroeconomics the cornerstone of his campaign and made job creation his first economic priority. He and his advisers argued that job generation would not raise inflation until the unemployment rate dropped below 5 percent. Carter specifically rejected wage and price controls and pledged to balance the budget by the end of the presidential term.

Interpreting his victory as a mandate for these objectives, President-elect Carter and his economic team began immediately after the election to devise the specific measures they would submit to the Democratic Congress. Although there was general agreement within the group of advisers and officials-designate who developed the program that a stimulus of tens of billions was in order, there was less agreement on the composition of the fiscal injection into the economy. The main issue was the emphasis to be given either to tax reduction or to direct job creation, public works, and other spending programs. Between the November election and the inauguration, the AFL-CIO, black leaders, and the Democratic congressional leadership, among others, argued vigorously for the stimulus to be weighted toward spending and job-creation programs. Business representatives and some designated cabinet officials supported tax-reduction measures. Charles Schultze, slated to become the president's chief economic adviser, argued that a rebate on 1976 income taxes was the quickest method of stimulating the economy.

The program Carter chose in early January favored tax cuts and amounted to $31 billion spread evenly over 1977 and 1978. To stimulate the economy as soon as possible, the Carter team proposed a $50 rebate on 1976 income taxes for virtually every American as part of this program.[40] The president stated in his first cabinet meeting that he expected to act as a restraining influence on spending by the Democratic Congress. Schultze announced that the stimulus was necessary to be sure that the economy would not slide into recession again. With the stimulus, the incoming administration predicted, unemployment could be expected to decline from just under 8.0 percent in the fourth quarter of 1976 to 6.6 percent by the end of 1977.

Treasury Secretary Michael Blumenthal, Schultze, Undersecretary of State for Economic Affairs Richard N. Cooper, and Assistant Secretary of the Treasury for International Affairs C. Fred Bergsten argued in administration economic planning meetings—and publicly after the inauguration—that it was necessary for Germany and Japan to stimulate their economies as well. The new president, himself a strong advocate of cooperation among the United States, Japan, and Western Europe, stressed this in a telephone conversation with Schmidt before the inauguration.[41] After the administration's stimulus package had been proposed, Blumenthal testified to Congress:

> By adopting this stimulus program, the United States will be asserting leadership and providing a better international economic climate. We will then ask the stronger countries abroad [Germany and Japan were cited] to follow suit. This program itself implicitly calls on them to undertake stimulus efforts of proportionately similar amounts to ours.[42]

Few if any of the architects of the domestic economic package, however, seem to have believed in early 1977 that the effectiveness of the American stimulus was contingent on the willingness of the Germans and Japanese to go along. Nor did the administration condition its support for the package on any foreign action.

Conflicting analyses of reflation. As the world economic recovery had stalled in the second half of 1976, proponents of coordinated reflation had gathered renewed strength. The OECD secretariat, the Callaghan government in the United Kingdom, the Carter administration, many private economists in the summit countries, and some governments in the smaller countries shared this prescription. The view was well expressed by a group of economists from Europe, Japan, and the United States, who met at the Brookings Institution in early November 1976, recommending that

> Germany, Japan, and the United States should now adopt domestic economic policies geared to stimulating economic activity. Stronger economic expansion in the three countries, each of which has recently experienced a lull, need not intensify inflation problems, but should reduce domestic unemployment and provide benefits to other countries, both developed and developing.[43]

The proposal was reiterated by the OECD secretariat in its *OECD Economic Outlook* in December 1976 and by principal members of the incoming Carter administration, not least the president-elect himself. After his inauguration the new president immediately dispatched Vice President Walter Mondale with messages to major allies around the world. Prominent among the issues on Mondale's agenda was the joint stimulus proposal. The plan proved to be very controversial. As a result, analytical macroeconomic issues, as well as differing macroeconomic values, received a full hearing in the international deliberations that followed.

Carter had brought with him into the executive branch a group of analytic, Keynesian economic advisers. As such they differed with neoclassical analysts over the appropriate response to oil price increases, the discretionary use of fiscal policy, and the inflationary dangers associated with it. Carter administration officials were defiant toward the constraints the recent oil price increases placed on real income, in contrast with the resignation of the Germans and Japanese. The oil price increases represented a tax, the deflationary effects of which could be offset by an expansionary fiscal policy.[44] Such a stimulus to demand would pose little threat of inflation under conditions of substantial unemployment. Nor would monetary expansion lead to greater inflation, given significant capacity underutilization. The analysis of the U.S. and world economies by the Council of Economic Advisers during 1977–78 is illustrative:

> A program for achieving full recovery in the industrial economies must begin with measures to raise domestic demand and capacity utilization. Only then is sufficient investment likely to be forthcoming to achieve structural objectives such as reducing dependence on export demand and forestalling potential imbalances between capital stocks and labor forces. Both monetary and fiscal policy can make a contribution. With excess capacity everywhere, world recovery can proceed without undue concern that reasonable expansionary policies will trigger a new round of inflation.[45]

Furthermore, the prescription for a more expansionary fiscal policy in the United States was not generated simply by economists affiliated with the left wing of the Democratic party. Rather, there was a fairly broad consensus among labor, business, the economic profession, both political parties, and even some fiscal conservatives that a stimulus of some magnitude was in order. That sentiment was shared by a southern Democratic president with fiscal conservative instincts. The tax cut put forth by the Ford administration and adopted by Congress in 1975 had been substantial, amounting to 1.5 percent of GNP. The tax measures put forward by the Carter administration in early 1977 were not that large. Thus, although the composition of the stimulus was a matter of some contention, there was a fairly strong consensus behind the principle of an expansionary program when it was proposed by the new administration.

In Germany, by contrast, the active, countercyclical use of fiscal policy had dubious legitimacy in the eyes of the most influential economists and economic advisers of policymakers. The German Council of Economic Experts had often issued economic advice very different from that of the U.S. Council of Economic Advisers, its near counterpart. The German experts had been consistently analytically neoclassical. First, they contended that national income was largely determined on the supply side, and that unemployment in the mid-1970s was due to excessive wages, not to insufficient demand. Second, the proper role of demand management policies should therefore be limited to speeding the adjustment of demand to supply that market forces would eventually produce anyway. Third, over the business cycle (the medium term), the budget deficit should be neutral.[46]

The German council took the position that the oil price increases represented a transfer of income abroad that had to be accepted at home, particularly by the trade unions. The council calculated the scope for wage increases by taking the increase in real GNP per worker, adjusting for terms of trade effects (as well as for changes in social security contributions), and concluded that real wages had been excessive.[47] An expansionary monetary policy would simply provide greater room for inflation, despite unused capacity. German economic experts recognized that investment lagged despite lower interest rates, but they attributed this lag to low profitability, due in turn to high wages. Providing a fiscal stimulus, rather than raising profitability, would induce trade unions to demand larger wage increases and would cause corporations to expect higher taxes, further depressing investment.

The central principles of this analysis were shared broadly within Germany among the five major economic institutes, the economics profession, the Bundesbank, and politicians within the three main political parties. Some disagreed, however, whether a stimulus would be useful in bringing aggregate demand into better balance with productive capacity. German trade unions and the left wing of the SPD were more favorably disposed to stimulative fiscal measures. The trade unions, of course, rejected the notion that high wage settlements would reduce economic growth but nonetheless were considerably more prudent than trade unions in other European countries.

The chancellor had shown himself to be flexible on questions of macroeconomic analysis and values during his public career. After becoming minister for economics and finance upon Karl Schiller's resignation in 1972, Schmidt had coined the slogan "better 5 percent inflation than 5 percent unemployment." This echoed Willy Brandt's declaration a few years earlier that unemployment was not an acceptable tool to maintain price stability and clearly implied a Keynesian trade-off between the two goals, which had been denied by many in Germany. Schmidt's statement was controversial among his inflation-conscious countrymen, and he refrained from making similar statements in the German press throughout his tenure as chancellor.

Schmidt had put forward several initiatives for domestic and international reflation in 1974–75, but by the outbreak of the 1976–78 controversy about reflation he was consistently recommending anti-inflationary policies.

The Carter administration makes its case. Vice President Mondale and his aides, including Cooper and Bergsten, presented an array of arguments to their counterparts in Bonn.[48] First, they contended that the world economic situation was gloomy and even dangerous. Some industrial and developing countries had gambled that the recession would be short, had therefore pursued expansionary policies to offset it, and had incurred payments deficits in so doing, and they had now got into serious trouble. The result might be not only international financial instability but increased support for the extreme left within these countries as well. Economic hardship, they maintained, was strengthening the left in several important European countries— France, Italy, and Portugal in particular—and in some developing countries, such as the Philippines.

Second, the United States and Germany, as well as Japan, had large amounts of unused capacity and high rates of unemployment. All these countries, moreover, had succeeded in reducing inflation to relatively low levels and were collectively running a substantial surplus on current account, which exacerbated the payments problems of the other non-OPEC countries. Third, these leading industrial countries were in an excellent position, the Carter envoys reasoned, to administer fiscal stimuli to their economies, to mutual and third-country benefit. Through direct transmission of growth and reduction of the balance-of-payments constraint on the expansionary policies of the deficit countries, the United States, Japan, and Germany could lead the rest of the world resolutely out of the recession.[49]

The Germans were aggressive in refuting the Americans' economic argument. They disputed the proposition that there was wide "room for maneuver" for noninflationary fiscal stimulus in Germany. They queried the Americans on what specific measures they prescribed for the German economy. The U.S. delegation advised that the Germans further reduce taxes and defer or cancel the planned VAT increases, not unlike the Carter administration's consumer-oriented economic program. The Germans argued that, because a large portion of the proposed tax cuts would be saved, business would be discouraged from investing, and trade unions would demand higher wage increases. Additional stimulus would not have the expansionary effects the Carter administration predicted and would increase German inflation. When the Americans explained their own domestic economic program, the chancellor asked their estimate of its inflationary impact. Bergsten responded that the program was expected to raise the inflation rate by only 0.3 percent. Schmidt was incredulous. Finally, the Germans contended that, owing to the alleged thinness of international macroeconomic transmission channels and to flexible exchange rates, faster German growth would not have as strong a beneficial impact on partner countries as the Americans predicted. The Germans cited a Citibank study concluding that a rise of 1 percent in German growth could cut U.K. unemployment by only 50,000–100,000 people, while risking a renewal of inflation in Germany.[50]

On arriving in Bonn, members of the American delegation had received signals from a high German official that they understood to mean that international pressure to reflate would assist the chancellor in overcoming domestic political resistance to policies he personally wanted to implement. (The British, too, had received clear hints, most recently at a bilateral summit in October 1976, that Schmidt would not mind being pushed into additional expansion.) The Americans may have presented their argument more forcefully as a result in the meetings with the chancellor and other SPD and FDP cabinet and subcabinet officials. They left Bonn with the impression that they had got their point across, and that the meetings had gone well. While remaining noncommittal on the future course of his economic policy, the chancellor was publicly conciliatory.[51] On their return to Washington, however, the Mondale team learned that the chancellor privately was very resentful. In particular, he complained of being lectured to by inexperienced American academics.[52] The fundamental political-economic gap that had opened between the Americans and the Germans with the advent of the Carter administration was reflected in an exchange between Schmidt and Mondale about Ford's tight-fisted treasury secretary, William E. Simon. "We owe a lot to Bill Simon," noted Schmidt, admiringly. Mondale agreed: "We owe Bill Simon everything—without him we wouldn't have won the election."[53]

It is significant that the U.S. delegation had gone beyond merely presenting their domestic economic program and urging Schmidt to reflate. The Americans served notice on Bonn that their domestic program would be implemented regardless of what the chancellor chose to do. The Americans predicted that if he chose not to stimulate the German economy, the American current account deficit and the German surplus would grow, with predictable effects on the foreign exchange markets. Were the German government to continue its restrictive course, it should be prepared to countenance the domestic economic ramifications of substantial appreciation of the deutsche mark relative to the dollar. Although an appreciation of the deutsche mark would tend to correct the payments imbalance eventually, that adjustment process would be less efficient than the locomotive proposal. German concern at the time of the Mondale trip about American complacency toward the dollar would be sharpened a few months later when they perceived Treasury Secretary Blumenthal to be "talking down the dollar."

From Bonn, Mondale and his delegation traveled on to other European capitals and to Tokyo. The Americans presented the same argument to the Japanese, who had been the object of strong criticism in the United States for holding the yen artificially low during 1976. A few days before their arrival, the Japanese government had passed a supplemental budget touted as a concession to foreign pressure to expand domestic demand. The package was criticized both at home and abroad as being insufficient to shift substantially the Japanese economy from foreign to domestic sources of demand. Nonetheless, the Mondale team suspended heavy public criticism of Japanese fiscal policy, pending further developments in Japan's growth rate and its external position. As with German fiscal measures, Carter administration officials soon became discontented, and the U.S.-Japanese controversy about reflation continued in parallel with the U.S.-German dispute.[54] These issues would inevitably occupy much of the energy of the leaders when they gathered for Carter's first Western summit, scheduled for London in May 1977.

Precursor to Bonn: The 1977 London Summit

Fiscal policy in Germany and the United States. During the January Mondale trip and for two months afterward, Chancellor Schmidt kept the size and timing of the ZIP public investment program unspecified. He reportedly had been eyeing the fortunes of Carter's economic proposals before making his own decision on the investment package. With its passage through the Bundestag in March 1977, the ZIP was fixed at DM 16 billion, to be financed jointly by the federal and *Land* governments and to be spread over four years. A small increase in the magnitude of the program over the amount previously considered was hailed as a conciliatory gesture to the Carter administration.[55] Also that spring, the Bundesrat passed the final version of the tax reform package, scaling it down but retaining its fiscal neutrality.[56]

Meanwhile, Carter's proposed tax and spending program was undergoing a metamorphosis as it was negotiated through Congress. The tax rebate, in particular, ran into difficulty. With the business community pressing for tax reductions that would benefit them directly, such as investment tax credits, and with labor unenthusiastic about the Carter proposal, preferring instead job-creation measures, the rebate lacked strong advocates on Capitol Hill. Furthermore, the American economy had performed very well in the first quarter, with growth near 9 percent on an annual basis, and Carter's economic advisers were privately becoming concerned about inflation. Consequently, the president decided in April to withdraw the rebate from congressional consideration, along with the business investment tax credit. This reduced the size of the proposed stimulus package by $14 billion. Nonetheless, the measures Congress finally adopted provided a stimulus of $32.2 billion, mostly in tax reductions, concentrated in 1978.[57] Schmidt and his colleagues lost no time claiming vindication by this apparent recognition of the dangers of inflation.

Carter's National Energy Plan. Concurrent with the negotiation of Carter's fiscal package through Congress and the preparations for the May 1977 London summit, a small group of officials and advisers, headed by James Schlesinger, were formulating the energy policies the administration would pursue with Congress over the next several years. Although not the immediate focus of discussion at the London summit, American energy policy would become controversial among the summit countries as the U.S. current position deteriorated and the dollar began to fall precipitously in autumn 1977. Because American energy policy would become a critical element in the Bonn summit agreement, its origins in the Carter administration bear consideration here.[58]

Schlesinger and his team were saddled with legislation enacted under the Nixon and Ford administrations. A two-tiered pricing system for domestically produced oil—designed to encourage production at the margin but to prevent large windfall profits on "old oil"—had been established under Nixon's wage and price controls, and this system was incorporated into congressional legislation at the outset of the first oil shock in November 1973. Subsequent attempts by the Nixon Treasury and Council of Economic Advisers to decontrol the price of old oil gave way, in large part because of congressional pressure, to a program whereby refiners were entitled to buy price-controlled oil in proportion to their refining capacity. This program equalized refiners' costs and held the prices to American consumers far below the world price. The policy held American demand high and had the indirect effect of subsidizing oil imports.

President Ford tried to bring U.S. oil-pricing policy back to free market principles, coupling decontrol with excise and windfall profits taxes in his proposals to Congress in 1975. Like Nixon, however, he failed in his efforts to put together a majority coalition to support his proposals. Despite widespread concern about excessive U.S. dependence on foreign oil, the issue was still framed in mostly domestic terms: would free market prices actually reduce domestic consumption and increase domestic production? In any event, would not decontrol merely redistribute income from middle- and working-class consumers and small businesses to the giant oil companies? Republicans favored decontrol but would not accept tax increases, whereas many Democrats sought to tighten and extend price controls beyond the scheduled expiration date in late 1975. Nor did the oil industry support President Ford, for the oil men gambled that when the current legislation expired they could have decontrol without windfall profits taxes. In essence, this same alignment of forces would continue to deadlock congressional action on decontrol until Carter finally moved to cut the Gordian knot in 1979.

The battle between Congress and President Ford was hard fought, with Congress voting to rescind executive discretion to levy oil import fees and only narrowly sustaining Ford's veto. By December 1975, Ford, unwilling to bear the political onus of sole responsibility for higher oil prices, had retreated to accepting an extension of mandatory price controls through June 1979, under the Energy Policy and Conservation Act. Without a successful linkage between a free market oil price and taxes on producers, a winning political coalition could not be built to support an oil-pricing policy—the key to any comprehensive American energy program—that curtailed the heavy effective subsidy to foreign imports.

Energy issues, surprisingly, held a low profile during the 1976 elections, with the exception of Carter's promise to decontrol "new" natural gas. Carter did not make any promises with regard to oil pricing before his election but pledged that he would submit a comprehensive energy program to Congress within the first ninety days of his administration. With the presentation of the National Energy Plan in April, Carter announced his view that price controls on domestic oil should be retained as long as world prices were arbitrarily determined by OPEC's exercise of monopoly power.

The plan's main objective was the reduction of American dependence on imported crude oil. Schlesinger and his team were determined to end the effective import subsidy without also giving cartel-determined profits to American oil companies. Although the plan comprised over a hundred separate initiatives, ranging from natural gas deregulation to energy conservation measures, its keystone was the crude oil equalization tax. By taxing producers the difference between the controlled price of oil and the world price, the tax was designed to "achieve the effects of free markets on the demand side but not the supply side."[59] Oil discovered before 1975 would be controlled indefinitely, rising in price along with inflation. Oil discovered after 1975 would be brought gradually up to the 1977 prevailing world price, frozen there, and allowed to increase from that point at the rate of inflation. "Stripper" oil would remain uncontrolled. The tax would be applied at the wellhead on all price-controlled domestic oil. Revenues from the new tax would be distributed to all taxpayers through income tax credits, and thus would represent no net gain or loss to either consumers or the government. But higher domestic prices would nonetheless be expected to encourage conservation.

The crude oil equalization tax was an elegant device designed not only to insulate the American economy from the adverse internal redistributive effects of the exercise of monopoly power in the world oil market, but also to muster an appropriate national response to the price increases. The brainchild of Schlesinger, it was developed within the energy group under the pressure of Carter's ninety-day deadline. The group was closed; the rest of the administration, including the Council of Economic Advisers, Treasury, and the White House domestic policy staff, not to mention Congress, was kept virtually in the dark about proposals that were being developed. Other officials were reportedly dismayed when the National Energy Plan was eventually unveiled, believing the equalization tax to be politically unappealing: the administration was asking for sacrifices from consumers without offering compelling benefits to producers.

Thus, after an initially friendly reception in Congress, by autumn 1977 this part of the package had lost the momentum it needed to clear both houses. At the time of the London summit in the spring, however, it still appeared that under the Carter administration the U.S. government might indeed be able to overcome the internal political impediments that had blocked previous administrations from mounting an effective national response to the energy problem.

Multilateral preparations. At meetings of the OECD in February 1977 and of the "sherpas" (the senior officials charged with preparing the summit) in March, the Americans continued their pressure on the Germans for added fiscal stimulus, with strong support from the British. Similar demands were made on the Germans in meetings of the EC finance ministers. In addition to the battery of counterarguments already outlined, the German representatives insisted that German growth for 1977 was likely to be in the 4.5–5.5 percent range, considerably stronger than forecast by the OECD. Despite German growth in the first quarter at less than half that rate, Schmidt personally assured Carter of the plausibility of this forecast in a meeting of the two men in advance of the summit. American growth, by contrast, had been strong during the first months of 1977—strong enough to warrant the withdrawal of the tax rebate and investment tax credit. Carter was thus asking Schmidt to stimulate the German economy with expansionary fiscal policy, while his own economy was being buoyed largely by the private sector. The revocation of the tax rebate only weeks before the summit had relieved some of the political pressure on Schmidt to follow suit. Carter, nonetheless, continued to press the chancellor and announced: "When we are selfish and try to have large trade surpluses, and a tight restraint on the international economy, then we make the weaker nations suffer too much." Schmidt, however, responded indirectly: "I do not believe that the French or the President of the United States will ask us in London to make more inflation. The English might like to see others make a bit more inflation, but I think it would be desirable for the rest of us to help them, as we have been doing until now, to come down from their inflation rate of 18 percent."[60]

The 1977 London summit. Prime Minister Callaghan opened the Downing Street summit by stressing the social costs and political risks of slow growth. He noted the current economic forecasts of the German and Japanese governments, and he urged them to redouble their efforts to make sure those targets were actually met. He welcomed the U.S. reflation but noted that it would inevitably cause an adverse shift in the balance of payments for the Americans over the next year. President Carter supported Callaghan's concerns about the surplus countries and promised continued U.S. growth. Later in the meeting, Chancellor of the Exchequer Denis Healey was blunter, discussing the problems of deficit countries and denouncing (from his recent personal experience) excessive IMF-imposed rigor. He hinted at protectionist responses to continued recession and singled out Germany and Japan for special criticism. In response, Chancellor Schmidt restated his concerns about inflation, but pledged "great efforts" to achieve the German growth targets. Japanese Prime Minister Takeo Fukuda, the oldest of the summiteers, movingly recalled his attendance at the 1933 London "world economic conference," whose failure had opened the floodgates to protectionism, depression, and war, and he said Japan would do its share to stimulate growth.

Meanwhile, officials worked on communiqué language to balance the conflicting concerns about inflation, unemployment, and growth. Over U.S. objections, and with the help of the French, who were seeking language that would be helpful in defending French Prime Minister Raymond Barre's austerity plan at home, Karl-Otto Pöhl, the German representative, succeeded in inserting the phrase that "inflation does not reduce unemployment. On the contrary, it is one of its major causes." This endorsement of the Germans' basic stance on economic policy was quoted in all German press commentaries following the summit, and would be hailed by Germans years later as one of the most significant achievements of German summit diplomacy.

The Americans and British did obtain their tactical objective in the very next sentence, in which the summiteers agreed to "commit our Governments to stated economic growth targets or to stabilization policies which, taken as a whole, should provide a basis for sustained non-inflationary growth in our own countries and worldwide, and for reduction of imbalances in international payments." Although the Germans and Japanese avoided the inclusion of specific figures in the communiqué itself, it was widely acknowledged that the Germans were aiming for 5.0 percent, the Japanese for 6.7 percent, and the Americans for nearly 6.0 percent. In addition, the three largest summit countries pledged to "keep their policies under review, and commit themselves to adopt *further policies*, if needed, to achieve their stated target rates and to contribute to the adjustment of payments imbalances."[61] Unfortunately, the German chancellor was unaware that, as he was making this promise at the summit, his statistics bureau and Economics Ministry at home were learning that the German economy had slowed early in the second quarter from the already low rate of the first quarter. The *Frankfurter Allgemeine Zeitung* noted with foreboding that Germany had

> committed itself to reach real growth of five percent this year. That is surprising and dangerous. . . . Perhaps the Government is saying to itself that the commitment does not mean much, since new stimulus measures have already been introduced, and the year is already half over. But even if the practical significance for this year is modest, a regrettable precedent is established for the future. Must the Federal Republic commit itself again next year?[62]

Meanwhile, Carter, who had just submitted the National Energy Plan to Congress, maneuvered to include helpful energy language in the summit communiqué that committed the participants to "conserve energy and increase and diversify energy production, so that we reduce our dependence on oil." Like the German growth target, this seemingly innocuous sentence embodied what would become a major item of contention during the 1978 summit.

With respect to trade, French President Valéry Giscard d'Estaing and Prime Minister Barre stressed the structural changes under way in the world economy and the consequent need to approach trade barriers in an "organized" way, a code word for resistance to free trade. The Americans, Germans, and Japanese succeeded in getting a commitment to "seek this year to achieve substantial progress" in the Tokyo round negotiations, but French, British, and Italian resistance diluted the communiqué language on trade, and French briefings afterward stressed the qualifications that had been introduced. Nevertheless, although no progress had even been attempted on the substantive issues in the GATT negotiations, U.S. Trade Representative Robert Strauss had received what he chose to interpret as his marching orders, and in July the Geneva talks moved into a more intensive phase.

The fate of the London summit's growth targets. The economic news for Germany worsened over the following weeks. When the chancellor learned that the economy had grown in the second quarter at an annual rate of merely 1.2 percent, he called an emergency meeting of the economic cabinet in the middle of the summer vacation. Schmidt stressed his personal stake in seeing that growth not fall too far below the 5 percent target reaffirmed in London. The chancellor told the group, meeting at his home in Hamburg, that because of the growth shortfall he had been *blamiert* ["shamed" or "made to look ridiculous"]. At this meeting, the economic cabinet laid the groundwork for a new package of expansionary measures, which was passed in the autumn by the Bundestag. It comprised mainly tax reductions for individuals and was expected to reduce revenue by more than DM 10 billion.[63]

The autumn 1977 tax package, however, came too late to boost growth before 1978. Privately, some German officials expressed embarrassment at the chancellor's having agreed to the 5 percent target in the first place. Aware that growth would fall significantly short, at the November 1977 OECD meeting the chairman of the German delegation to the Economic Policy Committee, Hans Tietmeyer, rejected the secretariat's call for further stimulation of the German economy and dismissed the idea of the locomotive theory as "naive."[64] By the end of the year it was apparent that German growth had reached barely half of the stated target. Further, although German inflation remained moderate, unemployment jumped dramatically in the third quarter of 1977 to 4.7 percent and remained high into the following year.[65] At the end of the year, the government predicted that with the latest tax package, 1978 growth would be 3.5 percent, consumer prices would increase by 3.5 percent, and unemployment would remain steady at 4.5 percent or would decline.[66] The government also announced that no further expansionary measures would be considered until the spring of 1978.

By contrast, the U.S. economy came quite close to meeting the London commitment, registering 5.5 percent growth in 1977.[67] The U.S. Council of Economic Advisers noted that the United States was the only major country to achieve its London target. (Japan's growth slowed abruptly from 7.1 percent in the first half of 1977 to barely half that in the second half.) From December 1976 to December 1977, the U.S. unemployment rate dropped 1.4 percent, to a three-year low of 6.4 percent. Inflation, brisk in the first half of 1977, moderated to 4.5 percent in the second half.[68]

The Winding Path to the Bonn Summit, 1977–78

The German policy debate evolves. The German Council of Economic Experts, the five national economic institutes, and the Bundesbank broadly agreed on the major economic issues facing Germany during 1977. Fiscal policy should have a circumscribed role in economic management, and consolidation of the budget should be its medium-term goal. German policymakers were caught by surprise, however, by the dramatic shortfall in growth in 1977, and they agreed that this situation represented one of the rare circumstances under which stimulative fiscal policy could properly be applied. In both the spring and fall of 1977, the institutes noted that, although all of the necessary conditions for robust growth were present, the recovery had stalled. They recommended that fiscal policy temporarily depart from the medium-term consolidation objective.[69] The council interpreted the growth shortfall as a confirmation of its late 1976 warning that a small economic package would be useful at that time, although growth was off even further than the council had expected without the measures.[70] In acquiescing in the autumn 1977 stimulus, the Bundesbank cited the deflationary effects of deutsche mark appreciation as an additional reason why an expansionary package would be acceptable. But it added that even a more "powerful" stimulation of domestic demand could not guarantee the neutralization of the dampening effects of the rising mark.[71]

In the exceptional event that a fiscal stimulus was necessary, these bodies of experts mostly recommended tax cuts, although some of the institutes advocated public investment projects. Preferably, those tax cuts would be directed toward the supply side of the economy to facilitate investment. Income tax cuts should be offset in the medium term by increases in the VAT, they argued.[72]

The three bodies were unanimous in their analysis that the primary cause of unemployment was excessive real wages. It was for this reason that they argued that fiscal expansion would in general not be helpful. Cognizant that the trade unions were threatening a difficult round of negotiations in the winter, the council repeatedly urged moderation in wage increases, as it had throughout the mid-1970s. These experts went so far as to argue that there was a short-term inverse relationship between wage increases and real growth. In late 1977 the council said that if wages were increased by 5.5 percent rather than 3.5 percent, growth would be 1.0 percent lower in 1978.[73] This was too extreme for the institutes and the Bundesbank, and the report had to be disavowed by the usually sympathetic Economics Ministry on the grounds that it would take longer than a year for the benefits of wage moderation to be realized.

Both the council and the institutes agreed that the Bundesbank should concentrate primarily on restraining money expansion to limit the scope for price increases. They adopted the "gradualist" monetarist position that the margin by which nominal growth exceeded real growth, permitted by increases in the money supply, should be reduced incrementally over the medium term. They did not criticize the Bundesbank for overshooting the 1977 growth targets, however, recognizing that foreign exchange intervention during the year increased the money stock. They did emphasize, however, as did the Bundesbank, that money growth would have to come back down in 1978 to target rates.

The FDP was sympathetic to this relatively austere policy approach, as was the Economics Ministry, headed by FDP Vice Chairman Count Otto Lambsdorff. The FDP and the Economics Ministry had not favored increasing the size of the budget deficit in early 1977, although they did favor a shift from current expenditure toward investment expenditure within the existing level of spending. The business community was broadly supportive of this stand, arguing that expansionary fiscal policy would aggravate inflation and create public finance problems that could not be easily resolved without an increase in taxes. Larger deficits would discourage investment by generating inflationary expectations and encouraging high wage demands. If a fiscal stimulus were to be administered, however, it should be in the form of tax cuts to corporations, particularly in trade, payroll, and property taxes.[74]

Important factions within the SPD and the trade unions disagreed. The unions were strongly in favor of fiscal stimulus through public investment projects and were diametrically opposed to the FDP and business groups on the issue of wage increases. In January 1977, after Schmidt had announced the ZIP but had left its size and timing unspecified, the trade union association president had demanded that the investment program be at least 1 percent of GNP.[75] It was largely to appease the trade unions and the left wing of the SPD that the program had been proposed in the first place. Nonetheless, the SPD often acted as a check on trade union demands during this period, arguing that overzealousness could embarrass the government and ultimately damage union interests. Sympathetic but realistic members of the SPD's left wing urged moderation in wage demands and discouraged the trade unions from pressing for more expansionary programs. The Finance Ministry was under SPD control but was in general resistant to using the federal budget to stimulate the economy.

Chancellor Schmidt mediated between the contending views and interests within this coalition, restraining the left wing of his party while prodding the FDP to be flexible. After the failure of the large post–oil shock deficits to spark a self-sustaining recovery in Germany, Schmidt's economic strategy, as publicly articulated, had shifted to reliance on private investment to generate the upswing. He was reported to believe that private investment would come about only if he could demonstrate to the business community that the deficits were indeed under effective political control. His private views, however, may well have remained closer to those of his earlier years in the chancellery and Finance Ministry. Indeed, Schmidt was the prime instigator of the 1977 stimulus package. That package appears to have been a well-balanced compromise between the different factions of his coalition. Although the measures did not specifically give advantages to investment, they were tax reductions rather than spending increases; although they were not the high-powered public investment programs the left had been advocating, the tax cuts were for individuals across the board rather than for narrow groups. The cuts, moreover, placed the government in a stronger position to argue for moderation in wage increases.

The opposition's ability to influence economic policy was hindered by its lack of strong leadership and by the absence of an authoritative spokesman on economic issues. After the first oil shock, the CDU-CSU had not proposed a credible and coherent alternative economic program, and when growth stalled again in 1976–77, they put forth no strong alternative solutions, although they did in general take the business community's view on the composition of any fiscal stimulus. Although Chancellor Schmidt had to be concerned to protect his political flanks and to retain his credibility as a sound and prudent manager of the German economy, the initiative on economic issues remained his.

American Economic Policy under Pressure. At the beginning of 1978, Jimmy Carter undertook the second major macroeconomic initiative of his administration. Announced in January, the package centered on a proposed series of personal and corporate tax reductions and reforms that amounted to a net $25 billion stimulus to take effect in October 1978. The administration predicted that this would create a million jobs and reduce the unemployment rate to 5.5–6.0 percent by late 1979. With these tax measures, growth could be maintained at 4.5–5.0 percent in both 1978 and 1979, but without them, growth would begin to fall in late 1978 and would hit only 3.5 percent in 1979. The president also put forth a voluntary program of wage and price restraints whereby 1978 wage and price increases would be kept below the average of the preceding two years. In addition he reaffirmed his medium-term objective of a balanced budget, but proclaimed his support for the Humphrey-Hawkins employment bill being developed in Congress, which would have committed the government to further spending on job programs.[76]

Carter noted the relatively slow growth in the rest of the world economy, reaffirmed U.S. responsibility to help ensure world prosperity, and restated his administration's view of the importance of German and Japanese reflation. More important, he publicly acknowledged for the first time that U.S. reflation could not proceed independently of the other major capitalist economies:

> The problems we face today are more complex and difficult than those of an earlier era. We cannot concentrate just on inflation, or just on unemployment, or just on deficits in the Federal budget or our international payments. Nor can we act in isolation from other countries. We must deal with all of these problems simultaneously and on a worldwide basis.[77]

This recognition did not imply (at least in the view of the administration), however, that the United States should adjust its own macroeconomic policy. Rather, the Americans were still calling on other countries to move into line. International constraints did not figure prominently in internal administration deliberations on the matter in the winter of 1977–78. The president added:

> The first priority in our international economic policy is continued economic recovery throughout the industrial world. Growth of the U.S. economy—the largest and strongest in the world—is of vital importance. The economic program that I have proposed will ensure that America remains a leader and a source of strength in the world economy. It is important that other strong nations join with us to take direct actions to spur demand within their own economies. World recovery cannot proceed, if nations rely upon exports as the principal source of economic expansion.[78]

The worsening U.S. payments position gave Carter an incentive to strengthen his appeal for foreign stimulus. The Ford and Carter administrations had both argued that the American external deficit was helpful to the world economy, in particular to the payments position of the weaker European countries. However, during 1977 the current account deficit had grown beyond the point where it could be defended as salutary. In just two years the U.S. current account had shifted into the red by $30 billion and registered a deficit of $18.5 billion—small by comparison with the deficits later reached in the 1980s, but in 1977 a postwar record. The overall balance on official settlements was $30 billion in deficit, implying substantial capital outflows financed by foreign intervention.[79] The administration cited this drag on American growth as a reason to implement the proposed 1978 tax cut.

Accordingly, just as the U.S. delegation at the time of the Mondale trip had predicted, downward pressure on the dollar ensued. During 1977 the dollar depreciated 10.8 percent against the mark, 22.3 percent against the yen, 18.0 percent against the Swiss franc, and 10.5 percent against the British pound. Appreciation against the Canadian dollar of 7.2 percent left the trade-weighted effective rate of the dollar down only 2.4 percent for the year.[80] Nonetheless, the major central banks intervened in large amounts in an effort to dampen the depreciation of the dollar against the European currencies and the yen, mostly in the fourth quarter of 1977.

However, the Council of Economic Advisers argued that foreign exchange intervention would not significantly stem the dollar's slide, which reflected underlying "fundamental" factors, mainly the current account deficit, and was rarely "disorderly" during the year. Furthermore, it would not be "appropriate" for a large country such as the United States "to modify domestic objectives for economic growth in order to reduce the current account deficit," since the "economic cost of changing domestic growth is large relative to the improvement in the current account that would result." The council further argued that exchange rate changes that did occur should be supported with domestic demand policies to bring about international adjustment; it urged that the adjustment of policies should be greater in those countries whose performance diverged most from established targets—that is, Germany and Japan.[81]

The U.S. Treasury appeared to take a less than neutral position with regard to the dollar. On May 25, 1977, when underlining the London summit commitments, Treasury Secretary Michael Blumenthal asserted that Germany and Japan had agreed not to resist market pressures for the appreciation of the yen and mark.[82] This was the first of a series of comments widely interpreted as a deliberate attempt to "talk down the dollar." Blumenthal made similar statements to the OECD ministers' meeting in June and at the annual meetings of the World Bank and IMF the following September. It appears that Blumenthal's remarks may actually have been taken out of context and misinterpreted, and that he did not intend to depress the dollar on the foreign exchange markets by his public statements. Nevertheless, these remarks followed criticism by Carter administration officials of others' exchange rate policies (Japan's in particular) and insistence by the administration (supported by the managing director of the IMF and the chairman of the Board of Governors of the Federal Reserve System) that surplus countries not resist upward pressures on their currencies. In this context, Blumenthal's failure to express optimism for the dollar was likely to be interpreted by the markets as at least willful neglect, if not an outright attempt to depress the dollar's value.[83] The public consensus, in any case, was that the secretary was indeed trying to depress the value of the dollar. This view was reinforced by the projected current account deficits for the United States, for many observers attributed Blumenthal's remarks to concern over those deficits. European officials noted that Blumenthal's trade negotiation background in the Kennedy and Johnson administrations gave him an acute awareness of the implications of the exchange rate for trade competitiveness. The exchange markets steadied through the summer, with the exception of the gradual depreciation of the dollar against the yen. During autumn 1977, however, the dollar began to fall precipitously.

American monetary policy, which had been quite expansionary during the first ten months of 1977, was tightened by the Federal Reserve in October. Accordingly, interest rates began to increase in the second half, with the prime rate reaching 8.0 percent in January 1978. For 1977 as a whole, currency plus demand deposits (M1) grew 7.9 percent. The Fed had thus broadly accommodated growth during the recovery sufficiently to please the Carter administration. For 1978 it maintained its long-term money growth objective of 4.0–6.5 percent, although this range was exceeded during the first three quarters.[84] In early 1978 the reins of monetary policy were transferred from Arthur Burns to Carter's nominee, G. William Miller. With Carter's man in office, there was little likelihood that monetary policy would threaten the recovery against the advice of the administration, within the next several months at least. Despite modest interest rate increases, therefore, the markets were not convinced that monetary policy would be used to defend the dollar.

Germany responds to the falling dollar. The response of the Germans to the declining dollar during 1977–78 was two-pronged: first, private and public criticism of the Carter administration policies; second, monetary loosening, largely through extended intervention in the foreign exchange markets, to slow the rise of the mark. The international reserves of the Bundesbank rose by $5.3 billion during the year, and by another $2 billion in the first quarter of 1978. This was combined with increases amounting to $6.6 billion for the Bank of Japan, and $16.2 billion for the Bank of England, reflecting the dramatic turnaround of the British external balance.[85] Moreover, in December 1977 the Bundesbank dropped the rediscount rate to an eighteen-year low of 3 percent.

As a result, German monetary growth overshot the central bank's targets for the year. Central bank money (the high-powered money base) grew at 9 percent rather than 8 percent. Currency and demand deposits grew at the more rapid rate of 11.4 percent.[86] Through most of 1977 the money supply expanded beyond the target rate, although without the express concurrence of Bundesbank officials. Toward the end of the year, as foreign exchange intervention became more intensive, the overshooting of the money supply was openly accepted. But the Bundesbank announced that the target rate of growth for central bank money would again be 8 percent in 1978 and—since money expansion in 1977 nearly exhausted the room for overshooting—the 1978 target would be adhered to.[87]

The Bundesbank complained repeatedly about having to intervene unilaterally to defend the dollar (that is, to prevent appreciation of the mark) and thus to finance the American payments deficit. Bundesbank officials argued publicly and privately that the American deficit had to be financed in the short run and significantly reduced in the medium term, and it was the Americans' responsibility to do both. The German central bank identified high U.S. growth rates and America's heavy imports of expensive oil as the prime causes of the current deficit.[88] In contrast to the growing U.S. deficit, the German current account surplus amounted to $4 billion during 1977, and official settlements were near balance.[89]

The measures taken in December 1977 and early January 1978 by the Carter administration ostensibly to support the dollar—expressions of concern, a publicly unspecified augmentation of the $2 billion currency swap lines between the U.S. Federal Reserve and the Bundesbank, and a half-point increase in the discount rate—proved to be largely symbolic. The basic exchange rate policy of the administration continued to be complacent in the face of accentuated day-to-day fluctuations in the markets during the first quarter of 1978. When this became clear to the Bundesbank, its president, Otmar Emminger, declared that "the surplus of dollars in world markets had become not only the key problem of the international monetary system but also a possible obstacle to world economic recovery and to an upswing in the German economy" in 1978.[90]

By early spring 1978, harsh criticism of German and Japanese trade surpluses in virtually every international forum was accompanied by increasing uneasiness about U.S. neglect of the dollar. Johannes Witteveen, managing director of the IMF, for example, called past expansionary moves by Germany and Japan "quite disappointing" and urged them to do more, but also called for more active U.S. intervention in defense of the dollar to offset its payments deficit.[91] As the dollar's difficulties continued, several schemes were proposed to stabilize it. Witteveen, supported by the British, pressed for a "substitution account" to spread the dollar's "burden" as a reserve currency. The Japanese expressed interest in a "target zone" exchange rate regime. Some European bankers called for the United States to raise large foreign loans. But neither the Americans nor the Germans were much attracted by these ideas. Both preferred to address "the fundamentals" behind the dollar's problems, although they could not agree whether the German (and Japanese) trade surpluses or U.S. oil imports and inflationary pressures were more fundamental.

On March 2, 1978, the dollar dropped below DM 2.00, a record low. This depreciation and widespread international criticism prompted the Carter administration to respond to German demands for concrete action, although the U.S. response was modest. In mid-March, the U.S. and German governments announced a bilateral pact designed to stabilize the foreign exchange markets. The United States agreed to a doubling of the existing currency swap lines to $4 billion, selling the Bundesbank $740 million equivalent in IMF special drawing rights (SDRs) for marks and expressing its willingness to draw on its IMF tranches if necessary to defend the dollar. The Bundesbank hailed this as a watershed because it was the first time since the switch to floating rates that the United States had expressed its willingness to use its own foreign exchange reserves to defend the dollar. In April the German central bank, upon the entering into force of Article IV of the Second Amendment to the IMF Articles of Agreement, reminded the United

States and the world that Washington had committed itself to anti-inflationary policies by agreeing "to direct economic and financial policies toward the objective of fostering orderly economic growth with reasonable price stability."[92]

However, the German-American agreement did not spare the Bundesbank from having to choose between appreciation of the mark and overshooting of the domestic monetary target. In April Emminger explained that the Bundesbank was following a "two-dimensional" policy of moderate appreciation of the mark coupled with foreign exchange intervention.[93] In early June, the Bundesbank officially reaffirmed its determination to hold money growth to the 1978 target, though adherence was becoming increasingly difficult.[94]

Meanwhile, unconvinced that the foreign exchange measures the Americans agreed to in March represented a significant departure from previous policy, Chancellor Schmidt had blown new wind into the sails of the becalmed European Monetary System (EMS) initiative that had been launched in late 1977 by the president of the European Commission, Roy Jenkins. Calling in April 1978 for a "zone of monetary stability" in Europe, Schmidt appeared to have two motives. First, he argued that by joining in a group with the other European currencies, Germany could minimize the effects of the appreciation of the mark against the dollar.[95] Second, it is also likely that Schmidt and Giscard saw the EMS as a way of reinforcing the relatively austere Barre plan in France. The EMS was debated during the same EC meetings as the joint reflation program, and at times the EMS was the primary object of negotiation. The proposed system would also constrain the international monetary policy of the Bundesbank, and thus it was strongly opposed in Frankfurt. However, the German government and central bank were in agreement on the appropriate short-run monetary response to the dollar depreciation. These developments set the monetary backdrop for German policy deliberations surrounding the economic summit scheduled for Bonn in July 1978. The dollar, while fluctuating in the second quarter, followed a roughly even trend during the three months preceding the summit.

International pressure on Germany. In the diplomatic maneuvering over German macroeconomic policy, the Americans had important allies abroad. Despite improvements in the balance-of-payments positions of France and Britain, and despite signs of improvement in Italy's external situation, a recovery sufficiently strong to reduce unemployment in German's EC partners was not a likely prospect. The smaller

European countries were also expected to lack strong demand and to see some rise in unemployment, but they were not expected to experience the same reduction in current account deficits as their larger partners. Meanwhile, the OECD projected that the German current surplus would rise to $5.2 billion in 1978.[96] Therefore, the other European countries continued to join the United States in pressing Germany to expand domestic demand. This pressure was applied in most of the international meetings and organizations that brought representatives of the advanced capitalist countries together, including the OECD, the EC, the IMF, and the summit preparatory sessions.

The reflation proposals were colored somewhat differently after the failure of most of the London summit participants to meet their growth targets. Greater emphasis was given to spreading the responsibility for collective macroeconomic management, with the deficit countries adopting anti-inflationary obligations, and the surplus countries adopting expansionary policies. There was also greater emphasis on *policy* commitments, which governments could directly control, as opposed to commitments on economic *performance*, over which they had less control.

The job of following up the London summit had been given to the OECD, and at the June 1977 ministers' meeting the governments agreed to submit to the secretariat in October their national current account and growth projections for 1978. After compiling these forecasts in the fall, the secretariat calculated that the governments expected a collective OECD growth rate of 4.5 percent in 1978. The secretariat believed, however, that this estimate was unrealistically high, given the national policies in place at the time, and predicted that without further stimulative measures the OECD growth rate would not exceed 3.5 percent, the outcome for 1977. However, the secretariat recommended a "differentiation" between policies of individual countries, permitting each to focus on different objectives that would collectively raise growth and improve the pattern of current account payments.[97]

The secretariat presented this argument at the November 1977 Economic Policy Committee meeting. In subsequent meetings of the Executive Council in Special Session in January 1978 and the EPC in February, the secretariat received encouragement to develop a detailed proposal for a joint reflation program. On the basis of this mandate, the secretariat asked each member government (1) the extent to which it could take expansionary measures, (2) what specific measures these might be, and (3) what would be the effects on it if other countries took hypothetical expansionary or anti-inflationary measures. The secretariat, working sometimes very closely with U.S. officials, then constructed a program of what it argued could be mutually consistent policy actions. This program was presented to member countries at the EPC meeting in May 1978. In the package, nine countries were to take expansionary action, a few small countries were to give more emphasis to the fight against inflation, and the rest were to continue the policy course already established. Germany and Japan, of course, were to take expansionary action, as were Belgium, Britain, Canada, France, Italy, Switzerland, and the Netherlands. The United States was not to take any further expansionary policy action beyond the measures already planned.

At the OECD in June 1978, barely a month before the heads of government were to meet in Bonn, their ministers agreed in principle to the joint reflationary plan developed by the secretariat. Moreover, they encouraged countries to raise domestic energy prices to world levels and stressed the importance of the United States adopting a comprehensive energy policy.[98] The particular macroeconomic measures that each country was expected to implement as part of the joint strategy were laid out in the secretariat's plan, but these measures were left conspicuously unspecified in the communiqué. The countries on whom the program essentially depended remained noncommittal until the heads of government met at the economic summit in Bonn in July.

Pressure on the Germans for faster growth was mounting within the EC as well. In April 1978 the European Council endorsed in principle a "concerted action" plan aimed at accelerating European recovery. All recognized that the strategy would entail additional German expansion. At the same meeting, Schmidt and Giscard put forward their startling proposal to create a "zone of monetary stability in Europe," and some observers thought they detected a link between the two initiatives: the Germans would agree to additional fiscal stimulus if the others would agree to the monetary discipline implicit in tying their currencies to the deutsche mark in the EMS. As in the OECD, Germany was isolated on the question of reflation. Under siege, and amid growing expectations of a German stimulus, Schmidt kept his cards close to his vest.

The July European summit held in Bremen, just ten days before the seven-power Bonn summit, was devoted largely to negotiations over the EMS. The same meeting broadly endorsed the European reflationary program, and the specific obligations of each country *except* the hosts were known. Because the Germans were withholding their commitment for the Bonn summit, however, national contributions were left unspecified in the Bremen communiqué, too. It ambiguously stated that "countries without inflation and balance-of-payments problems will do more to increase domestic demand, in particular investment demand, and the rate of economic growth," and added, "countries with steeply rising prices will first concentrate in particular on undesirable inflationary developments."[99] Despite the ambiguity of the German position, it was the widespread impression of European officials present at Bremen that the meeting was so well stage-managed that it would have been surprising had the German government not undertaken a significant stimulus at Bonn. Schmidt did not want to give away his hand before the Bonn meeting, the only forum in which he could extract any concession from the American president.

The issue of U.S. oil prices. While the Germans (and the Japanese) were becoming isolated on the macroeconomic question in autumn 1977 and winter 1978, the Americans were becoming isolated on energy policy. Over the course of 1977 the effects of a lack of a comprehensive energy plan were becoming clear. The economic recovery in the United States and the deliberate maintenance of oil prices below world levels caused an increase in total consumption, when conservation was needed instead. After declining in 1974 and 1975, oil consumption and total energy consumption had resumed their upward climb in 1976 and 1977. The increase in consumption, coupled with the temporary decline in domestic production pending the coming on stream of Alaskan oil in September 1977, generated increases in oil imports of 20 percent in 1976 and 18 percent in 1977. The increased quantity of imports and higher prices combined to raise the oil import bill ninefold over the course of 1972–77, from $5 billion to $45 billion. These imports weighed heavily on the American trade account. The comparison with other advanced industrial states is particularly striking. Whereas crude oil imports elsewhere in the West declined over 1973–76, American imports rose by over 60 percent.[100] Thus, in addition to a larger current deficit and downward pressure on the dollar, American policy also generated an increase in world crude oil demand that threatened to make the resource more expensive for all countries. The allies castigated what they saw as American exploitation of their own efforts to curb consumption.

Despite the clear consequences of inattention to the energy problem, Congress was unwilling to adopt the bold provisions of Carter's National Energy Plan. The plan had been divided into five separate bills, dealing with conservation, coal conversion, utility rates, natural gas pricing, and energy taxes (including the crude oil equalization tax). The first three passed through both houses and the House-Senate conference committee with relative ease. However, natural gas pricing and the equalization tax generated discord. Just before the August 1977 recess, the tax had squeaked through the House, 219–203, under the stewardship of Speaker Thomas P. O'Neill. By the fall, however, the Bert Lance affair had abruptly ended Jimmy Carter's honeymoon period, and the equalization tax had run aground in the Senate Finance Committee, chaired by Russell Long of Louisiana, a long-standing advocate of oil company interests. Supported both by his colleagues who wanted continued controls but opposed further taxes and by those who wanted outright decontrol, Long replaced the equalization tax with a series of generous tax credits to industry for conservation and conversion. Virtually no progress on this issue was made on Capitol Hill during the rest of the session. However, both the president and Schlesinger—now secretary of the new Department of Energy—continued to invest their hopes in the proposal. Despite Long's announcement in March 1978 that the "White House is beating a dead horse when they talk about that [crude oil equalization] tax," and that it would not pass the Senate "under any imaginable set of circumstances,"[101] some senior administration officials continued to hope for its passage until well into the autumn of 1978.

America's economic partners were increasingly critical, registering their discontent at the November 1977 EPC meeting and elsewhere. With the exception of Canada (which, with substantial domestic production, also maintained prices below world levels), OECD criticism was unanimous. The EPC's chairman, Charles Schultze, duly reported the foreign complaints about U.S. energy policy to the press and to his colleagues in Washington. The strong perception among the allies that the fall of the dollar was linked to the fate of the administration's energy package in Congress was widely shared within the U.S. government. Measures that reduced U.S. oil imports were expected to help the dollar, at least over the long term. That perception gave additional reason to press Congress strongly for a more rational oil-pricing policy.

Because of the international implications of domestic oil price controls, foreign economic policy officials within the administration were particularly sensitive to the need for a remedy. Frustrated by the lack of movement on this most important part of the national energy plan, some administration officials actually encouraged foreign criticism of U.S. energy policy, in the hope that the criticism would help generate the necessary impetus to pass stringent measures. Many administration officials whose responsibilities were mainly in domestic economic affairs were less sensitive to the international disequilibrium caused by holding oil prices down and less sanguine about the domestic political usefulness of foreign complaints. Some economists in the Department of Energy and elsewhere favored higher prices on the grounds of general economic rationality. For most key domestic officials, however, the potential political costs of higher oil prices and the risks of accelerating inflation outweighed the international arguments. Their position reminded one senior official of the Augustinian prayer, "Let me renounce sin, O Lord, but please not yet." Thus, in early 1978 a division on oil price decontrol began to emerge within the administration, especially between officials with domestic political responsibilities, such as Vice President Mondale, Chief Domestic Adviser Stuart Eizenstat, and White House Chief of Staff Hamilton Jordan, on the one side, and those concerned with international economics, such as Richard Cooper and Henry Owen, Carter's sherpa for Western summits. Schultze, Schlesinger, and others were caught in the middle, between their appreciation for the virtues of simple free market pricing and their sensitivity to various competing priorities, including the mounting risks of inflation and the still faint hope of resuscitating the crude oil tax.

Progress in the trade talks. Meanwhile, in the aftermath of the London summit commitment to "substantive progress" by the time of the Bonn rendezvous, the first significant progress in the Tokyo round of trade talks had been made in Geneva. Negotiations were in full swing in three important areas: tariff reduction, nontariff barriers (NTBs) to trade, and revisions to the GATT articles, which were of interest to developing countries. Trade issues were not the responsibility of the summit sherpas. The sherpas instead monitored the progress being made by Robert Strauss; his EC and Japanese counterparts, Wilhelm Haferkamp and Nobuhiko Ushiba; and their colleagues in Geneva. The summit was then used to ratify the tentative agreements and to give further impetus to the negotiations.

On issues of trade, unlike macroeconomics and energy, the Germans and Americans were closely allied. At French insistence, but with occasional support from the British and Italians, the EC negotiators had been dragging their feet in Geneva, as the Americans and Germans saw it. Privately, President Giscard already recognized that a deal was unavoidable, given French isolation on the issue. However, he intended that his acquiescence would be accepted as his contribution to the Bonn package, and he was naturally also concerned to minimize the risks to French interests.

The most important and problematic of the trade issues were NTBs. Governments tried to negotiate "codes of conduct" in six separate areas: technical standards, subsidies and countervailing duties, safeguards, government procurement, customs valuation, and import licensing. Since the London summit, important progress had been made in all these areas. In mid-1978, however, safeguards and subsidies and countervailing duties remained particularly contentious. The parties were also split on tariffs and agriculture. To prepare an agreement for the summit, the head negotiators redoubled their efforts during June and July.[102]

On the question of subsidies and countervailing duties, the United States was anxious to proscribe not only export subsidies but also production subsidies, which confer export advantages. The EC was staunchly opposed to this position, particularly because many of the large member countries such as the United Kingdom, France, and Italy relied heavily on production subsidies as instruments of government economic policy. Under pressure of the impending Bonn summit, negotiators were able to produce an "Outline of an Arrangement" that established the conceptual structure of the agreement finally reached in subsequent negotiations. On the issue of safeguards, the EC and developing countries were mostly opposed, with the United States taking an intermediate position, but one that was still unacceptable to the Europeans. Language on safeguards agreed on in mid-July proved controversial even at the summit; indeed, no final accord was ever reached in the Tokyo round on this issue. Similar texts outlining areas of agreement were drawn up in the other NTB areas in the final days preceding the summit. The presummit drafts on government procurement, customs valuation, and technical standards put agreements into nearly final form, and from the beginning there had been a broad consensus among the negotiating parties on import licensing. Deliberations on tariffs, a nondivisible set of negotiations, were not accelerated for the benefit of the summit. Agriculture continued to be too contentious an area for Tokyo round, much less summit, agreement. Many of the agreements on NTBs were negotiated in Geneva during the week before the summit and were rushed to Bonn for presentation to the heads of government.

U.S.-German diplomacy in the summit preparations. The preparations for the Bonn summit itself took place in parallel with the development of the joint reflationary program in the EC and OECD. The sherpas met three times before the summit. Their assistants, in turn, held a series of meetings to establish common ground on the economic issues before the summit. It was in these preparatory meetings, and in bilateral sessions between the heads of government themselves in the spring and early summer, that the outlines of the Bonn summit "deal" began to take shape.

Because the United States and Germany had mutual grievances on the macroeconomic and energy issues—and were joined in both criticisms by a broad international consensus—an exchange of concessions was a logical point on which the two sides might converge. Such an agreement would require domestic political support within each country for the necessary policy changes. Between the German announcement in January that the next summit would be held in Bonn and the actual meeting in July, the two sides cautiously moved toward an accord, bringing in the other summit countries as well. International initiatives formally laid out the prospective agreement, but it was not clear until July 1978 that domestic political forces would permit international expectations to be fulfilled. What seemed on the surface to be the result of hard international bargaining entailed hard domestic bargaining as well.

At the outset it was not clear that President Carter would attend the 1978 summit. In February, Treasury Secretary Blumenthal visited Bonn, driving home U.S. views by threatening that the Americans might skip the meeting unless an advance understanding could be reached on German growth.[103] Though the Germans correctly surmised that the Americans were bluffing, Schmidt did offer private assurances that he would move on the growth issue if the United States did its part. On March 12, the administration announced that it would indeed attend the summit, and the internal politics over the growth and energy issues heated up.

U.K. Prime Minister Callaghan was the first head of government to propose that an explicit exchange be made between the Americans and Germans. Callaghan held a unique position between the two sides. First, the British government perceived itself to be a bystander, along with others, caught in the middle of a dangerous game of "chicken," wherein Bonn and Washington would blame one another for foreign exchange instability and general international economic problems.[104] Second, Callaghan saw himself as an honest broker between his mutually distrustful colleagues, Carter and Schmidt. Third, Callaghan wanted desperately to relax the international constraints on British growth in time for an election in autumn 1978. Thus, in mid-March, he visited Bonn and Washington to suggest the outline of a comprehensive package deal for the summit: the Germans would accelerate growth; the Americans would agree to conserve energy and to share more broadly the burdens of managing the international monetary system; the French and British would agree to liberalize trade; and all would increase aid to the developing world. Neither the Germans nor the Americans liked the U.K. ideas on currency reform, but the notion of a package of offsetting concessions from the summit participants was attractive. The Americans suggested that their part of the bargain should include energy conservation and inflation fighting, two issues on which the Carter administration could use some international support domestically.[105] Callaghan's initiative was an important step forward and contained virtually all the elements of the eventual Bonn settlement. The outlines of this package were sanctioned at the first meeting of the summit sherpas in Bonn at the end of March. Despite a bitter exchange between Carter and Schmidt at this time over the issue of production and deployment of the neutron bomb, Schmidt and Henry Owen, Carter's sherpa, discussed the idea of exchanging assurances at the summit—the Americans on energy, and the Germans on macroeconomics.[106]

The summit paper on macroeconomic issues was the province of a committee, chaired by Charles Schultze, consisting of the EPC representatives from the other summit countries. After soliciting comments from the other representatives and circulating a draft to them in April 1978, Schultze convened the group in Washington in mid-May to finalize the paper. The German delegate, Hans Tietmeyer, remained noncommittal on the subject of a stimulus during the Washington meeting, but he did not reject as totally out of the question Schultze's suggestion that the German stimulus be 1 percent of GNP. Concurrently, the chorus favoring stimulus received amplification from outside the summit process. At an IMF interim committee meeting in Mexico City, German Finance Minister Hans Matthöfer faced nearly unanimous complaints about the restrictiveness of his government's policies. Although rejecting expansionary measures at Mexico City, he seemed to leave the door open for a later policy shift and privately confided to Americans that he expected new stimulus measures to be introduced by his government.[107]

Schultze presented the macroeconomic paper to the summit sherpas in Washington at the end of May. They in turn prepared a draft summit communiqué that left blanks for the crucial passages covering the size of the German stimulus and the date for U.S. oil price decontrol. The nascent summit deal was then presented to both governments. In Washington, Henry Owen first outlined the deal in detail to the White House Economic Policy Group and then to the full cabinet on June 5. Meanwhile in Bonn Horst Schulmann, Schmidt's sherpa, made his report. The bargain at this point remained uncertain, and there was much maneuvering within each capital on the macroeconomic and oil-pricing issues.

Formulating the U.S. contribution. In the United States, growth had slowed to 1.9 percent on an annual basis in the first quarter of 1978 but reaccelerated to 8.3 percent in the second quarter, while unemployment hovered slightly above 6.0 percent. After abating in the second half of 1977, however, inflation had doubled in the first half of 1978. In April Schultze reported to the cabinet that consumer prices had increased 8.2 percent on an annual basis during the first quarter, and producer prices even more. The next month he reported that the administration was fifteen months ahead of schedule in the reduction of unemployment. (In January 1977, Schultze had anticipated that the 6 percent level would not be reached until the end of 1979.) Nonetheless, Schultze continued to argue that a substantial tax cut was necessary, and there was no vocal opposition to this view within the Economic Policy Group or the cabinet at this time. Treasury Secretary Blumenthal, for example, agreed that the risks were on the down side.

But the inflation news did persuade the administration to adjust the size and timing of the stimulus. In May 1978, for the second time in as many years, the administration announced that it was reducing its proposed tax cut, to $20 billion, and rescheduled it to take effect at the beginning of 1979, rather than October 1, 1978. In part this move was thought necessary to calm the anxious Federal Reserve and to help to avoid a further increase in interest rates. At the same time, Schultze announced to the OECD that the United States would not participate in the joint reflationary program by stimulating the economy beyond the tax cut program. U.S. officials at the May EPC meeting said it was "desirable and necessary" that the United States not grow by more than 4.0–4.5 percent in 1978 because of inflation and balance-of-payments considerations.[108]

Despite unexpectedly low unemployment and high inflation, there is no evidence that any high administration official strongly advocated a wholesale change toward demand restraint during the spring of 1978. Since taking office in January 1977, the administration had faced a dilemma—should it forgo demand expansion or institute stronger incomes policies? Forgoing demand expansion would alienate core supporters within the Democratic party. Both business and labor opposed incomes policies to restrain price increases. As inflation surged again in the winter and spring of 1978, this dilemma sharpened. The initial reaction within the administration was to consider more seriously administrative measures, wage-price guidelines, and intensive consultations with labor and business to scrutinize major labor agreements and pricing decisions. These functions would reside in the Council on Wage and Price Stability, which would be given expanded powers. However, the widespread unpopularity of incomes policy ensured that phase one of Carter's anti-inflationary program would be entirely voluntary. Blocked from instituting a strong incomes policy—and not yet willing to bite the political bullet by shelving the tax cut or tightening monetary policy—the administration refrained from serious anti-inflationary measures throughout the Bonn summit and into the following autumn. Nor were the Americans seriously pressed by their foreign interlocutors to make domestic stringency a part of their contribution to the emerging summit package.

Instead, the Americans were facing ever-sharper complaints about oil policy. As the summit approached, the domestic politics of this issue also became more heated. Carter and Schlesinger were determined to push the crude oil equalization tax until all possibilities for congressional passage had been exhausted. They adopted a new tactic, threatening to act unilaterally if Congress did not approve the tax. With the aim of passing the tax before July 1978, they threatened to impose a $5–$6 per barrel import fee on crude oil. Foreseeing this tactic, Robert Dole, the ranking minority member of the Senate Finance Committee, and thirty supporters sponsored a Senate resolution stating that the president should not impose import fees. This reiterated an earlier clause, inserted in the Senate version of the energy tax bill, that prohibited the president's imposing such fees except in "time of war or national emergency."

But as the summit neared, Carter reaffirmed his determination to act alone if Congress failed to act. In a White House meeting with key legislators at the end of June, Carter noted in his diary, "I got all of those who would speak out to advise me . . . to tell our partners at the Bonn economic summit meeting that if Congress did not act to raise the domestic price up to the world level by 1980, then I would act administratively."[109] Senator Dole, however, emerged defiant from the meeting, and on June 27 the Senate passed an amendment sponsored by him that would prohibit the president outright from imposing either fees or quotas on oil imports. The Senate debate over the amendment revealed the importance of the upcoming gathering of heads of government for oil-pricing policy. Speaking for the amendment's supporters, Senator Edward Brooke announced, "It is essential that the President receive a clear message that he is not yet in a position to commit our Nation to an import restriction program at the [Bonn] economic summit meetings."[110]

Opponents to the Dole amendment argued that the president should be given free rein to bargain at Bonn. Anticipating the summit, Senator Herman Talmadge of the Finance Committee said, "I do not think we should deliberately tie the hands of the President." Senator Henry Jackson agreed:

> To severely limit the President's options before the tax bill is complete, and on the eve of his departure to the economic summit, would unnecessarily damage the prospects for success at the summit and underscore our energy paralysis for the rest of the world.[111]

Aware that the Senate's action threatened to undermine faith in his ability to fulfill his part of the nascent summit deal, Carter sent Majority Leader Robert Byrd to Bonn to assure Chancellor Schmidt that the prospects for eventual legislative success were still good. Nevertheless, on the eve of the summit, key members of the U.S. delegation were privately worried more about their ability to deliver their own part of the deal than about the contributions of the other summiteers.

Of course, the administration's options were not limited to the crude oil tax, import fees, or import quotas, even though these were apparently the main alternatives under consideration before the Bonn summit. Outright price decontrol was the other means of reducing American oil consumption and was considered (but not emphasized) among the president's options before the summit. The administration could act without the consent of Congress to raise prices as early as June 1979, and discretionary price controls would automatically expire in October 1981 unless Congress extended control legislation. Allowing domestic oil prices to increase, however, would generate windfall profits for producers of "old oil," and that had been a key stumbling block all along. To be sure, producers could be prevented from reaping monopoly rents through a tax on the windfall to the oil industry. Such a tax, the administration would later discover, would be easier to pass through Congress once the decision had already been taken to raise prices to world levels. In most important respects, the end results would be the same as originally envisioned by the Carter plan: domestic oil prices to consumers would be raised to world levels, and the oil companies would be prevented from reaping unseemly profits. But there proved to be fundamental political differences between the two alternative routes to the same objective. Once the president had taken the heat for higher prices, Congress would come under strong pressure to ensure that the result did not merely enrich the oil companies.

Thus the summit would help to break the deadlock on oil policy in part by separating the decision on *whether* and *how soon* to raise prices to world levels from the *means* to accomplish that goal. In addition, the gathering international debate about American energy indiscipline increasingly influenced the domestic debate, both within the administration and between it and the Congress. The issue of domestic oil prices was no longer defined, as it had been between 1975 and 1978, almost entirely in domestic terms, and this shift would accelerate after the Bonn summit accord was reached.[112] In effect, the advocates of decontrol within the administration were gaining support from a transnational alignment of forces.

As the president prepared to leave for Bonn, officials at the Treasury Department, the National Security Council, and the State Department, as well as Henry Owen, favored pledging an early move to world prices. The White House staff thought such a pledge would be unwise, unnecessarily exposing the president to domestic criticism in advance of the 1980 elections. Stuart Eizenstat and his domestic policy staff were particularly sensitive to the demands of Carter's political constituency and to the risks of the president's taking responsibility for raising oil prices. They also worried that an oil price pledge at the summit would incite congressional action to restrict the president's authority to act unilaterally. Energy Secretary Schlesinger, still hoping to breathe life back into the crude oil equalization tax, was supportive of the pledge but wary that the summit might complicate his negotiations with Congress. He advised that the administration be willing to go to world oil prices by 1980 or 1981, but he urged that nothing be done that would weaken his hand with Congress. Schultze, who occupied the middle ground throughout the controversy, wrote the president on the eve of his departure that

> over the next week, you will have to decide specifically what to say about energy policy at Bonn. . . . Summing up the benefits and the risks, I conclude that *in the absence of major gains at the Bonn Summit, I would recommend not committing to administrative actions at this time.* The risks for the economy, the increased inflationary pressures, and the political expression of Congress on this subject argue against the wisdom of this commitment at this time, *unless there is an offsetting quid pro quo.*[113]

Despite widespread awareness that such a deal was in the offing, there was apparently no unambiguous administration decision before the summit to pledge early decontrol, in contrast to the readiness on the part of both coalition members in Bonn to proceed with the German stimulus. The outlines of the summit deal had been presented to the White House Economic Policy Group and the cabinet in early June, and the possible summit concession was clearly uppermost in the minds of members of Congress, as well as the president. But the deliberations over the pledge within the administration were incomplete. Those officials on the international "track" within the administration thought that the oil-pricing pledge had been thoroughly discussed and that while the president might not have made a formal decision, he was clearly leaning toward making the pledge. But those on the domestic track had a very different perception of the presummit deliberations. As Carter left Washington, his domestic policy staff was evidently unaware that the president was about to commit the administration to raising domestic oil prices. The president did not receive a full briefing of the domestic political consequences of the summit decision before his departure. When later informed by Henry Owen in a phone call from Bonn that the president had agreed that "the prices paid for oil in the United States shall be raised to the world level by the end of 1980," Stuart Eizenstat and his assistant for energy policy,

Katherine Schirmer, were shocked. For them, that commitment was only the beginning of debate within the administration, not the end.

Formulating the German contribution. In Bonn, meanwhile, the Schmidt government was on the verge of reversing its oft-repeated and adamant refusal to contemplate additional reflation. It is worth pausing at this point to ask how this about-face could have occurred. The simple myth, then and now, is that a reluctant government, led by a reluctant chancellor, was forced to take an unwise step by overwhelming international pressure. The facts are more complex and more interesting.

During spring 1978 a domestic political process, inspired by foreign pressures but orchestrated by expansionists within the German government, led to a situation in which a revision of German economic policy would have been highly likely, even if the international pressure had eased. In effect, those closest to Schmidt confide, the chancellor "let himself be pushed" into a policy that he probably favored on domestic grounds but would have found costly and perhaps impossible to pursue without the "tail wind" provided by the summit.[114]

As 1978 opened, support within German domestic politics for additional expansion was visible only in the trade union movement and the SPD. Those forces were heartened by the international clamor for faster German growth, but alone they provided an inadequate basis for policy change. At the time of Treasury Secretary Blumenthal's February visit, for example, both the German Chamber of Industry and Commerce and the opposition CDU economics spokesman cheered the chancellor's rejection of additional stimulus, as did virtually all the German press. Most senior officials in the Finance and Economics ministries opposed further reflation; indeed, Finance Minister Hans Apel had resisted foreign pressure in that direction for more than four years. An even more important adversary was FDP Economics Minister Otto Lambsdorff, given the coalition's narrow parliamentary margin. Finally, the powerful Bundesbank maintained its traditional defense of fiscal and monetary rectitude.

Within four months, however, each of these partners in Germany economic policymaking had become members—some reluctant, some enthusiastic—of a broad consensus for additional fiscal stimulus. In February 1978, the replacement of Apel by Matthöfer meant that the Finance Ministry was represented by someone less inclined to argue against reflation. Meanwhile, the mood in broader economic circles began to shift. Updated economic indicators encouraged these conversions to some extent, for the latest data showed continued undershooting of growth targets and rising unemployment, caused in part by appreciation of the mark.

Chancellor Schmidt himself remained publicly noncommittal on the subject of the stimulus and occasionally was even hostile to the idea. There is strong evidence, however, that he was privately much more favorably disposed to the stimulus at the time. By early 1978, several of Schmidt's closest economic advisers had privately concluded that a reflationary program was in Germany's own interest, rather than merely internationally desirable. Their line of argument was strikingly similar to that of the OECD, the Americans, and their allies. Outlining the basic summit package, his closest economic adviser counseled the chancellor in mid-May 1978 that the stagnation of the German economy would continue without new stimulative measures, that inflation would remain low for the foreseeable future, that international macroeconomic interdependence necessitated collective action, and, therefore, that Germany should accede to the concerted reflationary program at the upcoming summit. This German official reasoned:

> Only with a more equilibrated balance of payments situation in the OECD area will there also be more calm in the exchange rates between the currencies of the deficit and surplus countries. Our economies have grown close together in recent years. For this reason, the idea of a concerted strategy among the industrialized countries has won more and more friends. If the Federal Republic takes part in such a concerted action, it does so not out of altruism, but out of solid national interest. Given the export dependence of our economy, a higher employment level can be achieved only if our exports rise more strongly. This assumes that we put our partners in a position to import more goods from the Federal Republic. Essentially, that must happen through higher imports by the Federal Republic, and that in turn assumes that domestic demand here at home rises more sharply than is to be expected according to current trends.[115]

Equally important, the chancellor's advisers were acutely aware of his political need to plan for adequate economic growth during the approach to the 1980 elections.

In retrospect, all evidence suggests the chancellor shared the views of his advisers on the desirability of additional reflation in terms of his own and Germany's interests. But there were two good reasons for him to disguise his preferences. First, as the reconciler of the diverse views within his coalition, Schmidt could not push his personal position too strongly until the right moment. He had to wait for the more conservative members of his coalition, the Bundesbank, and the business community to move closer to supporting reflation. (Early in 1978 domestic political advisers in the chancellor's office had urged that the summit be held before the June elections in Hamburg and Lower Saxony, so that the SPD could profit at the polls from the aura around the chancellor at the meetings; Schmidt chose instead to host the summit in mid-July, in part because he expected that the FDP would be more favorably disposed to a stimulus later in the year.) Most important, disguising his true preferences permitted the chancellor to maintain his reputation as a sturdy defender of German interests and, above all, of price stability.

Second, Schmidt's public opposition to reflation increased his bargaining leverage with the Americans and the other European countries. If international demands for German reflation continued—a good bet—the chancellor might win energy restraint from the Americans and concessions on trade policy from the British and French, while ensuring timely German expansion and reinforcing his stature both nationally and internationally. In short, the chancellor was following Br'er Rabbit's "please don't throw me in the briar patch" strategy. Rarely has a strategy in international political economy been played with such skill or success.

In their spring 1978 report, the five economic institutes endorsed the fiscal stimulus, although they disagreed with the SPD's left wing and the trade unions on the composition of an expansionary package. They forecast that growth would fall 1.0 percent short of the government's 3.5 percent target and recommended a 5.0 percent across-the-board tax reduction and income tax reforms to redress the shortfall.[116]

Economics Minister Lambsdorff had been steadfastly opposed to the idea of an immediate stimulus. During a trip to Washington in early February, he said that the German government would wait to see the effects of the stimulus administered at the beginning of 1978 before considering further measures. Although he did not completely reject the possibility of adopting stimulative measures later, Lambsdorff argued that formulating one program just after instituting another would provoke inflation and paralyze decisionmaking within the business community, and that the United States should stop pressuring the Germans on the issue. Furthermore, he warned the United States that fighting inflation and reducing oil imports would be necessary to stabilize the dollar and correct the U.S. payments deficit. During the spring, Lambsdorff reiterated that the autumn 1977 tax cut package had pressed Bonn's fiscal policy efforts to "the limits of what is feasible in political and economic terms," and rejected as "senseless" the recommendation of the German economic institutes for a stimulus.[117]

Over the months preceding the summit, economic and political events conspired to nudge Lambsdorff toward stimulus. Not only did the autumn 1977 tax cut fail to revive the economy in the second quarter of 1978, but the FDP suffered significant defeats in June elections in Hamburg and Lower Saxony, where the Liberals formed governments with the SPD and the CDU, respectively. In Lower Saxony, the FDP vote declined by one-third, to 4.2 percent. In Hamburg, the FDP lost more than half of its previous vote and polled 4.8 percent. Because it failed to reach the 5 percent threshold, the FDP lost all representation in both *Land* parliaments.[118]

With these political difficulties in mind, Lambsdorff publicly announced his support for tax cuts during a June visit to Washington, although he remained noncommittal about any specific stimulus. Officials within the Economics Ministry were also reported to have pointed out to the minister that a stimulus could be defended on sound conservative economic grounds. In early July Lambsdorff sent a letter to Schmidt saying that the time was now ripe for a stimulus. That letter was then leaked to the press on the eve of the summit.[119] Hearing early reports of Lambsdorff's shift, Chancellor Schmidt smiled triumphantly at one senior aide. His strategy had worked: domestic and international pressure had at last removed the primary obstacle within his coalition to further reflation.

The position of the German business community, once fairly solidly opposed to increasing the size of the budget deficit, became split during the approach to the summit. Beyond the effects of slow growth, the appreciation of the mark had further damaged the profitability of German firms. Moreover, there were particular sectors and firms that stood to gain directly from a possible stimulus. Thus the Federation of German Industry criticized the locomotive strategy in its May 1978 annual report but stressed the need to maintain economic growth and reiterated that reducing corporate taxes in Germany could stimulate growth without any medium-term increase in budget deficits. On an international scale, the business community endorsed the joint reflationary stratagem, provided that spending and inflation were not raised.[120] Like Lambsdorff, business leaders had now moved from the issue of *whether* to the issue of *how*, and they were intent on ensuring that stimulus would take the form of tax cuts rather than spending increases.

Bundesbank president Otmar Emminger was perhaps the most staunch opponent to the stimulus in early summer, remaining steadfast while allies previously opposed to stimulus were wavering or had already shifted to supporting expansion. After a central bank council meeting in Hannover at the beginning of June, Emminger announced that business activity had resumed sufficiently so that it was unnecessary to make a reflationary commitment at the upcoming summit.[121] When Arthur Burns visited Germany shortly before the summit, Emminger secretly enlisted his help in trying to dissuade the chancellor from proceeding with a stimulus package. The chancellor was apparently unmoved.

However, Bundesbank officials apparently were not unanimous on either the monetary or fiscal issue. Karl-Otto Pöhl, who had left the Finance Ministry to become vice president of the Bundesbank and was soon to succeed Emminger, was critical of U.S. monetary and foreign exchange policy. But three weeks after Emminger had delivered his sharpest attack yet on the Carter administration, Pöhl stated that recent criticism of U.S. monetary officials had been "exaggerated."[122] Some Bundesbank officials felt that the central bank faced a dilemma between allowing the mark to appreciate and approving a domestic fiscal stimulus. They tended to be more favorably disposed to a fiscal stimulus in light of continued slow growth, stable domestic prices, and widening external surpluses. A rapidly rising mark threatened further to reduce future growth. Before the summit, some officials made public statements to the effect that monetary policy would be sufficiently loose so that a fiscal stimulus, should it occur, would not crowd out private investment. In the end, the central bank council agreed to tell the government how large a fiscal deficit would be permissible in the bank's view, in effect agreeing to a monetary policy that would accommodate the stimulus program.

By June the domestic stimulus movement had taken on such momentum that the chancellor tried to dampen the flames—*not* because he did not want to see a stimulus, but out of fear that his bargaining position in relation to the United States would be undercut. "Let's wait a while, until after the summit," he told his colleagues. "Make them [the Americans and their allies] force me to do it." As the summit neared, Schmidt kept his hand well concealed, even from people within his own government. During this period, although he consulted frequently with cabinet officials, he consulted very little with representatives of interest groups on the macroeconomic issue. In the end, the Bonn summit decision was presented as a fait accompli to the hold-outs in the business and banking community, who subsequently acceded to the agreement.

In short, the *fact* of a significant German stimulus program was driven in the final analysis as much by domestic as by foreign pressures. The foreign pressure had catalyzed a reaction in domestic politics that then became self-sustaining. The *composition* of the program was clearly determined by domestic politics, in particular by Lambsdorff's tactical victory over those Social Democrats who wished to increase social spending and investment grants rather than cut taxes. Whether the *size* and *timing* of the program would have been the same without the foreign pressures is less certain, in part because the question involves conjectural history.

On the one hand, throughout the mid-1970s the German government had resorted to occasional tax cuts to offset fiscal drag, and the summit package might be cast as merely the latest example of this policy (see Gerald Holtham's chapter in this volume). On the other hand, we have found little evidence, either in our interviews with virtually all the participants on all sides of the policy debate or in the documentary evidence available to us (including internal memoranda), that would support the view that fiscal stimulus of the sort agreed at Bonn would have emerged from purely domestic deliberations. Most German participants believe that without the international factor it would have been very difficult for the government to put through the Bundestag so sizable a boost to the budget deficit, and many believe that the chancellor himself was persuaded of the specific numbers only at the summit itself. Yet the figure agreed to in the communiqué—1 percent of GNP, or approximately DM 12 billion—had been used in internal discussion for several months before the summit. Thus the bargaining over numbers at the summit, like the presummit international bargaining over whether there would be a stimulus program at all, may have been shadowboxing. The conclusion best supported by the available evidence is that the domestic and the international pressures were singly necessary, but only jointly sufficient, to account for the final decision.

Policies in other summit countries. During the final approach to the Bonn summit, the primary focus of attention was on Germany and the United States. Six months earlier, however, Japanese policies had been a major source of controversy. During November and December 1977, U.S. foreign economic diplomacy had been directed mainly at bilateral relations with Japan. By then it had become clear that Japanese Prime Minister Fukuda's London targets were going to be badly under-achieved. Growth for the year was not 6.7 percent but 5.3 percent, and in place of a predicted trade deficit of $700 million, Japan's exporters racked up a trade surplus of $10 billion despite the yen's appreciation. Pressures to restrict trade with Japan were building in the U.S. Congress, as they were in Europe. Although international demands for greater domestic stimulus in Japan paralleled the pressures placed on Germany, both the Japanese and the Americans apparently preferred to handle the Japanese issue primarily through bilateral channels.[123]

Within Japan a coalition of business interests, the Ministry of International Trade and Industry (MITI), the Economic Planning Agency, and some expansion-minded politicians within the Liberal Democratic Party (LDP) pushed for substantial additional domestic stimulus, using U.S. pressure as one of their prime arguments against the stubborn resistance of the Finance Ministry. Fukuda, despite his reputation as a "stingy" former finance minister, was by all accounts eager to be accepted as a responsible world statesman, conscious of his unfulfilled promises of London and concerned about trade frictions with the Americans and (less vitally) the Europeans. In late November he reshuffled his cabinet, bringing in several of the LDP expansionists and charging Nobuhiko Ushiba, his original Japanese sherpa and now minister for external economic affairs, with the task of seeking an accommodation with the Americans.

Within six weeks Ushiba and U.S. Trade Representative Robert Strauss had reached an accord. The Japanese agreed to a 7 percent growth target for 1978, to be attained through additional fiscal stimulus and thus to be led by domestic demand, not exports. Ushiba and Strauss also settled several bilateral trade issues. In return, the Americans pledged in much less concrete terms to bring down oil imports and control inflation. This agreement—asymmetrical though it was— served as an important building block for the package deal arrived at in Bonn, where Fukuda reconfirmed (and in certain respects, amplified) the Strauss-Ushiba understanding.

Over Finance Ministry objections, the government in Tokyo adopted a budget for the Japanese fiscal year 1978 that envisioned an unprecedented deficit, exceeding 30 percent of total government spending for the first time. Nonetheless, the 7 percent Japanese growth commitment negotiated in the Strauss-Ushiba accord was expected to require a supplemental budget in the autumn. The reflationary coalition within Japan favored a large supplemental budget, whereas the Finance Ministry argued for a smaller supplemental. Prime Minister Fukuda was aware that he would be making the decision on the supplemental budget within weeks after the Bonn summit.

During a state visit to Tokyo by German President Walter Scheel and Foreign Minister Hans-Dietrich Genscher in April 1978, Ushiba noted that Japan had voluntarily committed itself to the 7 percent growth target and urged the Germans to make more effort.[124] During the approach to the Bonn meeting, Fukuda repeated the growth target so often that in Tokyo he was nicknamed "Mr. Seven Percent." Anxious to show cooperation, the Japanese government announced three days before the summit that it would hold the volume of its exports constant in 1978, would spend $4 billion on an emergency import program, and would double development assistance within the next three years.

As in the case of the American pledge to decontrol oil prices and the German concession to undertake stimulus, the interplay between domestic and international politics was quite striking in the Japanese decision to raise its growth target and to adopt a supplemental budget if necessary to achieve it. Without the alignment of forces within Japan pressing for reflation, it is unlikely that the American demands would have been met. Without the U.S. pressure, however, and later legitimation by the multilateral summit commitment, it is even more unlikely that the Japanese expansionists could have overridden the powerful Japanese Finance Ministry. "Seventy percent foreign pressure, thirty percent internal politics," was the private judgment of one Finance Ministry insider. "Fifty-fifty," guessed an official from MITI.

Meanwhile, in Great Britain Prime Minister Callaghan was giving every impression that he would call a general election for autumn 1978. At the same time, the trade unions were becoming increasingly restless over continuing wage moderation. Consequently, Denis Healey masterminded a decidedly stimulative budget, which was adopted by Parliament in the early spring. The Labour government was thus eager for a stimulus in Germany, which had become significantly more important than the United States to British macroeconomic performance. Although the British current account was running in the black, it was not yet clear how fundamental the shift in Britain's external position had become, in part because of the flow of North Sea oil. The British therefore kept up their nearly constant pressure on Bonn for a stimulus. At the OECD ministers' meeting in May 1978, Healey delivered a particularly eloquent speech, explaining that there were many ways that countries could avoid adjustment, that the appreciation of the mark indicated that Germany had been doing so, and that it was incumbent on the Germans to stimulate their economy.

In Paris, Prime Minister Raymond Barre, with Giscard's support, had imposed an austerity plan on the French economy. The Barre plan, as it came to be called, provided for reduced budget deficits in an attempt to exorcise inflation from the economy and stabilize the external balance. After Giscard had staved off the long-feared victory of the left in the March 1978 elections to the National Assembly, he undoubtedly felt considerably more independent of the German decision on macroeconomic policy than did Callaghan. Nonetheless, by French calculations, the costs of the austerity program in terms of growth and unemployment could be minimized if the Germans would stimulate, and Giscard privately encouraged Schmidt to do so.

Agreement at Bonn and Its Aftermath

Bargaining at Bonn, July 16–17, 1978. When the summiteers gathered in the German capital for their climactic exchanges, the prepared script was reasonably clear, but it was not certain, even to their aides, whether the leaders could summon the political will to follow it. The first item on their agenda was macroeconomics, and as expected, Schmidt and Fukuda were exhorted to accelerate growth. For his part, Fukuda repeated his commitment to the 7 percent growth target, to be achieved through expansion of domestic demand, and reaffirmed his intention to institute additional measures in August or September 1978, should they be necessary to achieve that rate of growth. The outstanding issue remained the German commitment, and the German and American sherpas were asked to work out acceptable language on that question, as well as on the U.S. energy commitment. Ironically, each negotiator privately favored the policy being urged on his country by the other during their overnight session.

The luncheon meetings of the second day were reserved for intra-governmental conferences. Present at the German table were Schmidt, Genscher, Lambsdorff, Matthöfer, and summit aides. It was here that the FDP ministers finally assured their support for a sizable stimulus, making the group unanimous in favor of reflation. There was a surprisingly long discussion on the merits of the phrase "up to 1 percent" as opposed to simply using a 1 percent figure. Poker-faced to the end, Schmidt resisted agreeing to a specific size for the stimulus program until the last plenary session, when everyone's final offer was on the table. In the final communiqué, the German economic cabinet agreed to the following commitment (for this and subsequent excerpts, see the full text given in the appendix to this chapter):

As a contribution to avert the world-wide disturbances of economic equilibrium the German Delegation has indicated that by the end of August it will propose to the legislative bodies additional and quantitatively substantial measures up to 1 [percent] of GNP, designed to achieve a significant strengthening of demand and a higher rate of growth.

Carter also made commitments in the macroeconomic area that, although vaguely worded, would later prove significant. He declared that reducing inflation was his top economic priority and pointed to the reduction in the size of the 1979 tax cut, cutbacks in government spending for 1978 and 1979, the voluntary wage and price program, and efforts to eliminate inflationary government regulations as evidence of his seriousness. He also indicated that the 1980 federal budget would be tight in relation to previous years. However, the American commitments in the macroeconomic field were not nearly so specifically negotiated as the German commitment had been. The anti-inflationary commitment was of secondary importance, for Carter's oil price concession was to be the decisive quid pro quo for the German stimulus.

Formally speaking, each of the other summit countries shared in the macroeconomic undertakings. France agreed that its 1978 budget deficit would be FF 10 billion larger than earlier forecast. Italy repeated earlier commitments to cut public current expenditure while increasing public investment. Canada restated its existing growth target of "up to 5 percent." Great Britain reckoned that its budget announced earlier in the spring contributed to the concerted recovery. In substance, however, only the Germans and Japanese promised new macroeconomic initiatives; the others simply reaffirmed measures already in the pipeline.

The second item on the summit agenda was energy. Fukuda, expressing a widely shared view with uncharacteristic assertiveness, told Carter that most of the world's economic woes could be traced to the inability of the United States to reduce its oil imports. In reply, the president detailed the domestic politics of the issue, expressing confidence that the essential elements of his energy program would receive congressional approval, but offering assurances that if the legislation were unsatisfactory, he would take unilateral action to cut oil imports. Schmidt had apparently been persuaded during a presummit bilateral meeting with Carter that this approach was acceptable, if appropriate language could be drafted, and the others expressed understanding for the president's political dilemma.

President Carter was not accompanied in Bonn by any domestic political advisers, and their absence may perhaps have been a factor in his agreement to the specific language of the communiqué. In general terms, the Americans promised to "have in place by the end of the year a comprehensive policy framework . . . that will result in oil import savings of approximately 2.5 million barrels a day by 1985." More specifically, the U.S. pledges included (1) the filling of a billion-barrel strategic petroleum reserve; (2) a two-thirds increase in the rate of U.S. coal production; (3) maintaining the ratio between growth of GNP and growth of energy usage at or below 0.8; (4) keeping the growth of oil consumption below the growth of energy consumption; (5) reducing the volume of oil imports in 1978 and 1979 below that of 1977; and (6) the most crucial and controversial pledge of all: "that the prices paid for oil in the U.S. shall be raised to the world level by the end of 1980."

Most of these pledges could be readily squared with the truncated version of Carter's National Energy Plan that was already assured of congressional passage, particularly given that Alaskan oil was coming on stream, reducing American import requirements. The oil price commitment was much more portentous, however, for in effect it ruled out one politically convenient solution to the president's difficulties: as one of his senior energy advisers later described it, "to take the three crummy little bills [that had been approved by Congress] and declare victory." Whether and how to fulfill this oil price pledge—by the crude oil equalization tax (however improbable), by import fees (however un-

popular), by decontrol itself (however costly), or perhaps not at all—
would preoccupy American policymakers for much of the next nine
months.

Having taken on this heavy burden, Carter avoided making any further commitments to support the dollar on the exchange markets. The
discussion of monetary issues was considerably less satisfactory than
the deliberations on the other issues. Fukuda, Schmidt, Giscard, and
Jenkins criticized U.S. neglect of the dollar. Carter answered by restat-
ing the U.S. view that world currency stability could be achieved only
by addressing its fundamental causes, a view that was reflected in the
final communiqué. The three Europeans explained the Bremen initiative for European monetary integration, asking for endorsement of
that proposal from the others. With quiet encouragement from Prime
Minister Callaghan, who was himself uneasy about the EMS idea, the
Americans and Japanese closely questioned Giscard, Schmidt, and
Jenkins about the details. Although expressing general sympathy for
the ideal of European unity, the non-Europeans did not provide the
desired endorsement. After a year of recrimination, international
monetary policy was relegated somewhat incongruously to the very
end of the communiqué, ranking behind even some innocuous language on North-South relations.

The substantive contribution of Great Britain, France, Italy, and
Canada to the summit package was in the area of trade, the most controversial topic during the proceedings themselves in Bonn. The summiteers spent a heated half-day on this subject. The French were un-
happy about the framework reached the previous week, complaining
that the EC negotiators had made excessive concessions to the Americans, particularly on subsidies. When Robert Strauss and his European colleagues arrived in Bonn to present their achievements to the
summit, a frantic round of bilateral discussions was held late into the
night between the Americans and the French, the French and the Germans, the Americans and the Japanese, and finally the Commission
of the EC and the Americans. These sessions found solutions for several specific problems, including a procedural finesse for the contentious question of safeguards, although the communiqué noted candidly that "some difficult and important issues remain unresolved."
But the leaders' commitment "to conclude the detailed negotiations
by December 15, 1978" did serve as a statement of political will that
the bargainers subsequently were able to exploit to overcome internal
obstacles. As one aide later put it, "The summits created an atmo-

sphere in which those of us working on the negotiations could legitimately say that it was unthinkable to fail."

A missed opportunity for tightening U.S. macroeconomic policy? Because there had been so much international and domestic criticism of the failure of the Carter administration to institute more restrictive demand policies, why Schmidt did not bargain more energetically at Bonn for stronger anti-inflationary commitments from the Americans is something of a puzzle. There are several possible explanations. First, Schmidt might have felt that he did not have a strong enough bargaining position to ask for more than the oil price concession. Second, the oil price concession might have been more valuable to him because it was more "verifiable" (he could hold Carter accountable), whereas the relative restrictiveness of anti-inflationary measures would be disputable. Third, Schmidt apparently believed that the fall of the dollar was due at least as much to U.S. energy policy as to demand management, if not more so. In fact, criticism of the Carter administration's anti-inflationary policy might even accelerate appreciation of the mark. Last, the chancellor was fully aware of differences within the U.S. government over oil pricing, but at least during the preliminaries to Bonn, differences within the administration over demand management were not nearly so salient. At the time of the summit, Schmidt probably saw no way to lend encouragement to anti-inflationary forces within the United States, as he could (and did) give to the forces for decontrol. There is some evidence that this calculation about internal American politics was essential to the German strategy.

In retrospect, however, this calculation may have been mistaken, in the sense that stronger pressure at the summit might actually have influenced the course of American fiscal policy during the following months. One participant has written that pressure from Schmidt might have been well received within the United States and the Carter administration:

> The major lost opportunity of the Bonn summit agreement was that not enough pressure was put on the United States to face squarely its inflation problem and take stronger measures early enough to bring inflation under control. . . . A more specific program of action, mirroring the quantitative undertaking of the countries which agreed to stimulate demand, should have been proposed. And it might very well have gone through.[125]

This view seems particularly plausible in light of the restrictive monetary measures that were instituted over the course of the following three and one-half months. In the early autumn it became evident that Congress had radically revised the planned 1979 tax cut that had been negotiated for the administration by Treasury Secretary Blumenthal. According to inside accounts, the president came close to vetoing the tax cut as it emerged from Congress. In particular, Carter objected to the distributive effects of the cuts. He felt torn between, on the one hand, the practical politics of vetoing a Democratic bill on the eve of a midterm election and the advice of Schultze and others that a stimulus was needed to ensure against a relapse into recession, and, on the other hand, the advice of the Office of Management and Budget, which sought to reduce further the budget deficit, and the warnings of others about inflationary trends. Because the decontrol pledge made at Bonn appears to have influenced the president on an issue on which he might have gone either way, a stronger anti-inflationary pledge at Bonn might have been enough, at the margin, to persuade him to reject the tax cut package, and that in turn would have enhanced the credibility and effectiveness of the administration's subsequent struggle against inflation.

Implementing the German and Japanese pledges. During the months after the Bonn summit, Chancellor Schmidt further broadened the reflationary coalition within Germany so that, when finally instituted, the stimulus program had support among virtually all of the important domestic actors. In the early autumn the Bundesbank officially sanctioned an increase in the public-sector borrowing requirement for 1979 to DM 60 billion and communicated that decision to the cabinet.[126] The members of the Central Bank Council had three factors in mind when they acceded to the stimulus. First, the expansion had already been agreed to at the summit. Second, the appreciation of the mark had slowed growth and squeezed out inflation to the point where a more expansionary fiscal policy could be countenanced, if not actively encouraged, and the seemingly inexorable rise of the mark accelerated in late summer and early autumn. Finally, Bundesbank officials believed that by conceding a fiscal stimulus in late 1978 or early 1979, they might avoid an additional program during the 1980 election campaign.

With the cabinet unanimous on the rough size of the stimulus, after its submission to the Bundestag, politics in Bonn centered on the composition of the package. In the end, there was something for everyone, although the FDP skillfully used its earlier reticence to tilt the largest share of the program toward tax reductions. The final package consisted of tax cuts for individuals, reductions in the trade taxes for corporations, and expenditure increases in the form of children's benefits and investment incentives. The stimulus also had the legislative support of the opposition. The CDU-CSU used their dominance in the Bundesrat to add DM 1.2 billion in measures, raising the total package to DM 13.5 billion. The Bundesbank estimated that the budget deficit would be increased by a further DM 15 billion in 1980 as a result of these measures.[127] Altogether, the German budget deficit for 1978–79 was larger (probably by somewhat more than 1 percent of GDP) than would have been expected on the basis of presummit trends.[128]

In Japan, within weeks after the summit, Prime Minister Fukuda began working to augment the autumn supplemental budget with additional expenditures of 1.5 percent of GNP. Convinced that this program was a sincere effort to administer a Keynesian stimulus to the Japanese economy, Carter wrote Fukuda to acknowledge fulfillment of his summit pledge, despite American expectations that Japanese growth would nonetheless fall short of the 7 percent target. By the end of the year, Japanese growth was a full point below Fukuda's 7 percent target, although domestic demand was up to the mark. In addition, Japanese exports in 1978 were 2 percent below 1977, Japanese imports were 10 percent higher, and Japanese foreign aid in 1980–81 exceeded the 1977 levels by 130 percent measured in dollars, or 90 percent measured in yen. In each respect the Japanese fulfilled commitments made at Bonn.

Fukuda's 7 percent target was the object of considerable criticism during LDP leadership elections in December. As probably anticipated by prior agreement among the LDP factions to rotate the top post, Fukuda was unseated by Masayoshi Ohira during the vote. On becoming prime minister, and realizing that the supplemental budget would not satisfy the growth objective, Ohira repudiated the target. Carter thereupon dispatched a sharply worded letter to the new head of government, interpreted by Japanese officials as an implicit threat that the American president might not attend the next summit meeting, to be held in Tokyo. Despite some sentiment within the Carter administration to continue pressure against the Japanese, however, the macroeconomic dispute dissipated after the first quarter of 1979, owing in part to shifts in the Japanese current account position as the effects of the dollar's depreciation in relation to the yen began to appear. The 7 percent pledge by Japan was the only significant Bonn commitment that was not fully met, but the U.S. sherpa, Henry Owen, testified the following spring that "it is our view that Japan made a good-faith effort to achieve its Bonn target."[129]

Renewed depreciation of the dollar and the German response. Whatever its other virtues, the summit agreement failed to have much visible effect on the foreign currency markets. In the first half of the year, the U.S. current account deficit had grown to nearly $11 billion, and predictions differed about whether it would decline in the second half. Inflation abated only slightly over the summer. Moreover, the Carter administration did not demonstrate that its exchange rate policies would part with the past. It had become clear that the administration did not place as much stock as the Germans did in the arrangements agreed to the previous March. Accordingly, after the announcement of July's disappointing trade figures in mid-August, the dollar began another slide, which lasted until the beginning of November. The slide accelerated over the ten-week period, despite increases in the Federal Reserve's discount rate, which had begun in May, amounting to 2.25 percentage points by the end of October and paralleled by prime rate increases to 10.25 percent over the same period. The market also seemed to ignore projections for a reduction in the current deficit and a forecast reduction in U.S. growth in 1979.[130] With the dollar dropping against all major currencies, its depreciation amounted to 8.9 percent on an effective basis between September 1977 and September 1978.[131]

Although the Federal Reserve had not compromised domestic monetary policy to prop up the dollar, the depreciation was having definite, undesirable effects on the American economy. The dollar's slide would tend to correct the current account deficit in the medium term, but it also aggravated domestic inflation. The Council of Economic Advisers estimated that the direct and indirect effects on the price level of a 10.0 percent depreciation would be roughly 1.5 percent over two to three years, with approximately half of the increase coming in the first year.[132] Analysts at the Fed subsequently concluded that the dollar's slide in 1977 and 1978 had raised the level of consumer prices by 1 percent by the end of 1978 over what prices otherwise would have been. They predicted that if the dollar remained low, the full impact would be a 2.25–2.67 percent increase.[133]

In the face of the growing German current account surplus, which was to register $8.7 billion for 1978, the mark climbed by 2.5 percent in effective terms in 1978, as it had in 1977.[134] The Bundesbank had to intervene heavily in the exchange markets to prevent the mark from appreciating further than this, however. First primarily to support the Narrower Margins Arrangement (which preserved stability between the mark and the currencies of the smaller European countries) and then to support the dollar, the Bundesbank's international reserves grew by $8 billion from July through October 1978, and by nearly $4 billion from mid-October through December.[135] Total intervention by the fourteen central banks that participated in daily concerted action in the international currency markets removed almost $50 billion during the year, although some of this was replaced during periods of relative dollar strength. The Bundesbank claimed that the U.S. payments deficit was responsible for 75 percent of the growth of world monetary reserves of $40 billion during the year, on top of net dollar intervention of $35.8 billion and growth of world monetary reserves of $57 billion in 1977.[136] In contrast, American intervention amounted to a mere $1.0 billion in 1977 and only $2.8 billion through October 23, 1978.[137] The Bundesbank was becoming increasingly critical of U.S. policies and resolved in August to do all it could to transfer further burdens of exchange stabilization onto the "irresponsible" Americans.

Foreign exchange intervention by the Bundesbank was coupled with continued easy domestic monetary policy. At the same time that the central bank reaffirmed its determination to adhere to the 8 percent target for money growth, it announced measures to increase bank liquidity through open market operations and the raising of rediscount quotas. Loose domestic monetary policy and low interest rates were an important part of the strategy to suppress mark appreciation. As a result, currency and demand deposits rose 14.1 percent over the course of the year.[138] There was little strong public criticism of the overshooting of the target by the Bundesbank during 1978, for it was widely recognized that the alternative—appreciation of the mark—would stunt growth. But Bundesbank officials had serious misgivings about continuing this policy of rapid money expansion for very long. By the end of summer 1978 the bank had decided that monetary policy would soon have to take a decidedly more restrictive stance.

Making that restrictive shift in monetary policy was out of the question, however, as long as the dollar was depreciating, and the mark appreciating, at the pace that developed in early autumn. Had the German central bank taken restrictive measures under those conditions, as one Bundesbank official later put it, "The world would have thought we were crazy." The shift in German monetary policy had to await stability on the exchange markets, which by autumn 1978 could be provided only by a dramatic change in American foreign exchange and domestic monetary policy.

Just as the Bundesbank was deciding that more restrictive monetary measures were around the corner, American officials urged that the Germans take action that would have precisely the opposite effect. When the dollar began to depreciate anew in August, President Carter expressed renewed concern and directed Treasury Secretary Blumenthal and Federal Reserve Board Chairman G. William Miller to seek ways to bolster the currency.[139] The Americans reportedly asked for large increases in the swap arrangements and for a German commitment to intervene decisively to arrest the depreciation of the U.S. currency—measures that would place the burden of exchange stabilization even more squarely on the shoulders of the Bundesbank and that threatened to increase the German money supply further.

German officials reacted sharply. Although they reaffirmed the availability of the $4 billion swap arrangement—only roughly $1 billion of which the Americans had so far used—the German side reportedly flatly rejected the additional American requests. They argued that to arrest the slide of the dollar, the Americans had to reverse the stance of U.S. economic policy, particularly monetary policy. It is unclear how far the Germans were willing to go to secure more restrictive American monetary policy, but they were persistent and adamant. German officials correctly perceived that drastic dollar depreciation and domestic inflation had placed the United States in a dilemma as well. More restrictive American policies were imminent if Germany refused to change its own policy course. Heightened German intervention could only serve to take the pressure off the Carter administration to tighten policies.[140]

The dollar crisis and rescue: U.S. policy turns. A few weeks later, on October 24, 1978, President Carter announced new anti-inflationary policies to the nation. The centerpiece of the new program was a set of voluntary wage and price standards limiting increases to 7 percent. These standards were to be monitored by the Council on Wage and Price Stability, headed by Alfred Kahn. Although this program was supported by incentives for compliance, such as government procurement limitations on firms that failed to comply, it was essentially voluntary. In his announcement Carter repeated that fighting inflation was his first priority and that fiscal policy would be considerably tightened in 1980. However, the American business community and foreign markets greeted the message with dismay at the president's failure to institute firm anti-inflationary policies. The dollar dropped precipitously. In the four days after Carter's inflation speech, central banks intervened repeatedly in the markets, the Fed alone to the tune of $977 million. Nonetheless, intervention failed to prevent the dollar from sliding to record lows of 176 against the yen and 1.71 against the deutsche mark on October 31, 1978. At that time, against the mark the dollar stood 20 percent below its level of early August, 23 percent below its value of the beginning of the year, and 34 percent below the rate of July 1976.[141]

The rapidity of this depreciation was unprecedented. All the more significant was that the dollar's fall had occurred in the face of heavy intervention. It gave American officials reason to fear that there might be a panic run on the dollar unless the administration acted decisively to tighten domestic monetary policy. Secretary Blumenthal thereupon secretly directed Undersecretary of the Treasury for Monetary Affairs Anthony Solomon to construct an unprecedented package of measures to support the dollar in cooperation with the Fed. The Americans hastily negotiated with the Bundesbank an augmentation of the swap line by $2 billion, which the Germans reluctantly accepted after persuasion from the Fed. The Germans readily agreed to the U.S. Treasury's issuing mark-denominated bonds in German capital markets—an idea Emminger had been promoting for some time.[142]

President Carter was briefed on the recent events in the markets and the package that had been prepared to counter them. Although he and Miller were wary of inducing a recession, they were urged to authorize even more extensive foreign exchange intervention and a tightening of domestic monetary policy. Blumenthal argued most forcefully for the package, in contrast to his public image as one who had been talking down the dollar. To other Carter advisers, his arguments sounded similar to those Schmidt and Lambsdorff had been making. Among other things, Blumenthal argued that further dollar depreciation would disrupt international trade, increase the likelihood of bank failure, provide further inducement for OPEC to raise dollar-denominated oil prices, and increase domestic inflation.[143] The importance to the allies was also discussed. British Prime Minister Callaghan had privately communicated his deep concern about the falling dollar to both Carter and Blumenthal. Callaghan reported that Schmidt and Giscard believed that Carter did not grasp the seriousness of the dollar's decline. According to several inside accounts, however, it was the argument that continued depreciation of the dollar would undermine his anti-inflationary program that carried the greatest weight with the president in persuading him to adopt the proposed package.[144]

The dollar's rescue package was announced on November 1, 1978. On the international side, it provided for an unprecedented $30 billion equivalent in foreign exchange to be placed at the disposal of the Federal Reserve and U.S. Treasury for the purpose of intervention. (This amount of money was never actually needed and was never fully assembled, but the figure did impress the markets.) This amount included the increase in the swap arrangement with the Bundesbank to $6 billion, as well as increases in the swap lines with the Bank of Japan and the Swiss National Bank. "Up to $10 billion" was slated to be raised in German and Swiss capital markets through the issuance of "Carter bonds," as they came to be called. On the domestic side, the discount rate was raised one full point to 9.5 percent, and a supplementary reserve requirement was imposed by the Federal Reserve. Carter described the package as "a major step in the anti-inflation program." Solomon, one of the prime architects of the package, said it represented the administration's commitment to "massive intervention," if that were necessary to calm the markets. Both he and Blumenthal assured the public that these measures would provide stable foundations for future growth rather than cause a recession.[145]

On the morning the measures were announced, the New York Federal Reserve Bank was virtually the only major net buyer of dollars in the market. As one participant described the trading, "It was us against the world." During that day, the New York Fed purchased $1.6 billion. The markets responded enthusiastically. Within a matter of minutes, the dollar bounced back an enormous 7.5 percent against the Swiss franc, 7.0 percent against the mark, and 5.0 percent against the yen. The business community was generally very supportive of the package. The New York Stock Exchange registered a record single-day gain. By November 20, the dollar rose to DM 1.94. By the end of January, it was clear that the currency had established a floor beneath which it was unlikely to fall and from which, with the declining current account deficits, it was more likely to rise. During the six-month period of August through January, U.S. intervention amounted to $9.4 billion, by far the largest share in marks.[146]

Although the Bundesbank had agreed to an increase in the swap lines, it was not anxious to see them used. Indeed, when they were announced, Emminger took pains to make it known that he expected that they would not have to be drawn on.[147] There was apparently an understanding between the German and American central banks that the supplement to the swap line would be drawn on only as a last resort. As it turned out, the Federal Reserve and Treasury did use most of the German credit but were able to repay the Bundesbank relatively quickly. U.S. intervention after the beginning of November was financed mostly by drawings on the IMF and by the Carter bond issues.[148]

The issue of Carter bonds fit very conveniently into the Bundesbank's plans to tighten monetary policy. The bonds would, of course, temporarily soak up German money until the marks were resold to support the dollar in the foreign exchange markets, and the Bundesbank announced no efforts to counteract this effect. (The Swiss, in contrast, did.) The first issue was floated in early December, raising DM 3 billion. Another would be sold in February for another DM 2.5 billion. The timing was well coordinated with the Bundesbank's purposes and represented the first moves toward a more restrictive monetary policy in Germany. Shortly after the first Carter bond issue, the Bundesbank lowered rediscount quotas, reducing the growth of the money supply further. In mid-January, the Lombard rate was raised half a point to 4 percent, and reserve requirements were raised 5 percent, among other restrictive measures.[149]

The Bundesbank had thus successfully negotiated German monetary policy around the restrictive bend. Once the Carter administration had agreed to tighten domestic monetary policy and to intervene to support the dollar, the Bundesbank had much greater latitude to correct for its recent overshooting of money growth without putting renewed upward pressure on the mark. Within weeks of the American decision, the German central bank moved to take advantage of that latitude. Thus, by the end of 1978 monetary policy in both countries had become decidedly more restrictive. The Bank of Japan followed suit in April 1979. Fiscal policy in the three largest countries was loosened with the activation of Germany's stimulus as agreed on at the Bonn summit, Fukuda's supplemental budget, and the Carter administration's tax cut package, although Carter had promised a tight budget for 1980. With these changes, the summit countries no longer disputed one another's macroeconomic policy. By 1979, the great "locomotive" reflation controversy had effectively come to a close.

Carter fulfills his pledge on oil prices. Carter's bold commitment on oil pricing at Bonn had impressed his critics and shocked some of his own aides. The *Frankfurter Allgemeine Zeitung* (no friend of the president) observed afterward that "Carter took on the biggest commitments," and one of his closest advisers judged in retrospect that the president had "embraced this package and the oil price pledge without knowing exactly how to fulfill it." [150] Speaking of the 1980 price target, administration spokesmen maintained that Carter "still hopes to achieve it via his energy plan now before Congress"—that is, the crude oil equalization tax. [151] Had the tax passed, the lingering conflict among his foreign policy and domestic advisers about the Bonn promise would have subsided. Controls would have been retained, but domestic prices would have been raised for consumers, thus discouraging consumption and keeping Carter's promise. Throughout the summer and into the fall, however, the deadlock in Congress over oil pricing dragged on, the tax's prospects dimmed, and the administration's search for alternatives intensified, reopening the conflict over the Bonn pledge.

Shortly after the summit, some congressmen had privately advised the administration that the crude oil tax was not yet beyond resuscitation. All action on oil pricing was temporarily suspended, however, by delicate negotiations over proposed decontrol of natural gas prices. A bill offered by House Majority Leader Jim Wright that would have decontrolled the price of about half the oil produced in the United States (by redefining it as unregulated "stripper" oil) was suppressed in order not to jeopardize the emerging but fragile compromise on natural gas. By the time the natural gas issue was resolved, the congressional elections were approaching. An amendment to limit the president's authority to impose oil import fees and quotas was rejected by a seven-vote margin in the House on September 4, but the narrowness of this outcome made clear that stiff reprisals within Congress and even within the Democratic party would inevitably greet any presidential move to impose import fees. With remaining support for the crude oil tax fading rapidly, and with import controls seemingly beyond the president's power (politically, if not yet legally), Carter was faced once again with the alternative that both Nixon and Ford had tried in vain to implement: decontrol.

The final passage of the five-part National Energy Act, signed by the president amid much fanfare in early November, merely confirmed the dilemma. "We have declared to ourselves and the world our intent to control our use of energy and thereby to control our own destiny as a nation," Carter proclaimed, but the words rang hollow, for the bill contained no provision for raising oil prices to world levels, as he had promised his colleagues in Bonn.[152]

The administration now had difficult choices to make. Under the existing 1975 legislation, the president would have the authority, as of June 1, 1979, to act without the consent of Congress in fixing (or decontrolling) oil prices until discretionary controls expired on October 1, 1981. Congress was judged highly unlikely either to extend the period of mandatory controls or to end discretionary controls before the 1981 expiration date.[153] Thus, for better or worse, the president alone would control (or decontrol) oil prices during that twenty-eight-month period. Therefore the administration had to decide, first, whether to (1) decontrol immediately, (2) decontrol gradually between June 1979 and October 1981, (3) maintain controls until October 1981, or (4) ask Congress to extend controls beyond 1981. (The third option—and even more blatantly, the fourth—would flout both the letter and the spirit of the Bonn commitment.) If the administration decided to decontrol, it would then have to decide whether and how to tax the resultant windfall profits back from the oil producers. If he wished to impose such a tax, moreover, the president needed a strategy to get the tax through Congress, perhaps by linking it to the decontrol decision.

In the administration's renewed deliberations during the winter of 1978–79, a variety of arguments were adduced for and against decontrol. Conventional microeconomic analysis emphasized the advantages of the market: higher incentives for production of domestic oil and other energy sources, inducements for conservation, and elimination of the maze of inefficient regulatory controls. Yet the prospect of windfall profits continued to be a powerful deterrent to decontrol, as it had been in the previous two administrations. Now, in addition, mounting concerns about inflation and the credibility of the administration's wage-price guidelines argued against willfully unleashing a new round of oil price increases. These were all essentially domestic arguments, although some opponents of decontrol astutely cited the president's Bonn pledge to make inflation fighting a top priority. The international context provided even more powerful arguments for the decontrollers. The trade deficit and the weak dollar made reduction of U.S. oil imports more urgent. Above all, the president himself had put his credibility with the allies on the line with his Bonn pledge on oil prices. As John Ikenberry has pointed out, "After Bonn, oil pricing was manifestly an international issue, even in meetings with domestic staff." [154]

Stuart Eizenstat noted the president's predicament in an important memorandum on January 3, 1979: "The choices which you will face in deciding this issue are not easy, and your advisors have widely divergent recommendations." [155] Those foreign policy advisers who had prepared the summit at which Carter made his decontrol pledge (especially Cooper and Owen) considered that step to have been the watershed in the decision process, and they took a lower profile in subsequent administration discussions of domestic oil pricing policy. Nonetheless, the achievements of those anxious to commit the president to decontrol at Bonn were exploited by some who had been less involved in the summit, and those "achievements" were regretted by the opponents of decontrol, as well as (occasionally) by the president himself.

In internal discussions on oil pricing between the signing of the National Energy Act in November 1978 and the final decontrol decision in April 1979, Blumenthal and Solomon supported early decontrol, arguing that the sooner the political bad medicine was taken, the sooner the economic benefits—reduced oil dependence and a more stable dollar—could be enjoyed. Schlesinger, who had conceded defeat on the crude oil tax, now supported immediate decontrol as well and also argued for additional taxes to prevent windfall profits from going to producers. Decontrol plus the tax would achieve by a two-step process what the crude oil tax had been more elegantly designed to achieve in one: increases in domestic prices to encourage conservation and prevention of excessive rents accruing to oil producers. These advocates of prompt decontrol recalled the Bonn pledge to the president on a number of occasions.

Schultze, as the president's chief economic adviser, and Alfred Kahn, as chief inflation fighter, were torn: on the one hand decontrol was economically rational, but on the other it would exacerbate the already difficult inflation problem. Schultze recommended decontrol in principle, with the proviso that domestic oil prices would come under new restraints should world prices shoot up unexpectedly. Because of the inflation problem, Schultze recommended gradual, "back-loaded" decontrol by September 1981. He noted the summit pledge, but added that the Germans would not be worried about a one-year slippage that helped to restrain American inflation and maintain growth. Schultze also supported a tax on oil producers if decontrol were to be decided on.

The White House staff, led by Eizenstat and Mondale, continued to oppose early decontrol. Decontrol would happen automatically by 1981 anyway, and by accelerating its pace the president would be taking a large and unnecessary political risk in advance of the 1980 election. Early decontrol would increase the threat from the left. (Apparently, the argument that decontrol might bring the president political gains on the right was not made forcefully within the administration.) Senator Edward Kennedy, a potentially strong rival for the Democratic nomination, was himself a staunch advocate of controls. The opponents of decontrol added that the summit commitments were inconsistent: if the president was to make good on his anti-inflationary commitments, he could not proceed with decontrol too quickly. By early 1979 inflation had become the most urgent argument against decontrol. As the president's advisers summarized the issue for him on January 3: "Should our energy policies and international commitments on energy be deferred or delayed in their implementation so as to minimize the near-term inflation effects which an increase in U.S. prices to world levels would entail?"[156]

The president faced a sharp dilemma. On the one hand, he had acquiesced in tighter monetary policy, had agonized over spending limitations, and nearly had vetoed the tax bill, in part because of the inflation problem. As he observed in a meeting with his key domestic advisers on January 3, 1979 (at the outset of another series of OPEC price increases), the worst political situation in 1980 would be rising prices and rising energy costs. On the other hand, he appreciated the argument that decontrol would encourage a more rational allocation of resources. To delay or forgo decontrol, moreover, would violate the Bonn accord and would require him to persuade Schmidt and the other summit participants that inflation now posed the greater threat. Perhaps fighting inflation was of greater importance than living up to the Bonn pledge, the president mused, and he would simply accept the consequences. Frustrated at the looming (and perhaps unanticipated) domestic costs associated with the Bonn accord, he remarked almost plaintively that he "did not know how the Bonn commitment had been made, but that all of a sudden everyone had been pushing him for it."[157] The president could not lightly dismiss his commitment, but he was not easily reconciled to complying with it. At a press conference on January 17, 1979, he called oil pricing "a difficult decision" and added that "those decisions have not yet been made." [158]

At this difficult juncture, the debate about decontrol was drastically complicated by the Iranian revolution and the second oil shock. The new increases began in December 1978, when OPEC announced a modest $0.60 increase, to $13.30 per barrel for Saudi Arabian light crude. Spot market prices more than doubled, to $22.00, with the fall of the shah. Some American officials argued that the time was not right for decontrol and that the political reception was likely to be hostile. Schlesinger, however, thought that he saw a brief opportunity for making the decision to decontrol, between the time when OPEC's initial action highlighted the need for conservation and the time when the cartel fully matched the higher spot market prices.

The final decision to decontrol was made following an "economic summit" of virtually all the administration's top domestic officials at Camp David on March 19, 1979. Each of the major figures rehearsed his established arguments. Schlesinger invoked the Bonn decontrol pledge, among other arguments, in pressing for a decision to decontrol, the sooner the better. When Carter repeated that he was perplexed at having made the Bonn commitment to bring domestic oil prices to world levels by the end of 1980, Blumenthal, pressing for immediate decontrol, reminded him that it was part of an explicit trade with the Germans and Japanese. He added that the decision would help the dollar and that the effect on inflation would be marginal. Mondale, however, speaking for the liberal wing of the party and supported by Eizenstat, argued that decontrol would "blow every fuse in the economy and lead to greater inflation and incredible profits." Carter replied that his "heart went out to Fritz [Mondale]," but that delaying decontrol would lead to the same higher prices without the prospect of winning a tax on the oil companies' windfall. It was eventually decided to decontrol definitively, but incrementally through October 1981, a delay of some months past the deadline agreed to at Bonn. (White House officials had consulted the Germans on this modest slippage of the decontrol deadline and had correctly advised the president that Schmidt and his senior economic officials would acquiesce.)

The Camp David meeting also crystallized the option eventually chosen by the president to deal with the windfall gains to the oil companies. He would petition Congress for a heavy windfall profits tax, but decontrol would not be made formally contingent on the tax, although the administration could threaten to reinstitute controls if the tax were not passed. Senator Kennedy had argued publicly (as Mondale had privately at Camp David) that, by decontrolling first, the president would undercut the prospects for a tax. Kennedy proved to have misjudged the fundamental change in the political balance that took place once the president announced his decision to lift controls in the face of escalating OPEC prices. A modified version of the windfall profits tax proposed by the administration was passed by Congress within a year, given impetus by OPEC price increases to $26.00 a barrel and the prospect of truly enormous oil industry profits. The tax was repealed in the 1988 trade act, but a decade later U.S. oil pricing policy remained essentially that decided on at Camp David and announced by President Carter on April 5, 1979.

In sum, in early 1979 the president (and indirectly the Congress) had to decide whether to extend oil price controls or allow them to expire. Similar choices had confronted the two branches of government on at least two earlier occasions during the 1970s. Earlier, two presidents had reluctantly acceded to congressional pressure to extend controls. In 1979, the outcome was different. Why was a Democratic president willing to take the responsibility for raising domestic crude oil prices, an act that most concede took a major and largely predictable toll on Carter's political fortunes, when Congress was unwilling to share that responsibility with him?

One possible answer is that the climate of opinion toward energy price controls and government regulation among energy experts, among the national political elite, and even among the broader public had slowly shifted, and that the second oil shock underscored the need for serious measures to curb American oil imports. This change in the background to energy policymaking clearly played some part in the 1979 decisions. When the president convened a diverse group of congressmen in March 1979 to discuss the energy dilemmas, he sensed growing support for "higher prices for oil and a big tax on the resulting profits."[159] Yet the fact remains that, when faced with a similar national crisis during the first oil shock, Congress had insisted on price controls and Carter's predecessors had declined to act alone. Political coalitions and the basic economic interests on which they rested had not changed fundamentally in the interim.

Thus an important second part of the explanation for the different outcome in 1979 is that international criticism of American oil imports—crystallized in and reinforced by Carter's pledge made at Bonn—had an effect on the president's final decision. The Bonn pledge is an element that was not present during the earlier decisions by Nixon and Ford to acquiesce in continued controls, whereas it was prominent during the deliberations that led to Carter's decision to decontrol. The summit pledge clearly worked against the president's domestic political interests. It may not have fundamentally changed the positions taken by the agencies and advisers within the administration from what those positions would otherwise have been. But those officials who sought to raise American oil prices to the world level seem to have used the summit process effectively to steer the president and his policies toward their objective, and after the summit the Bonn commitment was increasingly cited in congressional debates as well.[160] No one, inside the administration or out, argued that the Bonn pledge was legally binding or politically conclusive, but it did have weight with the man who signed his name to the communiqué. As one of the decontrol proponents later said, "If a president commits himself to something at a summit, and you can cite that in a meeting, that's a damn powerful argument. The rest of the government may not be impressed, but the president is."

The summit, moreover, affected the U.S. oil-pricing decisionmaking by helping to separate the question of whether and when oil prices would be raised from the question of the means for doing so. Because alternative mechanisms for raising oil prices to world levels would affect the interests of producers and consumers differently, the method of the domestic oil price hike was a contentious issue. When questions of method were linked to the issue of whether oil prices should be raised at all, as they were effectively in the debate over the crude oil equalization tax, disagreement over the method blocked an accord on both questions. When separated, however, a presidential decision on pricing was able to elicit a congressional response on taxes. Thus the pledge at the summit represented an important stage in the decisionmaking process that led the administration to agree firmly on decontrol, loosely coupled with a tax on windfall profits.

Neither a purely domestic interpretation nor a purely international one can fully account for the outcome of American energy policymaking in 1977–79, for domestic and international forces became inextricably entangled. At a minimum, however, the Bonn summit agreement was an important element in the 1979 decision to decontrol U.S. oil prices.

The Bonn trade commitment: completing the Tokyo round. The Bonn summit initiated a new phase in the Tokyo round of trade talks. Before the summit, countries were able to defer many difficult decisions. After the summit, those decisions were made. Despite European objections to negotiating under the threat of imposition of countervailing duties in the United States, at the beginning of 1979 a code governing subsidies and countervailing duties was arrived at. Substantial tariff reductions and amendments to the GATT articles were agreed on. The negotiations were concluded, and the agreement signed, in April 1979. The results of the Tokyo round are in general regarded as the most comprehensive set of trade agreements since the inception of GATT. Economic summitry played an important role in winning accession on the part of those Western governments that had had the strongest internal opposition to trade liberalization. The Bonn summit provided an opportunity for the major parties to take stock of the progress of the negotiations and provided an important intermediate deadline for them.[161] Notwithstanding the minor overshooting of the deadline set at the summit for the conclusion of the negotiations, the mid-December date (buttressed by the coming into force of U.S. legislation on countervailing duties) generated the necessary incentives for timely closing of the trade talks.

The Bonn Story in Synthesis

The foregoing account makes clear that the Bonn summit of July 16–17, 1978, was merely the most memorable moment of a multifaceted process of international policy adjustment that required more than three years to unfold from its inception in 1976 until its consummation in 1979. Conceived in the first half of the decade as a response to the problems of Western recovery from the first oil shock, the suggestion for a coordinated program of global reflation, led by the "locomotive" economies of the United States, Germany, and Japan, received a powerful boost from the incoming Carter administration. This proposal was warmly supported by the weaker countries, as well as by the OECD and many private economists, who argued that it would overcome international payments imbalances and speed growth all around. The Germans and the Japanese, in contrast, protested that prudent and successful economic managers should not be asked to bail out spendthrifts. This issue dominated Western economic diplomacy during 1977 and 1978.

At London in 1977 the summiteers could agree only to play for time on the key questions. Although the Germans and Japanese accepted ambitious growth targets, they avoided commitments to fiscal expansion. Over the next year, the solitary American locomotive moved under full steam, triggering a steady decline in the dollar. Schmidt and others complained about the Americans' uncontrolled appetite for imported oil and their apparent lack of concern for monetary stability. All sides conceded that the world economy was in serious trouble, but it was not clear which was more to blame—tight-fisted German and Japanese fiscal policies, or slack U.S. energy and monetary policies.

Throughout the spring of 1978, negotiations that sprawled across a half-dozen bilateral and multilateral forums produced the outline of a possible package deal for the forthcoming Bonn summit. The heart of the bargain would be German agreement to specific reflationary measures, in return for specific American commitments on energy, especially the decontrol of U.S. oil prices. Other elements in the proposed accord were Japanese export restraint and reconfirmation of an earlier commitment to domestic growth, American recognition of the risks of inflation, and acquiescence by the other countries (particularly the reluctant French) in a successful conclusion of the multilateral trade negotiations. At the summit itself in Bonn in July, after some dickering about the details, this package was approved, the clearest case of a summit deal that left all participants happier than when they arrived. Indeed, at the time most international economic observers, including such defenders of orthodoxy as the IMF and the Basel club of central bankers, welcomed the policies agreed to at Bonn.

As we have shown, agreement was possible at Bonn only because a powerful minority within each key government actually favored on domestic grounds the policy being demanded internationally. Within Germany, a political process catalyzed by foreign pressures was surreptitiously orchestrated by expansionists inside the Schmidt government. Contrary to the public mythology, the Bonn deal was not forced on a reluctant or "altruistic" Germany.[162] In effect, while protesting publicly, the chancellor let himself be pushed into a policy that he favored privately on domestic grounds but would have found costly and perhaps impossible to enact without the summit's package deal. Similarly, in Japan officials favoring stimulus exploited the American pressure. Without internal divisions in Tokyo, it is unlikely that the foreign demands would have been met; without the external pressure, it is even more unlikely that the Japanese expansionists could have overridden the powerful Ministry of Finance.

In the American case, too, internal politicking reinforced, and was reinforced by, the international pressure. Key officials within the Carter administration strongly favored a tougher energy policy, but they were opposed by the president's closest domestic advisers. After the summit, the president's commitment to his colleagues at Bonn played a central role in the heated intramural debate about the administration's energy policy, and was probably crucial in the final decision to decontrol oil prices.

In the end, each leader believed that what he was doing was in his nation's interest and his own, even though not all his aides agreed. Yet without the summit he probably would not (or could not) have changed policies so easily. In that sense, the Bonn deal successfully meshed domestic and international pressures.

Remarkably, virtually all the crucial pledges of the Bonn summit were redeemed:

—Two months after the summit the Schmidt government introduced a substantial pump-priming program, and by November 1978 a DM 13.5 billion measure had been approved by the Bundestag, producing a budget deficit significantly higher than would have been expected on the basis of earlier trends.

—In September 1978, in light of an apparent shortfall in growth, Japan adopted a substantial additional public works program, which the Americans regarded as a good-faith effort to achieve domestically led expansion. As promised at Bonn, the Japanese trade surplus fell significantly in 1978, and Japanese foreign aid was put on a higher growth path.

—The essential elements of the Tokyo round trade negotiations were successfully concluded within the deadline set at Bonn. Final approval of the entire package was delayed by a last-minute Franco-American procedural wrangle, but the agreement was signed in April 1979.

—In October 1978 Congress passed a weakened version of Carter's energy package, thus meeting his summit commitment to have a long-range energy program in place by the end of the year. As had been foreseen at Bonn, the president was forced to resort to administrative action to raise U.S. oil prices to world levels. His domestic advisers won a delay of some months in the effective date of full decontrol, but in the end, the essential American energy pledges made at Bonn were fulfilled.

—Worries about the dollar and about the Carter administration's anti-inflationary policies played a secondary role in the background to

Bonn and in the summit communiqué, and not until November 1978 did the Americans grasp the nettle, sharply tightening monetary policy and putting together an international support package for the dollar. Mounting administration concern about domestic inflation—and *not* international policy considerations—was apparently the crucial factor in this policy shift. It remains an open question whether the low salience of this issue in the Bonn bargaining represented a major "lost opportunity."

In short, the Bonn accord represents a genuine case of discretionary, international coordination of economic policy. Policy changes were pledged by the key participants, and those policy changes were implemented. Moreover—although this counterfactual claim is necessarily more difficult to establish—those policy changes would very probably not have been pursued (certainly not on the same scale and within the same time frame) in the absence of the international agreement at Bonn.

Theoretical Implications of the Bonn Summit

The 1977–78 experience raises serious questions about some basic tenets of standard theories of international economic policy coordination. In this final section, we address several of these fundamental assumptions.

Cheating

Most game-theoretic dilemmas discussed in the literature on international economic policy coordination arise from the assumption of international anarchy. The possibility that nations may resolve these dilemmas through mutually binding contracts is often recognized but is quickly dismissed. Given the centrality of the assumption that fear of cheating inhibits cooperation, it is perhaps surprising that so little attention has been paid to the incidence of, and incentives for, cheating in international economic diplomacy. We are unaware of any systematic treatment of this issue in the context of international economics, in contrast to the rather extensive discussion of comparable issues in the literature on international security negotiations, above all, on arms control.[163]

The problem of cheating (or reneging) can be broken into three distinct issues: (1) the problem of *good faith*, (2) the problem of *verification*, and (3) the problem of *the ability to deliver* on an agreement. We consider each problem in turn.

Good faith. Most interpretations of international economic policy coordination assume that "unfortunately, policy makers generally have an incentive to cheat."[164] This approach is also characteristic of the so-called Realist school of international relations. In an anarchic, "self-help" international system, dilemmas of collective action (such as the well-known "prisoners' dilemma" of game theory) are rife. Public goods are undersupplied, public "bads" oversupplied, and free-riders abound.[165] The fundamental problem is simple: nations may promise to cooperate, but there is no third party to prevent their reneging.

In considering the importance of this problem for international cooperation, it is useful to distinguish between what we shall call *voluntary* and *involuntary* defection. Voluntary defection refers to reneging by a rational egoist in the absence of enforceable contracts—the much-analyzed problem posed, for example, in the prisoners' dilemma and other dilemmas of collective action. Involuntary defection instead reflects the behavior of an agent for a nonunitary actor who is unable to deliver on a previous promise. Even though these two types of behavior may be difficult to disentangle in some instances, the underlying logic is quite different, as we shall explain below.

Voluntary reneging is actually much less common, particularly in dealings among Western governments, than a simple-minded view of international anarchy might imply. One plausible explanation is that governments (and politicians) have an interest in maintaining their reputations for keeping their word. As Axelrod, Keohane, and others have recently pointed out, the temptation to engage in voluntary defection is dramatically reduced among players who are concerned for their reputation, and in any situation of recurrent interaction a rational player will be concerned for his reputation:

To a government that values its ability to make future agreements, reputation is a crucial resource; and the most important aspect of an actor's reputation in world politics is the belief of others that it will keep its future commitments even when a particular situation, myopically viewed, makes it appear disadvantageous to do so.[166]

Concern for one's reputation rests in part on anticipation of future games. It is well recognized, for example, that cooperation in prisoners' dilemmas is more common when the games are indefinitely repeated.[167] This is clearest for players who expect to encounter one another again, as Western summiteers usually do. In the real world, however, reputations are often generalized across other players, so that "the failure to stick by one's word reduces the scope for making agreements with *other* countries in the future."[168]

Equally important, reputation is also generalized across different games at a single point in time, so that in a loose sense the outcomes of all those games are linked. The density of contemporary interdependence means that the major Western governments are continuously engaged in negotiations on a myriad of important, although highly disparate issues. They are not only one another's most important trading partners, but also one another's most important military allies. On any given issue, a deal is usually possible only if the parties are mutually credible. Hence, as a first approximation, each party's credibility has a value to it equal to the sum of the net benefits in all those deals—a value almost surely higher than the benefit of reneging on any single deal.

To be sure, this formulation assumes that reneging on any single deal will destroy a party's credibility in all other negotiations. The damage to credibility from a single defection depends, among other things, on the visibility of the defection and the "vengefulness" of the other players.[169] If the reneging negotiator appears to be a single agency or a low-ranking official, the assumption of generalized credibility is probably false. But the assumption of generalized credibility is surely true when the reneging negotiator is the chief executive. Hence, the costs of reneging on a deal that has been struck (or publicly sanctioned) by the chief executive are extremely high. That, of course, is why deals struck at the summit are inherently more credible.[170]

Even among Western chief executives, reneging occasionally occurs, although almost always in a context in which the terms of the agreement were sufficiently vague that verification is problematic. But even when an agreement is only implicit, or when its sanction by the chief executive is ambiguous, the costs of appearing to renege are high. One notable example is President Carter's decision in March 1978 not to deploy the so-called neutron bomb, despite earlier suggestions by American emissaries to NATO that he would. This policy shift by the American president traumatized—the word is not too strong—virtually all his senior advisers, regardless of their views of the merits of the issue, precisely because they recognized the extremely high costs of reneging by a Western chief executive.[171]

If one takes seriously the claim that policymakers in an anarchic world are constantly tempted to cheat, certain features of the Bonn story—certain things that did *not* happen—seem quite anomalous. We have found little evidence that the negotiations were hampered by mutual fear of reneging. For example, even though the Bonn agreement was negotiated with exquisite care, it contained no special provisions about phasing or partial conditionality that might have protected the parties from unexpected defection. Moreover, the Germans and the Japanese both irretrievably enacted their parts of the bargain in September, more than six months before the president's decision on oil price decontrol and nearly two years before decontrol was implemented.

Once the Germans and Japanese had fulfilled their parts of the bargain, the temptation for the U.S. president to renege should have been overpowering, if the standard account of international anarchy is to be believed. What is more, the domestic political pressure on him to renege was clearly very strong, and this was precisely the advice he received from his principal domestic advisers. But virtually no one on either side of the final debate on decontrol dismissed the Bonn pledge as irrelevant. The president's own comments about the pledge during that debate suggest some second thoughts about the wisdom of the Bonn package, but little eagerness to cheat. When weighing actions that might have infringed on the agreement, the president seemed to recognize that he should clear those actions with his foreign colleagues; when he did delay implementation of decontrol by some months, he sent a personal emissary to Schmidt to seek his understanding. In short, the Bonn "promise" had political weight. We conjecture that this weight derived, not primarily from Carter's personal sense of morality, but rather from the fact that Western governments are involved in so many continuing policy games that reneging would have had very high political and diplomatic costs.

The primary evidence against the assumption that fear of voluntary cheating prevents international cooperation is not that cheating rarely occurs, for of course if rational governments had a well-founded fear of cheating, they would not expose themselves to defection by their partners in the first place. Rather, the point of the Bonn experience is that governments did not act as if they feared intentional cheating, and they did not exploit what might have seemed, myopically viewed, opportunities to cheat their partners. Concern for reputation seems to be one plausible interpretation for this behavior.

The conclusion is not that all international pledges can be trusted, but that some would be very costly to break. The temptation for *voluntary* reneging varies widely in the international political economy, depending on the visibility and solemnity of the commitment, its verifiability, the frequency of dealing among the contracting parties, the value that they attribute to those other deals, and the number of other parties "observing" the game.[172] As a practical matter, it seems unlikely that fear of intentional defection can explain all, or even most, of the unconsummated opportunities for mutually beneficial cooperation, particularly among Western nations.

Verification. Even if players in general trust one another or have full confidence in enforcement of their promises (as they would within a framework of commercial law, for example), if an agreement is to be credible, the players must be able to tell when it has been broken. Concern about verification played an interesting role in the economic diplomacy of 1977–78. It has been pointed out that verification is simpler in the case of agreements about policy settings than in the case of agreements that specify policy targets, since policy instruments are directly controlled by governments, but failures to achieve policy targets can be blamed on external events.[173] Both approaches were tried during 1977–78.

At the London summit, agreement was stated in terms of growth targets, but Germany and Japan fell far short of their targets.[174] These failures might be interpreted as reneging on the London agreement, but it is probably more accurate to explain the shortfalls as the result of the uncertainty and unpredictability that pervade international economics. Recall Chancellor Schmidt's privately expressed concern that he had been "shamed" by the shortfall in growth. Over the following year, the negotiators came to recognize the superiority of agreements that specified policy moves, and the Bonn agreement was for the most part framed in terms of policy choices, not economic outcomes. We conclude that international agreements are easier to verify—and hence easier to make in the first place—when they are instrument based rather than outcome based.

The ability to deliver. The credibility of a negotiator depends not only on trust in his good faith and on the verifiability of his promises, but also on confidence in his ability to fulfill those promises. Particularly in a democratic political system, the credibility of an official commitment can be low, even if the commitment is perfectly verifiable and even if the negotiator is personally trusted by his foreign counterparts, for the negotiator may be unable to guarantee that the commitment will be ratified in domestic politics. (As used here, "ratification" refers not merely to formal legislative endorsement, but to any domestic action needed to implement the agreement.) Europeans often claim that this problem is particularly severe in the American case, given our constitutional separation of powers, but in principle the problem is universal. Examples of this kind of credibility gap are particularly common in trade; the failure of Congress to ratify abolition of the "American selling price" method of customs valuation for chemicals, as agreed on during the Kennedy round, is a classic instance. Similarly, a key obstacle to macroeconomic coordination in 1985–87 was the Germans' fear that the Reagan administration would be politically unable to carry out any commitment it might make to cut the U.S. budget deficit, no matter how well-intentioned the president.

Concern about "deliverability" was a prominent element in the Bonn negotiations. In the joint postsummit press conference, President Carter stressed that "each of us has been careful not to promise more than he can deliver." A major issue throughout the preparation of the agreement was Carter's own ability to deliver on his energy commitments. The Americans worked hard to convince the others, first, that the president was under severe domestic political constraints on energy issues that limited what he could promise, but, second, that he could deliver on what he was prepared to promise. To address this issue was the sole purpose of Senator Robert Byrd's presummit trip to Europe, and the domestic politics of energy was also the focus of bilateral meetings between Carter and Schmidt on the eve of the summit.

Thus the Bonn experience suggests that concern about cheating is somewhat misplaced. The negotiators in 1977–78 sought to make their mutual promises as verifiable as possible, and they sought to be sure that no one had promised more than he could deliver.[175] But they also behaved as if they assumed their counterparts would act in good faith, rather than renege at the first opportunity. Negotiators seemed to follow this presumption about one another: "He will do what he has promised, so long as what he has promised is clear and within his power."

In other words, the frustrating inability to make a binding contract that helps to define the prisoners' dilemma was *not* a prominent feature of the Bonn negotiations. We attribute this surprising lack of concern about "voluntary cheating" to the very high importance that rational policymakers will attribute to their reputation for reliability. If that conclusion is valid and general, it suggests that the strategic dilemmas that are at the center of most current theories of international economic policy coordination may be less frequent than is sometimes supposed. If that is so, then cheating and fear of cheating may be a less important constraint on international economic policy coordination than other factors, such as uncertainty, transaction costs, and domestic politics.

Deliverability raises important issues about the feasibility of international economic policy coordination, but in our view it is not useful analytically to assimilate these issues to the question of voluntary cheating that lies at the heart of most standard game-theoretic interpretations. Involuntary defection, and the fear of it, can be just as fatal to prospects for cooperation as voluntary defection. To an analyst committed to a "unitary actor" model of state behavior, moreover, failure to deliver might appear indistinguishable from intentional cheating. However, involuntary defection derives from a quite different source and cannot be accurately understood within a framework limited to unitary actors. Conversely, it should not be assumed that domestic political pressures invariably tend to undermine international agreements. When some domestic actors themselves favor the policy agreed to internationally, they will tend to act as "enforcers" of the international agreement. This seems a plausible interpretation of the activities of the forces supporting decontrol during the post-Bonn maneuvering within the Carter administration over oil prices. In short, the analysis of a negotiator's ability to deliver on his promises requires an assessment of the domestic political game that underlies his international strategy, a task we consider next.[176]

Unitary or Pluralistic National Authorities

In the light of our analysis of the Bonn accord, the most problematic tenet of current theories of international economic policy coordination is the assumption that the behavior of national governments can be interpreted in terms of a unitary utility function and a stable preference schedule. Of course many economic analysts recognize that the assumption that the national government is a unitary actor is unrealistic. As Bryant notes, for example, "The concept of a centralized policy authority within the national government is a fictional construct greatly at variance with political reality. . . . In all countries, for better or for worse, the ship of state has more than one captain and stabilization decisions are not fully coordinated." [177]

Not only economists intent on formal theories of policy coordination adopt the simplifying assumption that the international behavior of national governments can be interpreted in terms of a unitary utility function and a stable preference schedule. Indeed, within the literature of political science the dominant Realist interpretation of international relations argues that domestic dynamics can be safely ignored. The earliest attempt within political science to analyze Western economic diplomacy during 1977–78 in game-theoretic terms assumed an undivided set of national preferences; as Keohane explained this approach, "By major objectives I mean those foreign economic policy objectives that *any* nonrevolutionary U.S. government, responding to the interests of individuals and groups within the United States, would find it desirable to pursue." [178]

That some important national objectives have this undisputed status can hardly be doubted. However, *not* every American government sought German and Japanese reflation, and *no* administration before Carter's had mustered the political will to decontrol oil prices. Hence, by Keohane's definition, these cannot have been "major objectives," although they were obviously central to U.S. foreign economic policy in this era. The replacement of Ford by Carter (and, of course, the subsequent replacement of Carter by Reagan) had powerful effects on the apparent "American" preferences in international economic diplomacy. This discrepancy illustrates how domestic politics can condition prospects for international economic policy coordination. The discrepancy also suggests that the assumption of a unitary actor is unrealistic. (Keohane recognizes these complications, but they are not accommodated in his game-theoretic analysis.)

But the unitary-actor assumption is powerfully parsimonious. If the goal is theoretical simplification, as it must be, then merely showing that this assumption is unrealistic is not adequate grounds for discarding it. If (as Henri Bergson quipped) "the chief advantage of time is that it prevents everything from happening at once," then (as Jagdish Bhagwati has added) "the chief advantage of economic theory is that it prevents us from considering everything at the same time." [179] Perhaps analysts of international economic policy coordination can safely leave the "black box" of domestic politics closed. The right question is not whether the unitary-actor assumption is unrealistic, but whether it is misleading. Unfortunately, we believe that it is the latter.

From the point of view of most political scientists analyzing national policymaking, the utility functions and preference schedules postulated by unitary-actor models represent a (possibly unstable) coalition of political parties, interest groups, bureaucratic agencies, politicians, and officials. This is true, of course, regardless of whether or not the government is formally a coalition government. Indeed, it is probably especially true of American politics, in which formal party coalitions are almost unknown. If the governing coalition (of parties, agencies, private groups, and so on) is itself highly stable and cohesive, then the unitary-actor model, though unrealistic and incomplete in its account of national policy preferences, may not be misleading from the point of view of international economic policy coordination. But if the governing coalition is internally divided, finely balanced, or unstable, then the national utility function imputed by formal models will itself be unstable.

International pressures may actually "reverberate" within domestic politics, tipping the domestic balance and producing, in effect, a shift in the utility function that may, in turn, feed back into the international negotiations. As James A. Caporaso puts the point:

> Interdependence is not simply a relationship of one country against another. Beneath the national envelop lies a myriad of groups, each with its distinctive cost-benefit calculations in the interdependence relationship. In some cases the domestic-international alignments may be so distinctive as to affect the domestic policy process.[180]

These cautions about the unitary-actor assumption are strongly supported, we believe, by the history of economic diplomacy in 1977–78. The story of the Bonn accord makes clear that this parsimonious assumption would produce not simply an incomplete, but a radically misleading, interpretation of this case of international economic policy coordination. The 1978 agreement was possible only because *none* of the key national authorities was a unified actor. Each of the three governments called on to make the most specific contributions to the bargain—the United States, Germany, and Japan—was internally divided. Within each, one faction supported the policy shift being demanded of their country internationally, but in each case that faction was initially outnumbered in the domestic political arena.

As the preparations for Bonn began, the American government was divided but inclined to be against oil price decontrol. A coalition of the president's international and economic advisers favored a move to world price levels, but they were opposed by the president's key domestic aides and a strong majority in Congress. Not until nine months after the summit would it become clear that the advocates of decontrol had carried the day. Similarly, as the international negotiations got under way, the German government was divided but inclined to be against more rapid expansion of its economy. Here the advocates of the policy shift were in an even smaller minority than were their American counterparts, although they were unusually well placed. They included a few officials in the Economics Ministry and the chancellery, as well as the leaders of the labor unions and the left wing of the Social Democrats, but they had a silent partner at the head of the government. Against this group were arrayed the Free Democrats, the Bundesbank, most economic officials in the government, and most of the business and banking community. Finally, as 1977 opened, the Japanese government was divided but inclined to be against additional fiscal stimulus. Here the expansionist forces were more numerous but less powerful than in Germany. They included some business interests and some LDP politicians, but they were implacably opposed by the Ministry of Finance, the most powerful agency in Japanese government.

In each case the domestic advocates of the internationally desired policy were able to use the summit process (and the associated negotiations during the eighteen months before the Bonn summit) to help shift the internal balance of power in their favor. In each case these advocates of the internationally desired policy acted (in the words of one of the Americans) as a kind of benevolent "conspiracy," and in each case they signaled to their foreign counterparts that additional international pressure would be welcome.[181]

On the one hand, without that domestic resonance international forces would not have sufficed to produce the accord, no matter how balanced the package of concessions and no matter how attractive it might have seemed to outside economic analysts. On the other hand, the international pressure, coupled with the balanced character of the final package, allowed policies to be "sold" domestically that would not have been feasible otherwise. As one Japanese participant-observer put it, "For a snowflake, you need not only the right temperature and humidity; you need some particle as a precipitant. Foreign demands can provide that precipitant." Despite the uncertainties of conjectural, "what-if" history, it seems probable that international pressure and this sort of domestic division were singly necessary and jointly sufficient to produce the policy shifts in all three cases.

Divisions within a government are often thought to hamper international cooperation.[182] The Bonn case suggests, however, that domestic divisions may actually foster, rather than impede, coordination. Dieter Hiss, the 1978 German sherpa and one of those who believed that a stimulus package would be in Germany's own interest, later wrote that summits are likely to effect changes in national policy

> only insofar as they mobilize and/or change public opinion and the attitude of political groups. . . . Often that is enough, if the balance of opinion is shifted, providing a bare majority for the previously stymied actions of a strong minority. . . . No country violates its own interests, but certainly the definition of its interests can change through a summit with its possible trade-offs and give-and-take. . . . The results of the summit meetings, inserted efficaciously into the domestic decision process, make it easier to steer this process in a direction that produces positive results not only from the narrower national point of view, but also in the international context.[183]

From a theoretical point of view, the appropriateness of the unitary-actor assumption in any particular case depends on the robustness and balance of the political aggregation function (which is related to, but not the same thing as, a social welfare function). If the political aggregation function is relatively robust (that is, if a substantial majority of the relevant political actors, weighted for political influence, favor a particular course of action or have very similar utility functions, so that the loss function of the incumbent authorities is highly stable), then the assumption of unitary policy authorities is acceptable. If, however, the political aggregation function is complex or closely balanced, then the assumption of unitary actors is quite misleading.[184] If international pressures "reverberate" within the domestic arena, changing the internal balance of forces and thus altering the political aggregation function, then the results of the international negotiation may well be altered, as they were in 1977–78.

Precisely this interpretation of the process in Tokyo in 1978 was offered by a senior politician, closely involved on the expansionist side of the dispute, who explained how summit pressures and domestic politics became intertwined:

> When the bureaucracy is unanimous, their position cannot be beaten at the summit, because the other heads of government are not audacious enough to engage in harsh criticism [of one another], and national sovereignty survives. But in some cases the arguments within Japan could go either way, as in the locomotive case, and then one can "draw authority" from the summit.

Like a small child jumping on one end of a packed but balanced teeter-totter, international pressure can have disproportionate effects on the domestic balance. Reverberation need not always be positive, however, for under other circumstances external pressures can trigger a backlash in domestic politics. For example, during 1986 U.S. public pressure on the Germans to accelerate their economy was probably counterproductive. Despite rumored support within the Bundesbank for a September discount rate cut, pressure from the Reagan administration was so well publicized that officials in Frankfurt, loathe to appear submissive to their own government in Bonn, not to mention Washington, deferred the decision for four months. Distinguishing positive from negative reverberation must, of course, not be left as pure "ad-hoc-ery." Probably the crucial determinant is the character of the preexisting domestic balance of forces, and (more precisely) the degree to which the external pressure finds a domestic "sponsor," as it did in the 1978 case.

It is probably not uncommon in instances of international cooperation that government leaders or other domestic actors have successfully exploited international pressure to enable them to do what they privately wished to do but were unable to do with only their domestic political resources. For example, this pattern probably characterizes most cases of successful stabilization programs that are said (misleadingly) to be "imposed" by the IMF. For example, in the 1977 negotiations between Italy and the IMF, conservative Christian Democrats apparently exploited IMF pressure to facilitate policy moves that were otherwise infeasible in terms of domestic politics.[185]

From the viewpoint of orthodox social choice theory, this sort of reverberation may seem problematic, for it implies a certain interconnectedness among the utility functions of independent actors, albeit across different levels of the game. Two rationales may be offered to explain reverberation within a context of utility-maximizing egoists. First, consider the long-run or cross-issue calculus of domestic actors. In a complex, independent, but often unfriendly world, offending foreigners may be costly. "To get along, go along," may be a rational maxim. This rationale is likely to be more common in more dependent nations.

The second possible rationale takes into account cognitive factors and uncertainty. In practice, negotiation (especially internationally) is more than mere bargaining over a fixed, known payoff matrix. Much of what actually happens is attempted persuasion. Behaviorally at least, our account of the events of 1977–78 suggests that it is highly misleading to disregard the degree to which policymakers, negotiating internationally, actually try to convince one another that their respective models of the world and even their respective preferences are mistaken. Under uncertainty, international communications and persuasion can change minds, move the undecided, and hearten those in the minority, domestically speaking. As one reluctant German latecomer to the "locomotive" cause in 1978 explained his conversion, "In the end, even the Bank for International Settlements supported the idea of coordinated reflation." To appreciate the political utility of international pressure—and its limits—we need to develop a better understanding of reverberation.

In short, at least under some circumstances, the results of international bargaining may be quite different from the outcome that would have been predicted by simply examining the *ex ante* preference schedules of the contending national authorities. A further hypothesis suggested by the Bonn case, but not yet proved, empirically or theoretically, is that explicit international policy coordination is more likely to occur when the political aggregation function is complex or closely balanced; that is, when the government is sharply divided. In some cases, transnational alignments may emerge, tacit or explicit, in which domestic interests pressure their respective governments to adopt mutually supportive policies. This is, of course, our interpretation of the 1978 Bonn summit accord.[186] In any event, if the 1977–78 negotiations provide any guide, the parsimonious unitary-actor assumption is not merely unrealistic, but positively misleading. Theories of international economic policy coordination must encompass domestic policy games as well as international ones.

We find it useful to conceive international economic policy coordination as a two-level game. Games at both the domestic and international level are played simultaneously, so that national policies are in some sense the result of both the domestic and the international parallelograms of forces. Neither of the two games can be ignored by policymakers, so long as their countries remain interdependent yet sovereign democracies. Each national political leader appears at both game boards. Across the international table sit his foreign counterparts, and at his elbows sit diplomats and other international advisers. Around the domestic table behind him sit party and parliamentary figures, spokesmen for the great domestic ministries, representatives of key domestic interest groups, and the leader's own political advisers. Domestic interest groups may be players not because of their direct lobbying, but because of their anticipated reactions to possible moves, as interpreted by their bureaucratic patrons or by the leader's political counselors. The absence of overt party or interest group involvement in international economic policy coordination by no means proves that the interests and preferences of those groups are irrelevant to the process.

The special complexity of this two-level game is that moves that are rational for a player at one board (such as raising energy prices or limiting automobile imports) may be quite irrational for that same player at the other board. Nevertheless, there are powerful incentives for consistency between the two games. Players (and kibitzers) will tolerate some differences in rhetoric between the two games—which is why each summiteer gives his (or her) own news conference after the summit—but in the end, either energy prices rise or they do not; either auto imports fall or they do not.

The political complexities for the players in this two-level game are staggering, quite apart from the technical economic complexities. Any key player at the international table who is dissatisfied with the outcome may upset the game board. Conversely, any national leader who fails to satisfy an adequate number of his fellow players at the domestic table risks being evicted from his seat. For example, the move by Canadian Prime Minister Joe Clark in 1979 to raise Canadian oil prices pleased his foreign counterparts, but it contributed to his fall from power. Each national leader, moreover, already has made a substantial investment in building a particular coalition at the domestic board, and he will be loathe to try to construct a different coalition simply to sustain an alternative policy mix that might be more acceptable internationally. For example, international complaints about the U.S. fiscal deficit did not cause President Reagan to alter his policies, despite domestic pressure in the same direction. We believe that it is political complexities of this sort, as much as the purely economic uncertainties, that explain why it took so long to complete the Bonn deal. On occasion, however, clever players will spot a move on one board that will trigger realignments on other boards, enabling them to achieve otherwise unattainable objectives. This two-table metaphor captures the dynamics of the 1977–78 negotiations better than any model based on unitary national actors.

Metaphors are not theories, but we are comforted by Max Black's observation that "perhaps every science must start with metaphor and end with algebra; and perhaps without the metaphor there would never have been any algebra." [187] If our interpretation of the Bonn summit accord is approximately correct, then the development of two-level game theory should have high priority, not only for explaining the conditions for successful international macroeconomic policy coordination, but also for understanding other instances of international influence on national policies, as in the case of IMF conditionality agreements.[188]

Several cautions need to be added at this point. First, we do not deny that unitary-actor models that focus on interstate conflicts of interest are also relevant to understanding international policy coordination. Indeed, the unitary-actor approach could be used to explain some aspects of the pattern of economic relations among the United States, Europe, and Japan in 1977–78. The depreciation of the dollar against the deutsche mark and yen, for example, created economic incentives for governments to shift toward more expansionary policies in Japan and Germany, as well as toward more restrictive policies in the United States. These incentives could be used to explain the position of governments and central banks during the debate leading up to the November 1978 foreign exchange intervention package and their monetary policies afterward. These same incentives, of course, operated on the heads of government at the Bonn summit, but as we have argued at length in our narrative, an examination of domestic politics is necessary for a complete understanding of how and why international cooperation succeeded. Similarly, we conjecture that features of the domestic games in the United States and Germany are also crucial for understanding why (in a situation parallel in many respects to 1977–78) transatlantic cooperation was so difficult during 1985–87.

Second, if our analysis is correct, the domestic game is probably *not* best modeled as pitting a unified government against a unified private sector. Kenneth Rogoff, for example, has disaggregated countries into monetary authorities, on the one hand, and labor and business, on the other. In his model, the central bank and the private sector contend over the real wage. Private wage setters therefore view collusion among central banks with suspicion, fearing that monetary authorities will agree jointly (and thus without fear of currency depreciation) to expand money supplies in order to increase employment through the effects of inflation on the real wage. Although Rogoff does highlight the effects of international cooperation on the domestic game, the dynamics of this domestic game are highly simplified, and their effect on international negotiations—our main interest—are unexplored.[189] In short, we are not here alluding to the issue of the credibility of government policy pronouncements that is raised by rational expectations theories.

Third, it is important to avoid premature simplification of the structure of the domestic game. For example, so-called median-voter models of domestic economic policy argue that policy reflects the preferences of the median voter in an n-dimensional policy space. But such models abstract from important institutional features of politics and government that affect the political aggregation function. In the Bonn summit case, for example, it is implausible to suppose that the position of the median German voter on macroeconomics or of the median American voter on energy pricing shifted sharply in the summer of 1978. In other words, minorities of various sorts almost always play a more important role in national decisionmaking than median-voter models allow. It is important, moreover, to avoid building a sequential assumption into the two-level model; that is, to avoid assuming that the domestic-level games are completed before beginning the international-level game. This assumption would simplify the mathematics of the models, but it would prevent exploration of precisely the kind of interaction between the levels that was crucial in the 1977–78 case.

Finally, it is worth noting that this two-level approach would complicate (properly, in our view) any calculation of the gains from international economic policy coordination. For example, the pioneering calculations of Oudiz and Sachs rest on the assumption that current policy reflects "revealed preferences" of the national authorities. The apparent U.S. indifference to current account and fiscal deficits that appears in their results probably reflects an impasse in the domestic political game about the budget deficit, rather than a considered national choice.[190] In 1977–78 the American "gains" from the Bonn policy trade were negative from the point of view of Stuart Eizenstat and the White House domestic policy staff, but they were positive from the point of view of Henry Owen, Richard Cooper, and Anthony Solomon. Who better reflected "the national authorities" in that case? Similar questions could be posed about the Ministry of Finance and the Economic Planning Agency in Tokyo or about the Social Democrats and the Bundesbank in Germany. To respond that the ultimate arbiter is the chief executive would be to posit a political aggregation function that is unrealistic and misleading, as almost any president would testify.

Given the character of international economic negotiation as a two-level game, it is a false dichotomy to ask whether a given policy decision (such as any of the policies agreed to at Bonn) is to be explained in domestic *or* international terms.[191] Interpretations cast in terms either of domestic causes and international effects or of international causes and domestic effects represent merely "partial equilibrium" analyses and miss an important part of the story—that is, how the domestic politics of several countries became entangled by means of an international negotiation. The events of 1977–78 illustrate that we must aim instead for "general equilibrium" theories that account simultaneously for the interaction of domestic and international factors.

Multiple-Issue Games

Most formal models of international economic policy coordination assume that the bargaining involves the single domain of macroeconomics. Game-theoretic dilemmas and calculations of Pareto optimality assume that side payments on issues other than macroeconomics are excluded.[192] This assumption radically simplifies the analysis, but it entails important costs in terms of realism, as the 1977–78 case makes clear.

It is well known that side payments facilitate the solution of games. It is sometimes supposed that political "linkage" among functionally unrelated topics hampers the resolution of international conflict, but it can be shown formally—and Bonn demonstrated practically—that without cross-issue linkage, many important positive-sum international games may never be concluded.[193] Thus the potential gains from international economic policy coordination may be much greater in a multi-issue context than when coordination is confined to "policy barter" within a single domain. We agree with Oudiz and Sachs that "the case for coordination must rest on the demonstration of a Pareto improvement in the economic outcome."[194] However, the Pareto bounds on joint welfare improvement may be expanded, perhaps considerably, when multiple issues are simultaneously negotiated.

Particularly within the context of Western summitry, single-issue analysis can be quite misleading. The major Western nations are continuously involved in negotiations on multiple issues—not only on economic matters, but also on broader matters of foreign policy and security. Because in the modern state distinct issue areas are normally handled by different agencies and respond to different domestic constituencies, cross-issue deals rarely can be accomplished without the active involvement of the chief executive. However, the head of government may be able to compel one sector to make what is for it an uncompensated concession, and he can balance those costs against the benefits that will presumably flow from the counterpart concession by the other party.

It is important to distinguish clearly between "substantive" and "strategic" issue linkage. Substantive linkage refers to causal connections in the real world such that the outcome on one issue (say, monetary policy) has direct implications for the outcome on another (say, trade flows). Strategic linkage refers to instances in which agreement in one domain is conditioned, by at least one of the actors, on agreement in some other domain. There is no reason to suppose that opportunities for successful strategic linkage presuppose substantive linkage, and negotiating a strategic linkage may actually be simpler among substantively unrelated issues. Artis and Ostry argue that the suggestion that strategic linkage may improve the odds for successful cooperation is "something of a red herring," for "negotiation and computation costs rise very rapidly with an increase in the spread of issues under negotiation."[195] We agree that there may be a point of diminishing returns to injecting new issues into negotiations, arising out of transaction costs and depending on the number of countries involved, the pattern of domestic divisions, and the complexity of the issues. But we believe that the comparison of the costs and benefits of cross-issue strategic linkage is not so straightforward as their argument implies, and the 1978 case seems to support our relatively more favorable assessment of strategic linkage.

Although the Bonn accord is sometimes described elliptically as a "macroeconomic policy package," energy and trade matters were also intrinsic to the deal, as we have shown. An accord might conceivably have been struck without the inclusion of the trade issue, but a game limited to energy policy could not have been played, for there was no plausible German (or Japanese) concession in that domain that could have elicited the American commitment to world oil pricing. We have discussed the possibility of an exclusively macroeconomic package under the rubric of "a missed opportunity." This hypothetical bargain would have traded German and Japanese reflation for American fiscal and monetary restraint.[196] The Bonn summit communiqué is nominally consistent with this sort of deal, in that the Americans pledged restraint, but both sides actually saw energy, not macroeconomics, as the crucial American concession. The climactic midnight bargaining in Bonn pitted German reflation against American commitments on energy, not macroeconomics. Moreover, we find no evidence that the Bonn accord was a relevant consideration in the administration's subsequent deliberations about monetary restraint in the autumn of 1978, in marked contrast to the prominent role of the summit pledge during the deliberations about oil price decontrol in the spring of 1979. In short, the Bonn episode is evidence that multi-issue international policy coordination is possible, but it is not a case of purely macroeconomic policy coordination.

One kind of issue linkage is absolutely crucial to understanding how domestic and international politics can become entangled in a two-level game. Suppose that a majority of domestic constituents oppose a given policy (say, oil price decontrol), but that some members of that majority would be willing to switch their vote on that issue in return for more jobs (say, in export industries). If bargaining is limited to the domestic table, that trade-off is not technically feasible, but if the chief negotiator can broker an international deal that delivers more jobs (say, by means of faster growth abroad), he can, in effect, overturn the initial outcome at the domestic table. Such transnational issue linkage was a crucial element in the 1978 Bonn accord.

Note that this strategy works not by changing the preferences of any domestic constituents, but rather by creating a policy option (such as faster export growth) that was previously beyond domestic control. Hence, we refer to this type of issue linkage that alters the domestically feasible outcomes as *synergistic linkage*. Economic interdependence multiplies the opportunities for altering domestic coalitions (and thus policy outcomes) by expanding the set of feasible alternatives in this way—in effect, by creating political entanglements across national boundaries. Thus, one should expect synergistic linkage (which is, by definition, explicable only in terms of two-level analysis) to become more frequent as interdependence grows.

Issues for Future Analysis

Important issues remain that may be illuminated by a closer examination of Western economic diplomacy in 1977–78. One, for example, is analytic agreement as a precondition for international economic policy coordination. Some analysts have stressed analytic disagreements as a crucial—perhaps even "the" crucial—stumbling block to international cooperation (see Richard Cooper's paper in this volume). As a general proposition, we suspect that governments can reach practical policy agreements with one another even if they do not agree on the underlying model of the world economy. Two actors may well agree on what to do, despite conflicting interests, *precisely because* they have different expectations about the consequences of the agreed action.[197] We are not certain, however, whether the Bonn episode supports our suspicion.

A related (and, we believe, highly plausible) proposition is that uncertainty is a powerful deterrent to international economic policy coordination. Certainly, it is difficult to exaggerate the degree and multiplicity of the uncertainties that pervade economic diplomacy— uncertainties about how the respective domestic economies work, about how the international economy works, about the potential benefits from coordination, and about how to formulate a deal that meets the minimal political needs of each party. In 1977–78, for example, the negotiators were usually wrong in their assessments of domestic politics abroad; most American officials did not appreciate the complex domestic game that Chancellor Schmidt was playing over the issue of reflation.

It is important here to distinguish what we might call "model uncertainty"—that is, uncertainty about the relationship of means to ends—from uncertainty over current economic conditions and trends and political uncertainties over upcoming elections, the viability of formal and informal coalitions, the positions of major actors, and so on. Careful analysis may reveal special features of the Bonn accord, and of the process that produced it, that tended to reduce uncertainty.

For example, the extended period of discussion may have been important because it allowed crucial uncertainties to be resolved.

In economic terms, of course, it is arguable that the Bonn decisions, both on energy and on macroeconomics, came a year too late. If those policy changes could have been achieved in 1977, as their proponents originally had hoped, the benefits might have been clearer and the risks of adverse side effects lower. But the politics of international policy coordination, as our story has shown, are so complex that timely action is difficult at best. Politically, the Bonn decisions could hardly have been reached much earlier, even if, economically, they may have come too late. This suggests, finally, the desirability of greater attention to the institutional context of international economic policy coordination.

Appendix: The Bonn Summit Conference Declaration, July 17, 1978

[What follows is the full text of the Bonn summit communiqué.]

The Heads of State and Government of Canada, the Federal Republic of Germany, France, Italy, Japan, the United Kingdom of Great Britain and Northern Ireland and the United States of America met in Bonn on 16th and 17th July 1978. The European Community was represented by the President of the European Council and by the President of the European Commission for discussion of matters within the Community's competence.

1. We agreed on a comprehensive strategy covering growth, employment and inflation, international monetary policy, energy, trade and other issues of particular interest to developing countries. We must create more jobs and fight inflation, strengthen international trading, reduce payments imbalances, and achieve greater stability in exchange markets. We are dealing with long-term problems, which will only yield to sustained efforts. This strategy is a coherent whole, whose parts are interdependent. To this strategy, each of our countries can contribute; from it, each can benefit.

Growth, Employment and Inflation

2. We are concerned, above all, about world-wide unemployment because it has been at too high a level for many years, because it hits

hardest at the most vulnerable sections of the population, because its economic cost is high and its human cost higher still. We will act, through measures to assure growth and develop needed skills, to increase employment.

In doing this, we will build on the progress that has already been made in the fight against inflation and will seek new successes in that fight. But we need an improvement in growth where that can be achieved without rekindling inflation in order to reduce extremes of balance of payments surpluses and deficits. This will reduce destabilizing exchange rate movements. Improved growth will help to reduce protectionist pressures. We need it also to encourage the flow of private investment, on which economic progress depends; we will seek to reduce impediments to private investment, both domestically and internationally. Better growth is needed to ensure that the free world is able to develop to meet the expectations of its citizens and the aspirations of the developing countries.

3. A programme of different actions by countries that face different conditions is needed to assure steady non-inflationary growth. In countries whose balance of payments situation and inflation rate does not impose special restrictions, this requires a faster rise in domestic demand. In countries where rising prices and costs are creating strong pressures, this means taking new measures against inflation.

—Canada reaffirmed its intention, within the limits permitted by the need to contain and reduce inflation, to achieve higher growth of employment and an increase in output of up to 5%.

—As a contribution to avert the world-wide disturbances of economic equilibrium the German Delegation has indicated that by the end of August it will propose to the legislative bodies additional and quantitatively substantial measures up to 1% of GNP, designed to achieve a significant strengthening of demand and a higher rate of growth. The order of magnitude will take account of the absorptive capacity of the capital market and the need to avoid inflationary pressures.

—The President of the French Republic has indicated that, while pursuing its policy of reduction of the rate of inflation, the French Government agrees, as a contribution to the common effort, to increase by an amount of about 0.5% of GNP the deficit of the budget of the State for the year 1978.

—The Italian Prime Minister has indicated that the Government undertakes to raise the rate of economic growth in 1979 by 1.5 percentage points with respect to 1978. It plans to achieve this goal by cutting public current expenditure while stimulating investments, with the aim of increasing employment in a non-inflationary context.

—The Prime Minister of Japan has referred to the fact that his Government is striving for the attainment of the real growth target for fiscal year 1978, which is about 1.5 percentage points higher than the performance of the previous year, mainly through the expansion of domestic demand. He has further expressed his determination to achieve the said target by taking appropriate measures as necessary. In August or September he will determine whether additional measures are needed.

—The United Kingdom, having achieved a major reduction in the rate of inflation and improvement in the balance of payments has recently given a fiscal stimulus equivalent to rather over 1% of GNP. The Government intends to continue the fight against inflation so as to improve still further the prospects for growth and employment.

—The President of the United States stated that reducing inflation is essential to maintaining a healthy U.S. economy and has therefore become the top priority of U.S. economic policy. He identified the major actions that have been taken and are being taken to counter inflation in the United States: Tax cuts originally proposed for fiscal year 1979 have now been reduced by $10 billion; government expenditure projections for 1978 and 1979 have been reduced; a very tight budget is being prepared for 1980; steps are being taken to reduce the direct contribution by government regulations or restrictions to rising costs and prices; and a voluntary programme has been undertaken to achieve deceleration of wages and prices.

—The meeting took note with satisfaction that the common approach of the European Community already agreed at Bremen would reinforce the effectiveness of this programme.

Energy

4. In spite of some improvement, the present energy situation remains unsatisfactory. Much more needs to be done.

5. We are committed to reduce our dependence on imported oil.

6. We note that the European Community has already agreed at Bremen the following objectives for 1985: to reduce the Community's dependence on imported energy to 50 per cent, to limit net oil imports,

and to reduce to 0.8 the ratio between the rate of increase in energy consumption and the rate of increase in gross domestic product.

7. Recognizing its particular responsibility in the energy field, the United States will reduce its dependence on imported oil. The U.S. will have in place by the end of the year a comprehensive policy framework within which this effort can be urgently carried forward. By year end, measures will be in effect that will result in oil import savings of approximately 2.5 million barrels per day by 1985. In order to achieve these goals, the U.S. will establish a strategic oil reserve of 1 billion barrels; it will increase coal production by two-thirds; it will maintain the ratio between growth in gross national product and growth in energy demand at or below 0.8; and its oil consumption will grow more slowly than energy consumption. The volume of oil imported in 1978 and 1979 should be less than that imported in 1977. In order to discourage excessive consumption of oil and to encourage the movement toward coal, the U.S. remains determined that the prices paid for oil in the U.S. shall be raised to the world level by the end of 1980.

8. We hope that the oil exporting countries will continue to contribute to a stable world energy situation.

9. Looking to the longer term, our countries will review their national energy programmes with a view to speeding them up. General energy targets can serve as useful measures of the progress achieved.

10. Private and public investment to produce energy and to use it more efficiently within the industrial world should be increased. This can contribute significantly to economic growth.

11. The further development of nuclear energy is indispensable, and the slippage in the execution of nuclear power programmes must be reversed. To promote the peaceful use of nuclear energy and reduce the risk of nuclear proliferation, the nuclear fuel cycle studies initiated at the London Summit should be pursued. The President of the United States and the Prime Minister of Canada have expressed their firm intention to continue as reliable suppliers of nuclear fuel within the framework of effective safeguards. The president intends to use the full powers of his office to prevent any interruption of enriched uranium supply and to ensure that existing agreements will be respected. The Prime Minister intends that there shall be no interruption of Canadian uranium on the basis of effective safeguards.

12. Coal should play an increasing important role in the long term.

13. Joint or co-ordinated energy research and development should

be carried out to hasten the development of new, including renewable, energy sources and the more efficient use of existing sources.

14. In energy development, the environment and human safety of the population must be safeguarded with greatest care.

15. To help developing countries, we will intensify our national development assistance programmes in the energy field and we will develop a co-ordinated effort to bring into use renewable energy technologies and to elaborate the details within one year. We suggest that the OECD will provide the medium for co-operation with other countries.

16. We stress the need for improvement and co-ordination of assistance for developing countries in the energy field. We suggest that the World Bank explore ways in which its activities in this field can be made increasingly responsive to the needs of the developing countries, and to examine whether new approaches, particularly to financing hydrocarbon exploration, would be useful.

Trade

17. We reaffirm our determination to expand international trade, one of the driving forces for more sustained and balanced economic growth. Through our joint efforts we will maintain and strengthen the open international trading system. We appreciate and support the progress as set forth in the Framework of Understanding on the Tokyo Round of Multilateral Trade Negotiations made public in Geneva, July 13th, 1978, even though within this Framework of Understanding some difficult and important issues remain unresolved.

The successful conclusion of these negotiations, the biggest yet held, would mean not just a major trade liberalisation programme extending over the 1980s but the most important progress yet made in the GATT in relation to non-tariff measures. Thus the GATT rules would be brought more closely into line with the requirements of the next decade—particularly in relation to safeguards—in ways which would avoid any weakening of the world trading system and be of benefit to all trading countries developed and developing alike. A substantially higher degree of equity and discipline in the international trading system would be achieved by the creation of new mechanisms in many fields for consultation and dispute settlement. Uniform application of the GATT rules is vital and we shall move in that direction as soon as possible.

In all areas of the negotiations the Summit countries look forward to working even more closely with the developing countries. We seek to ensure for all participants a sound and balanced result, which adequately takes into account the needs of developing countries, for example, through special and differential treatment, and which brings about their greater participation in the benefits and obligations of the world trading system.

At last year's Downing Street Summit we rejected a protectionist course for world trade. We agreed to give a new impetus to the Tokyo Round. Our negotiators have fulfilled that commitment. Today we charge them, in co-operation with the other participants, to resolve the outstanding issues and to conclude successfully the detailed negotiations by December 15, 1978.

18. We note with satisfaction the renewal of the pledge to maintain an open market oriented economic system made by the OECD Council of Ministers last month. Today's world economic problems cannot be solved by relapsing into open or concealed protectionism.

19. We welcome the statement on positive adjustment policy made by the OECD Ministers. There must be a readiness over time, to accept and facilitate structural change. Measures to prevent such change perpetuate economic inefficiency, place the burden of structural change on trading partners, and inhibit the integration of developing countries into the world economy. We are determined in our industrial, social, structural, and regional policy initiatives to help sectors in difficulties, without interfering with international competition and trade flows.

20. We note the need for countries with large current accounts deficits to increase exports and for countries with large current accounts surpluses to facilitate increases in imports. In this context, the United States is firmly committed to improve its export performance and is examining measures to this end. The Prime Minister of Japan has stated that he wishes to work for the increase of imports through the expansion of domestic demand and various efforts to facilitate imports.

Furthermore, he has stated that in order to cope with the immediate situation of unusual surplus, the Government of Japan is taking a temporary and extraordinary step of calling for moderation in exports with the aim of keeping the total volume of Japan's exports for the fiscal year of 1978 at or below the level of fiscal year 1977.

21. We underline our willingness to increase our co-operation in

the field of foreign private investment flows among industrialized countries and between them and developing countries. We will intensify work for further agreements in the OECD and elsewhere.

22. In the context of expanding world economic activity, we recognize the requirement for better access to our countries' markets for the products of the developing countries. At the same time we look to increasing readiness on the part of the more advanced developing countries to open their markets to imports.

Relations with Developing Countries

23. Success in our efforts to strengthen our countries' economies will benefit the developing countries, and their economic progress will benefit us. This calls for joint action on the basis of shared responsibility.

24. In the years ahead the developing countries, particularly those most in need, can count on us for an increased flow of financial assistance and other resources for their development. The Prime Minister of Japan has stated that he will strive to double Japan's official development assistance in three years.

We deeply regret the failure of the COMECON countries to take their due share in the financial assistance to developing countries and invite them once more to do so.

25. The poorer developing countries require increased concessional aid. We support the soft loan funds of the World Bank and the three regional development banks. We pledge our governments to support replenishment of the International Development Association on a scale that would permit its lending to rise annually in real terms.

26. As regards the more advanced developing countries, we renew our pledge to support replenishment of the multilateral development banks' resources, on the scale needed to meet the growing needs for loans on commercial terms. We will encourage governmental and private co-financing of development projects with these banks.

The co-operation of the developing countries in creating a good investment climate and adequate protection for foreign investment is required if foreign private investment is to play its effective role in generating economic growth and in stimulating the transfer of technology.

We also refer to our efforts with respect to developing countries in the field of energy as outlined in paragraph 15 and 16.

27. We agreed to pursue actively the negotiations on a Common

Fund to a successful conclusion and to continue our efforts to conclude individual commodity agreements and to complete studies of various ways of stabilizing export earnings.

International Monetary Policy

28. The erratic fluctuations of the exchange markets in recent months have had a damaging effect on confidence, investment and growth throughout the world. Essentially, exchange rate stability can only be achieved by attacking the fundamental problems which have contributed to the present large balance of payments deficits and surpluses. Implementation of the policies described above in the framework of a concerted program will help to bring about a better pattern of world payments balances and lead to greater stability in international exchange markets. This stability will in turn improve confidence and the environment for sustained economic growth.

29. Although exchange rates need to respond to changes in underlying economic and financial conditions among nations, our monetary authorities will continue to intervene to the extent necessary to counter disorderly conditions in the exchange markets. They will maintain extensive consultation to enhance these efforts' effectiveness. We will support surveillance by the International Monetary Fund, to promote effective functioning of the international monetary system.

30. The representatives of the European Community informed the meeting of the decision of the European Council at Bremen on 6/7 July to consider a scheme for a closer monetary co-operation. The meeting welcomed the report and noted that the Community would keep the other participants informed.

Conclusion

31. It has been our combined purpose to attack the fundamental economic problems that our countries confront.

The measures on which we have agreed are mutually reinforcing. Their total effect should thus be more than the sum of their parts. We will now seek parliamentary and public support for these measures.

We cannot hope to achieve our purposes alone. We shall work closely together with other countries and within the appropriate international institutions, those among us whose countries are members of the European Community intend to make their efforts within this framework.

We have instructed our representatives to convene by the end of 1978 in order to review this Declaration. We also intend to have a similar meeting among ourselves at an appropriate time next year.

Notes

1. For accounts of economic diplomacy in the 1980s, see C. Randall Henning, *Macroeconomic Diplomacy in the 1980s: Domestic Politics and International Conflict among the United States, Japan, and Europe*, Atlantic Paper no. 65 (London: Croom Helm, for the Atlantic Institute for International Affairs, 1987); and Yoichi Funabashi, *Managing the Dollar: From the Plaza to the Louvre* (Washington: Institute for International Economics, 1988).

2. Koichi Hamada, "Macroeconomic Strategy and Coordination under Alternative Exchange Rates," in Rudiger Dornbusch and Jacob A. Frenkel, eds., *International Economic Policy: Theory and Evidence* (Johns Hopkins University Press, 1979), p. 321.

3. See Robert O. Keohane, "U.S. Foreign Economic Policy toward Other Advanced Capitalist States: The Struggle to Make Others Adjust," in Kenneth A. Oye, Donald Rothchild, and Robert J. Lieber, eds., *Eagle Entangled: U.S. Foreign Policy in a Complex World* (New York: Longman, 1979), pp. 107–09; Robert O. Keohane, *After Hegemony: Cooperation and Discord in the World Political Economy* (Princeton University Press, 1984); Duncan Snidal, "The Game *Theory* of International Politics," *World Politics*, vol. 38 (October 1985), pp. 25–27, as well as other papers in the issue, which has been republished as Kenneth A. Oye, ed., *Cooperation under Anarchy* (Princeton University Press, 1986).

4. This chapter is based in part on Robert D. Putnam and Nicholas Bayne, *Hanging Together: Cooperation and Conflict in the Seven-Power Summits*, rev. ed. (Harvard University Press, 1987); C. Randall Henning, "The Politics of Macroeconomic Conflict and Coordination among Advanced Capitalist States, 1975–1985" (Ph.D. thesis, Fletcher School of Law and Diplomacy, 1985); and Robert D. Putnam, "Diplomacy and Domestic Politics: The Logic of Two-Level Games," *International Organization*, vol. 42 (Summer 1988), pp. 427–60. The historical account of the events of 1977–78 draws on confidential personal interviews with virtually all the key participants.

5. See Richard N. Cooper, "Economic Interdependence and Coordination of Economic Policies," in Ronald W. Jones and Peter B. Kenen, eds., *Handbook of International Economics*, vol. 2 (Amsterdam: North-Holland, 1985; New York: Elsevier, 1985).

6. Compare Ralph Bryant's definition of coordination—"agreements among national authorities to implement instrument settings different from those that would be chosen in the absence of the agreements"—in Ralph C.

Bryant, *Money and Monetary Policy in Interdependent Nations* (Brookings, 1980), p. 465.

7. See Bryant, *Money and Monetary Policy,* pp. 477–78.

8. In terms of formal game theory, Nash and Stackelberg outcomes are two prominent subtypes here. In the Nash (or Cournot-Nash) equilibrium, each government regards other governments' policy choices as independent of its own. The Stackelberg equilibrium is distinguished by one nation (the "leader") taking into account the probable reactions of others (the "followers") to its own policies.

9. Stabilization programs of the International Monetary Fund (IMF), too, often have the function of strengthening a government's ability to do what it believes it should be doing anyhow.

10. Ronald I. McKinnon, "Currency Substitution and Instability in the World Dollar Standard," *American Economic Review,* vol. 72 (June 1982), pp. 320–33; and McKinnon, *An International Standard for Monetary Stabilization,* Policy Analyses in International Economics no. 8 (Institute for International Economics, 1984).

11. Important studies in this area include Koichi Hamada's pioneering works, recapitulated in *The Political Economy of International Monetary Interdependence* (MIT Press, 1985). See also Lief Johansen, "A Note on the Possibility of an International Equilibrium with Low Levels of Activity," *Journal of International Economics,* vol. 13 (November 1982), pp. 257–65; Matthew B. Canzoneri and Jo Anna Gray, "Two Essays on Monetary Policy in an Interdependent World," International Finance Discussion Paper no. 219 (Board of Governors of the Federal Reserve System, February 1983); Gilles Oudiz and Jeffrey Sachs, "Macroeconomic Policy Coordination among the Industrial Economies," *Brookings Papers on Economic Activity, 1:1984,* pp. 1–75; Willem H. Buiter and Richard C. Marston, eds., *International Economic Policy Coordination* (New York: Cambridge University Press, 1985); Michael Artis and Sylvia Ostry, *International Economic Policy Coordination* (London: Routledge and Kegan Paul for the Royal Institute of International Affairs, 1986); Ralph C. Bryant and Richard Portes, eds., *Global Macroeconomics: Policy Conflict and Coordination* (London: MacMillan, 1987); Bryant, *Money and Monetary Policy;* and Cooper, "Economic Interdependence and Coordination." For a sharply constrasting view, skeptical of the merits of international policy coordination, see Roland Vaubel, "International Collusion or Competition for Macroeconomic Policy Coordination? A Restatement," *Recherches Economiques de Louvain,* vol. 51 (December 1985), pp. 223–40; and Vaubel, "A Public Choice Approach to International Organization," *Public Choice,* vol. 51, no. 1 (1986), pp. 39–57. For a useful critical overview of much of the recent literature in this field, see Peter B. Kenen, "Exchange Rates and Policy Coordination," Brookings Discussion Papers in International Economics no. 61 (Brookings, October 1987).

12. On the importance of this factor, see Cooper, "Economic Interdependence and Coordination." The utility functions of national authorities typically exclude outcomes in other countries, but even in the rare instances in which governments seem to care what happens abroad, this concern may not ease

international cooperation. One objective of U.S. foreign economic policy in 1981–82 reportedly was to bring French Socialists to a more austere, market-oriented domestic policy, and accounts of Anglo-American negotiations in 1976 suggest that Ford administration officials had a similar objective in dealing with the Callaghan government. See Henry R. Nau, *International Reaganomics: A Domestic Approach to World Economy*, Significant Issues Series, vol. 6 (Georgetown University Center for Strategic and International Studies, 1984); and Stephen Fay and Hugo Young, *The Day the Pound Nearly Died* (London: The Sunday Times, 1978).

13. Bryant, *Money and Monetary Policy*, p. 469, argues that agreement on a model of the world economy is a precondition for international economic policy coordination, so that the national authorities can jointly distinguish Pareto-optimal and suboptimal policies. For a similar argument, see Richard N. Cooper, "International Cooperation in Public Health as a Prologue to Macroeconomic Cooperation," in this volume.

14. Canzoneri and Gray, "Two Essays on Monetary Policy." This issue is treated at greater length below.

15. See Bryant, *Money and Monetary Policy*, especially pp. 168–74; and Oudiz and Sachs, "Macroeconomic Policy Coordination," p. 56, and the sources cited there.

16. On the relationship between "distributive" bargaining and "integrative" (or cooperative) bargaining, see Richard E. Walton and Robert B. McKersie, *A Behavioral Theory of Labor Negotiations: An Analysis of a Social Interaction System* (McGraw-Hill, 1965).

17. See Oudiz and Sachs, "Macroeconomic Policy Coordination." Subsequent studies have so far tended to confirm the Oudiz-Sachs estimates of the modest gains from coordination. For a recent review, see Kenen, "Exchange Rates and Policy Coordination."

18. Oudiz and Sachs, "Macroeconomic Policy Coordination," p. 2. In addition, Charles R. Bean, "The Case for Co-ordination: Theory and History" (London School of Economics, March 1984), describes the Bonn accord as the "only . . . episode [in recent historical experience] during which there was any positive attempt to co-ordinate policies" (p. 17).

19. Anthony M. Solomon, "A Personal Evaluation," in George de Menil and Anthony M. Solomon, eds., *Economic Summitry* (New York: Council on Foreign Relations, 1983), p. 47.

20. See Oudiz and Sachs, "Macroeconomic Policy Coordination," pp. 43–44; and Nau, "International Reaganomics." Oudiz and Sachs hint that, given the utility functions of the U.S. authorities in the respective periods, the potential gains to international economic policy coordination may have been greater in 1976–78 than in the mid-1980s period that is the focus of their detailed calculations.

21. Several official postmortems, incomplete and still confidential, reach divergent conclusions on this point. For a systematic assessment of the economic impact of the German contribution to the Bonn accord, see Gerald Holtham, "German Macroeconomic Policy and the 1978 Bonn Economic Summit," in this volume.

22. *Economic Report of the President, January 1978*, p. 187. Gasoline excise taxes in these countries (already higher than the $0.12 in federal tax per gallon in the United States at the time of the first oil shock) ranged between $0.55 and $1.48 by 1977.

23. For a review of the development of the summits as an institution, see Putnam and Bayne, *Hanging Together*, chaps. 1–5, 11.

24. James Reston, "Bonn Chancellor Bids Ford Act with Care on Inflation," and "Excerpts from Interview with Chancellor Helmut Schmidt of West Germany," *New York Times*, August 25, 1974, pp. 1, 26.

25. *Financial Times* (London), November 19, 1974.

26. David Binder, "Recession Seen Lingering until Late '75: Ford, Schmidt, Carter," *New York Times*, December 7, 1974.

27. *The Times* (London), December 13, 1974.

28. *International Herald Tribune*, July 14, 1975.

29. For an excellent account of these negotiations, see Fay and Young, *The Day the Pound Nearly Died.*

30. For an account of the negotiations between Italy and the IMF, see John R. Hillman, "The Mutual Influence of Italian Domestic Politics and the International Monetary Fund," *Fletcher Forum*, vol. 4 (Winter 1980), pp. 1–22. For the dispute with Germany over the inclusion of Communists in the Italian coalition government, see *Financial Times* (London), September 9, 1976.

31. *Economic Report of the President, January 1977*, p. 118.

32. For an extensive analysis of this election, see Karl H. Cerny, ed., *Germany at the Polls: The Bundestag Election of 1976* (Washington: American Enterprise Institute for Public Policy Research, 1978).

33. See David P. Conradt, "The 1976 Campaign and Election: An Overview," and Heino Kaack, "The FDP in the German Party System," in Cerny, ed., *Germany at the Polls*, pp. 45, 101. See also *International Herald Tribune* (Paris), February 2, 1976.

34. *Le Figaro* (Paris), January 7, 1977.

35. *OECD Economic Surveys: Germany* (May 1976), pp. 33–34.

36. *International Herald Tribune* (Paris), September 13, 1976; and *Financial Times* (London), August 17, 1976.

37. Report of the five German economic research institutes, as translated and summarized in "German Prism: The Economic Situation in the Federal Republic," *Intereconomics*, vol. 11 (November 1976), pp. 318–20; and *Financial Times* (London), November 24, 1976. The Council of Economic Experts proposed a package consisting of increased depreciation allowances and measures to increase the geographic mobility of the unemployed. The council is a government-appointed but independent advisory body.

38. *OECD Economic Surveys: Germany* (July 1977), p. 55, and (July 1978), annex II, p. 66.

39. *International Herald Tribune*, November 25, 1976.

40. *Economic Report of the President, January 1978*, pp. 50–52.

41. I. M. Destler and Hisao Mitsuyu, "Locomotives on Different Tracks: Macroeconomic Diplomacy, 1977–1979," in I. M. Destler and Hideo Sato,

eds., *Coping with U.S.-Japanese Economic Conflicts* (Lexington Books, 1982), p. 248.

42. *Conduct of Monetary Policy*, Hearings before the House Committee on Banking, Finance, and Urban Affairs, 95 Cong. 1 sess. (Government Printing Office, 1977), p. 9.

43. "Economic Prospects and Politics in the Industrial Countries" (Brookings, 1977), pp. 9–10.

44. For an example of the intellectual underpinnings of U.S. foreign macroeconomic policy under the Carter administration, see Richard N. Cooper, "Global Economic Policy in a World of Energy Shortage," in Joseph A. Pechman and N. J. Simler, eds., *Economics in the Public Service* (Norton, 1982), pp. 84–107.

45. *Economic Report of the President, January 1978*, pp. 114–15.

46. See Charles C. Roberts, "Economic Theory and Policy Making in West Germany: The Role of the Council of Economic Experts," *Cambridge Journal of Economics*, vol. 3 (March 1979), pp. 83–89; and Henry C. Wallich, "The American Council of Economic Advisers and the German Sachverstaendigenrat: A Study in the Economics of Advice," *Quarterly Journal of Economics*, vol. 82 (August 1968), pp. 349–79.

47. Konrad Zweig, *Germany through Inflation and Recession: An Object Lesson in Economic Management, 1973–1976* (London: Centre for Policy Studies, 1976), p. 25.

48. Cooper, "Global Economic Policy."

49. Although this later came to be called the "locomotive" approach or theory of growth, apparently no one in the Carter administration officially used the locomotive metaphor to describe the plan. Richard N. Cooper speculates that he used the term "engine" of growth in an interview with a Japanese journalist, after which the Japanese phrase was retranslated into English as "locomotive." Hans Tietmeyer, then of the German Economics Ministry, was the first to use the term in international discussions—derisively—at an OECD meeting in November 1976.

50. *Financial Times* (London), January 20, 1977.

51. Craig R. Whitney, "Schmidt Asserts 'Irritations' Will Not Divide U.S. and Bonn," *New York Times*, March 21, 1977. Schmidt seemed to support the American program, but hedged: "It is of great importance that President Carter's economic program succeeds. I'm not going to comment on the situation in Italy, France, and Britain, but generally speaking, I do see possible linkages between high rates of inflation, social unrest, and domestic political instability in general."

52. Before the delegation had arrived in Bonn, Schmidt caused considerable controversy by saying that the Carter administration officials who recommended reflation as the solution to Germany's economic problems should "please better shut their mouths." Craig R. Whitney, "A Refreshed and Newly Confident Schmidt Resumes Active Role," *New York Times*, January 24, 1977. But the Mondale team had been under the impression that this bad feeling had been assuaged before their arrival and further resolved during their meeting with the chancellor.

53. *Washington Post*, May 26, 1977.

54. For a full account of U.S.-Japanese macroeconomic discussions during this period, see Destler and Mitsuyu, "Locomotives on Different Tracks," pp. 243–69.

55. Whitney, "Schmidt Asserts 'Irritations' Will Not Divide U.S. and Bonn"; and Whitney, "Bonn, Bowing to U.S., Adding $1.7 Billion to Stimulus," *New York Times*, March 23, 1977.

56. *OECD Economic Surveys: Germany* (June 1978), p. 65. The package reduced certain wealth and income taxes, increased family allowances, and provided for a 1 percent increase in the VAT.

57. *Economic Report of the President, January 1978*, pp. 51–52.

58. Useful reviews of U.S. energy policy during the 1970s include Neil de Marchi, "The Ford Administration: Energy as a Political Good," and James L. Cochrane, "Carter Energy Policy and the Ninety-fifth Congress," in Craufurd D. Goodwin, ed., *Energy Policy in Perspective: Today's Problems, Yesterday's Solutions* (Brookings, 1981), pp. 475–600; Richard H. K. Vietor, *Energy Policy in America since 1945: A Study of Business-Government Relations* (Cambridge University Press, 1984); Ann Pelham, ed., *Energy Policy*, 2d ed. (Washington: Congressional Quarterly, 1981); and G. John Ikenberry, "Market Solutions for State Problems: The International and Domestic Politics of American Oil Decontrol," *International Organization*, vol. 42 (Winter 1988), pp. 151–77.

59. Cochrane, "Carter Energy Policy," p. 572.

60. *The Times* (London), May 3, 1977; and *Daily Telegraph* (London), May 6, 1977.

61. *Keesing's Contemporary Archives*, July 29, 1977, p. 28470 (italics added).

62. *Frankfurter Allgemeine Zeitung*, May 9, 1977. See also *Die Zeit*, May 13, 1977.

63. *Report of the Deutsche Bundesbank for the Year 1977*, p. 17.

64. Paul Lewis, "U.S. Voices Concern on Further Slowing of World Economy," *New York Times*, November 22, 1977.

65. *OECD Economic Outlook*, vol. 25 (July 1979), p. 136; and *International Financial Statistics* (October 1979), pp. 164–66.

66. *OECD Economic Surveys: Germany* (June 1978), p. 66.

67. On a fourth-quarter-to-fourth-quarter basis, as calculated from *Economic Report of the President, January 1979*, p. 184.

68. *Economic Report of the President, January 1978*, pp. 35, 44, 46, 107. Preliminary figures available at the time led the CEA to conclude that the 5.75–6.0 percent target had been met. Although revised figures show that U.S. growth was one-quarter point short of this goal, the United States still came closer to achieving its target than did the other summit countries.

69. "The Economic Situation in the World and in West Germany in Spring 1977," *Economic Bulletin* (Berlin), vol. 14 (Spring 1977), supplement; and "The Economic Situation in the World and in West Germany in Autumn 1977," *Economic Bulletin* (Berlin), vol. 14 (Autumn 1977).

70. Council of Economic Experts, *Jahresgutachten 1978* and *Jahresgutachten 1977*; Roberts, "Economic Theory and Policy Making in West Germany."

71. *Report of the Deutsche Bundesbank for the Year 1977*, pp. 2, 48.

72. See Council of Economic Experts, *Jahresgutachten 1978*, pars. 9, 10, 11, 12, 21, and 22.

73. *OECD Economic Surveys: Germany* (June 1978), p. 38.

74. Bundesverband der Deutschen Industrie (BDI), *Jahresbericht 1977–78*, p. 17; and BDI, *Joint Strengthening of the Forces of Growth*, special reprint from the BDI *Annual Report 1977–78*, p. 9. Corroborated by interviews, Germany, 1982.

75. Leonard Silk, "Germany Intends to Keep Economy 'in Good Shape,'" *New York Times*, January 24, 1977.

76. *Economic Report of the President, January 1978*, pp. 11–12.

77. *Economic Report of the President, January 1978*, p. 4.

78. *Economic Report of the President, January 1978*, p. 21.

79. *OECD Economic Outlook*, vol. 23 (July 1978), p. 61.

80. *Economic Report of the President, January 1978*, p. 111.

81. *Economic Report of the President, January 1978*, pp. 125–26.

82. *Financial Times* (London), May 26, 1977.

83. Stephen D. Cohen and Ronald I. Meltzer, *United States International Economic Policy in Action: Diversity of Decision Making* (Praeger, 1982), pp. 16–23, have carefully tried to explain the miscommunication between Blumenthal and the foreign exchange markets in the "talking down the dollar" debacle.

84. *Economic Report of the President, January 1978*, pp. 56–60; and *Economic Report of the President, January 1979*, pp. 50, 251.

85. *Economic Report of the President, January 1978*, p. 121.

86. *OECD Economic Surveys, Germany* (July 1978), p. 73.

87. *Report of the Deutsche Bundesbank for the Year 1977*, p. 32.

88. *Report of the Deutsche Bundesbank, 1977*, pp. 50–51.

89. *OECD Economic Outlook*, vol. 23 (July 1978), p. 71.

90. Leonard Silk, "Bonn's Response to Critics Who Say It Stifles Growth," *New York Times*, February 3, 1978.

91. Mario A. Millctti, "Witteveen Presses Germany and Japan to Spur Economies," *New York Times*, February 16, 1978, p. D1.

92. Bundesbank, *Monthly Report* (August 1977), p. 22; and *Report of the Deutsche Bundesbank for the Year 1977*, pp. 42–49.

93. See Otmar Emminger, *Frankfurter Allgemeine Zeitung* (April 4, 1978).

94. Bundesbank, press release (Hannover, June 1, 1978), pp. 7–10.

95. Peter Ludlow, *The Making of the European Monetary System: A Case Study of the Politics of the European Community* (London: Butterworth Scientific, 1982), pp. 69–77.

96. *OECD Economic Outlook*, vol. 22 (December 1977), pp. 94–95, 99–101, 109–10, 111–15, and vol. 23 (July 1978), pp. 71, 75–77, 79–82, 90–91.

97. *OECD Economic Outlook*, vol. 22 (December 1977), pp. 7–8.

98. OECD, press release (Paris, June 15, 1978), pp. 4–6.

99. Commission of the European Communities, Directorate-General for Economic and Financial Affairs, *The Economic Situation in the Community* (1978), pp. 3–10 (quotation on pp. 3–4).

100. *Economic Report of the President, January 1978*, pp. 182–87.

101. In Pelham, ed., *Energy Policy*, p. 41. See also Richard Corrigan, "Last Rites Being Delivered for Carter's Crude Oil Tax," *National Journal*, June 24, 1978, pp. 1020–21.

102. For a detailed account of the trade negotiations under the Tokyo round, see Gilbert R. Winham, *International Trade and the Tokyo Round Negotiation* (Princeton University Press, 1986), especially chaps. 5–7, to which the discussion in the following paragraphs is indebted.

103. "We don't need a new economic summit that would only send empty platitudes floating down the Rhine," Blumenthal was quoted as saying. See *Daily Telegraph* (London), February 14, 1978.

104. *Guardian* (London), February 21–22, 1978.

105. This initial suggestion from the American side—that the American contribution to the summit package should include a macroeconomic commitment—was apparently not followed up in later discussions. This point is discussed later under the rubric of "a missed opportunity."

106. In reaction to Carter's decision against production of the neutron bomb, Schmidt had called the U.S. president "an unfathomable dilettante . . . incompetent to fill the shoes of the Western leader." *Observer* (London), July 9, 1978. The coexistence of this acrimony with the incipient summit deal is striking confirmation that international policy coordination does not require personal sympathy among the summiteers.

107. *Frankfurter Allgemeine Zeitung*, May 5, 1978.

108. Paul Lewis, "U.S. Shuns O.E.C.D. Growth Plan," *New York Times*, June 1, 1978.

109. Jimmy Carter, *Keeping Faith: Memoirs of a President* (Bantam, 1982), pp. 103–04.

110. *Congressional Record*, June 27, 1979, p. 19094.

111. *Congressional Record*, June 27, 1979, p. 19091.

112. Ikenberry, "Market Solutions for State Problems," emphasizes this development.

113. Charles L. Schultze, "Memorandum for the President: Economic Effects of Alternative Outcomes at the Summit," July 7, 1978 (italics in the original).

114. Of interest in this context, a senior German politician spoke of "the authority of the summit," precisely the same phrase used by his Japanese counterpart in discussing the analogous episode in Japan. The following account of German decisionmaking, although anchored at crucial points by documentary evidence, is based primarily on extensive confidential interviews with virtually all key participants in the 1978 German decisions.

115. Chancellor's office memorandum from Horst Schulmann to Helmut Schmidt, written in mid-May 1978. Different parts of the memorandum, as translated by the authors, are excerpted together here.

116. John Vinocur, "West Germany Seen Facing a Slowdown in Economic Growth," *New York Times*, April 25, 1978.

117. Youssef Ibrahim, "Faster German Growth Is Rejected," *New York Times*, February 1, 1978; John Vinocur, "Battered Dollar Hits 1.99 Marks in

West Germany, A Record Low," *New York Times*, March 2, 1978; Otto Graf Lambsdorff, "West Germany's Economic-Growth Program," *New York Times*, March 2, 1978, p. A19; and Vinocur, "West Germany Seen Facing a Slowdown in Economic Growth." At about this same time, however, Hans-Dietrich Genscher, chairman of Lambsdorff's FDP and foreign minister in Schmidt's cabinet, reportedly told the chancellor that the dispute over economic growth was needlessly threatening U.S.-German relations.

118. Carol Carl-Sime and Jane Hall, "The *Land* Elections in West Germany 1978/79 and the '*Kanzlereffekt*,'" *Parliamentary Affairs* (London), vol. 32 (Summer 1979), p. 318.

119. *Frankfurter Allgemeine Zeitung*, July 17, 1978, cited by Peter Ludlow in *The Making of the European Monetary System: A Case Study of the Politics of the European Community* (London: Butterworth Scientific, 1982), p. 130.

120. *Report of the Deutsche Bundesbank for the Year 1978*, p. 20; *Economic Report of the President, January 1979*, p. 42; and Federation of German Industries, *Joint Strengthening of the Forces of Growth*, pp. 3–5, 9–11. See also *A Policy for the Eighties*, special print from the *Annual Report 1978–79* of the Federation of German Industries.

121. Bundesbank, press release (Hannover, June 1, 1978), p. 2.

122. "U.S. and Bonn Agree to Cease Disputing Economics in Public," *New York Times*, February 23, 1978.

123. This is an interesting parallel between the diplomatic maneuvering of 1977–78 and the comparable maneuvering in 1985–87. In both cases, the Americans pressed for faster domestic growth in Germany and Japan; in both cases, the crucial negotiations with Japan (unlike those with Germany) were primarily bilateral; and in both cases, the Japanese reached a settlement with the Americans long before the negotiations with the Germans reached their climax. In this chapter, we devote less attention to the Japanese issue, in part because it was less central than the German and American contributions to the negotiations culminated in Bonn, and in part because the U.S.-Japan negotiations have been ably recounted in Destler and Mitsuyu, "Locomotives on Different Tracks."

124. *Japan Times* (Tokyo), April 19, 1978.

125. Anthony M. Solomon, "A Personal Evaluation," in de Menil and Solomon, eds., *Economic Summitry*, p. 48.

126. The final figure for 1979 was actually only DM 43 billion. See Bundesbank, *Monthly Report*, vol. 33 (January 1981), p. 16.

127. *Report of the Deutsche Bundesbank for the Year 1978*, p. 15.

128. This is the consensus of several unpublished studies by various national and international financial agencies. For a discussion of relevant methodology, see *European Economy*, Technical Annex (November 1982), pp. 186–87.

129. *Oversight of International Economic Issues*, Hearings before the Subcommittee on International Economic Policy of the Senate Committee on Foreign Relations, 96 Cong. 1 sess. (GPO, 1979), p. 139.

130. For the best accounts of the tribulations of the dollar in autumn 1978,

see Alan R. Holmes and Scott E. Pardee, "Treasury and Federal Reserve Foreign Exchange Operations," *Federal Reserve Bank of New York Quarterly Review*, vol. 4 (Spring 1979), pp. 67–87; *Economic Report of the President, January 1979*, pp. 26–30; and Herman Nickel, "The Inside Story of the Dollar Rescue," *Fortune*, December 4, 1978, pp. 40–44.

131. *Economic Report of the President, January 1979*, p. 42. On a multilateral basis, the depreciation amounted to 13.8 percent. Of course, these figures do not include the substantial depreciation in October 1978.

132. *Economic Report of the President, January 1979*, p. 43.

133. Peter Hooper and Barbara R. Lowrey, *Impact of the Dollar Depreciation on the U.S. Price Level: An Analytical Survey of Empirical Estimates*, Staff Studies no. 103 (Board of Governors of the Federal Reserve System, April 1979).

134. *OECD Economic Outlook*, vol. 25 (July 1979), p. 105; and *Report of the Deutsche Bundesbank for the Year 1978*, p. 20.

135. *Federal Reserve Bulletin*, vol. 65 (March 1979), p. 205; and *Report of the Deutsche Bundesbank for the Year 1978*, p. 47.

136. *Report of the Deutsche Bundesbank for the Year 1978*, pp. 46–47, 53; and *Report of the Deutsche Bundesbank for the Year 1977*, p. 52.

137. Calculated from *Federal Reserve Bulletin*, vol. 64 (September 1978), p. 718; and *Federal Reserve Bulletin*, vol. 65 (March 1979), pp. 204–05.

138. *OECD Economic Surveys: Germany* (June 1981), p. 73.

139. *Federal Reserve Bulletin*, vol. 65 (March 1979), p. 204.

140. At least one credible German source recounts that they threatened not to intervene at all in the exchange markets unless the United States agreed to institute more restrictive domestic policies to support the dollar. This account has not been confirmed by the American side.

141. *Federal Reserve Bulletin*, vol. 65 (March 1979), pp. 205, 208.

142. For another account, see F. Lisle Widman, *Making International Monetary Policy* (Georgetown University Law Center, International Law Institute, 1982), pp. 175–84; and Cohen and Meltzer, *United States International Economic Policy*, chap. 2.

143. For Blumenthal's argument for the package after the fact, see his congressional testimony in *Oversight of International Economic Issues*, Hearings, p. 3.

144. Nickel, "The Inside Story of the Dollar Rescue," p. 42.

145. Richard J. Levine, "Dollar Dilemma: Bold Currency Support Announced by the U.S. Raises Recession Risks," *Wall Street Journal*, November 2, 1978.

146. *Federal Reserve Bulletin*, vol. 65 (March 1979), pp. 203, 206–07.

147. Bundesbank, press release (Berlin, November 2, 1978).

148. *Federal Reserve Bulletin*, vol. 65 (March 1979), p. 206.

149. Bundesbank, press releases (Frankfurt, December 14, 1978, and January 18, 1979); and *Report of the Deutsche Bundesbank for the Year 1978*, p. 14. The government in Bonn appears to have been split over this restrictive shift in monetary policy. Otto Schlecht, state secretary in the Economics Min-

istry, declared in mid-December that it was necessary, but Manfred Lahnstein, state secretary in the Finance Ministry, came out strongly against it in mid-January.

150. *Frankfurter Allgemeine Zeitung* (July 18, 1978); and confidential interview. See also Richard Corrigan, "Putting Himself on the Spot," *National Journal,* July 22, 1978, p. 1178.

151. "Possible Solution to Carter's Summit Pledge," *Congressional Quarterly Weekly Report,* July 22,1978, p. 1881.

152. *Congressional Quarterly Almanac 1978,* vol. 34 (1979), p. 639. The National Energy Act covered the categories of conservation, power plants and industrial fuels, public utility regulation, energy taxes, and natural gas. The new policies for the first four were in general expected to reduce U.S. oil imports by about 1.5 million barrels a day by 1985. The effect on oil imports of the natural gas bill—which eliminated the artificial distinction between intrastate and interstate markets for natural gas and gradually raised prices—was controversial, with the administration claiming a savings on the order of a million barrels a day by 1985 and opponents claiming that it would actually increase American imports. See Cochrane, "Carter Energy Policy," pp. 584–87.

153. Ann Pelham, "Impact of OPEC: Administration Facing Tough Decision on Oil Pricing," *Congressional Quarterly Weekly Report,* December 23, 1978, p. 3465.

154. Ikenberry, "Market Solutions for State Problems," p. 171. Ikenberry quotes extensively from a joint memorandum to the president, cited below.

155. Memorandum for the President, "Domestic Crude Oil Pricing—Information," January 3, 1979. This joint memorandum, from Schlesinger, Blumenthal, Cooper, Schultze, Kahn, James McIntyre, Owen, and Eizenstat, placed the pricing decision in the context of energy, economic, and foreign policy considerations.

156. Memorandum for the President, "Domestic Crude Oil Pricing," p. 3.

157. Carter meeting with Mondale, McIntyre, Barry Bosworth, Schultze, Kahn, and Eizenstat, as recorded in the diary of Stuart Eizenstat, January 3, 1979. For evidence on the internal deliberations of the administration between November 1978 and April 1979, including the Camp David "economic summit," we are particularly grateful to Stuart Eizenstat for his detailed daily diaries.

158. Ann Pelham, "Few Political Goodies: Congress to Face Difficult Energy Decisions This Year," *Congressional Quarterly Weekly Report,* February 3, 1979, p. 206.

159. Carter, *Keeping Faith,* p. 110.

160. See, for example, the statement by Charles Vanik, *Congressional Record,* September 7, 1978, pp. 28363–64.

161. This is Winham's conclusion as well. See Winham, *International Trade and the Tokyo Round Negotiation,* chap. 6.

162. Even some advocates of internationally coordinated stimulus programs propagate this myth. Michael Stewart claims, "In 1978, . . . Germany had reluctantly taken expansionary measures on essentially 'altruistic' grounds—measures it would not have taken had it been concerned with the

immediate welfare of its own citizens alone." See Stewart, *The Age of Interdependence: Economic Policy in a Shrinking World* (MIT Press, 1984), p. 75.

163. The recent flurry of attention to the problem of "time inconsistency" is relevant here, of course, although for the most part the economic literature on time inconsistency addresses the credibility of a government's commitments to its own private sector, rather than to another government. In any event, this literature is based on the assumption that governments cannot issue binding promises about their future behavior; as we explain below, we find that assumption problematic, at least in the context of the present analysis.

164. Canzoneri and Gray, "Two Essays on Monetary Policy," p. 1.

165. A recent exposition of this approach to problems of the international political economy is Bruno S. Frey, *International Political Economics* (New York: Basil Blackwell, 1984), especially chap. 7.

166. Keohane, *After Hegemony,* p. 116. For a useful, albeit technical, exploration of reputational effects in such diverse contexts as public accountancy, double-agent espionage, and brand-name consumer goods, see Robert Wilson, "Reputations in Games and Markets," Technical Paper 434 (Stanford, Calif.: Institute for Mathematical Studies in the Social Sciences, November 1983).

167. See Robert Axelrod, *The Evolution of Cooperation* (Basic Books, 1984), and the sources cited therein.

168. Oudiz and Sachs, "Macroeconomic Policy Coordination," p. 35 (emphasis added).

169. See Axelrod, *The Evolution of Cooperation.* In some cases a ruined reputation may be restored after a number of plays in which an actor behaves properly. See also Robert J. Barro and David B. Gordon, "A Positive Theory of Monetary Policy in a Natural Rate Model," *Journal of Political Economy,* vol. 91 (August 1983), pp. 589–610; Barro and Gordon, "Rules, Discretion, and Reputation in a Model of Monetary Policy," *Journal of Monetary Economics,* vol. 12 (July 1983), pp. 101–21; and Christopher J. Waller and Jo Anna Gray, "A Note on Rules, Discretion and Reputation," Washington State University, Department of Economics, April 1985. Note, however, that Alt and Eichengreen argue that "pooling of the incentive constraints" across several issues may in some circumstances actually encourage simultaneous defection by a given player in each of the otherwise separable games: James E. Alt and Barry Eichengreen, "Parallel and Overlapping Games: Theory and Application to the European Gas Trade," *Economics and Politics,* forthcoming.

170. An official at the International Energy Agency, commenting on the oil import restraint agreement reached at the Tokyo summit of 1979, recalls privately that "we decided at the official level on 1–2 March that we would all bring down our oil demand by 5 percent, but real action at the national level was very, very rare. When you have ministers take a commitment to their colleagues, it has a different political weight, and if heads of state engage themselves at the level of the Seven [G-7], you have even stronger policy."

171. The Carter administration's subsequent desire to rebuild its credibility within NATO was an important motivation for the controversial decision to deploy the so-called Euromissiles, but that is another story.

172. In addition to the sources previously cited, see Charles Lipson, "International Cooperation in Economic and Security Affairs," *World Politics*, vol. 37 (October 1984), pp. 1–23; and Robert Axelrod and Robert O. Keohane, "Achieving Cooperation under Anarchy: Strategies and Institutions," *World Politics*, vol. 38 (October 1985), pp. 226–54.

173. Bean, "The Case for Co-ordination," pp. 10–11.

174. Germany pledged 5.0 percent growth for 1977 but managed only 2.5 percent, whereas Japan pledged 6.7 percent but achieved only 5.0 percent. *Economic Report of the President, January 1978*, p. 107.

175. The question of deliverability and reputation were linked in an interesting way in the American case. Before the summit several of the president's closest domestic advisers argued against a far-reaching commitment on energy, for fear that he would be unable to fulfill such a commitment at home. They believed that apparent reneging, even if unintentional on the president's part, would undermine the president's credibility at home and abroad. Practical politicians devote much more attention to credibility than most simple game-theoretic analyses acknowledge.

176. For example, Canzoneri and Gray, in "Two Essays on Monetary Policy," argue that even if governments understand the need to abide by an international agreement, their publics will not, and "the political pressure to cheat could well be enormous" (p. 16). This observation correctly highlights the importance of the domestic political game, but it rests on a very simple view about the uniformity and shortsightedness of public preferences.

177. Bryant, *Money and Monetary Policy in Interdependent Nations*, pp. 12, 315.

178. Keohane, "U.S. Foreign Economic Policy toward Other Advanced Capitalist States," pp. 92, 107–09 (italics added).

179. Leonard Silk, "Economic Scene: Complexity and Control," *New York Times*, October 24, 1984, p. D2.

180. James A. Caporaso, "Interdependence and the Coordination of Foreign and Domestic Policies in the Atlantic World," in Wolfram F. Hanrieder, ed., *Economic Issues and the Atlantic Community* (Praeger, 1982), p. 8.

181. These domestic agents of international cooperation had to walk a fine line between fostering international agreement and betraying their trust as national officials, but in none of the cases did their behavior provoke serious accusations of disloyalty from their domestic opponents.

182. In one recent example among many, Artis and Ostry, *International Economic Policy Coordination*, pp. 75–76, imply that domestic unity—what they call "domestic policy coordination"—is an important precondition for international coordination.

183. Dieter Hiss, "Weltwirtschaftsgipfel: Betrachtungen eines Insiders [World Economic Summit: Observations of an Insider]," in Joachim Frohn and Reiner Staeglin, eds., *Empirische Wirtschaftsforschung* (Berlin: Duncker and Humblot, 1980), pp. 286–87.

184. Because economic policies of the sort considered here usually have important distributional consequences, it seems plausible to suppose that the

political aggregation function will typically *not* reflect a broad national consensus, but this is hard to predict in the abstract. In any event, the form of the political aggregation function will depend heavily on specific institutional and constitutional factors.

185. See Hillman, "The Mutual Influence of Italian Domestic Politics."

186. It is not our claim here that domestic disunity is, in general, either a necessary or a sufficient condition for international cooperation, but rather that domestic discord may—under conditions yet to be specified—facilitate cooperation. For further discussion of the logic linking domestic disunity and international cooperation, see Putnam, "Diplomacy and Domestic Politics."

187. Max Black, *Models and Metaphors: Studies in Language and Philosophy* (Cornell University Press, 1962), p. 242.

188. Compare Bryant, *Money and Monetary Policy in Interdependent Nations*, pp. 12, 315. For another example of how domestic politics affect the prospects for international cooperation, see Donald J. Puchala, *Fiscal Harmonization in the European Communities: National Politics and International Cooperation* (London and Dover, N.H.: Frances Pinter, 1984), wherein (p. x) he writes that "successful international cooperation requires high degrees of mutual sensitivity on the part of interacting governments, particularly regarding one another's domestic politics." Note, too, the analogy to theories of labor-management bargaining, as illustrated in Walton and McKersie, *Behavioral Theory of Labor Negotiations;* and John T. Dunlop, *Dispute Resolution: Negotiation and Consensus Building* (Dover, Mass.: Auburn House, 1984). For a more detailed and slightly more formalized discussion of two-level games, including a "theory of ratification," see Putnam, "Diplomacy and Domestic Politics."

189. Kenneth Rogoff, "Productive and Counterproductive Cooperative Monetary Policies," Federal Reserve Board International Finance Discussion Papers no. 233 (December 1983).

190. See Oudiz and Sachs, "Macroeconomic Policy Coordination," and Olivier J. Blanchard, "Comments and Discussion," pp. 67–68.

191. This is one difference between our analysis of the 1978 agreement and that of Holtham, "German Macroeconomic Policy and the 1978 Bonn Economic Summit," in this volume.

192. See, for example, Oudiz and Sachs, "Macroeconomic Policy Coordination," pp. 24, 26.

193. Robert D. Tollison and Thomas D. Willett, "An Economic Theory of Mutually Advantageous Issue Linkages in International Negotiations," *International Organization*, vol. 33 (Autumn 1979), pp. 425–49; and James K. Sebenius, "Negotiation Arithmetic: Adding and Subtracting Issues and Parties," *International Organization*, vol. 37 (Spring 1983), pp. 281–316.

194. Oudiz and Sachs, "Macroeconomic Policy Coordination," p. 3.

195. Artis and Ostry, *International Economic Policy Coordination*, p. 19.

196. Note that this hypothetical deal would *not* have involved the sort of joint expansion, or joint restraint, that is most often discussed in formal models of international economic policy coordination. This highlights the obvious fact

that the appropriate target for international cooperation is international "compatibility" of national policies, not international "convergence" of national policies. See Putnam and Bayne, *Hanging Together;* and Artis and Ostry, *International Economic Policy Coordination,* p. 72.

197. See Charles E. Lindblom, *The Intelligence of Democracy: Decision Making through Mutual Adjustment* (New York: Free Press, 1965).

German Macroeconomic Policy and the 1978 Bonn Economic Summit

GERALD HOLTHAM

T HERE ARE TWO common and conflicting views about the 1978 Bonn economic summit. The first holds that it was an unequaled instance of international economic policy coordination that was tragically unlucky in being followed by the fall of the shah of Iran and the second oil price crisis—events that changed the priorities of policymakers worldwide and made the Bonn agreement rapidly obsolete. The second view, held particularly strongly in Germany, is that the summit resulted, among other things, in Germany's reluctantly and altruistically taking expansionary policy action; this turned out to be a procyclical change that contributed to the acceleration of inflation and a seriously adverse balance of payments in Germany.

Not surprisingly, such different views lead to different policy prescriptions. Supporters of the summit argue that it shows what could be achieved, and they deplore the apparent contrast between its accomplishments and subsequent failures of the larger OECD countries to agree on macroeconomic policy. Detractors of the summit, especially in Germany, argue that it shows the dangers of "demand management" and means Germany should resist pressure from other countries to adopt inflationary policies.

The seven summit countries all agreed at Bonn to follow certain policies, although those measures agreed to by the United States, Japan, and the Federal Republic of Germany were much the most important. This paper looks only at German policy moves following the Bonn summit and assesses their effect on the German economy. The restricted ambitions of the paper should be emphasized. Because it

I am grateful for comment from or discussion with Ralph Bryant, Hermann-Josef Dudler, Randall Henning, Edith Hodgkinson, Giles Keating, Stephen Marris, and Robert Putnam. I am also grateful for research assistance from Rebecca Goodway and Jon Gruber. Some of the comment on this study was extensive and led me to reconsider substantially some earlier views. Nonetheless, probably not one of my discussants agrees with all of my conclusions. I alone am responsible for errors of fact or interpretation that remain.

does not consider the effects of the U.S. and Japanese actions, it is not an assessment of the Bonn summit agreement as a whole. It cannot even be said to evaluate the impact of the summit on the German economy because, for example, the U.S. measures to raise domestic oil prices to world levels, which are not examined, must certainly have affected the German economy. Indeed, the existence of "spillover" effects from the actions of one government to other economies is the justification for, and basis of, any economic policy coordination.

Yet, in view of the strongly divergent views that exist on the effects of the German policies on the German economy, a narrower focus can be justified. Few, in Germany or elsewhere, would now argue that the oil price or trade liberalization measures stimulated by the summit were misconceived. Criticism of the substantive agreement centers on the reflationary macroeconomic measures, particularly those adopted in Germany.

Ideally, an assessment should have a clear hypothetical counterfactual situation with which actual developments may be compared. The desirable counterfactual has two components: the policies that would have been followed in the absence of the summit and the effects of the policy divergence that occurred. Unfortunately, a clear counterfactual is not available. The summit was an influence on German policy, particularly fiscal policy. The paper by Putnam and Henning in this volume provides evidence that the summit was critical to resolving a debate within Germany on the appropriate stance of fiscal policy. In effect, expansionists within the German administration used the summit to carry the argument in favor of tax cuts. The measures adopted were, however, consistent with the ethos of German policymaking during the 1970s; moreover, the circumstances of 1978 were similar to those in other years when policy changes were made. The summit made a difference, but perhaps more in the scale and timing of tax measures than as to whether they would ever have been adopted at all.

No specific agreements on monetary policy were announced at the summit. German monetary policy tightened at the start of 1979 when the fiscal measures announced at Bonn were coming into effect. That tightening was not due in any direct way to the fiscal policy, but to other events. However, it is obviously possible that policymakers' judgments about monetary policy were colored by knowledge of the stance of fiscal policy. In sum, it would be naive to simply ascribe the fiscal policy measures of January 1979 to the Bonn summit and to ignore monetary policy. This study looks at both fiscal and monetary policy following the Bonn summit and compares them with a conventional counterfactual of "no policy change" after mid-1978. This reflects the difficulty of identifying the "true" counterfactual policies that would have been followed if, for some reason, the summit had not occurred. It does not imply that in those circumstances "no policy change" was necessarily the most likely outcome.

The fiscal measures came at a time when demand in the German economy was stronger than policymakers realized. However, demand appears to have been slowing down, so the measures were not clearly procyclical. In any case, I conclude that their effect was small. They almost certainly added, modestly, to the German current balance deficit of 1979–81, which was part of their purpose, and they made only a small contribution to inflation. However, when monetary policy is considered, overall German macroeconomic policy in 1979 was anti-inflationary. The effect of the measures on inflation and even on the current account was swamped by the effect of the oil price increases of 1979.

The Agreement and the German Policy Measures

At the summit, the United States promised a series of energy policy measures designed to reduce U.S. imports of oil. The most important of these was a pledge to raise the price of oil in the United States to world levels by the end of 1980. A controlled oil price for domestic crude production had encouraged U.S. consumption and hence import demand. Other countries viewed this as exacerbating the U.S. current account deficit and tending to raise world oil prices to the detriment of all oil-importing countries. Japan and Germany, as a quid pro quo for this American promise, promised to stimulate the level of demand in their economies. The Americans, and analysts at the OECD and IMF, viewed this as likely to lead to a reduction of those countries' current account surpluses and a consequential fall in the U.S. external deficit that could be achieved without restrictive U.S. measures that might carry the risk of recession.

Japan reaffirmed its commitment to a 7 percent growth target for GNP and promised a supplementary budget in 1978 in order to achieve the target. It also made certain commitments for the voluntary restraint of exports.

Germany promised to take fiscal policy measures to stimulate the growth of domestic demand. The size of the promised measures was "up to 1 percent of GDP," or some DM 12 billion. The precise nature of this stimulus was not specified in the summit communiqué but was understood to largely be in the form of tax cuts.

In the event, the expansionary measures undertaken by Germany following the Bonn summit amounted to DM 15.75 billion, or 1.2 percent of 1979 GDP.[1] Most of the measures were scheduled to take effect on January 1, 1979. Of these, the principal tax measures were as follows (with expected revenue effect in a full year shown in parentheses): a change in income tax schedules reducing direct taxes on household factor incomes (DM 11 billion); an increase in children's allowances (DM 1.75 billion); and an increase in early retirement options (DM 1 billion) and maternity benefits (DM 0.75 billion). There was also an increase in federal expenditures of DM 2.75 billion. Offsetting that was a 1 percent increase in the value-added tax rate worth DM 6.5 billion in additional revenue. The estimated net revenue loss from those measures taking effect in 1979 was thus DM 10.75 billion. Further tax measures scheduled for 1980 were an increase in the tax-free income allowance and tax deductibility of educational expenses (DM 2.25 billion) and a reduction in business taxes (DM 2.75 billion net).

The measures taken, therefore, went beyond the bare commitment made at the Bonn summit. The tax measures alone amounted to a sum consistent with the summit communiqué; the 1979 tax changes were worth 0.6 percent of GNP, and the 1980 tax measures amounted to 0.34 percent of GNP.

Although the commitments made by Japan and Germany at the Bonn summit were essentially macroeconomic in nature—that is, they were promises to use fiscal policy in an aggregative sense to stimulate domestic demand—no specific commitments were made about monetary policy. References to monetary measures were confined to an undertaking to intervene in foreign exchange markets to "counter disorderly conditions."

However, a sentence in the summit communiqué indicates that the Germans were not committing themselves to any monetary accommodation of the changes in fiscal stance. The sentence states that "The order of magnitude [of the fiscal stimulus] will take account of the absorbtive capacity of the capital market. . . ." Clearly, the state of the capital market is relevant to the extent that the government intends to issue debt to make up for lost revenue or extra expenditure, as opposed to borrowing from the banking system or the central bank and thereby expanding the money supply. This way of qualifying the commitment to fiscal expansion is consistent with the constitutional position in Germany, which affords the Bundesbank independent responsibility for monetary policy and does not require it to finance government deficits.

German Fiscal Policy after the Summit

The timing of fiscal policy measures in Germany during the past thirty years, together with contemporaneous commentary, suggests three motives have influenced the German government. The first and constant requirement has been the periodic need to offset fiscal drag— the tendency of average tax rates to rise owing to both inflation and real income growth.

A second motive has been to move the federal budget nearer to balance. The size of the public-sector borrowing requirement is limited by law to covering public investment expenditures, though borrowing in excess of this limit is permitted to offset "macroeconomic disequilibrium." Legal restrictions on deficit financing are, therefore, very weak in practice. Yet a balanced budget has considerable political appeal, and the objective of achieving one has become more important during the 1980s. A cyclically indifferent policy, giving precedence to the requirement for a balanced budget, was followed in the recessionary years 1982–85 in reaction to what were then seen as the mistakes of the 1970s, which had left the country with a government deficit of over 4 percent of GNP.

A third motive prompting fiscal actions has been to use budgetary policy for countercyclical management of demand. It appears to be unique to the period from 1967 to 1981, when Social Democratic governments were in office. Contemporary comment ascribed demand-management motives to tax reductions in 1975 and 1977.

In January 1975 there was a DM 4 billion reduction in direct taxes and a DM 10 billion increase in family allowances, together raising personal disposable income by about 2 percent. These measures certainly came at a time of recession when the unemployment rate was on its way to a record. They also came in the year after income tax receipts had reached a record proportion of GDP that was to be exceeded only once, in 1977 (table 1).

TABLE 1. *German Tax Receipts, Government Lending, and Unemployment Rates, 1970–87*
Percent of GDP

Year	Total taxes[a]	Income tax[b]	Net government lending	Unemployment rate[c]
1970	34.70	8.95	0.21	0.55
1971	36.03	9.76	−0.16	0.68
1972	36.62	9.60	−0.51	0.91
1973	38.64	10.89	1.20	1.01
1974	39.34	11.49	−1.30	2.15
1975	39.56	10.63	−5.59	4.00
1976	40.45	11.11	−3.38	3.98
1977	41.13	11.68	−2.41	3.88
1978	40.46	10.99	−2.43	3.72
1979	40.16	10.53	−2.55	3.25
1980	40.63	10.85	−2.89	3.27
1981	40.75	10.51	−3.66	4.64
1982	40.85	10.40	−3.29	6.66
1983	40.20	10.09	−2.53	8.18
1984	40.07	10.05	−1.91	8.20
1985	40.14	10.28	−1.14	8.28
1986	39.61	10.12	−1.21	7.95
1987[d]	39.64	10.13	−1.74	8.15

SOURCE: *OECD Economic Outlook*, no. 42, December 1987, data diskette.
a. Total direct taxes, indirect taxes, and social security contributions of households.
b. Direct taxes on households.
c. Unemployment rate as percent of labor force.
d. OECD estimates.

There was a recovery in the German economy in 1975–76. High growth was recorded, but it then slackened. The 1977 tax measures were adopted against that background. A preoccupation of German policy in the period of slower growth since 1973 has been the need to increase business fixed investment. Policymakers have preferred "investment-led growth," and this preference has been reflected in the structure of periodic tax reductions. In January 1977 "double taxation" of corporate profits was abolished, partly offset by increases in excise taxes on tobacco and alcohol. In September depreciation allowances were increased and personal taxes were decreased. All told, the measures reduced tax revenue by an estimated DM 1.7 billion in 1977 and DM 10.3 billion in 1978.

Much outside comment assumed that these 1977 measures, as well as those agreed to at the Bonn summit for enactment in 1979, were motivated by considerations of aggregate demand. No doubt such considerations were present. For one thing, only four or five years had elapsed since the first oil price crisis, which brought to an end more than a decade of real growth at 5 percent a year. Growth of 3 percent in the German economy, regarded as rapid or even reckless in the 1980s, was still thought disappointing in the mid-1970s. Unemployment of 4 percent in the mid-1970s was compared with the rates of less than 1 percent in an earlier period and was regarded as a serious problem. What is most striking in looking back at the period from 1977 to 1979 is how much official ambitions and aspirations were to decline in the following ten years.

The German fiscal measures agreed to at the Bonn summit were not, therefore, without precedent. Moreover, tax cuts at about that time were necessary to offset fiscal drag. This is not to say that early in 1978 the German government was unanimous in favoring tax cuts nor that the tax package, or its timing, would have been the same without the summit. The summit was apparently a factor in determining the timing of tax cuts. That is a far cry, however, from the claim that the German government reluctantly but altruistically agreed to something at the summit that was contrary to its own interests. Putnam and Henning give a detailed account of political dealings within the German government at the time, which made tax cuts possible. Here, I concentrate on the objective economic circumstances that justified tax cuts and that, in my judgment, made them likely at some point.

In 1977 total tax revenues were at record levels in relation to GDP in Germany; the same was true of revenues from personal income tax (table 1). To explain how this came about, it is necessary to say something about the German tax system.[2]

The income tax recognizes four basic bands of income: an initial band that incurs no tax; a lower band that is taxed at a proportional rate of 22 percent; a middle range where the marginal tax rate is not constant but is a function of income, rising progressively from 22 to 56 percent; and an upper band with a fixed proportional rate of 56 percent.

The effect of inflation on the system is to make more of the population liable for tax and to propel more and more of the taxpayers into and up the progressive middle band. Incipient fiscal drag is therefore high in Germany and periodic discrete tax cuts are necessary to offset it. Tax changes, including those in 1975, 1977, 1978, and 1980, compensated for inflation so that in real terms the shape and position of the marginal rate curve changed little after 1965. In terms of real income, the starting point of the progressive middle tax band was held constant by the periodic tax changes.

Even so, the general rise in real incomes propelled an increasing number of taxpayers into the progressive middle band. In 1965 only 6 percent of taxpayers were in that band, and it yielded only a small proportion of income tax revenue. In 1974 some 40 percent of taxpayers were in the middle band, and 35 percent remained in it in 1979. In 1980 the middle band contributed 78 percent of total income tax receipts. In the early 1960s the average tax rate was 7 percent (16 percent including social security contributions); by 1982 the average rate had risen to 17 percent (31 percent with social security contributions).

Periodic tax cuts have therefore been routine in Germany. The tax measures agreed to in 1978 following the undertaking at the Bonn summit—cuts in income tax, partially offset by increases in indirect taxes—were consistent with a general pattern and do not look in any way exceptional in scale or composition. Earlier measures have been noted already, but others followed those agreed to in 1978.

For example, in December 1979, the government proposed a tax relief program that was accepted by the Bundestag in July 1980. It was for a package of measures extending over 1980–82 worth a total of DM 16.4 billion, most of it falling in 1981. The more substantial elements were changes in income tax rates (DM 6.1 billion), increases in family and housing allowances (DM 2 billion), and improvements in special deductions (DM 3.6 billion). Again there was some increase in indirect taxes. Duties on oil and alcohol were increased as of April 1981, a measure worth DM 2.5 billion. It seems extraordinary that the package announced in 1978 should be blamed for the "crisis" of 1980–81 in Germany when in 1980 and 1981 the government was implementing another similar package without any suggestion of foreign pressure.

The German governments of the 1970s were coalitions of the majority Social Democratic party and the smaller Free Democrats. After the election of October 1982, the Social Democrats lost office and the new government was a coalition in which the Christian Democrats were dominant with the support of the Free Democrats. With the change of government, the style of German fiscal policy changed in the early 1980s. Between 1981 and 1985 the government deficit was reduced by nearly 1.5 percent of GDP despite the concurrent recession, which tended to swell the deficit. Most of the fiscal retrenchment was effected via expenditure cuts, especially in the 1983 budget. A substantial part, though, consisted in simply not offsetting the continuing effect of fiscal drag on income tax revenues. Income tax schedules remained unchanged from 1981 until 1986. Another cut scheduled originally for 1984 was postponed in the interests of reducing the budget deficit. The average tax rate increased by 1.5 percent in 1981–83 and by around 2 percent in the period up to 1986, when cuts in income tax worth some DM 11 billion, or 1 percent of household disposable income, were implemented. This "tax reform," which raised the threshold for income tax, increased deductions for children, and lowered marginal tax rates, was explicitly motivated by the need to offset fiscal drag. It was no doubt facilitated by the earlier success in reducing the budget deficit from some 4 percent of GDP to 1 percent.

As of 1987 it appeared that the average tax rate could increase by another 1 percent between 1986 and 1989, based on reasonable projections for growth and inflation in the German economy. Hence further tax measures for offsetting fiscal drag were scheduled for early 1988. These were originally for a reduction of income tax progressivity costing DM 9 billion. That figure was subsequently increased to DM 14 billion as evidence accumulated of continuing sluggishness in the German economy and continuing weakness in the U.S. balance of payments and the dollar. While some of the pressures on German policy in 1986–88 were similar to those of a decade before, tax changes in 1986 and 1988 were planned without overt agreement with other countries and were widely regarded as inadequate in the United States.

German fiscal policy in the 1980s has been in conscious reaction to the policy of the 1970s, which resulted in a large budget deficit but did not prevent unemployment from rising over the decade. In the 1980s the deficit was reduced, but unemployment increased further from below 4 percent to around 8 percent. It is difficult to argue that the Bonn summit resulted in a deleterious change in the general thrust of German policy. It is perhaps easier to maintain that the post-Bonn measures typified a whole era of German macroeconomic policy that with hindsight has come to be regarded as a failure. The policies of the 1980s have not been conspicuously more successful in terms of economic growth or unemployment than the policies of the 1970s; indeed, in those respects the German economy has performed substantially worse in the present decade.

TABLE 2. *Annual Growth and Target Growth of German Monetary Aggregates, 1974–83*
Percent

Year	Central bank money[a]	Target	M1[b]
1974	6.3	. . .	11.1
1975	9.8	8.0	14.5
1976	9.2	8.0	4.1
1977	9.0	8.0	11.3
1978	11.4[c]	8.0	14.3
1979	9.0	6–9	3.9
1980	4.8	5–8	4.2
1981	4.4	4–7	− 0.8
1982	4.9	4–7	6.7
1983	7.3	4–7	8.1

SOURCE: *Report of the Deutsche Bundesbank for the Year 1980*, p. 31; *1986*, p. 35.
a. CBM data are year over year to 1975 (based on daily averages of the last month of the period and the last month of the previous period, respectively). After 1975 the data are on an annual average basis.
b. Currency in circulation and sight deposits.
c. Adjusted for break in series.

German Monetary Policy after the Summit

It is important to note the behavior of German monetary policy in assessing the plausibility of assertions that German macroeconomic policy, under the influence of the Bonn summit, was responsible for the ills that befell the German economy in 1979 and 1980.

At the start of 1979, when the Bonn fiscal measures came into effect, monetary policy swung decisively toward restriction. If the thinking behind the Bonn summit was that Germany and Japan should stimulate their economies to lead a "convoy" of countries to faster growth, the Bundesbank clearly was no longer on board the ship.[3]

Central bank money (CBM) was the targeted aggregate in Germany between 1975 and 1987. After running consistently above target for four years (1975–78), its growth rate dropped sharply during 1979 and subsequently fell below the target range (table 2). The growth rate of other monetary aggregates such as M1 also fell sharply. That was not the result of the Bundesbank passively accommodating a shift in asset preferences. Consider short-term interest rates (table 3). The discount rate doubled in 1979 from 3 to 6 percent. The Lombard rate, the key policy-guided short-term rate at that time, more than doubled from 3.5 to 7 percent. Other rates responded, but the initial policy moves in the first quarter of 1979 resulted in both a reduction of the spread between the Lombard rate and other short-term rates, such as the

TABLE 3. *German Interest Rates, 1978–79*[a]

Percent

Rate	1978:3	1978:4	1979:1	1979:2	1979:3	1979:4
Discount rate	3.0	3.0	4.0	4.0	5.0	6.0
Lombard rate	3.5	3.5	5.0	5.5	6.0	7.0
Frankfurt						
3-month rate[b]	3.7	4.1	4.5	6.5	7.9	9.6
Bond rate[b,c]	6.0	6.3	6.8	7.8	7.5	7.9

SOURCE: OECD and Bundesbank, quoted by Datastream database.
a. End-of-quarter data.
b. Daily average, final month of the quarter.
c. Index of secondary market public bonds with life of three to fifteen years.

TABLE 4. *Changes in German Foreign Exchange Reserves, 1974–80*

Billions of deutsche marks

Item	1974	1975	1976	1977	1978	1979	1980
Change in net external assets of Bundesbank at transactions values, from balance of payments accounts	−1.9	−2.2	8.8	10.5	19.8	−5.0	−27.9
Net foreign exchange flows to Bundesbank from monetary accounts	−2.8	−2.1	8.3	8.4	20.3	−5.2	−24.6

SOURCE: *Report of the Deutsche Bundesbank, 1980*, pp. 24, 31.

three-month Frankfurt rate, and a shallower yield curve as short rates gained on longs.

As table 2 shows, money supply consistently overshot targets during the early years of targeting. This was largely due to intervention in foreign exchange markets to brake deutsche mark appreciation. Consequent increases in foreign exchange reserves could not be entirely sterilized, and thus they inflated the money supply (table 4). Wide currency fluctuations and repeated foreign exchange market intervention in 1978 led to a particularly large acquisition of reserves in that year and a substantial overshoot of the monetary target as CBM grew by about 11½ percent. The Bundesbank was becoming concerned at the growth of the money supply and at this point resolved to rein it in. In January 1979 it raised the Lombard rate by half a percentage point to 4 percent and reduced rediscount quotas by DM 5 billion. In February there was a 5 percent increase in required reserve ratios.

The contraction was made easier at that time by a change in U.S. monetary policy in November 1978, signaling the end of a policy of indifference toward the exchange rate of the dollar. There was consequently a marked strengthening of the dollar in the first quarter of

1979 and a return flow of speculative funds from the deutsche mark to
the dollar. This enabled the Bundesbank to tighten monetary conditions without driving up the exchange rate.

When price inflation threatened to rise after the second oil shock,
German monetary policy not only failed to accommodate the increased inflation, it tightened further, as did policy in other countries.
In March both discount and Lombard rates were increased by one percentage point. There was some increase in rediscount quotas in April
to counteract the liquidity effects of a loss of foreign exchange, but the
Lombard rate was increased in June. In July further increases took
discount and Lombard rates to 5 and 6 percent, respectively. Credit
restrictions were tightened in September. Renewed capital inflows did
not deflect monetary policy. Instead, the deutsche mark was revalued
by 2.15 percent within the exchange rate mechanism of the European
Monetary System, which had gone into operation in March 1979. The
discount rate went to 6 percent in November and 7 percent in February
1980.

The progressive tightening of monetary policy through 1979 was
largely to counter the actual and prospective inflation following the 60
percent increase in traded oil prices during the first six months of the
year. Monetary policy was to stay tight for some time. There was an
undershooting of the target for money growth in 1980.

Was the initial tightening in the first two months of 1979 a deliberate effort to offset the effects of the Bonn agreement? That is extremely improbable. A broadly monetarist view has generally been influential in German policy circles, though it has taken a pragmatic
form in which monetary targets have been tempered by a good deal of
discretionary over- and undershooting in response to other indicators,
like the exchange rate or inflation. Nonetheless, the prevalent view
regards money as primary in determining nominal GNP and inflation,
and this view was held especially strong in 1979. Fiscal policy was
consequently regarded as having little or no sustained effect on nominal GNP in the absence of a monetary accommodation. The Bundesbank's control of the money supply was seen as the ultimate safeguard
against inflation, whatever the government policy. The initial restriction early in 1979 was in response to previous rapid growth of the
money supply, particularly in 1978, caused by foreign exchange intervention. The tightening was not in response to the fiscal measures. Of
course, it cannot be entirely excluded that the monetary authorities'

view of the need for restriction was reinforced, if only marginally, by awareness that fiscal policy had moved to a more expansionary stance.

Consequences of Policy Changes, 1978–79

In this section, I assess the effects of German economic policy after the 1978 summit on the German economy. I first examine the consequences for aggregate demand and then turn successively to effects on the balance of payments, inflation, and government debt.

Aggregate Demand

German officials have claimed that the experience of 1978–79 confirms the proposition that stimulatory fiscal policy does not raise GDP because it pushes up budget and current account deficits and the rate of inflation, and thus weakens confidence and serves to reduce domestic investment.[4] What occurred in 1979, however, was not a simple expansionary fiscal policy but a more complicated twist in which a discretionary fiscal expansion was accompanied by monetary restriction. Moreover, the fiscal expansion would be considered mild if compared with a demand-neutral fiscal policy that sought to offset fiscal drag.

A fiscal expansion through tax cuts tends to raise domestic demand, especially private consumption, thus increasing import demand.[5] The tax cuts also raise the government's demand for credit (borrowing has to replace tax revenues). Hence the fiscal expansion also pushes up interest rates, tending to dampen interest-sensitive expenditures. Higher interest rates tend to appreciate the exchange rate, unless the central bank is expected to monetize the incremental deficit. Both the absorption effects (due to higher income and expenditure) and the expenditure-switching effects (due to exchange rate appreciation) of fiscal expansion thus work to worsen the current account.

Monetary restriction accompanying the fiscal expansion would generally result in interest rates and the exchange rate rising still more, thus worsening the trade balance further. By lowering import prices in domestic currency, the exchange rate appreciation should tend to slow inflation (which would otherwise be tending to rise because of higher domestic demand following the fiscal expansion). Furthermore, higher interest rates discourage certain interest-sensitive domestic expenditures, notably housing investment and perhaps credit-financed purchase of consumer durables. To the extent that domestic demand is reduced by higher interest rates, domestic activity and inflation are dampened and the trade account tends to improve. It is unclear a priori which effect of higher interest rates caused by tighter monetary policy dominates: the exchange rate effect or the domestic-demand effect. So it is unclear whether the effect of tighter money, on its own, is to improve or make worse the current account balance; the net effect may well be small.

The combined fiscal and monetary measures are likely to cause a shift in expenditures, therefore, with higher consumption expenditure, lower net exports, and, probably, less housing investment. Another way to view the matter is that the economy as a whole will save less (lower current account surplus or larger deficit), reflecting the lower saving or extra dissaving of the public sector (larger public-sector deficit). The effect on total demand is indeterminate a priori.

Of course, many other influences beyond the policy changes were at work on the German economy in 1979. It cannot be assumed that in the absence of those policy changes there would have been no changes in the composition of aggregate demand. The compositional shifts that did occur are not, therefore, direct evidence of the effects of the policy changes. Nonetheless, it is interesting that by no means all of the shifts in aggregate demand components predicted by theory are visible from German national accounts in late 1978 and 1979 (see table 5). That fact could suggest that the influence of the policy changes was not overwhelming.

There was no substantial increase in the proportion of GNP going to private consumption in late 1978 or early 1979, and in the second half of 1979 the proportion fell. The fall may have been due to rising inflation; in Germany, as in other countries, the observed savings rate rises with inflation.[6] Equally unexpectedly, there was a slight rise in the proportions of housing investment and business investment in 1979 over 1978. More predictably, there was a clear deterioration in net exports, although these had also been deteriorating in 1977 and 1978.

The slight growth in business fixed investment is perhaps suggestive evidence against the proposition that the increased budget deficit was bad for business investment. Indeed, the increase has been cited by supporters of the Bonn measures to argue that the German govern-

TABLE 5. *Demand Components of German GNP, Selected Periods, 1977–86*
Percent of GNP at 1980 prices

Year and period[a]	Private consumption	Business investment	Housing investment	Net exports[b]	Growth of business investment[c]
1977:1	56.2	11.2	6.6	1.6	12.1
1977:2	57.0	11.2	6.4	0.9	0.9
1978:1	56.9	11.3	6.5	1.3	6.9
1978:2	57.0	11.7	6.5	0.5	9.7
1979:1	57.0	11.9	6.6	− 0.4	8.1
1979:2	56.4	12.2	6.8	− 0.8	8.1
1980:1	56.2	12.2	6.9	0	3.4
1980:2	57.1	12.3	6.7	− 0.4	− 1.1
1985:1	54.9	11.7	5.6	5.3	− 0.3
1985:2	55.0	12.0	5.6	5.1	9.5
1986:1	55.9	12.2	5.3	4.4	3.5
1986:2	55.9	12.0	5.5	3.7	0.4

SOURCE: *OECD Economic Outlook*, no. 42, December 1987, data diskette.
a. Average for the half-year periods.
b. Goods and services.
c. Seasonally adjusted annual rate.

ment's preoccupation with "investment-led growth" would best be served by expansion of aggregate demand; they argue that a lack of demand is responsible for sluggish investment.[7] However, the increase in business fixed investment in the second half of 1978 is inconclusive. The share was at a historical low in 1974–76, but rose somewhat in 1977. It rose further in 1978 and 1979 and went on to reach a cyclical peak in late 1980 before falling back during the recession of the early 1980s. It picked up in 1986 and in the second semester rose above its 1979 level. The investment share has been a slightly lagging indicator of the business cycle, and its behavior in 1979 seems unexceptional viewed in that light.[8]

Apart from influences on the pattern of demand, the issue of whether domestic demand overall is raised by the combined effect of monetary tightening and fiscal easing cannot be asserted a priori and depends on empirical characteristics of the economy. These are not known with certainty. Consider, however, what might be predicted by the Bundesbank's own econometric model of the German economy.

Table 6 shows the Bundesbank model of the effects on GNP of a fiscal stimulus equal to 1 percent of baseline GNP and of a policy-induced increase in interest rates of 1 percent.

To apply these estimates to the experience of 1979, it is necessary

TABLE 6. *Simulation Properties of Two Models of the German Economy*
Percent deviation from baseline

	Response and year					
	Year 1		Year 2		Year 3	
Simulation and model	Real GNP	PGNP[a]	Real GNP	PGNP[a]	Real GNP	PGNP[a]
Fiscal expansion[b]						
Bundesbank	1.02	0.6	0.8	0.96	0.3	1.24
Increase in interest rates[c]						
Bundesbank	−0.13	−0.2	−0.2	−0.12	−0.21	−0.24
INTERLINK	. . .	. . .	. . .	. . .	−0.85	−1.7

SOURCE: James H. Chan-Lee and Hiromi Kato, "A Comparison of Simulation Properties of National Econometric Models," *OECD Economic Studies*, no. 2 (Spring 1984), pp. 123, 128.

a. Price deflator for nominal GNP.

b. The simulation is of an increase in government expenditure equal to 1 percent of GNP as it was before the shock. Monetary policy is assumed to be nonaccommodating and to maintain monetary aggregates growing at baseline rates. A reduction in taxes equal ex ante to 1 percent of GNP would generally have a somewhat smaller effect, as part of the tax cut would be saved, not spent. Results of a simulated tax cut are not published for the Bundesbank model.

c. The simulation is of an increase in policy-controlled short-term interest rates of 1 percentage point. In both simulations, the exchange rate is assumed to float freely.

to assume the model gives roughly linear responses, so that the effect of a three-percentage-point increase in interest rates, for example, is approximately three times as great as the response to a one-percentage-point increase.

The published multipliers for a fiscal stimulus also refer to an increase in government expenditure. Much of the fiscal package implemented after Bonn consisted of tax cuts. Increased government expenditure amounted to about 0.25 percent of GNP in 1979, while tax cuts and allowances were worth about 0.6 percent of GNP. Further tax cuts taking effect in 1980 were worth another 0.34 percent of that year's GNP. In general, the demand effect of tax cuts is less than that of an increase in government expenditures, even when the two have identical immediate effects on government revenue; some of the extra income due to tax cuts is saved by households, whereas all of the government spending boosts demand. Applying the Bundesbank's multipliers (appropriate to an expenditure increase) to the Bonn measures would lead to overestimation of the demand effect of the measures, even if the model is correct.

The multiplier effect on GNP of a tax reduction is smaller than that of a government expenditure increase by a factor depending on households' marginal propensity to consume. There may be other differences owing to the different goods being demanded, the different supply potential of the economy for different goods, and different consequences for imports and income distribution. However, a very crude adjustment would be to take the effects of expenditure increases, derived from the Bundesbank model's published expenditure multipliers, and multiply them by an estimate of household marginal propensity to consume, ignoring consumption dynamics. The marginal propensity to consume is, in general, a function of the interest rate and the inflation rate, consumer confidence, and the growth rate of the economy. However, since 1973 the average savings rate of the German personal sector has been broadly constant in the range of 11–12 percent, which suggests the marginal savings propensity could be similar. This implies a marginal propensity to consume of 0.88–0.89.

To avoid spurious precision, I adjust the post-Bonn tax cuts, measured as a percentage of GNP, by a factor of 0.9 to get the change in government expenditure that would have a similar demand effect. The fiscal boost for 1978 is thus taken to be 0.25 percent of GNP (expenditure increases) plus 0.55 percent of GNP (0.6 × 0.9, adjusted tax increases). In 1980 the additional fiscal stimulus is taken to be 0.3 percent of GNP. The Bundesbank multipliers are applied to these fiscal stimuli.

On that basis, in 1979 the fiscal boost would have contributed some 0.8 percent to GNP. In 1980 the combined effect of the 1979 and 1980 fiscal measures would have put GNP very nearly 1 percent above baseline (that is, where it would have been in the absence of the measures). That would have been the peak of the fiscal effect. In 1981, as the fiscal boost wore off, GNP would have been nearly half a percent above baseline. (Later fiscal measures having nothing to do with the Bonn summit are not being considered.) The effect on growth rates in the three years would have been 0.8, 0.1, and − 0.5 percentage points.[9]

Such effects would be adding to a baseline GNP slowed by fiscal drag. But, in any event, the effects were also counteracted by the monetary tightening. It is difficult to calibrate the monetary tightening that occurred in 1979 and 1980, because the fiscal boost would have been responsible for some rise in interest rates, unless monetary policy were actually relaxed to accommodate the higher GNP. As the monetary tightening was progressive through 1979 and 1980 and did not occur neatly at the beginning of each year, there is a further difficulty in assessing the size of the policy multiplier to apply in each year.

The Lombard rate, a purely policy-determined rate, was on average 2.5 percentage points higher in 1979 than it was in 1980. Heroically, I interpret the rise in the Lombard rate as a measure of the sustained monetary tightening; hence I ignore the possibility that some of the interest rate rise may have been a passive following of tighter money market conditions and I also disregard the further interest rate increases that occurred in 1980. On that basis, the monetary tightening on its own would have left GNP about 0.33 percent below baseline in 1979 and about 0.5 percent below baseline in both 1980 and 1981. These are extremely crude estimates, making no attempt to accurately adjust the multipliers for the actual intrayear timing of interest rate changes. In particular, the effect for 1979 may be overestimated, while the effects for 1980 and later years are almost certainly underestimated.

The effect of the combined policy measures was, therefore, to add perhaps one-half of a percentage point to GNP in 1979 and the same or slightly less in 1980. In the third year after the initial policy change, according to the Bundesbank model, the monetary effect canceled, if it did not dominate, the fiscal boost, and GNP was no higher than it would have been in the absence of the policy changes. In the years after 1981, the combined policy changes of 1979 and the tax cuts of 1980 (decided on in 1978) served to depress demand in the German economy.

The inflation responses in the Bundesbank model may well be baseline dependent in the sense that the simulated increase in inflation depends on the degree of slack in the economy when policy changes are made. Nonetheless, the inflation responses shown in table 6 suggest that the 1979 measures would have had no net effect on the GNP deflator in that year, because the inflation resulting from the fiscal boost (0.5 percentage points on the GNP deflator) was negated by monetary contraction. By 1981 the GNP deflator could have been 0.33 percent below baseline as a result of the combined monetary and fiscal measures, representing a negligible change in average inflation over the period. Even considering the fiscal changes alone, the effect on inflation was small. The GNP deflator might have been 1.3 percent above baseline in 1981, implying an addition to average annual inflation over 1979–81 of less than half of one percentage point.

Simulated inflation responses are sensitive to the predicted path of the exchange rate. Unfortunately, the exchange rate response of the Bundesbank model is not reported. A version of the OECD INTERLINK model, by simulating an appreciation of some 10 percent in response to a 2 percent increase in interest rates, implies that monetary restriction has stronger depressive effects on domestic demand and in-

flation than does the Bundesbank model. The implications of the IN-
TERLINK result is that inflation was reduced, not increased, by the
combined fiscal and monetary measures in 1979 and 1980. The implied deterioration in the current account would be greater than in the
Bundesbank model, however, because of the exchange rate movement.

The belief that the post-Bonn measures gave rise to an inflationary
boom, therefore, is incompatible with empirically supported views of
the German economy embodied in economic models. Even without
monetary contraction, the models imply that the fiscal boost had a
moderate effect on GNP and a small effect on inflation. When the
monetary contraction of 1979 is considered as an offset, the net demand boost becomes still smaller. It was probably zero in two to three
years and negative thereafter. The effect on inflation was minuscule at
worst and, on plausible exchange rate responses, could have been negative. Certainly, the measures reduced the German current account
surplus relative to what it would otherwise have been. Far from being
a problem, the elimination of the German surplus contributed to more
balanced current accounts within the OECD area and hence can be
seen as a benefit of the policy measures.

It is possible to argue about small differences in the estimates of the
consequences of the post-Bonn policies, but I know of no reputable or
empirically grounded model of the German economy that would give
qualitatively different results from those summarized above.[10] This
view is fortified by the difficulty in identifying changes in the pattern
of demand that can be attributed to the measures and by the readiness
of German policymakers to authorize further tax cuts for 1980 beyond
those agreed to after Bonn.

In view of these points, how is it possible to argue that the post-
Bonn policy measures were somehow disastrous? The key lies in what
was happening in the world economy as the 1970s drew to a close. The
German economy was hit by the second oil crisis. The resulting deterioration in terms of trade was responsible for much, though not all, of
the deterioration in the current account; it was responsible for the entire acceleration of inflation. (These assertions are justified below.)
Meanwhile, what of the argument that the policy measures were procyclical, coming at a time of cyclical upswing? Or that policymakers
significantly overestimated the supply potential of the economy, which
was closer to full capacity than they realized?

Either proposition, of course, takes for granted that the combined
fiscal and monetary measures were on balance expansionary. Alter-

TABLE 7. *Forecasts and Outcome for German and European Economic Activity, 1978–79*[a]
Percent

| Year and forecast | Germany | | | OECD Europe |
	Real GNP	Final domestic demand	Consumer expenditure price deflator	Real GNP
1977:2				
Forecast A[b]	1.5	3.0	3.75	1.5
Forecast B[c]	1.25	2.75	3.5	1.0
Forecast C[d]	n.a.	n.a.	n.a.	n.a.
Forecast D[e]	2.0	3.0	3.5	2.1
1978:1				
Forecast A[b]	4.0	3.75	4.75	3.0
Forecast B[c]	2.25	2.25	2.75	2.75
Forecast C[d]	2.8	2.7	2.5	2.75
Forecast D[e]	3.9	4.8	2.5	3.5
1978:2				
Forecast A[b]	3.0	3.0	3.0	2.75
Forecast B[c]	3.5	4.25	3.5	3.0
Forecast C[d]	4.0	5.0	2.25	4.5
Forecast D[e]	3.25	3.5	2.5	3.1
1979:1				
Forecast A[b]	n.a.	n.a.	n.a.	n.a.
Forecast B[c]	2.75	3.5	3.0	3.0
Forecast C[d]	4.25	5.25	2.75	3.5
Forecast D[e]	3.5	5.5	3.8	3.1

SOURCE: *OECD Economic Outlook*, various issues.
n.a. Not available.
a. All figures are seasonally adjusted annual growth rate, each half-year on the preceding half-year.
b. OECD forecast of December 1977.
c. OECD forecast of July 1978.
d. OECD forecast of December 1978.
e. Outcome (*OECD Economic Outlook*), no. 38, December 1985; no. 39, June 1986, data diskettes.

natively, it could be argued that the fiscal measures were expansionary when viewed on their own and that they can be considered in isolation. They did, after all, represent the views of the Americans and others attempting to influence German policy. Was that pressure misguided as well as unlucky?

Table 7 shows the forecasts of German growth and inflation made by the OECD in December 1977, July 1978, and December 1978. It also shows the outcome according to the statistics available at the end of 1987. The forecasts were published almost two months after they were essentially completed, so the forecast of July 1978 was available to the summiteers before Bonn and would have been the operative one for policymaking at that time.

The July 1978 forecast was more pessimistic than the one made six months earlier. Growth in the second half of 1977 was thought by mid-1978 to have come in fractionally weaker than it had seemed in December 1977, while GNP in the first half of 1978 was thought to be running at an annual rate of 2.25 percent, compared with the 4 percent forecast the previous December. GNP growth was expected, nonetheless, to accelerate to 3.5 percent in the second half of 1978 before falling slightly in the first half of 1979.

The striking thing in retrospect is that the German government was prepared to countenance expansion at a time when the OECD was forecasting 3.5 percent growth and 3.5 percent inflation. In 1987 it was nervous about inflation running at below 1 percent and expressed satisfaction with any positive growth rate at all. Such changed attitudes no doubt underlie the contention that in 1978 the government was too sanguine about the supply potential of the economy.

By the end of 1978 the OECD had made an upward revision of its estimate of German growth in the first half of 1978. Historical statistics as of 1987 showed, moreover, that growth in the first half of 1978 was, in fact, stronger still—just as strong as had been originally forecast in December 1977. This must be the basis for asserting that the 1978 fiscal policy decisions were a mistake: the economy was growing faster than thought at the time of the Bonn summit.

Even more relevant to policy, however, were the growth forecasts for the second half of 1978 and for 1979. Growth turned out to be no faster in the second half of 1978 than was expected at the time of the summit. In fact, the growth of final domestic demand was significantly slower (3.5 percent rather than 4.25 percent). It did not appear so at the end of 1978, when estimates of growth in the second half were rather higher. These estimates were subsequently used to argue that the policy agreed upon at Bonn was mistaken. Supporters of the policy argued that the (supposed) faster growth during the second half of 1978 was probably caused by the summit itself. Although tax cuts did not take effect before January 1979, they could have been anticipated. However, later statistics show these disagreements to be academic; demand in the German economy slowed through 1978, just as the December 1977 forecast had foreseen, and was slower in the second half than the mid-1978 forecast estimated.

It must be accepted, therefore, that there was a forecasting error for the first half of 1978 and the German economy was much stronger than thought in midyear. Growth through the whole year turned out to be 0.75 percent faster than the July 1978 forecast predicted, and it was fractionally quicker than in the forecast made in December 1977 (though it did slow down during the year, as foreseen in that earlier forecast). Events ultimately confirmed that the German economy was slowing at the time of Bonn or was to slow shortly afterward.

The forecast error for real domestic demand was larger than that for real GNP for the first half of the year by 2.5 percentage points. That is a particularly large error. However, domestic demand also slowed in the second half, and to a slower growth rate than the mid-1978 forecast expected. The mid-1978 forecast can be viewed as unduly pessimistic about demand if the focus is on growth rates for the year as a whole. For the second half of the year alone, however, it was not pessimistic, and that fact arguably is more relevant for the policy being considered in midyear. It is impossible to assess the forecast's predictions for 1979, which were overtaken by the policy changes themselves and by the second oil crisis.

Although the German economy was slightly more vigorous than thought at the time, the forecast error for 1978 as a whole was not a large one; it was of the order of magnitude that users of economic forecasts must routinely expect. One must conclude either that the policymakers at Bonn and their advisers were fine-tuners of the most extreme naivete or that they could well have undertaken similar policy steps even if they had known what German growth would actually be in 1978. That is especially true when the time path of growth is considered. If so, the forecasting error was largely immaterial.

However, the strongest criticism of the post-Bonn measures is not that they were based on erroneous forecasts of aggregate demand in Germany, but that they were based on erroneous beliefs about aggregate supply potential. This issue is examined below, where the reasons for the deterioration of the current balance and the acceleration of inflation are discussed. Before leaving OECD forecasts, however, two points that bear on the question of potential supply are worth noting.

First, inflation turned out to be slower in Germany in 1978 than either the end-1977 or mid-1978 forecast had expected, even though the latter forecast was too pessimistic about growth. In other words, there was no excessive optimism about the "split" of any nominal income growth into real growth and inflation during 1978. Policymakers were not too optimistic about the supply side of the economy in that sense; if anything, they were too pessimistic. Second, the forecasts foresaw that domestic demand would be growing faster than GDP in Germany in late 1978, entailing a fall in net exports at constant prices. Moreover, the current account was expected to worsen without the influence of either policy changes or oil price increases, neither of which was in the forecasts. (The current balance forecast made sense in view of the rise of the trade-weighted exchange rate during the 1970s; the deutsche mark's trade-weighted index rose monotonically from 0.63 in 1970 to 0.86 in the second half of 1978.)

Together, those two points suggest that it was not German policymakers' estimation of the supply potential of the economy that changed in the 1980s, when the post-Bonn measures fell into disrepute. It was rather that policymakers' preferences changed and they became less inclined to risk higher inflation or budget and external deficits in pursuit of faster demand growth and lower unemployment. Higher rates of inflation following the second oil price crisis and a change of governing party probably both contributed to a change of preferences.

Balance of Payments

The events of 1979–81 that appalled German policymakers in retrospect and led to the subsequent anathema on the Bonn summit were the deterioration of the current balance into deficit and the acceleration of inflation.

In principle, to consider the effects on the balance of payments a clear counterfactual is necessary: what would the current account have done in the absence of the policy changes? Such a counterfactual is unavailable, but it seems reasonable to suppose that in the absence of policy change there would have been no substantial improvement in the current balance in 1979 and 1980. That supposition is consistent with forecasts made in 1978, which were for some deterioration in the balance owing to earlier rises of the deutsche mark. There were no obvious important forces at work making for a larger current account surplus. That is important because it allows the actual deterioration in the balance that occurred after 1978 to be regarded as an upper bound on the possible effects of the post-Bonn summit policies.

The analytical problem is then reduced to decomposing the deterioration in the German balance of payments during 1979 and 1980 into

FIGURE 1. *Components of Current Account Balance in Germany,*
1971–87
Billions of U.S. dollars (annual rate)

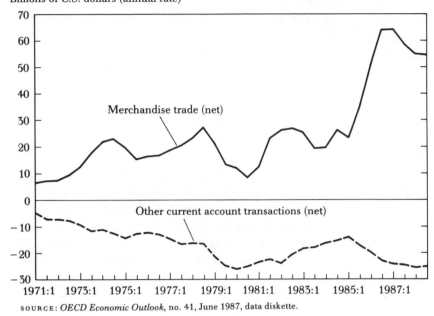

SOURCE: *OECD Economic Outlook*, no. 41, June 1987, data diskette.

those parts caused respectively by the rise in oil prices, the previous
real appreciation of the deutsche mark, and the fiscal stimulus following the summit. (As noted above, monetary policy changes may have
very small net effects on the current account; this is confirmed by most
international econometric models.) A judgment must also be made as
to whether the deterioration, and any part of it owing to the fiscal stimulus, should have caused the concern it did.

Figure 1 shows that the merchandise trade balance peaked in the
second half of 1978 and then declined until the second half of 1980,
though remaining in surplus throughout. The balance on current account transactions other than merchandise trade ("invisibles trade"),
which had been in steadily increasing deficit for years, also deteriorated sharply at the same time. That deterioration ended in the first
semester of 1980.

The invisibles balance is of subsidiary importance and can be analyzed quickly. Most of its components contributed to its deterioration.
There was an increase in net payments for foreign travel (over DM 2
billion in 1979 and DM 3.7 billion in 1980), part of which could be
attributed to tax cuts. There was also a deterioration in net factor in-

come flows, which fell by nearly DM 2 billion in 1979; this is less easily ascribed to tax cuts. Transfers also deteriorated, mostly owing to official transfers. More than half the worsening of the invisibles balance was in items that cannot plausibly be laid at the door of 1978 measures. Even if all the deterioration in travel and other nonfactor services was the result of the tax cuts, that accounts for little more than DM 4 billion in 1979 out of a deterioration of DM 9 billion in invisibles (in 1980, DM 3.3 billion out of DM 6.6 billion). Those are small numbers in relation to the total current account deterioration of DM 29 billion in 1979 and DM 17.5 billion in 1980. It seems reasonable, therefore, to concentrate on the merchandise trade balance.

The trade balance worsened by some DM 19.2 billion in 1979, as imports rose by over 20 percent at current prices while exports rose by only 9.7 percent. The equivalent figures for 1980 were DM 13.1 billion, 17.7 percent, and 11.5 percent. German trade in energy products alone deteriorated by DM 15.5 billion in 1979 and by DM 17.4 billion in 1980. That worsening of energy trade is entirely attributable to a larger import bill, mainly for oil, because energy exports actually increased. In 1979 energy imports increased in both value and volume. The volume increase was 5 percent and, at constant 1978 prices, would have added some DM 1.9 billion to the import bill. Higher energy prices alone added DM 13.6 billion to the import bill and about DM 13.3 billion to the deterioration in the balance of energy trade. That is nearly 70 percent of the total deterioration.

In 1980 energy imports fell in volume by 7.5 percent. The further deterioration in energy trade was therefore entirely due to higher prices. Moreover, the deterioration in energy trade was more than sufficient to explain the worsening of the overall trade balance; the trade balance in manufactures (SITC categories 6–8) was better in 1980 than in 1978 or 1979. The balance of trade in chemicals also improved over the two years.

Of course, it is possible to reject the initial supposition of this section and to argue that, without the energy price increase and the Bonn summit, the German trade balance would have been improving considerably in 1979 and 1980. The bare numbers for energy imports do not conclusively demonstrate that the summit measures had no effect on the trade balance. Energy prices are more than sufficient, however, to explain the actual deterioration in the trade balance over 1978–80.

The trade balance in goods at constant 1982 prices deteriorated by DM 11.4 billion between 1977 and 1978 and by DM 9.8 billion be-

TABLE 8. *Indexes of International Competitiveness for Germany, 1976–81*

Index 1982 = 100

Measure of labor costs	1976	1977	1978	1979	1980	1981
IMF	92.7	97.8	100.9	101.2	100.0	91.2
OECD	96.0	100.6	104.3	105.2	104.5	97.8
Relative export prices	103.7	106.4	110.5	109.7	106.8	99.0

SOURCES: International Monetary Fund, "Cost and Price Comparisons," *International Financial Statistics*, various issues; *OECD Economic Outlook*, no. 41, June 1987, data diskette.

tween 1978 and 1979, and then improved by DM 6.2 billion between 1979 and 1980. The maximum deterioration in volume flows in 1979–80 potentially ascribable to the fiscal measures was therefore not very large, unless the volume balance was on the verge of a substantial improvement in 1978, which seems unlikely. As noted above, the OECD projected some deterioration in the German current balance anyway due to the rise in the German exchange rate over 1976–78. Even allowing for relatively lower German inflation, there was a real deterioration in German competitiveness over the period. IMF and OECD measures both show a rise in relative unit labor costs in German manufacturing of about 8 percent over the three years (table 8).

Price elasticities of demand for German exports and imports of around − 0.4, applied to the average level of exports and imports over 1976–78, would be sufficient, in combination with the decline of competitiveness, to explain the entire deterioration in the merchandise trade balance at constant prices that occurred in 1978 and 1979.[11]

In fact, I do not argue that the fiscal measures had no effect on the trade balance. They increased domestic demand and tended to push up the exchange rate. Both of those effects must have resulted in more imports. (Higher demand would increase imports quickly, while an appreciated exchange rate would do so over a period of years.) Yet the effect of the fiscal measures on net exports cannot have been very large since it fails to show through in the data, unless it is assumed that German net exports were about to rise substantially in 1978. Adjusted for price changes, the deterioration in the trade balance in 1979 was smaller than that in 1978, and in 1980 there was no deterioration; there was an improvement.

In the end, one is not left looking for explanations for the deterioration in the current account that occurred in 1979 and 1980. There is a surfeit of explanations, and they can "explain" a larger deterioration

TABLE 9. *Annual Rates of Inflation in German Wages and Prices,*
1977–81
Percent

Year and period	Nominal wages	Unit labor costs	Consumer prices	Import prices			
				Manufactures	Raw materials	Energy	All import prices
1977:1	8.2	3.3	3.7	5.1	10.1	3.1	3.9
1977:2	4.6	4.0	3.4	0	−8.1	0	−2.1
1978:1	6.3	2.7	2.5	−1.0	−17.9	−12.4	−2.8
1978:2	5.3	3.9	2.4	6.4	0.5	−5.4	0.5
1979:1	6.4	3.3	3.8	5.4	10.0	48.8	7.6
1979:2	5.8	4.5	5.7	9.1	14.8	70.9	15.7
1980:1	8.4	7.7	6.1	10.4	11.1	46.5	13.2
1980:2	4.9	8.1	5.3	6.2	3.1	22.4	6.6
1981:1	1.2	3.2	6.4	12.8	16.0	53.8	14.0
1981:2	9.2	3.8	6.4	5.0	7.3	16.6	9.8

SOURCE: *OECD Economic Outlook*, no. 41, June 1987, data diskette.

than the one that occurred. Did the deterioration matter? The current balance caused concern at the time in Germany because the experience of a deficit contrasted with the period after the first oil shock, when the German current account never left surplus. With hindsight, however, it is possible to see that German trade performance was remarkably good considering the various factors at work: a significant previous decline in price competitiveness, domestic demand growing faster than that of trade partners, and a massive terms-of-trade loss due to energy prices. German trade was in fact showing a resilience that it has continued to show ever since.

The deterioration in the current balance and the ensuing deficit were small in relation to German current account surpluses before and since. In itself, the deficit should have been no cause for concern. Indeed, it represented the modest contribution to more balanced external positions among the OECD countries that authors of the Bonn agreement intended.

Inflation

The evolution of consumer prices, nominal wages, and unit labor costs during 1977–81 is shown in table 9. Nominal wage inflation was broadly stable in 1979, not accelerating significantly from its 1978 rate. Consumer prices, however, accelerated substantially and outstripped the rate of growth of unit labor costs. The obvious reason was a marked acceleration of import prices, caused largely by the rise

FIGURE 2. *Imported and Domestic Inflation in Germany, 1976–83*
Percent

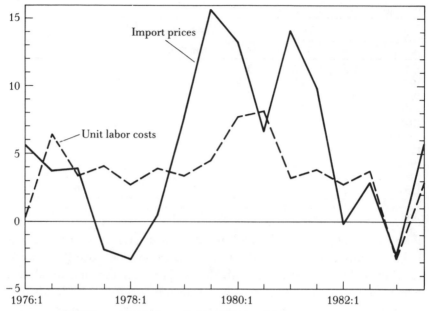

SOURCE: *OECD Economic Outlook*, no. 41, June 1987, data diskette.

in energy prices. The range and timing of increases in imported and domestic inflation, as represented in unit labor costs, is shown in figure 2.

Unit labor costs certainly accelerated in 1980. Clearly, this could have been a response to the earlier surge in consumer prices. However, it is also true that unemployment fell from 3.7 percent in 1978 to 3.3 percent in 1979 and remained at that level in 1980 before picking up to 4.6 percent in 1981. Could that drop in unemployment have contributed substantially to the increase in unit labor costs in 1980, if not 1979?

Econometric research suggests it could not have done so. A nominal wage equation of a standard augmented Phillips-curve type, estimated over the period between 1964 and 1979, produces a coefficient on the log of unemployment of −0.31:[12]

$$w = \begin{array}{l} 0.66 \ + \ 0.93p \ + \ 0.56 \times prod \ - \ 0.31 \times \ln U \\ (0.68) \quad (0.21) \quad\ \ (0.16) \qquad\qquad\quad (0.22) \\[4pt] \quad + \ 0.99D1 \ + \ 0.36D2, \\ \quad\ \ (0.31) \qquad\ (0.57) \end{array}$$

where
- w = growth of national accounts wages divided by private-sector employment;
- p = growth of national accounts–based deflator for private consumption, two-period moving average;
- $prod$ = real business-sector GNP divided by business-sector employment (productivity), two-period moving average;
- $\ln U$ = logarithm of unemployment rate;
- $D1$ = dummy variable for events of 1969 and 1970;
- $D2$ = dummy variable for unusual seasonal pattern.

A decrease of 0.4 percentage points in unemployment, a reduction of 12 percent, would have a negligible effect on the inflation rate (about 0.04 percentage points). Even adding two standard errors to the estimated coefficient produces an estimate of -0.75, which would give an inflation impact of only 0.1 percentage point.

The equation implies that the maximum increase in inflation in 1979 over 1978 that could be attributed to the decrease in unemployment was some 0.2 percentage points. That assumes the acceleration of wages in the first half of the year is fully passed into consumer prices, which then feed into wages again fully and immediately in the second half. Such assumptions are implausible. Thus the best estimate is that the short-run effect on inflation was much less than 0.2 percentage point. Even that incremental effect on inflation can be attributed to the fiscal measures only on the assumption that they were entirely responsible for the fall in unemployment that occurred.

Of course, the ultimate effect on inflation of even a small change in unemployment can be much greater. This is particularly so if the economy is thought to have a "natural" unemployment rate at which inflation is stable, while at other unemployment rates inflation tends to accelerate or decelerate without limit. This remains a popular theory of inflation, though less so now than it was in 1979, owing to the intervening experience of persistently rising unemployment with stable inflation (see appendix).

Perhaps the strongest case that could be made against the Bonn measures would be that they were applied to an economy at its natural unemployment rate, that they reduced unemployment below that rate and thus condemned the economy to a persistent, if slow, acceleration in the inflation rate. Is such a case plausible?

The first point to note is that the rises in consumer prices, average earnings, and unit labor costs were broadly stable or even declining between 1976 and 1978, so there is at least no evidence that German unemployment was below its natural rate, and may have been above it, at the end of 1978.

An estimate of the natural rate in 1979 can be inferred from the wage equation above plus a number of other assumptions, though such an estimate is highly uncertain. Moreover, the degree of the uncertainty (variance of the estimate) is unknown. Assume that consumer prices increase with the weighted average of increases in unit labor costs and of import prices, so

$$p = a \times (w - prod) + (1 - a) \times pm,$$

where pm is the rate of change in the import-price deflator, a is a parameter, and other variables are defined as above. Recall that the wage growth equation is

$$w = 0.65 - 0.31 \times \ln U - 0.56 \times prod + pe,$$

where pe is expected inflation. In equilibrium, when the economy has settled at its natural rate, actual and expected inflation will be the same and p can replace pe in the above equation. Now substituting the price equation into the wage equation and rearranging give an expression for wage inflation as a function of import prices, productivity, and unemployment:

$$w = [0.65 - 0.31 \times \ln U + (0.56 - a) \\ \times prod + (1 - a) \times pm] / (1 - a).$$

A necessary condition for a natural rate to be defined in an open economy, independently of the terms of trade, is that in equilibrium domestic unit (wage) cost inflation and import price inflation are proceeding at the same rate, that is, the exchange rate adjusts so as to maintain constant relative purchasing power. Then setting $w - prod = pm$ yields a relation between unemployment and productivity that can be rearranged as an expression for the natural rate of unemployment:

$$\ln U = [0.65 - (1 - 0.56) \times prod] / 0.31,$$

or

$$U = \exp \{[0.65 - (1 - 0.56) \times prod] / 0.31\}.$$

That formulation assumes that the constant in the wage equation is an exogenous element in the target growth of real wages, independent of the rate of productivity growth. On that assumption, the natural rate can be evaluated for plausible values of trend productivity.

Productivity growth in the range of 2–3 percent a year gives estimates of the natural rate of unemployment below 1 percent. (GNP per person employed grew at an average annual rate of 3.1 percent between 1973 and 1979.) No reliance can be put on these estimates in view of the badly determined constant in the wage equation. (With one standard error added to the constant, the natural unemployment rate is just over 8 percent.) Nonetheless, at historical productivity trends, the central estimate of the natural rate in 1979 is comfortably below the actual unemployment rate of 3.3 percent.

Other estimates in the literature show a tendency for the natural rate to increase during the 1970s after the terms-of-trade deterioration of 1973. The rise in the estimated natural rate has been used to argue that the supply potential of the German economy had grown more slowly than policymakers realized in 1978. The estimates in the literature are attended with the same uncertainties as the one made above. Nonetheless, estimates of the natural rate for the late 1970s generally put it just below the actual unemployment rate for 1978 and around the actual unemployment rate for 1979.[13]

In view of the impending deterioration in the terms of trade during 1979, the unemployment rate would certainly have had to be allowed to rise during the year if an increase in inflation was to be avoided. That says nothing about the position of the German economy in relation to its postulated natural rate during late 1978 (see appendix). The oil price increase would have led, at worst, to a one-time increase in the rate of inflation, given the 1979 unemployment rate; it would not have triggered an indefinitely accelerating inflation. In fact, the German authorities eventually opted to let unemployment rise in order to prevent the ratcheting up of the inflation rate and, indeed, to bring it down.

This change in policy, which was endorsed by election results, was the product of changed circumstances that contributed to changed preferences between inflation and unemployment. Nonetheless, it was perhaps natural for policymakers to justify difficult choices as being necessitated by the mistakes of predecessors. The German inflation after 1979 was not led by wages, however, as is evident from figure 2. There is nothing in the data to overturn the implications of the simulation results used above to conclude that the contribution of the post-Bonn measures to inflation was certainly small and probably negligible.

Government Debt

One effect of the fiscal policy measures implemented in 1979 and 1980 was a widening of the budget deficit. Net government borrowing had already reached 2.5 percent of GNP in 1978, which increased to 2.7 percent in 1979 despite a fall in unemployment.[14] The deficit went on to widen further as the economy went into recession, and it peaked in 1981 at nearly 4 percent of GNP. This was below the 1975 recession-induced peak of 5.7 percent, but was still viewed with concern. Public debt in Germany increased through the 1970s and on into the 1980s, only leveling off as a percentage of GNP in 1985–86 at 42.3 percent for gross public debt and 22.1 percent for net debt.

As noted above, in Germany balanced budgets or at least ostensibly sound public finances are valued for their own sake. A policy that led to an increase in a budget deficit that was already large by recent historical standards could be criticized on those grounds alone. The fiscal measures implemented after Bonn were clearly a step on the road to higher public debt. Even so, they were overshadowed as a source of public debt by the recession that followed. The deficit increased for cyclical reasons, and net public debt almost doubled between 1979, when it was 11.5 percent, and 1983, when it was 21.4 percent of GNP.

Some of the odium attaching to the Bonn episode in Germany does not pertain logically to policy coordination as such, but to a whole era of German policymaking in which the budget deficit was allowed to swell. The post-Bonn policies are seen as typical of this era. Some critics of the Bonn summit would perhaps have no objection to concerted policy involving German deflation, but they observe that German deflation is seldom if ever called for by the government of the United States.

Conclusion

In retrospect, it appears that both the significance of the Bonn summit for German macroeconomic policy and the effect on the German economy of those policies that were followed have been exaggerated. So strong is the view in Germany that the summit led to a period of disastrous expansionary policies that the myth may now prove ineradicable.

However, as Putnam and Henning show, there was majority support in Germany for fiscal measures by the time they were agreed upon at Bonn, although the summit process itself was important in mustering that support. The pattern of tax cuts earlier in the 1970s suggests that some tax relief would have occurred in Germany even without the summit, although in that case it would probably have come a year later. Indeed, some additional tax relief was passed a year later by the Bundestag. Moreover, as it happened, the easier fiscal policy coincided with tighter money, so German policy in 1979 did not move unambiguously to expansion.

The subsequent deterioration in the German current account balance was around three-quarters due to the oil price increases of 1979, and some remaining part was owing to the rise in the real value of the deutsche mark during the mid-1970s (that is, before the fiscal measures were announced). While the fiscal measures played some role, since the German current balance was not about to improve substantially in 1978, that role was small. It was nothing to worry about; on the contrary, it was a useful, if marginal, contribution to less unbalanced current account positions among OECD countries. The contribution of the fiscal measures to inflation was modest, perhaps half a percentage point a year. Taking monetary policy into account, German policy was disinflationary throughout 1979.

On the other hand, there is little or no evidence that the fiscal measures adopted after Bonn would have put the German economy on a durably higher or faster growth path in the absence of the oil price rises. There was some pickup in domestic demand, but how long it would have been sustained is unclear. The current generation of economic models implies that the effect of aggregate fiscal policy is short-lived if monetary policy does not accommodate it.

Fiscal policy can have more durable effects if it raises (or lowers) the level of investment and thereby contributes to a larger (or smaller) stock of productive capital. There was a modest increase in the ratio of investment to GNP in 1979. That increase was largely consistent with historical cyclical patterns; the same investment ratio was achieved in 1986, for example. The effect of the fiscal measures on investment remains uncertain. There is some faint circumstantial evidence that the boost to demand raised investment on balance, but the effect does not seem to have been overwhelming.

The 1978 Bonn summit has acquired a totemic significance in a broader debate in Germany about macroeconomic policy, which, in particular, compares the Social Democratic policies of the 1970s with the Christian Democratic policies of the 1980s. The weight of current opinion favors the latter approach. That debate raises issues not discussed in this chapter. On the narrower issue of the effect of the German post-Bonn policy measures, however, it is possible to conclude that the fiscal measures are simply not responsible for the evils attributed to them.

Appendix: The Natural Rate of Unemployment

There is some semantic confusion attaching to the term *natural rate of unemployment* and the term *NAIRU* (nonaccelerating inflation rate of unemployment), which is sometimes used as a synonym. It is worth clearing up. The natural rate of unemployment, as defined by Friedman, is a general equilibrium concept reflecting all the structural characteristics of labor and commodity markets.[15] In a wide class of economic models, so long as wage earners do not suffer from money illusion, there is a unique natural rate; it is the only unemployment rate consistent with stable inflation.

The economic literature sometimes suggests that the natural rate can be altered by terms-of-trade effects or changes in the rate of productivity growth. Yet, while these can alter either the price level or the rate of inflation, it is not clear they could cause inflation to accelerate indefinitely. The term *NAIRU* therefore has a systematic ambiguity. Is it synonymous with the natural rate, meaning the only unemployment rate at which inflation does not accelerate (or decelerate) without limit, or does it have a shorter-term connotation, meaning simply the unemployment rate that has to be maintained at any time to stop inflation from accelerating in a limited sense? This sort of NAIRU can be defined even if there is no unique natural rate; if the Phillips curve (the relation between nominal wage growth and unemployment) is not vertical and shifts owing to terms-of-trade effects, for example, it will be necessary to change the unemployment rate to maintain inflation unchanged (that is, to move along the curve to compensate for a shift in the curve).

As the German terms of trade deteriorated markedly in 1979 with the oil price increase, domestic inflation was bound to increase. If that was to be resisted at all costs, the only dependable means of doing so was to create unemployment. However, that does not mean the German natural rate had increased. If, for the sake of argument, German unemployment was supposed to have been at its natural rate in 1978 and had been maintained there, there would have been a surge in German inflation, but this would eventually have stabilized. An explicit aim of policy during and after 1979 was to prevent the inflation surge from becoming built in to the wage-price formation process. In other words, policy was aimed at preventing any permanent increase in inflation, so unemployment was allowed to rise. That had nothing to do with any increase in the natural rate. No worthwhile evidence has been adduced for an increase in the natural rate, strictly speaking, at that time.

The subsequent failure of German unemployment to fall back to 1978 levels, even though inflation is now below 1978 rates, casts considerable doubt on the stability of any natural rate or the operational usefulness of the concept. However, that is another issue.

Notes

1. The list of fiscal measures carried out after the Bonn summit is taken from various issues of the *OECD Economic Surveys: Germany*.

2. The German tax system in the late 1970s is described in *OECD Economic Surveys: Germany* (June 1982), pp. 29–45. See also *Income Tax Schedules: Distribution of Tax Payers and Revenues*, OECD Studies in Taxation (Paris, July 1981); and Annette Dengel, "The Tax System of the Federal Republic of Germany," Brookings Discussion Papers in Economics, April 1986.

3. The thinking behind the Bonn summit measures has been ascribed to a "locomotive" theory, whereby Germany and Japan towed other countries to economic growth. However, "convoy" was the preferred metaphor of the OECD secretariat; German expansion was supposed to relieve the external balance constraint on its trade partners, allowing them also to expand domestic demand (albeit by less than Germany), rather than just relying on a German locomotive. See John Llewellyn, Stephen Potter, and Lee Samuelson, *Economic Forecasting and Policy: The International Dimension* (London: Routledge & Kegan Paul, 1985), pp. 244–45.

4. See Paul N. Courant, "Fiscal Policy and European Economic Growth"

in Robert Z. Lawrence and Charles L. Schultze, eds., *Barriers to European Growth: A Transatlantic View* (Brookings, 1987), p. 439.

5. An argument has been made that the private sector does not increase consumption in such circumstances because it realizes that the government must increase taxes in the future to recoup the deficit and thus private households must increase savings to meet future tax liabilities. This means there is no increase in domestic demand as a result of tax cuts. See Robert J. Barro, "Are Government Bonds Net Wealth?" *Journal of Political Economy*, vol. 82 (November 1974), pp. 1095–1117. Another argument has been made, that private households will respond to lower marginal tax rates by increasing work effort and saving so that the economy will receive a supply-side boost. My interpretation of the evidence for Germany and elsewhere is that both effects are negligibly small for tax cuts in the range being discussed.

6. See Gerald H. Holtham and Hiromi Kato, "Wealth and Inflation Effects in the Aggregate Consumption Function," OECD Economics and Statistics Department Working Paper no. 35 (Paris, July 1986).

7. See Llewellyn, Potter, and Samuelson, *Economic Forecasting and Policy*, p. 248.

8. An exaggerated impression of the rise in the investment share is obtained by looking at it at current prices. Total fixed capital formation as a proportion of GNP rose from 20.6 percent at current prices in 1978 to 21.7 percent in 1979 and 22.6 percent in 1980; in 1986 it was at 19.3 percent. The same proportions at constant 1980 prices are 21.6 percent in 1978, 22.3 percent in 1979, 22.6 percent in 1980, and 20 percent in 1986. See *OECD Economic Surveys: Germany* (July 1987), pp. 75, 77. The relative price of investment goods appears to have been correlated with the price of oil.

9. The dynamic multipliers of an econometric model may be thought of as embodying the coefficients of the final-form equations relating the exogenous to the endogenous variables in the model. These coefficients can be recovered from simulation results if the model is (approximately) linear. This is set out by Ralph C. Bryant, Dale W. Henderson, and Steven A. Symansky in "Estimates of the Consequences of Policy Actions Derived from Model Simulations," in Bryant and others, eds., *Macroeconomics for Interdependent Economies* (Brookings, 1988), pp. 63–91. Recovery of the coefficients is particularly simple in the case of the Bundesbank simulations of table 6 as they refer to single, sustained shocks in the forcing policy variables.

10. In Bryant and others, *Macroeconomics for Interdependent Economies*, supplemental volume, model results are quoted for the effects on German output and inflation of a fiscal stimulus in a number of countries. None are strictly comparable with the results in table 6. The U.S. Federal Reserve Board's MCM model (1986 vintage) gives a multiplier for German GNP of 1.3 in the first year that rises to a peak of 1.7 in the second year, following a government expenditure stimulus equal to 1 percent of baseline GNP occurring simultaneously in Germany, Japan, the United Kingdom, and Canada. The consumer price index is 0.1 percentage points above baseline in the year of the shock, rising steadily to 2.2 percentage points above baseline five years later (an average inflation increase of less than half a percentage point). Given the large

share of exports in the German GNP, the simulated foreign fiscal stimuli contributed substantially to the higher multipliers compared with the Bundesbank results. Nonetheless, the effects of fiscal stimulus on the German GNP appear to be longer-lived in the MCM model. In that respect, the OECD INTERLINK model, vintage 1986, is intermediate between the MCM and the Bundesbank model.

11. Such price elasticities are certainly lower than the average in the econometric literature. See, for example, James M. Boughton and others, "Effects of Exchange Rate Changes in Industrial Countries," *Staff Studies for the World Economic Outlook* (Washington: International Monetary Fund, July 1986), p. 123.

12. Semiannual data, estimated for 1964:1 to 1979:1. Equation estimated by two-stage least squares; bracketed numbers are standard errors of parameter estimates. The specification follows that in James Chan-Lee, David T. Coe, and Menahem Prywes, "Microeconomic Changes and Macroeconomic Wage Disinflation in the 1980s," *OECD Economic Studies*, no. 8 (Spring 1987), pp. 121–57. They report results of an identical equation estimated to 1985:2 following a standard specification search.

13. Other estimates of the natural rate (or NAIRU) for this period are given in the *OECD Economic Outlook*, no. 40 (December 1986), p. 30; and in Olivier Blanchard, Rudiger Dornbusch, and Richard Layard, eds., *Restoring Europe's Prosperity: Microeconomic Papers from the Centre for European Policy Studies* (MIT Press, 1986). The respective estimates were for NAIRUs in Germany in the late 1970s of 3.1 percent and 3.5 percent. However, the OECD estimate is of a shorter-run NAIRU that does not abstract from terms-of-trade changes. Michael C. Burda and Jeffrey D. Sachs, in "Institutional Aspects of High Unemployment in the Federal Republic of Germany," Working Paper 2241 (Cambridge, Mass.: National Bureau of Economic Research, May 1987), report a marked rise in the estimated German NAIRU between the late 1970s and the mid-1980s.

14. The increase in the deficit, against the cycle, indicates that the cyclically adjusted or "structural" deficit increased. Estimates of changes in the structural deficit are given in Patrice Muller and Robert W. R. Price, "Structural Budget Deficits and Fiscal Stance," OECD Economics and Statistics Department Working Paper no. 15 (Paris, July 1984). Between 1973 and 1979, there was an increase in the structural deficit in Germany equal to 2.7 percent of GDP. Between 1980 and 1985, the structural deficit moved back toward surplus by an extent equal to 4 percent of GDP. Economic performance over the two periods is compared in Gerald Holtham, "Foreign Responses to U.S. Macroeconomic Policies," in Bryant and others, *Empirical Macroeconomics*, pp. 267–84.

15. See Milton Friedman, "The Role of Monetary Policy," *American Economic Review*, vol. 52 (March 1968), pp. 1–17.

International Cooperation in Public Health as a Prologue to Macroeconomic Cooperation

RICHARD N. COOPER

T HIS PAPER IS ABOUT THE HISTORY of international cooperation in public health, in particular international efforts to control the spread of contagious diseases in the nineteenth and early twentieth centuries. At first or even second glance that may appear to be a peculiar topic for an economist to address. I was drawn to the topic, however, while puzzling over the great difficulty in achieving cooperation among major countries in framing and managing their macroeconomic policies in the late twentieth century.

The world has become more interdependent. Extensive exchange of goods, services, and assets takes place among residents of different countries. This development makes more difficult the pursuit of economic policy on a purely national basis. At a minimum, governments must take into account "leakages" abroad, diluting the domestic effects of their actions. But leakages of one country can be disturbances to another, so each country must take into account possible compensatory or offsetting actions other governments may take. If one central bank tightens credit conditions, will that evoke an inflow of capital from abroad, thus possibly weakening domestic actions? But might that in turn induce some tightening action abroad, thus restoring some efficacy to the domestic actions? If one country engages in fiscal expansion to reduce unemployment, in a highly open economy some of the enlarged demand will leak abroad as demand for imports, weakening the impact of the action on home employment. It will also stimulate demand abroad, thus encouraging exports. If that is unwelcome abroad, will other governments tighten their fiscal stance and thereby weaken further the desired domestic effects? And when there is a global disturbance, such as a sharp increase in oil prices, how one country should best respond depends closely on how other major

I am grateful to David Hall for his extremely valuable research assistance.

countries respond. Overcoming world recessionary tendencies is potentially easier if many countries act together.

It is not surprising, then, that as countries have become more economically interdependent, the calls for economic cooperation, and even coordination of economic policy actions, have increased in number and intensity. During the deep 1982 world recession, for instance, a conference of twenty-six economists from the major countries urged a concerted program of expansion. A few months later former German Chancellor Helmut Schmidt made a similar suggestion.[1] More recently, thirty-three economists from an even wider geographic representation urged fiscal contraction by the United States, combined with fiscal expansion in Europe and Japan, to help correct large global imbalances yet avoid a world recession and ameliorate the economic difficulties of debt-ridden developing countries.[2]

Despite the almost commonplace calls for more international economic cooperation, there are few examples of coordinated macroeconomic policy actions. Among them are the coordinated reduction of interest rates agreed at Checquers (England) in 1967, the Plaza accord of 1985 on the need for a depreciation of the dollar, and, less convincingly, the Louvre accord of 1987 that attempted both to stabilize exchange rates and to encourage coordination of macroeconomic actions, but broke down before year-end and in any case did not contain operational commitments. Of the various attempts at macroeconomic coordination, the Bonn economic summit of 1978 stands out for the range and specificity of the commitments and for the follow-through.

Why is international economic cooperation of this type so rare? Is there something about *international* cooperation that makes it peculiarly difficult? This question prompted me to ask whether there were any areas where international cooperation occurred successfully, beyond such obvious areas as international air traffic control or postal exchange. There are, it turns out, many such areas, most quite technical in nature. None is quite so pervasive in its impact, nor has achieved so much, as international cooperation in public health. In proper historical perspective, the eradication of smallpox will be recorded as one of the two outstanding practical achievements—along with the splitting of the atom—of the twentieth century. And it was an international endeavor par excellence, merely more dramatic than other activities that are routinely coordinated internationally in matters of public health. It is now taken for granted that a system exists for monitoring outbreaks of contagious disease and limiting their spread and that one can get needed pharmaceuticals of known potency in any of the world's leading cities.

How did this extensive system of cooperation, so obvious on reflection, come about? And what if anything can that evolution tell one about international cooperation in other areas, particularly macroeconomic management? To many the self-evident answer is that macroeconomic management is a much more complicated matter, both in objectives and substance, than public health—particularly public health that is focused on infectious disease. But that turns out to be a decidedly late twentieth century view. Mainline international cooperation in public health is not controversial today, although extension to new activities such as mental health or family planning often is still controversial. But it took over half a century from the first call, by a French official in the 1830s, for international cooperation in inhibiting the spread of dreaded diseases to the time when the first tentative steps in that direction were agreed to and implemented in the 1890s, and another half century to get the existing organizational structure. In view of these long delays, the question really needs to be turned around: why did it take so long to achieve effective international cooperation in an area so apparently uncontroversial as control of the spread of contagious disease? And what lessons does that experience have for cooperation in other areas? As I will discuss, there are many forms of international cooperation, starting simply with the exchange of accurate and timely information. Coordinated national actions involve a much more ambitious form of international cooperation. By the late twentieth century public health has experienced a wide range of cooperation, including jointly financed joint action.

In the following pages I attempt to describe, without offering a comprehensive history, the major elements—including obstacles and false starts—in the evolution of international cooperation in public health, in the thought that this story may contain useful lessons for other areas of international cooperation. The story involves a complex interplay among epidemics of disease, public actions in response to them, diplomacy, commercial and other economic interests, and the advance of both scientific and practical knowledge.

The dominant theme that emerges is that there is more than one plausible explanation for any slightly mysterious phenomenon (such as the arrival and spread of cholera or yellow fever), that these contending plausible explanations often have radically different implications for public action, and that societies are reluctant to undertake costly or even merely inconvenient actions on the basis of contending theories of uncertain merit. Thus international consensus about practical knowledge, along with shared objectives, is a necessary condition for close international cooperation. That consensus was absent in the matter of epidemic disease until around 1900, and it is absent in macroeconomic analysis today. So long as costs are positive and benefits are uncertain, countries are not likely to cooperate systematically with one another; and so long as sharply differing views are held on the relationship between actions and outcomes, at least some parties will question the benefits alleged to flow from any particular proposed course of action.

The bulk of this paper is about the fumbling process by which the world reached its present comprehensive system of international cooperation in public health. I briefly describe the current system and contrast it with the situation that existed one and a half to two centuries ago, when each nation or city dealt with threats from disease as it saw fit at the time, with what are now known to be irrational action and heavy costs. The arrival of cholera in Europe triggered both local and international efforts to contain the spread of epidemic disease, which gradually led to the faltering, but ultimately successful, establishment of a cooperative system of public health. This system rested not only on shared objectives—containment of disease—but also on a common understanding of how the disease is propagated and what practical action can be taken to impede its propagation. I draw parallels between the fascinating but discouraging history of attempts at international cooperation in public health after 1850 and the evolution of international cooperation in macroeconomic management since 1920. The paper concludes by portraying the continuing disagreements on the causes of economic fluctuations as perhaps the major impediment to closer international macroeconomic cooperation.

The Present and the Distant Past

Two major international organizations currently participate actively in fostering international cooperation in public health and the containment of communicable diseases. The World Health Organization (WHO) is headquartered in Geneva and has global responsibility, as a technical arm of the United Nations, with more than 150 member nations. The Pan American Health Organization (PAHO), headquartered in Washington, is older than WHO and acts as its regional arm in the Western hemisphere, but has a legally autonomous existence and undertakes some of its own programs, unconnected with WHO.

In the early 1980s WHO had a biennial budget of about $500 million, augmented by $490 million in funds for special projects. PAHO has its own budget of about $150 million, of which about one-third comes from WHO. The United States provides about 20 percent of the WHO funds.

These organizations perform a variety of functions. They collect, compile, and report information on cases of communicable diseases. This is the earliest function of international collaboration on public health matters and will be discussed further below. They disseminate new scientific and technical information arising from medical research. They help train medical and public health auxiliaries and professionals, providing fellowships and financing training facilities. They provide technical assistance for medical research and for public health planning and management. In addition to these service functions, they carry out actual projects, usually financed outside their normal budgets. They have helped improve water and sanitation facilities in developing countries. They have fostered disease control or even eradication, as in the cases of malaria and smallpox. They have participated in large-scale immunization projects and in the control of diarrheal diseases and animal diseases in order to improve protein production or reduce transmission of diseases to people. Finally, they help organize and disseminate medical disaster relief.

As a result of these organizations' multifarious activities, people can travel around the world with fewer arbitrary impediments imposed by national health authorities. Travelers who have been exposed to infectious diseases are quarantined under internationally agreed standards. Pharmaceuticals are subject to standard measurements of potency (but not common standards of national acceptability or safety). There are standard guidelines for the disinfection of disease-contaminated ships or aircraft.

Many areas formerly visited by yellow fever, malaria, cholera, and plague are now free of these diseases. Most of the work was performed by national public health authorities, but without international cooperation it would have been difficult to avoid reintroduction of these diseases to areas that were cleared of them. The crowning achievement of international efforts at disease eradication was the elimination of smallpox in 1977. All this activity goes on at a low level of public attention, and except for the inevitable debate over new programs it occurs more or less automatically. It has been built into the system of world management, so to speak.

The Plague and Its Consequences

It was not always so. Two centuries ago, some dreaded diseases, such as smallpox and typhus, were endemic in Europe. In 1775, 95 percent of the European population had already contracted or could expect to contract smallpox, and one-seventh of the cases were fatal.[3] Disease, possibly fatal, was a part of life, making daily existence uncertain and frightening. But what was really terrifying was the sudden visitation of epidemic plague, often with some advance warning as the news traveled slightly faster than the plague itself. The onset of plague is characterized by sudden fever, chills, vomiting, diarrhea, and swelling of the lymph glands ("buboes") in the groin and armpits—hence the term "bubonic plague." In severe cases hemorrhaging occurs below the skin, which darkens before death, hence the "black death." Once the plague arrived in a city, it could often sweep away a substantial portion of the population. The plague of 1630–31 killed 24 percent of the population of Bologna, 33 percent of Venice, 46 percent of Milan, and 61 percent of Verona. The death toll amounted to 154,000 in these four cities alone.[4] The plague returned a quarter of a century later and in 1656–57 took away 19 percent of the population of Rome, 50 percent of Naples, and 60 percent of Genoa—218,000 in these three cities.

The responses to the arrival of the plague were various: If one could afford it, one could escape from the city to the clean airs of the countryside; one could pray for redemption; and one could be sequestered by the public health authorities if in any way thought to be exposed to the plague. There was much tension among the remedies. A prevalent view, promulgated by priests and ministers, was that the plague was the wrath of God visited on the unworthy, the sinful, and the depraved. But that did not prevent people from trying to escape from the city on the commonsense view that, God's omnipresence notwithstanding, proximity to sick people—and to bad airs—was not conducive to good health. Cities often emptied at the prospect of the plague.

Local public health authorities were given wide powers once a plague was in prospect. They often banned assembly of any kind, including church services, leading to substantial friction between the health authorities and the clergy, who were beyond the reach of the secular authorities but prompted large prayer meetings to deal with the plague. On at least one occasion this led to a strange mass in which the priests officiated while the participants stayed home. The public health authorities also often attempted to prevent people from leaving the city once the plague had actually arrived, by placing a cordon sanitaire around it. Defoe describes how those who had left plague-ridden London encountered hostile reactions from villagers, who often closed the roads through their villages. Special pesthouses were created in the larger cities, where the diseased were often interred for lengthy periods. In addition, whenever a member of a private household was stricken by the plague, the house was locked up by the public authorities with its inhabitants inside and put under watch for at least twenty-eight days.[5]

Given the high costs and personal tragedy associated with plague, there were high benefits to its prevention. How could that be done? The economic historian Carlo Cipolla describes the prevalent view of the etiology of plague in the seventeenth century:

The basic, predominant idea was that it originated from venomous atoms. Whether generated by rotting matter or emanating from infected persons, animals, or objects, the venomous atoms would infect salubrious air and make it miasmatic—that is, poisonous. It was indeed the corruption of the air that, according to the doctors of the renaissance, was the basic precondition for the outbreak of an epidemic of plague. Besides being deadly poisonous, the nasty atoms . . . would "stick" to inanimate objects, animals, and human beings in the same way that perfumes and foul odors permeate fabrics and other materials. When inhaled or absorbed through the pores of the skin by a person or by an animal, the venomous atoms would poison the body, cause infirmity and, owing to their extreme malignancy, in most cases would bring death. By direct contact or inhalation the atoms actually pass from one object to another, from one person to the next, from one object or an animal to a person and vice versa. It logically followed that the only way to avoid the spreading of the disease was to stop all intercourse with people, animals, and objects coming from areas afflicted by the plague.[6]

A nearly contemporary account of the 1665 London plague puts the point slightly differently, but with the same ultimate implication.

The calamity was spread by infection; that is to say, by some certain steams or fumes, which the physicians call effluvia, by the breath or by the sweat or by the stench of the sores of the sick persons or some other way, perhaps beyond even the reach of the physicians themselves, which effluvia affected the sound, who came within certain distances of the sick, immediately penetrating the vital parts of the said sound persons, putting their blood into an immediate ferment, and agitating their spirits to that degree which it was found they were agitated; and so those newly infected persons communicated it in the same manner to others.[7]

Since the plague would often suddenly appear in a town or city after a prolonged period in which there had been no cases, that suggested to contemporaries it was transmitted by travelers, particularly by ships. As far back as the thirteenth century Venice had established a forty-day period of isolation for foreign ships before allowing their crew or goods to enter the city without restriction. Hence the introduction of the "quarantine," said to be based on the length of time Moses had remained in isolation in the desert.[8] This system was introduced primarily to prevent introduction of the plague from the Middle East, and it was imitated by other seaports of the Mediterranean and later the Atlantic. In 1423 Venice established its first lazaretto, or quarantine station, where the passengers, crew, and goods of ships that did not have clean bills of health or had come from infected areas could be lodged for the requisite period. Quarantine could be avoided and free pratique obtained if the ship had a clean bill of health, an official document from the last port of call stating that the port was free of contagious diseases.

Quarantine regulations were taken very seriously. If ships' ports of origin were clearly infected, the ships could be denied entry altogether and sent on their way. Suspect goods were often burned. Penalties for avoiding quarantine requirements were severe: it was typically a capital offense. This not only disturbed trade, but also sometimes led to war.

In 1781 a plague-infected Venetian ship arrived at Malta. Most of the crew had died and the sailor still on board was very ill. Malta's health council met and decided to care for the diseased sailor in isolation; the doctor assigned was adequately compensated but had to agree to serve a quarantine of eighty days. The ship and its goods were towed to the open sea and set on fire. The owners of the merchandise were subjects of the bey of Tunis and claimed compensation for their cargo. Neither Malta or Venice would agree to compensation, so the bey declared war on Venice and captured fourteen Venetian ships. The combined fleets of Venice and Malta could not breach the defenses of Tunis and eventually compensation was paid.

Strong quarantine measures were continued into the nineteenth century. In the 1820s if a plague-stricken ship entered Malta the ship was emptied of her cargo and her hatches were opened to allow fresh air into the interior. Plague-stricken persons were transferred to a hospital for treatment while the rest of the passengers and crew were divided into small groups and sent to the lazaretto, where they were given a fresh set of clothing after they had been thoroughly washed with vinegar and water. If after a fortnight no fresh cases of plague appeared, the passengers and crew were collected together to spend another forty days in isolation from others. The ship was washed with lime, painted, and disinfected with fumigations of various kinds.[9] Papers and letters arriving by ship had to be fumigated and sometimes dosed in vinegar, and even the bill of health and oath by the captain that there were no diseased persons on board were taken from the ship with long tongs and dosed in vinegar before they were read by the local public health authorities.

Obviously such measures represented a real burden to travel and commerce. They involved what is now known to be greatly excessive costs.[10] Today both persons and goods move relatively freely across national boundaries, subject to quarantine requirements and (for some goods) prohibitions that are precise and pose little burden on travel and commerce. But it was an indication both of the concern about the spread of infectious diseases and the ignorance about the etiology of those diseases that these measures of quarantine were so severe and so widespread.

It is difficult these days to appreciate the range of emotion from deep anxiety to sheer terror created by the arrival of total disease: some perhaps can remember similar emotions evoked by polio epidemics in the early 1950s, or by the terrifying mystery that surrounded the arrival of AIDS in the early 1980s.

The Arrival of Cholera in Europe

By the end of the nineteenth century many efforts at international collaboration in the control of infectious disease had begun. The immediate provocation was the arrival of cholera in Europe. This Asian disease struck devastatingly on five major occasions between 1830 and 1894. Since the disease "obviously"—or so it seemed to many, although that too was at first disputed—came from afar, particularly from India, it seemed desirable to cooperate in inhibiting or preferably preventing its spread. As a result, twelve International Sanitary Conferences were held between 1851 and 1912. The existence of these international conferences reflected a view that there was a distinctive role that international cooperation could play in containing disease. The sharp disagreements and lack of results at most of the conferences reflected the difficulty of achieving international cooperation even for such a widely shared objective as limiting the spread of virulent and often fatal disease.

Cholera broke out of the confines of India in 1818 and moved successively—perhaps carried in part by British soldiers or their servants—through southeast Asia and into China and Japan, across the Arabian Sea to East Africa, and up through the Middle East to Syria and Palestine, reaching southern Russia near the Caspian Sea by 1822. There it stopped, but only after infecting for the first time in memory much of the inhabited world.[11]

Cholera broke out of India again in 1826. It reached eastern Russia by 1827 and despite extensive quarantine measures all of Russia's major cities had been stricken by 1831. Russian troops carried cholera to Poland, whence it moved to Germany, Hungary, and Austria; and by 1832 it had reached Paris. Simultaneously it moved into the Middle East and was spread by returning Moslem pilgrims to Egypt and along the coast of North Africa.

A ship from Hamburg brought cholera to England in October 1831, whence it spread to Scotland and Ireland and then across the Atlantic to Montreal and Quebec in June 1832. It reached London in February 1832 and New York in June 1832. Rarely has the arrival of a disease been so widely heralded, with weekly accounts of its progress in the cheap newspapers of the days. An estimated one-third of New York's population (70,000 out of 200,000) fled from the city. From New York and New Orleans, another port of entry, cholera moved both west and up the Mississippi valley and by 1833 reached the Pacific coast, having infected a number of Indian tribes on the way. It also spread south through Mexico, where it stopped in 1834, but only after killing a minimum of 10,332 people in Mexico City, out of at least 48,000 who contracted it.[12]

As cholera approached European cities, intensive efforts were made both to provide special hospitals or other places of seclusion for the stricken and to clean up the filth that adorned the typical concentrated urban area of the early nineteenth century. These actions represented responses suggested by the two contending medical theories concerning the propagation of cholera (of which more will be said below). Together they must have had some effect, for the actual death toll from cholera in London in 1832–33 was about 7,000, compared with around 60,000 deaths in the Great Plague of 1665–66, in a city that had become slightly larger in the intervening century and a half. But the preventive actions were nonetheless controversial. In Britain the quarantine and disinfectant regulations were seen as an intrusion on individual liberty, and in Paris the attempt to clean up the streets provoked riots among ragpickers and vagabonds as a threat to their livelihood.[13] Furthermore, since cholera was so little understood, and since its incidence fell heavily on the poorest and most congested members of urban society, the suspicion was raised that these people were being deliberately poisoned.

The symptoms of cholera are especially gruesome, and its only saving grace is that death, if it comes, comes relatively quickly, sometimes after only two or three hours. A marked aging and discoloration occurs during this time, as death is produced by massive dehydration of the soft tissues. The mortality rate varied considerably with the condition of the patient—some cases were even mild—but generally ran around one-third. The terror created by cholera is captured well by McNeill:

> Once swallowed, if the cholera bacillus survives the stomach juices, it is capable of swift multiplication in the human alimentary tract, and produces violent and dramatic symptoms—diarrhea, vomiting, fever, and death, often within a few hours of the first signs of illness. The speed with which cholera killed was profoundly alarming, since perfectly healthy people could never

feel safe from sudden death when the infection was anywhere near. In addition, the symptoms were peculiarly horrible: radical dehydration meant that a victim shrank into a wizened caricature of his former self within a few hours, while ruptured capillaries discolored the skin, turning it black and blue. The effect was to make mortality uniquely visible; patterns of bodily decay were exacerbated and accelerated, as in a time-lapse motion picture, to remind all who saw it of death's ugly horror and utter inevitability.[14]

The propagation of cholera was mysterious and remained a source of controversy for the rest of the nineteenth century. Some held, even as late as mid-century, that its source was divine and meant to serve as a lesson and a warning. Most medical circles, however, focused their debate on whether cholera was contagious (that is, whether it could be transmitted from one sick person to another person), or whether it was due to miasma, a condition of the ground or atmosphere that was conducive to illness. Thus two broad "scientific" schools of thought developed, with countless shadings and compromises in between. The contagionist school concentrated its social therapeutic efforts on isolating those who were sick and the persons and objects they had contacted. The miasmatists, in contrast, thought quarantine would offer no help at all since the disease was not contagious, and instead concentrated on cleaning up the urban environment, the filth on the streets and in the basements, which seemed empirically to be associated with outbreaks of cholera. Neither school of thought was wholly right or wholly wrong, and while in the end the contagionists were closer to being right on the theory, the miasmatists probably did more useful work through most of the century to contain the disease.

But this is getting ahead of the story. As noted above, the plague had brought about widespread quarantine regulations for ships and their passengers and cargo. Yet they differed substantially from place to place and were also redundant when taken together. When cholera arrived in Europe these quarantine requirements stiffened (especially in the Mediterranean, as cholera moved north and west before reaching many Mediterranean ports). In 1834 the secretary to the Higher Council of Health of France pointed to the needless difficulties imposed on commerce by these diverse quarantine restrictions and urged the French government to call an international conference to standardize the measures to prevent the spread of exotic diseases.[15] This appeal failed, but was renewed in 1850 after a second major cholera epidemic reached Western Europe and North America in 1848–49.

In Britain, where systematic records on the reasons for death had begun to be kept in the late 1830s, 53,293 persons died of cholera in 1848–49, a figure that was negligible compared with the cholera deaths in Russia. As the cholera epidemic swept north and west in 1830–31, Russian cities had taken elaborate precautions to prevent the spread of the disease, and even so an estimated 290,000 Russians had died of cholera. As a result the Russians concluded that quarantine measures had little effect, and declined to take them as the disease again made its way through Russia starting in late 1846. This time an estimated 880,000 Russians died.[16]

British Sanitary Reform

The situation was somewhat different in Britain. A great "reform movement" started with the Reform Act of 1832 and permeated many aspects of British social life, including prisons, child care, welfare, and public health. These issues had their origins in the eighteenth century, especially in John Howard's work on life in prisons, including "jail fever" (probably typhus) and other diseases. By the 1830s a new impetus to reform was given by the development of the factory system and the need for healthy industrial workers. For centuries there had been a flow of migrants into the great cities of Europe, but the cities, with their destitution and disease, were centers of death and their "natural" population growth was negative. It has been estimated that throughout the eighteenth century deaths in London exceeded births by an average of 6,000 a year, so the city needed constant replenishment from the countryside.[17] Unless death was quick, as with cholera, it was preceded by a prolonged period of sickness and debilitation. This chronic condition could not provide the basis for a vigorous and flexible urban labor force.

Edwin Chadwick, a disciple of Jeremy Benthem, headed a Royal Commission on the Poor Laws in 1832. The Elizabethan poor law had remanded the poor to the charge of each parish, of which there were about 15,000 in the early nineteenth century, with a total cost of 8 million pounds for maintaining the poor. This system of responsibility for the poor and vagrants discouraged labor mobility within Britain. Chadwick's commission recommended that the national government absorb some financial responsibility for the maintenance of the poor, but that the able-bodied poor should be required to work in work-houses to be established. This report provided the basis of the new poor law of 1834.

Chadwick's interest in public health and its effects on the working population was sharpened in this effort, and for some years he encouraged greater action—including the all-important collection of relevant data, such as the cause of death—germane to public health. "Fever"—probably an undifferentiated mixture of typhus, typhoid, and relapsing fever—was a common source of absence from the workplace and of death. A series of surveys pertaining to health and sanitary questions in London were undertaken by the Poor Law Commission.

In 1839 the government asked the commission to examine the health of the working population of England and Wales, later extended also to Scotland. In 1842 the *Report on an Inquiry into the Sanitary Condition of the Labouring Population of Great Britain*, in large measure the work of Chadwick, was published. George Rosen, the historian of public health, has called it "the fundamental document of modern public health."[18] It details vividly prevailing conditions, district by district, and relates them to mortality and to economic status. The *Report* presented a clear statement of the miasmatic theory of disease, which was said to be caused by miasmas arising from decaying animal and vegetable matter.

> The defects which are most important and which come most immediately within practical legislative and administrative control are those chiefly external to the dwellings of the population and principally arise from the neglect of drainage. . . . The great preventatives, drainage, street and house cleaning by means of supplies of water and improved sewerage, and especially the introduction of cheaper and more efficient modes of removing all noxious refuse from the towns, are operations for which aid must be sought from the science of the Civil Engineer, not from the physician.[19]

Thus the emphasis of effort in health matters was shifted from the physician to the engineer, from actions that impinged on persons to those that impinged on property. This report laid down the basic principles that governed sanitary reform and public health action both in Britain and, with a lag, in the United States for the next half century. It required extensive public works, and that in turn required an adequate level of economic development to support the required taxation. But the advocates of sanitary reform argued that the forgone productive effect, the costs of medical care, the costs of burial, and the costs of welfare for widows and children of men carried away by epidemic disease greatly exceeded the costs of taking the required preventive measures.[20]

The Chadwick report led directly to the establishment of a royal commission, which recommended in 1845 the passage of legislation that would centralize nationally the authority for regulating sanitary conditions in large urban communities. Opposition and unrelated events stalled the proposal, but the approach of cholera across Europe in 1848 led finally to the passage of the Public Health Act in August of that year. It created a General Board of Health, which was empowered to establish local boards in response either to petitions by 10 percent of the taxpayers or when mortality exceeded 23 per 1,000 over a period of seven years (data had been collected systematically since 1837). Local boards could in turn deal authoritatively with water supply, sewerage, control of offensive trades, provision and regulation of cemeteries, and other relevant matters.[21]

The Public Health Act was limited to a trial period. The board, under Chadwick's enthusiasm and drive, did its work so vigorously and aggressively that while deaths from cholera and other diseases were reduced in the areas covered, many enemies were created, and it was allowed to expire in 1854. *The Times*, which had supported the original act, reflected a more general sentiment when it observed that "Mr. Chadwick and Dr. Southwood Smith have been deposed, and we prefer to take our chance with cholera [which hit mainly the poor rather than the propertied classes] and the rest than be bullied into health."[22]

The urgency of the problem was less in the United States only because urban congestion was somewhat lower than in Britain. But it grew as immigration accelerated in the 1840s. John Griscom published *The Sanitary Condition of the Laboring Population of New York* in 1845. In 1850 Lemuel Shattuck issued his famous report in Massachusetts, in which at one shot he made recommendations that presaged later enactments of housing codes, food and drug regulation, weather observation (as a guide to epidemics), urban renewal, vaccination requirements, quarantine, clean air regulations, and health education as well as improvements in water and sewerage.[23] But the immediate effect was negligible and it took the cholera epidemic of

1865 and the yellow fever epidemic of 1878 to jolt the Americans into action.

First Efforts toward International Cooperation

Governments are rarely mobilized to action on the basis of hypothetical forecasts and a priori reasoning. It usually takes an actual crisis, possibly a minor disaster, followed by public calls for action. Accordingly, it took a second cholera epidemic, in 1848–89, and the resulting tightening of quarantines, to jolt the Europeans into an attempt at collaborative action. For years the French government had called for a meeting of the maritime powers on the vexing question of the efficacy of quarantine, and at last a conference convened in Paris in July 1851. It was to be merely the first of twelve International Sanitary Conferences, as they came to be called, between then and World War I (see table 1 for a list of the conferences from 1851 to 1938).

The First Two International Sanitary Conferences

The French government called the 1851 conference with the seemingly narrow stated objective "to regulate in a uniform way the quarantines and lazarettos in the Mediterranean." In fact it put a somewhat wider range of issues to the conference:

> Is cholera contagious? Are quarantine regulations against this disease necessary for public safety? In cases of plague, is it safe to adopt the system practiced by Austria of allowing the quarantine to commence from the date of the sailing of the vessel from its last port, instead of that of arrival at its port of destination? Is it advisable to form a general sanitary board representing all the maritime powers, and to appoint for each port where a quarantine shall exist a medical officer of health who shall represent not merely the country in which he resides but all the maritime powers, and whose declaration shall be conclusive, unless it be set aside by the decision of the board on the remonstrances to which it shall give rise?[24]

Twelve states attended the conference: Austria, France, Great Britain, Greece, the Papal states, Portugal, Russia, Sardinia, Spain, Turkey,

TABLE 1. *International Sanitary Conferences, 1851–1938*

Year	Site	Duration (in weeks)	Major topic	Outcome
1851–52	Paris	26	Quarantines for cholera and plague	Convention on quarantines (never took effect)
1859	Paris	20	Quarantines	Unratified convention
1866	Constantinople	32	Etiology of cholera	Report on cholera
1874	Vienna	4	Quarantine vs. inspection	Recommendation for an international commission on epidemics (unfulfilled)
1881	Washington	8	Yellow fever	Proposals for countries' consuls to authenticate bills of health and for international agency for notification of disease
1885	Rome	3	Quarantine regulations	Agreement that land quarantine useless; disagreement on maritime quarantine
1892	Venice	4	Cholera	First international sanitary convention to take effect

Tuscany, and the two Sicilies. Within fifteen years four of these states would be combined into Italy; but it should be recalled that Austria and Turkey were both vastly larger than they are today, and both were substantial maritime countries, while Spain, Portugal, France, and Great Britain each had a large overseas empire.

Each country sent two delegates to the conference—a diplomat and a physician—each of whom had a separate vote. The French conveners hoped that the conference would focus on concrete results, but much of the six-month-long event was devoted to debate over the nature of the propagation of major diseases, especially cholera. While it was vaguely accepted that plague, which had not been seriously epidemic in Europe west of Russia since the great Marseilles plague of 1720, was communicable from diseased persons, the transmissibility of cholera (and yellow fever) was hotly disputed. At the conference Britain

TABLE 1 *(continued)*

Year	Site	Duration (in weeks)	Major topic	Outcome
1893	Dresden	5	Restrictions on trade	Convention to relax some restrictions
1894	Paris	8	Cholera in Persian Gulf	Convention on treatment of ships carrying Mecca pilgrims
1897	Venice	4	Plague	Convention dealing with notification and inspection
1903	Paris	8	Consolidation of 1892–97 conventions	Proposal for creating a permanent international office (carried out in 1907)
1911–12	Paris	10	Yellow fever, cholera	More countries brought into international framework; further consolidation
1926	Paris	6	Update of knowledge since 1912	Agreement on disease notification
1938	Paris	1	Elimination of Maritime Health and Quarantine Council of Egypt	Transfer of responsibility to Egypt

was represented by Dr. John Sutherland from the General Board of Health, which had strong views in favor of miasma and against contagion. Dr. Guliemo Menis from Austria took the position that cholera attacked the dregs of society and "the best weapons against it were courage, resignation, spiritual calmness, and faith." He considered it "as a divine wind sent on earth to punish those who did not know how to look after themselves," and concluded that quarantine "was not only useless but eminently dangerous to the conservation and the civilization of peoples." The French medical delegate, summarizing the four-to-three majority conclusion of a technical committee set up to examine the question, argued that it was "humanly impossible to do anything useful or efficacious against such a scourge [as cholera], which fell like a storm on the country it reached." In particular, quarantine measures against cholera were "impossible, illusory, even dangerous in certain cases."[25] These countries argued that cholera should be totally excluded from quarantine regulations. Others insisted that cholera should be covered. Eleven weeks into the conference, when the issue was put to a vote, fifteen delegates favored the inclusion of cholera under quarantine, four were against, and four abstained.

The remainder of the conference was devoted largely to drawing up a convention governing quarantine regulations and provisions for the treatment of arriving ships. The convention called for mutually agreed, standardized provisions to govern all Mediterranean and Black Sea ports of the ratifying powers dealing with the treatment of arriving ships with respect to cholera, plague, yellow fever, and other diseases "reputed to be importable." Ships departing a port were to be given a bill of health stating the health conditions in the port of embarkation. Ship captains or surgeons were to keep accurate records of health conditions on the voyage and report them on arrival. If a ship arrived with a clean bill of health, its passengers, crew, and goods were to be given free entrance to the port. If it arrived with a foul bill of health, its passengers were to be quarantined, ten to fifteen days in the case of plague, five to seven days in the case of yellow fever, and five days in the case of cholera, including the passage time. (Note the drastic reduction from forty days. The lower figure for cholera was a diplomatic compromise, suggested by a Portuguese delegate, between the views of the pro- and anticontagionists.) A ship with disease on board was considered to have a foul bill of health. Goods were divided into three categories—those for which quarantine was required, those for which it was prohibited, and a middle category at the discretion of the local health officer. No ship could be refused entry into a port on grounds of health. Ports had to have adequate lazarettos for quarantine, managed as hospitals rather than as prisons. Fees were to be uniform and set to cover costs, not to raise general revenue. And each port was to have an official, paid by the central government, who was responsible for health matters, in consultation with local authorities and with the consular officials of other countries.[26]

This convention, signed by all the participating countries, represented a major rationalization of the diverse provisions that then existed. Unfortunately, it never universally came into effect. Only France and Sardinia ratified the convention, and Sardinia withdrew in 1865 at the onset of the fourth cholera epidemic in Europe. So, contrary to the intention of the conveners, the conference produced nothing concrete. But it presaged conventions to come much later.

France called another International Sanitary Conference in 1859, after so few countries ratified the 1851 convention, with a view to getting a more acceptable agreement. To eliminate what was thought to be fruitless and disruptive scientific debate, only diplomats were invited to this conference, and eleven of the twelve 1851 countries attended. (The Austrian delegate withdrew for three months while France and Austria were at war, but the conference went on and the Austrian delegate returned for the final days of the conference and signed the convention.) Britain argued for relaxation of the quarantine restriction of the 1851 convention, and in particular asserted that cotton goods could not transmit plague and therefore should be exempt from quarantine. Britain also argued that the advent of the railroad throughout Europe rendered "illusory" any maritime quarantine against cholera. Greece led the contagionists and wanted discretion to increase quarantine periods above the maximums allowed. A motion by the recently returned Austrian delegate to delete cholera from the list of contagious diseases was deadlocked five to five, broken in the negative by a vote of the chairman.[27] The 1859 convention was a slightly simplified version of the 1851 convention, and no country ratified it. The positions remained essentially the same, despite the emergence in the 1850s of important scientific discoveries (discussed below) that could have and should have had a bearing on the issue of quarantine, but did not.

Early Efforts to Prevent Cholera

Cholera visited London again in 1853–54. The mortality was much lower than in 1848–49, perhaps because of the sanitation measures that had begun to be taken under the guidance of the General Board of Health, with only 20,000 deaths recorded in England and Wales in 1850–58.[28] This epidemic is noteworthy because of the epidemiological work done by John Snow, famous also for his contributions to anesthesiology. Snow had already conjectured in 1849 that cholera was waterborne and absorbed into the body through the mouth.

In the mid-1850s London was served by two water companies, one of which drew relatively clean water from the upstream Thames and another that drew its water from a sewage-laden part of the Thames. Snow collected information showing that in a fourteen-week period there were only 2.6 cholera cases per 1,000 persons drawing water from the first company and 15.3 cases per 1,000 drawing their water from the second company.[29] Snow also observed that the water from the Broad street pump, serving an area of London rife with cholera, reeked of sewage. The local incidence of cholera was dramatically reduced by the simple expedient of removing the pump handle.

Snow's work was known not only in Britain but also elsewhere in Europe. He had won a French prize for his 1849 essay. However, his work was before the period of refined statistical analysis, and his results, while respected by some, were dismissed as inconclusive by others. In particular, a German school of thought under the leadership of Max von Pettenkofer derided the "drinking water" theory of propagation of cholera from its inception until the end of the century.

Also in 1854, an Italian microscopist, Filippo Pacini, discovered what he called the "vibrio cholera" in the fluid dejections from cholera patients and in the intestines of persons who had died from cholera. More will be said below about this remarkable discovery, which despite Pacini's persistence was disregarded until into the twentieth century and had to be rediscovered by Robert Koch in the 1880s.

Another cholera epidemic hit Europe in 1865, having proceeded more rapidly from India than the earlier epidemics had, this time via the Moslem pilgrims to Mecca and thence along the Mediterranean coast. The purported completeness of reporting on the causes of death had improved throughout Europe. In 1866, 90,000 persons died from cholera in Russia; 120,000 in what is now Austria, Hungary, and Czechoslovakia; 115,000 in Prussia; over 50,000 in Belgium and the Netherlands; but only 14,000 in England and Wales, presumably due to improved sanitation measures introduced after 1849. The following year 130,000 died in Italy, an equal number in Russia, and 80,000 in Algiers. The disease receded for several years but struck strongly again in 1872–73, killing another 120,000 in Russia and 190,000 in Hungary alone.[30]

The Americans had somewhat more time to prepare, and as the inevitable introduction of cholera approached, the state of New York overrode New York City politics-as-usual and in February 1866 created the Metropolitan Board of Health with extensive powers. Following the earlier British example, a massive cleanup campaign was begun in New York City, not only of city streets, but also of private lots and yards. Some 160,000 tons of manure were removed. In addition, the city was divided into health districts under the charge of qualified physicians who were to report cases of cholera to a central office by telegraph at once. Disinfectant teams were then dispatched to isolate and disinfect the excretions and soiled belongings of all those with symptoms of cholera. A quarantine station was established in the port for new arrivals with symptoms, with the assistance of the U.S. Army, but was rendered only partially effective due to preventive court injunctions against some of the board's numerous orders. Nonetheless, the emergency effort paid off. Only 591 cholera deaths were reported in New York in 1866, one-tenth the cholera deaths of 1849, in a much larger city. The success of New York thereupon set a standard for public health activities in other U.S. states and cities.[31]

The Third and Fourth International Sanitary Conferences

While this practical work was going on, another International Sanitary Conference had been called in 1866 by the Turkish government at the suggestion of the French. Seventeen countries were invited, including the United States. All except the United States attended. Cholera had clearly invaded Europe by sea on this occasion, in contrast with the earlier epidemics, despite extensive quarantine provisions in most Mediterranean ports. It had probably been brought by pilgrims returning by sea from Mecca via Egypt. The first task the conference assigned itself was to array the extant knowledge on the etiology of cholera. A technical committee was established to identify the key questions and the extent of agreement on answers to them.

The resulting report is a remarkable document.[32] It attempts to collect all the extant evidence on cholera and to infer how the disease is propagated. It is a committee report, representing the joint product of twenty-one doctors and three diplomats from many countries. It poses thirty-four key questions, arrays the available evidence, and records separate votes on each, the majority of which were adopted unanimously. The report thus offers a compendium on the received wisdom—and, by implication, the ignorance—about cholera that prevailed in 1866, along with an indication of which views were widely accepted and which were under dispute.

The report devotes considerable space to establishing that cholera is transmissible and that the main vehicle of transmission is human beings. The space devoted to these propositions indicates general doubt about them even in the mid-1860s.

The report is unclear as to exactly what causes cholera. It speaks here and there of a "morbific principle." "Whether the principle of cholera be called contagion, a germ, miasma, whether we suppose it formed of an organic substance or not, it always escaped all investigations, which have never been able to isolate it, and it is known to us only by its effects. In this respect, it does not differ from other morbific principles." (There is no acknowledgement of Pacini's work, first published in 1854, and only passing reference to Snow's work of the same year.)

One of the puzzling features about cholera, in contrast to plague, was the appearance of relative immunity; even in the worst cases only 20 percent of the population caught cholera and in "grave cases" only 5 percent caught it. Often far fewer seemed to be infected. And certain locations seemed to be relatively immune (the committee was unsure of the reasons), but this fact raised doubts about the contagiousness of the disease.

There is lengthy discussion of the effects of quarantine. Empirical evidence from the 1865 epidemic is adduced. The committee concluded that persons in quarantine were not exceptionally exposed—apparently having built up some resistance—but the people in nearby towns were very vulnerable. The worst case was at the Dardenelles, where 6 percent of a town of 6,000 located near a lazaretto died from cholera in July and August 1865. The committee concluded that quarantine was helpful in limiting spread of the disease, but was not decisive: "Hygienic measures are necessary to complement" quarantine.

At this time quarantine by regulation was five days for passengers on a ship without a clean bill of health and ten days for passengers on a ship with a case of cholera on board. Later in the epidemic quarantine was extended to ten days for everyone and even up to fourteen days if cholera appeared in the lazaretto. Turkey—from which the data were largely drawn and where the epidemic was mainly located in 1865—included Crete, Beirut, Salonika, Cyprus, and Benghazi, but not Alexandria, which was a source of many of the passengers. The report comments on the problems of documenting the exact propagation of the disease: "It would be a matter of the greatest interest to be able to say precisely in what manner things have happened at each of the above localities; but the want of precise information does not permit this. It is easy to understand, also, how many interests are opposed, in most of the cases, to the exact truth being known." With respect to the period of contagion, bearing on the period of quarantine that would be needed, "observation shows that the duration of choleraic diarrhea . . . does not extend beyond a few days." This was the most controversial of the findings, voted fourteen to four with one abstention. However, earlier in the report all agreed that the period of incubation was just a few days.

The report reviews the relevance of hygienic conditions and finds that misery, high temperature, "confined air," and bad water all contribute to the spread of cholera. "Water appears ... to contribute under certain circumstances to the development of cholera in some localities." The report cites Snow's work, relating cholera deaths in London to the source of water. It also cites Pettenkofer to the effect that "it is in the privies, the sewers, in the soil itself that we should see the principal receptacle of the cholera principle." It reports Pettenkofer's views on the importance of soil quality, but concludes: "The surrounding atmosphere is the principal vehicle of the generative agent of cholera; but the transmission of the disease by the atmosphere, in the immense majority of cases, is limited to a very short distance from the focus of emission." The report concedes that "water and certain ingesta may also serve as vehicles for the introduction into the organism of the generative principle of cholera." It follows from these two that "the passages by which the toxic agent penetrates the economy are principally the respiratory passages, and, very probably, also the alimentary canal. As for penetration through the skin, nothing tends to prove it" (adopted unanimously).

Despite this somewhat confused and misleading conclusion, the commission came to a direct and basically correct practical conclusion: "The matter of cholera dejections being incontestably the principal receptacle of the morbific agent, it follows that everything that is contaminated by these dejections becomes also a receptacle from which the generative principle may be disengaged, under the influence of favorable conditions; it follows also that the production of the cholera germ takes place very probably in the alimentary canal, to the exclusion, perhaps of all other parts of the system." And despite a focus on the respiratory passages, it rules out as improbable "pulmonary exhalation" as a source of transmission.

This intellectual effort is the most interesting product of the Constantinople conference. Some members of the conference proposed a ban on all pilgrims returning by sea from Mecca via Egypt in 1866 since that had been the route of cholera to Europe the previous year. Britain's diplomatic representative initially opposed this idea on the grounds that cholera was not transmissible (a position the British medical representative did not insist on in the technical report), and Turkey opposed it on grounds of impracticality—it would have a revolt on its hands. Turkey did agree, however, to construct a lazaretto in the Sinai for future use in quarantine. Otherwise little concrete emerged from what, at seven months, was the longest of the International Sanitary Conferences. Even the relatively broad agreement on scientific propositions proved not to be durable.

Cholera did not completely die out in Europe after 1866 and returned violently in 1872–73. New York was prepared and did not have a single case enter the city due to what was considered an exemplary system of medical inspection and observational quarantine.[33] However, cholera entered the United States through New Orleans and took its toll in Memphis and other cities on the lower Mississippi. It also showed up in Kentucky, Minnesota, and the Dakotas. After the cases were traced in detail, this led to the conclusion that soiled clothes and linen could carry the cholera "germ" in dried form for some time, and that the disease was introduced through hand luggage that had entered the United States with immigrants through New York and was not opened until their ultimate destination had been reached.

The year 1873 was to be the last in which cholera was epidemic in the United States. Its presence prompted a government report by John Woodworth, supervising surgeon of the U.S. Marine Hospital Service, assisted by Ely McClellan and others under the direction of the surgeon general of the U.S. Army. McClellan went further than the 1866 conference report and simply asserted that it had been amply demonstrated that cholera was infectious and that with accurate advance notice and observational quarantines the importation of cholera into the United States could be completely prevented. He was appalled by quarantine procedures on the lower Mississippi, and he also urged a national quarantine act to set standards and provide assistance to the states and cities that had actual responsibility for public health. He also called for the government to require its consular offices overseas to report regularly, by cable if appropriate, on health conditions in all areas from which people were emigrating to the United States. Timely information and adequate procedures were sufficient to keep the United States free of cholera.[34]

Under the influence of anticontagionist thinking, Britain had weakened its quarantine law in 1825, abandoned quarantine for plague in 1841, and shifted from quarantine to medical observation for cholera in 1873. Britain's last serious encounter with cholera was in 1866; the

1873 epidemic and subsequent epidemics did not affect Britain seriously.

But cholera raged in eastern Europe. In 1874 Russia called for another international conference to deal with the stringent quarantine requirements Turkey and other Mediterranean countries were imposing on ships originating in Russia. The conference was held in Vienna, with representatives from twenty-one states, including the great German epidemiologists Pettenkofer and Hirsch, and lasted only a month. It somewhat perfunctorily endorsed the scientific conclusions of the Constantinople conference of 1866—perhaps because they had already been heavily influenced by Pettenkofer's writings—and went on to vote twelve to eight in favor of substituting medical inspection for quarantine, in the end agreeing to allow each state to choose the system that it preferred. The conference also recommended, for the first time, the creation of a permanent International Epidemic Commission, with the fourfold tasks of promoting the study of epidemics, presenting reasoned proposals on quarantines, providing technical advice to states that desired it, and preparing agendas for International Sanitary Conferences.[35] Nothing came of this unanimous conference recommendation for over thirty years.

Technological Developments

Vienna marked the fourth International Sanitary Conference with no concrete outcome. In the meantime important technological developments had been taking place, with implications for the spread and control of epidemic disease. Every schoolchild learns the dates of certain "firsts"—Fulton's steamboat on the Hudson River in 1807, George Stephenson's "rocket" locomotive in 1829, Morse's telegraph message from Washington to Baltimore in 1844. Such dates are typically just one point chosen from what is really a continuous evolutionary development. Steam was first used on a transatlantic crossing in 1819, and regular steamship service began in 1840. Monthly steamship service to India, with an overland stretch at Suez, began in 1845. The introduction of steam power, both when it only supplemented sail and when it fully supplanted wind power, shortened greatly both the time and the cost of long sea passages. For instance, a packet boat typically took at least five weeks to travel from southern England to New England or

New York in the 1820s. By the early 1870s steamships in regular service could do the trip in twelve days. One dramatic result was an increase in immigration. The average number of immigrants to the United States in the 1830s was 60,000 a year; by the 1870s it had reached 280,000 a year, and in the 1880s it was an astounding 520,000 a year.

Travel became easier elsewhere as well. Railroads began in earnest in the 1840s; by 1900 Europe had nearly 200,000 miles of track. In 1859 a railroad was built across the Isthmus of Suez, greatly easing the arduous overland trip across the desert, and in 1869 the Suez Canal opened, so a ship could go directly from India (the source of cholera) to the Mediterranean and western Europe. The typical number of Moslem pilgrims to Mecca was about 50,000 a year in the 1850s. By the 1890s it had reached 200,000 a year.

Communication accelerated even more. In the 1820s news traveled over long distances only as rapidly as a man—and a contagious disease—could travel. In 1851 London and Paris were telegraphically linked through a cross-channel cable. And in 1866 the first successful transatlantic cable was laid, so it was possible for news—for example, of an outbreak of disease—to reach the United States nearly two weeks before persons or goods could arrive from Europe. (Advance news of an outbreak of disease on a ship at sea had to await Marconi's wireless in the twentieth century.) News was rapidly and widely disseminated by the popular press that had sprung up in all major U.S. and western European cities in the nineteenth century.

The improvements in transportation hastened the spread of contagious disease, but the developments in communication meant that advance warning of the progress of an epidemic (and of other relevant information) was also possible.

Yellow Fever and Its Consequences

Unlike cholera and the plague, yellow fever was—as far as Europeans knew—mainly a disease of the New World and the West African coast, where it originated. Yellow fever had devastated Napoleon's 40,000-man army sent in 1802 to suppress a revolution in Haiti and was largely responsible for his willingness to sell the Louisiana Territory to the United States. Yellow fever had also devastated Philadelphia in 1793. The leading American doctor of the day, Benjamin Rush, put forward the hypothesis that yellow fever was not contagious, but rather was probably caused by foul air arising from rotting coffee beans. Thus began the modern miasmatic theory of epidemic disease that was to capture most of the scientific community half a century later.[36]

In Europe, yellow fever wiped out 20 percent of the population of Cadiz in 1801 and 1805, and fatal epidemics broke out in Gibraltar in 1821 and 1828, in Lisbon in 1857, and in Madrid in 1878. But for the most part the concern with yellow fever was in Spanish America and the United States. Over the course of the nineteenth century, over 500,000 persons are estimated to have died from yellow fever in the United States and far more than that in the Caribbean.[37]

Yellow fever struck the southern Atlantic and Gulf ports of the United States frequently throughout the early nineteenth century, but gradually receded in importance as the disease became associated with ships arriving from the Caribbean or West Africa and greater care was devoted to handling their arrival. Medical information was not always accurate on ports of embarkation, however, and the U.S. quarantine arrangements—in principle the responsibility of the states but in practice in the hands of local authorities—were neither uniform nor seriously enforced. In 1878 a yellow fever epidemic worked its way up the Mississippi valley and killed 5,150 people in Memphis, about 10 percent of the city's population. The overall U.S. death toll in 1878 was over 20,000. This disaster, on top of the cholera epidemic five years earlier, finally galvanized the U.S. Congress into action. It passed the National Quarantine Act in 1878 and created the National Board of Health in 1879. The 1878 act empowered the surgeon general of the Marine Hospital Service—the only federal organ concerned with public health outside the army and navy—to enforce port quarantine so long as he did not contravene the laws or interfere with the procedures of the states. It was a symbolic gesture, since he was given no appropriations for the task. The National Board of Health was mandated to collect information on public health matters, to advise federal departments and state governments, and to recommend a plan for national action with special reference to quarantine.[38] The board's appropriations were terminated in 1883 and it soon went out of existence, again because of the antagonism of the states.

In the meantime, the American public, following the example of Britain, had been paying more attention to health questions. In 1872 the American Public Health Association was founded, and it played a major role in passage of the 1879 act. Between 1869 and 1877 nine states created state boards of health, starting with Massachusetts, where the Shattuck report had been issued nineteen years earlier.

As a part of this general movement, and in reaction to the yellow fever epidemic of 1878, the United States convened the fifth International Sanitary Conference, which met in Washington in 1881. It was the first in which the United States participated, and it focused on yellow fever, which had been acknowledged but not discussed extensively in the previous conferences. Twenty-six countries attended, including ten from the Western hemisphere, as well as China and Japan. Most countries were represented by their diplomatic representatives in Washington, but Spain sent a delegation from Cuba.

The conference was called by the U.S. government to carry out an injunction from Congress that aimed at limiting the importation of cholera and yellow fever. Every vessel sailing to the United States was to carry a certificate from a U.S. consular official setting forth the sanitary condition of the vessel before it left for the United States. This could be accomplished only through inspection of such vessels in the various ports of embarkation, and that in turn could be done only with the agreement of the foreign country of jurisdiction. The U.S. medical delegate to the conference proposed that "each government should bind itself to give to the consuls or accredited agents of the others access to all hospitals and all the records of the public health, as well as authority to make a thorough examination of vessels, both before and after taking in cargo, when such vessels are about to sail for any of the ports of the country represented by the examining officer."[39] He explained that this proposal would achieve the advantages of quarantine without the associated costs to commerce, since the inspection could be carried out before departure rather than after arrival, when it would hold everyone up. The requirement that officials from countries of disembarkation do the inspecting arose from the distrust with which some bills of health were then held. For example, a contemporary author notes that "in the West Indies one should never trust the rumor that there is no yellow fever. A ship of war is always a mine of wealth to the inhabitants of these colonial ports, and they are careful to keep silent about the sporadic cases of yellow fever that occur from time to time so as not to interrupt the shipping traffic and their own business." He adds that the same condition is even more true of merchant vessels.[40]

This proposal, a sensible if naive example of U.S. application of extraterritorial jurisdiction, affronted most other countries and was thoroughly rejected on grounds that it infringed on their sovereignty. A compromise proposal passed by a majority required a bill of health to be given by a responsible health official from the central government of the port of embarkation, but consular officials could be present at the inspection of a ship and could authenticate the bill of health and add such remarks as they wished. The U.S. representative voted against this proposal on the grounds, as he later explained, that the arrangement was fraught with difficulty: the consular officer would be faced with a choice between rubber-stamping the bill of health or dissenting from it and thus creating a diplomatic incident.[41] Such an agreement also might have been seen as a federal infringement of the rights of the states within the United States.

The 1881 conference also proposed establishing an international agency for notification of disease, with regional offices in Vienna and Havana, and with a budget to be apportioned among members, half based on their population and half based on their merchant shipping tonnage. Austria and Spain favored the proposal, along with eleven others, but the United States and France voted against it and the British delegation was absent at the time of that vote. Nothing came of it for over twenty years.

So the conference, like those before it, produced nothing tangible. It is noteworthy, however, for its implicit acceptance of the proposition that yellow fever was introduced by ship, a point that would have been contested not long before. Hirsch, the German epidemiologist, published his massive *Handbuch der historisch-geographische Pathologie* in 1881; on the basis of a comprehensive review of known cases, he asserts that apart from a few identified places the outbreak of yellow fever "*always* followed shortly after the arrival of ships from ports where the disease was known to be epidemically prevalent at the time of their sailing, or which were notorious as endemic foci of yellow fever," and that on the East Coast of the United States, "yellow fever has never occurred without an infected ship having arrived just before."[42] This view marked a major change from the earlier belief that yellow fever is miasmatic. Hirsch points out that yellow fever is not directly infectious, since medical workers and other patients where yellow fever patients were present in hospitals rarely contracted the disease, but that the disease never occurred away from the areas where it was endemic without the arrival of an infected person. So the nature of its communicability was a puzzle. The Cuban delegate to the Washington conference, Dr. Carlos Finlay, conjectured that some agent must be present that is "entirely independent for its existence both of the disease and of the sick man, but which is necessary in order that the disease shall be conveyed from the yellow fever patient to a healthy individual."[43] No notice was taken of this prescient statement. Finlay later in the year implicated the mosquito, but that was not proven until Walter Reed's work in 1900.

Four International Conferences, 1885–94

A cholera epidemic developed in Egypt in 1883, and once again quarantine restrictions around the Mediterranean were tightened in response to public apprehension. The Italian government (Italy had been formed from various states in 1866) convoked an International Sanitary Conference to address the "anarchy" that reigned in quarantine regulations. Sixty-three delegates, half medical, from twenty-eight countries met in Rome in May 1885. It was again agreed that quarantine of travelers by land was useless, and that most goods could not carry cholera and therefore did not have to be disinfected. Dispute erupted over proposals for maritime quarantine. A large majority favored a twenty-four hour observation period for healthy ships arriving from areas of cholera infestation, and a three- to six-day observation of apparently healthy persons arriving on infected ships. Britain, supported by the United States and Denmark, opposed these quarantine regulations and had no intention of carrying them out. That was especially relevant at the time, since Britain had occupied Egypt in 1881 and thus was in a position to determine whether ships passing from India to the Mediterranean should be quarantined at Suez, as many countries desired.

The British ambassador in Rome sent a lengthy memorandum explaining the British position to the chairman of the conference after its adjournment. Britain did not understand why other countries should object to the direct passage of ships from India to British ports, since they posed no danger to other countries. Indeed, the British revived the view that cholera was endemic to Egypt and Hejaz (where Mecca was located) and asserted that the notion that cholera was imported from India was unsupported by the evidence. In the previous year, 893 ships had arrived at British ports from India and China without introducing cholera. Adequate surveillance on board and adequate expenditures on water and sewerage systems were preferable to drastic quarantine and other emergency measures introduced only when cholera appeared. In any case, there was the practical problem of caring for 1,000–1,500 passengers on each ship while they were in quarantine. Britain also expressed concern that a required quarantine of five days at Suez would almost eliminate the seven-day advantage that ships gained by going through the Suez Canal, and that such a requirement when combined with the canal tolls would lead to diversion of ships to the Cape route around Africa, thus undermining the financial condition of the Suez Canal, in which, the British ambassador pointed out, the French also had a strong financial interest.[44]

British health practice with respect to cholera, adopted in 1883, was to inspect ships from cholera-infected areas on arrival. Cholera cases were sent to hospitals, and passengers with suspicious symptoms could be detained for forty-eight hours. All other passengers were free to travel to their destinations, but had to give the health authorities their names and exact destinations, and they were put under the surveillance of the well-developed local health authorities. The effects of cholera patients were carefully disinfected or disposed of.[45] The Americans had also adopted a system of medical inspection rather than quarantine in some of their ports.

The Egyptian cholera epidemic of 1883 is noteworthy for the work there, and subsequently in India, by the German cholera commission under the direction of Robert Koch, the discoverer of the tuberculous bacillus in 1882. This group (re)discovered the cholera bacillus and identified it positively as the cause of cholera in 1884.[46] The finding created a sensation when Koch returned to Germany, but was greeted with skepticism or even hostility outside Germany and even by Pettenkofer and his disciples within Germany. Koch was a medical delegate to the Rome conference, but there was no formal discussion, not even any mention, of his work in the transcript of the conference. At British insistence the conference eschewed any consideration of the origin and transmissibility of the disease.[47]

So the Rome conference too came to nothing. In subsequent years Koch's work was gradually and increasingly accepted, and by 1893 his clinical tests had become the standard for positive identification of cholera by British health authorities.[48] But it remained in contention well into the 1890s whether the Koch bacillus was a cause or a consequence of cholera.

A growing preoccupation of European health authorities was the

annual Moslem pilgrimage to Mecca. This brought increasing numbers of people together from many parts of the world, mingled them
in very crowded and unsanitary conditions, and dispersed them again.
Between 1831, when cholera first broke out among Moslem pilgrims,
and 1895 there were sixteen serious cholera epidemics, and there was
justifiable concern that pilgrims returning to Egypt or Algeria or the
Balkans would transmit it onward to the major European countries. By
this time returning pilgrims could embark from Jidda or Yanbu on the
Red Sea and reach the Mediterranean quickly through the Suez
Canal.

Cholera was epidemic in the Middle East in the early 1890s, and in
1892 at Austria's suggestion a Sanitary Conference met at Venice to
address the problem. The conference produced the first International
Sanitary Convention that went into force among many states. It reor-
ganized the Sanitary Council of Egypt (which had been an advisory
body of foreign physicians in Egypt since the 1830s); established a
quarantine station on the Sinai Peninsula where all returning pilgrims
would be required to undergo fifteen days of quarantine if cholera were
present at their ports of embarkation in the Hejaz; and provided that
all westbound ships through the Suez Canal would be required to undertake varying degrees of quarantine and disinfection if they had
cases of cholera on board, depending in part on whether the ships had
a doctor and a sterilizer on board. The agreement was ratified by
twelve countries and went into effect in 1893. The annex notes that
"the germ of cholera is contained in the digestive tracts of patients; its
transmission is effected principally by the dejections and vomited matter and, consequently, by linen, clothing, and soiled hands."[49] This was
the first recognition of the value of the sterilization of clothing and
linens by steam sterilizers, a device recently installed on steamships.

In 1892 cholera again struck Europe as so often before, arriving not
from the Mediterranean but through Afghanistan and Persia into Russia. An estimated 555,000 persons contracted the disease in Russia, of
whom 268,000—including the composer Peter Ilyich Tchaikovsky—
died, almost as many as in 1831–32. The epidemic was severe in Hamburg (8,605 deaths) and reached Paris, but only a few hundred cases
occurred in Britain.[50] In face of the disease's advance, many local and
some national authorities imposed many restrictions on the overland
movement of goods and persons. Germany called a conference at
Dresden in March 1893 to deal with the disastrous effects of these
restrictions on trade. The conference agreed that governments should

notify one another at once of any outbreak of cholera, that the only goods that should be subject to restriction (prohibition or disinfection, not quarantine) were used clothes and bed linen and rags, and that travelers by rail could be detained only if they actually had cholera-like symptoms. It was agreed in particular that all letters, newspapers, and books should be free of restrictions (contrasted with the dousing in vinegar to which letters were subjected early in the century). It was also agreed that noninfected ships coming from cholera-infected ports should undergo three days of medical inspection at Sulina before entering the Danube River system.[51] At this conference the British delegate for the first time noted that Britain did not reject the view that cholera could be transmitted from person to person, although it continued to deny the value of quarantine. Eleven states eventually ratified the convention, which went into effect in 1897.

A disastrous cholera epidemic occurred among the Mecca pilgrims in 1893: of some 200,000 pilgrims, over 30,000 died of cholera.[52] The areas in and around Mecca were strewn with decomposing bodies. Another conference was therefore called in Paris in 1894 to deal with Mecca and increasing problems with cholera in the Persian Gulf. Sixteen countries participated, including the United States. A convention was agreed that concerned mainly the conditions on pilgrim ships and the establishment of a quarantine station at the head of the Persian Gulf. A proposal for a "means test" for all pilgrims, concerning assured return passage, was rejected by Britain and Turkey as being inconsistent with the injunctions of Islam, and Britain rejected proposals for control of shipping in the Persian Gulf.[53]

In all, three International Sanitary Conferences were held in the early 1890s, all concerned exclusively with cholera and focusing on specific, limited objectives, and all resulting in conventions that ultimately went into force. Thus this period offered the limited inauguration of formal international cooperation in matters of public health. While the scientific debate on the etiology of cholera continued, serious disagreements at the intergovernmental level had ceased by the 1894 conference, and practical methods of containment were thought to be understood. And in fact cholera ceased to be a major scourge of Europe after 1893. Isolated cases have occurred in various European countries, mostly among travelers returning from Asia. A serious scare occurred in the late 1960s when an Asian cholera epidemic reached the Middle East and entered Russia in 1970. The apprehension cholera still evoked after so many years was reflected in the delay in the late 1960s of a westbound Oriental Express train from Istanbul for more than a week and requirements for the disinfection of mail and the prohibition of imports of tinned fruit and even iron beams from cholera-infected areas.[54] An international system of notification, monitoring, and rapid transmission of epidemiological information continues to attend all cholera cases.

Plague and the Venice Conference of 1897

The last major plague epidemic in Europe was in Russia, reaching Moscow in 1770. English and French troops were stricken with plague during the Egyptian campaigns of 1798–1801, and that kept the issue alive in European medical circles. There were isolated cases, and a minor epidemic occurred in several Greek islands in 1837. Writing in 1881, Hirsch reports the last known case in Turkey in 1841 and in Egypt in 1844, two areas considered to be the source of plague.[55] Therefore discussion of the plague in the International Sanitary Conferences of 1851 and subsequent conferences represented anxiety based on historical memory rather than contemporary events. Still, the plague existed in Mesopotamia and Arabia, and there was always the possibility of its reimportation into Europe. Indeed, a minor epidemic (about 600 deaths) occurred in southeast Russia in 1878, although plague was not diagnosed until the epidemic was over.

Like cholera, plague was a mysterious, often fatal disease of unknown origin and propagation. A favorite hypothesis was that it was caused by the effluvia from decomposing corpses.[56] But Hirsch in 1881 reports plague unambiguously as a contagious disease, transmissible from man to man. Curiously, he makes no mention of rats, even though rodents were long associated with plague, for example, in the Bible (I Samuel 5–6) and in DeFoe's 1722 discussion of the efforts to rid London of rats during the Great Plague of 1665.

Against this general background, a worldwide pandemic of plague began in the early 1890s, apparently in Yunnan Province in China. By 1894 it had reached Hong Kong. Two cases occurred in London in 1896, by 1897 Bombay was epidemic, and by 1900 it had reached Capetown and San Francisco. An International Sanitary Conference devoted solely to plague was held in Venice in 1897. It was a measure of how far bacteriology had advanced that the conference accepted without discussion the discovery by Alexandre Yersin of the culpable bacillus of plague in Hong Kong in 1894. It was recognized that rats and mice were susceptible to plague and that outbreaks among them often preceded human cases. The conference agreed that "the transmission of plague appears to take place by the excretions of patients (sputum, dejections), morbid products (suppuration of bubos, of boils, etc.) and consequently by contaminated linen, clothing, and hands." [57] This finding sounds suspiciously as though it were simply adapted from cholera, as was the recommendation that drinking water should be subject to strict surveillance.

There was no suggestion of an intermediary from rats to men. Masanori Ogata implicated the flea in the same year, but that link was not firmly established until 1907 by the Indian Plague commission. It is, however, a measure of the scientific enthusiasm stimulated by recent bacteriological discoveries that four national teams of scientists rushed off to Bombay soon after the plague epidemic was reported there.

The convention resulting from the 1897 conference stipulated that first cases of plague should be notified telegraphically to the other signatories. It also contained provisions dealing with disinfection and ships. Ships and passengers found to be healthy on arrival were to be given free pratique regardless of the bill of health received in the port of embarkation. This marked a major advance toward the British position favoring medical inspection over quarantine. The United States and Scandinavian countries did not sign the convention.

The plague reached San Francisco in 1900, probably from Hong Kong. Initially it struck exclusively in Chinatown, and continued until early 1904, with a total of 120 known cases and 112 deaths. It made a brief reappearance in 1907 with 160 cases and 77 deaths. It is a measure of the strength of commercial interests that most San Franciscans, including the newspapers and the governor of California, denied that plague was in the city, and they even hampered the work of the City's Board of Health and public health officials. An initial quarantine in Chinatown was reversed after sixty hours and public health officials were pilloried by the press. The governor affirmed in response to an inquiry from Secretary of State John Hay that there was no positive proof that plague existed there. [58] The health authorities, to their credit, persisted in their efforts, eliminating rats and disinfecting as well as they could and isolating new cases. In early 1903 a new, more cooperative governor came into office and the work of the health authorities became easier. [59]

The episode had international implications. In 1902 plague hit the

Mexican Pacific coast town of Mazatlan. It was identified early, the town and nearby villages were evacuated, 375 homes were burned, and much fumigation was undertaken to rid the area of rats and mice, but 351 deaths had occurred before the attack was ended. Mexican health authorities subsequently charged that the plague was introduced by a ship from San Francisco that had a false clean bill of health.[60]

Consolidation and Creation of an International Office

By the end of the nineteenth century four international conventions had been signed, and the 1897 conference called for consolidation of the previous agreements. A shipping conference in 1902 complained of continuing problems with quarantine regulations and urged that they be reduced and rationalized.[61] In addition, new advances had been made in understanding plague—particularly the role of rats in transmitting it—and yellow fever. In 1900 it was established definitively that yellow fever was transmitted by a particular species of mosquito. An International Sanitary Conference was called, at French initiative, in 1903, mainly to consolidate the 1892–97 conventions, and twenty-three states attended. It made a few changes. In particular, the minimum observation period of plague was reduced to five days, and measures were agreed to take against rats traveling on ships. A general injunction was given to take into account the role of the mosquito in transmitting yellow fever. And the conference invited the French government to propose creation of a permanent body to look after international health questions. Twenty countries signed the consolidated convention of 1903, and by 1907 sixteen countries had ratified it.

In the meantime, the breakthroughs in understanding the transmission of yellow fever had led to a conference of American republics in Mexico in late 1901. This conference urged that a convention of American health administrators formulate common agreements and regulations with the objective of reducing to a minimum quarantine requirements with respect to cholera, yellow fever, plague, smallpox, and any other serious pestilential outbreak.[62] Such a convention was held in Washington in December 1902, and a seven-member committee was established to receive reports on sanitary conditions in territories and especially ports of the American republics. It had an initial budget of $5,000, which was not increased until 1920. This "International Sanitary Bureau" was the first formal international organization dealing with public health. It represented the beginnings of what became the Pan American Health Organization, headquartered in Washington. Since the first staff member was not hired until 1921, the routine work of the International Sanitary Bureau was presumably carried out by the U.S. Public Health Service. Some members of the committee urged the United States to adapt its quarantine requirements, particularly in the Gulf coast states, to the new knowledge regarding yellow fever. But there was still sufficient uncertainty about whether the *Aëdes aëgypti* mosquito was the sole mechanism by which yellow fever was transmitted that the American delegates declined to be definitive on the point. Moreover, federal authorities could not compel changes in state health regulations.

In response to the injunction of the 1903 conference, France persuaded Italy to call an organizational conference in Rome in 1907 and put forward a proposal for what became the International Office of Public Hygiene, with an annual budget of 150,000 francs ($29,000). Nine countries attended the Rome conference, and the office at first had nine members. Germany, Austria, Turkey, and the Scandinavian countries were notable for their absence. The role of the office was to gather and disseminate information on cases of cholera, plague, and yellow fever and also to disseminate information of general interest on matters of public health. In addition, it was to help in establishing agendas for future International Sanitary Conferences. The office was to publish a monthly bulletin plus special reports as appropriate, covering the laws and regulations of the adhering states, the progress of infectious diseases, the measures taken, and general statistics on public health. Expenses of the office were to cover several salaried officers. Contributions were apportioned according to a schedule in which Brazil, France, Great Britain, British India, Italy, Russia, Spain, and the United States each had equal shares; Belgium, Egypt, and the Netherlands paid 60 percent of what the above countries paid; and Switzerland was to pay 40 percent of what the leading countries paid. The larger contributors also had greater weight in any voting that might take place.

The office was under the direction of a permanent committee, which first met in 1908. In that and other early meetings the focus of attention was on eliminating rats and fleas, which had lately come to be known as an intermediate vector in carrying plague from rats to humans; standardizing antidiphtheria serum; and standardizing public health reports, including the reporting week (for example, on what day it should begin). Subsequent meetings addressed the possibility that apparently healthy persons could be carriers of the cholera bacillus.

By 1911 the membership in the office had risen to twenty-two states. Early on it became engaged in what was later to become an important part of international health cooperation, namely the standardization of units of measurement for biological products used in medicine. The concrete issue was to assure that antidiphtheria serum produced in different countries was of equal potency.[63]

A cholera epidemic occurred in southern Italy in late 1910, and the Italian delegate urged that another International Sanitary Conference was needed because different countries were applying the 1903 convention in different ways. The twelfth International Sanitary Conference convened in Paris in November 1911. Forty-one countries attended; the new ones were mainly from Latin America but also included Siam and several others. More emphasis was placed on yellow fever than had been true of the other European-oriented conferences, as well as on the possibility of reducing the quarantine period for cholera. There was an extensive discussion of the role of the healthy carrier of cholera, but no agreement could be reached. Empirical evidence was adduced to show how few carriers there were among healthy people, and the point was made that it was too costly and too inconvenient to test all travelers in order to identify the healthy carriers. The upshot was that the health authorities of each country were left to require such bacteriological examinations as they considered to be necessary. The main effect of this conference was to bring many more countries into the framework of international cooperation in public health.

The first decade of the twentieth century thus marked the beginning of a new era. Organized international cooperation in matters of public health began to occur, involving both formal undertakings by governments as to their own behavior and the creation of two international organizations. The organizations were to collect and disseminate information, set agendas, draft regulations, and, not least, provide forums for chiding governments that were remiss in their undertakings. Meanwhile, important scientific developments were taking place between 1850 and 1910. These have been alluded to, but I will now discuss them in greater detail.

Advances in Medical Science, 1850–1910

Speculation about the origin and propagation of disease goes back to ancient times, but many age-old disputes were finally resolved by the early twentieth century, and in ways that would have greatly surprised those who held the dominant scientific views prevailing in the early or even mid-nineteenth century.

Differing Theories of Disease

In the mid-nineteenth century the dominant scientific view was that certainly yellow fever, probably cholera, and perhaps plague were all caused by miasmas—pestilential vapors exuded from some foul putrescence. The modern version of this miasmatic theory of epidemic disease seems to have originated with Benjamin Rush, the noted Philadelphia physician who determined that the yellow fever epidemic in 1793 must have been caused by coffee beans rotting on the docks. This view commanded more general appeal and was "confirmed" by Charles Maclean and other British students who investigated the yellow fever epidemics in Gibraltar in 1821. It was noted that people could work closely around yellow fever patients in hospitals, away from where the disease had been contracted, without themselves contracting it; but that when one person contracted the disease, others in the same or neighboring households also seemed to contract it. Moreover, the disease was very seasonal in nature: it appeared only in warm, moist periods when the rate of decay of the filth that was omnipresent in urban areas was at an apparent maximum.

The cumulative evidence that yellow fever was not contagious, yet epidemic and therefore from a common cause, was so persuasive that it carried the day. Moreover, while the evidence was not nearly so compelling, similar reasoning was carried over to both plague and cholera. A Frenchman appointed chief physician to the Egyptian army, A. B. Clot, later known as Clot Bey, was so convinced that plague was not contagious that to prove the point he inoculated himself in 1835 with pus from a plague-ridden patient, with no apparent ill effect. On the eve of the 1866 International Sanitary Conference he published his definitive "Last Words on the Noncontagion of Plague," in which he laments that the recent revival of contagionism represented a return to the ideas of the Middle Ages that was "deplorable and unworthy of our epoch. . . . Plague, according to my experience and deep conviction, is an epidemic and not a contagious disease." A generation earlier, Maclean had taken a post in the Greek Pest Hospital in Constantinople to work with plague patients and had contracted the disease. It did not, however, persuade him to change his anticontagionist views. When asked by a parliamentary committee later how he contracted the disease, he replied "by the air."[64] Similarly, Edwin Chadwick and his colleagues, including Dr. John Sutherland, who attended the 1851 International Sanitary Conference, were firmly convinced miasmatists and concluded that the only method for preventing epidemics was to get rid of the urban filth that most likely was the source of the miasmas.

There were of course other views. As early as 1836 John Riddell of the Cincinnati Medical College argued the cause of cholera must be organic, and he suggested "trans-microscopic corpuscles" similar to small fungi and algae as the source. In 1849 the Philadelphia *Medical Examiner* argued for a microorganism as the cause of cholera, citing among others a German biologist who in 1832 had found microscopic fungi in the dejections of cholera patients. The article noted that the English physician William Budd had adopted the "fungoid theory" and argued that the spread of cholera could be limited by using fungicide on the dejections of cholera patients. Samuel Henry Dickson, a professor at New York University, had believed in contagion of cholera since 1832. He was unsure of the exact nature of the cholera agent, but he was sure it was organic and ultramicroscopic. However, these views represented a minority opinion and were even considered bizarre. One professor wrote of the fungoid theory that it was "a fanciful hypothesis, which could only serve as a fresh occasion for sarcasm for those who search the annals of medical literature for subjects of ridicule or reproach."[65]

An indication of prevailing views is given by the remarkable story of Filippo Pacini, an Italian microscopist born in 1812. In the 1854 epidemic he had examined the intestinal contents of several cholera victims and found millions of "vibrios" that he identified as the cause of cholera. He published his findings in Italian, emphasizing that the cause of disease was an "organic, living substance of a parasitic nature, which can communicate itself, reproduce itself, and thereby produce a specific disease."[66] (A London microscopist, Arthur Hill, made a similar discovery in the same year and reported it to the General Board of Health. But, unlike Pacini, neither he nor the board appreciated the significance of his finding.) Pacini continued to work on the "cholera vibrio" for nearly thirty years, refining his analysis and accumulating evidence. He even worked out a mathematical model for the rate of dehydration as a function of the fraction of the surface area of the small intestine that was attacked by the bacillus.

A wealthy French chemist, John-Robert Breant, in the 1849 cholera epidemic willed a 100,000-franc prize, to be awarded by the Paris Academy of Sciences, to anyone who could discover the cause of cholera or find a cure for it, with the interest to be awarded annually to anyone who advanced knowledge on the question of cholera or other epidemic disease until the prize was won. The contest was opened in 1858. Among the 153 submissions were Pacini's 1854 paper and Snow's 1855 monograph implicating drinking water in the spread of cholera in London in 1854. The prize was not awarded, but special mention was given to two contributions. The first was to a Russian doctor who argued that the "virus" of cholera was the same as that of typhus, typhoid fever, and smallpox, and therefore that cholera patients should be inoculated with small amounts of smallpox pus. The second was to an English physician who reported that persons stricken with cholera could be helped by small oral doses of calomel taken every five minutes. Thus two fundamental discoveries were examined by one of the leading scientific institutions of the day and were rejected as unworthy even of special mention.[67] They would not be accepted by the scientific community until Robert Koch rediscovered the cholera vibrio thirty years later, and even then only after much controversy.

It would be wrong, however, to suppose that the scientific debate dichotomized neatly around miasma versus contagion. Even Clot Bey, a clear anticontagionist for plague and cholera, held that some diseases, such as smallpox and syphilis, were virulently contagious, and others, such as typhoid and malaria, fell into an intermediate category, where the disease could be transmitted by a diseased person under the right miasmatic conditions.[68]

One compromise theory on cholera was offered by Max von Pettenkofer, the Munich epidemiologist. Pettenkofer held that several conditions were necessary for cholera to occur. He conjectured that cholera was caused by an unknown x factor, probably a germ, which in the presence of an environmental y factor produced z, which was the real cause of cholera: $x + y = z$. Without both x and y, cholera would not occur. Pettenkofer and his students held that the y factor was specific to place and time and that the porousness and dampness of the soil were important. Pettenkofer's views were widely held from the early 1860s, and had a strong influence on thinking at the 1866 conference. His work drew attention to the importance of ground water, but he specifically rejected what he contemptuously called the "drinking water" theory of cholera propagation. After wide publicity had been given to Koch's discovery of the cholera bacillus in 1884, Pettenkofer conceded that Koch might have found the x factor, but that by itself it could not cause cholera. To prove his point, like Clot Bey, he performed a self-experiment in 1892 by drinking a pure culture of cholera vibrios, escaping with a brief bout of diarrhea. He committed suicide in 1901, but some of his students promoted his ground water theory of cholera into the 1920s.[69]

Ambiguous Evidence

In the face of these conflicting theories, one would think that medical scientists would have resorted to empirical evidence to distinguish among them. And so they did; the difficulty lay in the ambiguity of the evidence, which permitted various schools of thought to reconcile known facts with preferred theories, while admitting that an element of mystery remained. Part of the problem was that initially the diseases themselves were not clearly identified, so confirmatory evidence for a preferred theory could be drawn from what is now known to be irrelevant information. Throughout much of the nineteenth century typhus, typhoid, and relapsing fever, along with other ailments, were simply regarded as "the fever." Furthermore, "the idea of the transmutability of epidemic diseases was widespread [around 1850], and some held that plague, yellow fever, cholera, malaria, and typhus were all the same disease, manifesting itself in different guises according to the reigning epidemic constitution," that is, the atmospheric, climatic, and soil conditions. As discussed above, the Paris Academy gave special mention in 1859 to a Russian doctor who considered cholera to be the same disease as smallpox. As late as 1888, four years after Koch's rediscovery of the cholera vibrio, Sir Joseph Fayere—president of the Medical Board of the India Office in London, fellow of the Royal Society, and a highly honored physician—could declare, "I demur to a microbe being accepted as the solution of such a problem as the cause of cholera." He believed that cholera was a variant of malaria ("bad air"), caused by fluctuations in the electrical tension and degree of moisture in the atmosphere, despite the fact that the symptoms of the two diseases are very different.[70] William Farr devoted much of his long career at Britain's General Register Office to sorting out the various diseases and accurately recording the causes of death. Farr wrote in 1840:

> Each disease has, in many cases, been denoted by three or four terms, and each term has been applied to as many different diseases; vague inconvenient names have been employed, or complications have been registered instead of primary diseases. The nomenclature is of as much importance in this department of inquiry as weights and measures in the physical sciences, and should be settled without delay.[71]

A further problem in relying on evidence to distinguish among alternative theories was the fact that the same evidence could be used to support alternative theories. The British health authorities observed a decline in the incidence of cholera in those areas where they had removed the filth and provided sewers and clean water. Was not this standing proof that miasmas from the filth caused cholera? I have already recounted the linking of cholera to drinking water by Dr. John Snow and the correlation of incidence with the source of the water in 1854. But removal of the Broad Street pump handle came late in the epidemic, so the general recession of cholera could not be clearly linked to that action. Snow's analysis, now considered a model of epidemiological empiricism and inference, was undertaken without the benefit of modern statistical tests of significance; and since there were some cases of cholera associated with the relatively clean water source and many users of the sewage-polluted water who did not contract cholera, the results, while interesting, were not compelling. Indeed, William Farr's 1852 analysis of cholera mortality in the 1848–49 London epidemic as a function of mean elevation above the highwater mark of the Thames led him to support the miasmatic theory. As shown in figure 1, the fit is impressively close.[72] I have already discussed how the nontransmission of yellow fever to hospital employees and other patients in close proximity to yellow fever patients encouraged the notion that yellow fever was not contagious.

So the evidence was inconclusive for many years. Yet an accumulation of detailed epidemiological information, tracing the antecedents of every case of cholera that could be tracked down by the local health authorities in Britain, France, and Germany, led incontrovertably to

FIGURE 1. *Relationship between Cholera Deaths in England,*
1848–49, and Elevation above Thames River

Cholera deaths per 10,000

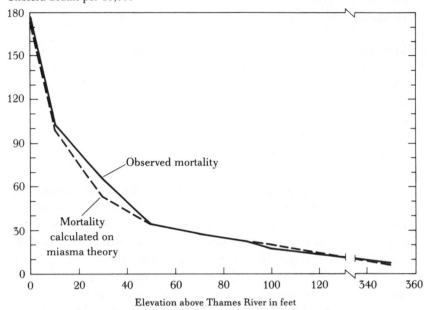

Elevation above Thames River in feet

SOURCE: Alexander D. Langmuir, "Epidemiology of Airborne Infection," *Bacteriological Review,* vol.
25 (1961), p. 174, drawn from New York Academy of Medicine, *Vital Statistics: A Memorial Volume of
Selections from the Reports and Writings of William Farr* (Metuchen, N.J.: Scarecrow Press, 1975), p. 346.

the conclusion that in many, if not all, cases it was transmitted by human beings. This was the general conclusion of the technical committee at the 1866 Constantinople conference. The assistant surgeon general of the U.S. Army, Ely McClellan, in analyzing the U.S. cholera
epidemic of 1873, simply took for granted that cholera was infectious.
So there was a gradual swing away from miasma to contagion.

Nonetheless, the issue continued to be controversial in the 1890s.
Hirsch, the great German chronicler of epidemics, writing in 1881,
takes an evenhanded view, calling the evidence as he sees it, and recognizing where it remains inconclusive. He asserts, "Only an obscu-
rantist adherence to preconceived opinions and vague notions can permit anyone nowadays to deny the communicability of plague," but also
concludes that it is not certain that plague is truly contagious, like
smallpox and typhus.[73] As noted above, he makes no reference to the
role of rats or fleas in transmitting plague.

On cholera, Hirsch is somewhat more circumspect. He reports that "the infectious character of cholera, and the communicability and re-production of the morbid poison, have been accepted as the general belief [and] there can no longer be any doubt that this morbid poison must be an organic one." But he goes on to say that "we should not be justified . . . in reckoning cholera among the *contagious* diseases prop-erly so-called, that is to say, among those diseases in which the morbid poison, after being eliminated from the sick and conveyed to other individuals, is able forthwith to unfold its infective power," such as smallpox and measles. Hirsch is impressed with Pettenkofer's ground water theory, that the "morbid poison" somehow needs a suitably po-rous and moist soil in which to multiply. He is agnostic with respect to the importance of drinking water.[74]

With respect to yellow fever, Hirsch laments that "hypotheses as to the nature of the yellow-fever poison, leaning sometimes to one side, sometimes to the other, have exhausted the ingenuity of the profession without advancing our knowledge by a single step." He then discusses various theories, uncharacteristically offering little judgment on them. He concludes from the evidence that yellow fever is communicable, because outside areas where the disease is endemic it occurs only upon arrival of a ship from an endemic area; but he asserts equally that "if we are to understand by *contagion* that kind of spreading of a disease in which we are concerned with infection of an individual by direct conveyance of a morbid poison reproduced in a specifically diseased organism and eliminated therefrom, then, for yellow fever, that mode of disease-conveyance has to be at once dismissed." He finds unhelpful the "obscure notions" of contagion and miasma.[75]

Developments in Applied Science

Such was the state of knowledge in 1881. In the meantime, work was going on by applied scientists that would revolutionize the under-standing of epidemic disease, although no mention was made of it at this time in the discussion of the diseases under consideration. In 1857 Louis Pasteur made the definitive discovery that fermentation (such as in beer) and the souring of milk were caused by minute organisms. A decade later, he showed through experiments with filtered air and in the pure air of the high Alps that these organisms were carried in nor-mal air, a controversial finding against the theory of spontaneous gen-eration, which was popular at the time. In 1865 he made important discoveries about the nature of a silkworm disease (silk making was then an important industry in France), in 1870 about the preservation of beer, and in 1881 about vaccination of cattle against anthrax. The Scottish surgeon Joseph Lister at once appreciated the implications of Pasteur's discoveries for surgery, where the main source of high mortality was infection. After he introduced antisepsis with carbolic acid into his Glasgow surgical ward in 1867, surgical mortality fell from 45 to 15 percent. Such was the opposition to "germ theory" among physicians at the time, however, that his use of antiseptic techniques in the Scottish provinces was not widely accepted until after he successfully performed an extremely difficult and risky kneecap operation in London, the center of British medicine, in 1877. The German scientist Robert Koch linked anthrax to a specific bacillus in 1876, sometimes claimed to be the first such linkage of a disease to a specific microorganism. He wrote about six different kinds of wound infection in 1878. In 1882 he isolated the tuberculosis bacillus, a subject to which he would return in the 1890s and for which he won a Nobel Prize in 1905.

In 1883 cholera broke out in Egypt, and the German government dispatched Koch there as head of a cholera commission to study it. Koch implicated the "comma bacillus" (so called because it was shaped like a comma), but the epidemic receded before he could be sure, so he requested permission to go on to India to continue his work. There he isolated the comma bacillus in pure culture and established to his satisfaction that it was the cause of cholera. He had hoped to make a decisive test by infecting animals, but all efforts at this failed. Nonetheless, the universal presence of the comma bacillus in cholera victims and its absence in bodies that had died from other causes persuaded Koch and his colleagues. In his research, Koch discovered that the comma bacillus cannot tolerate an acid environment and dies if dried for only a few hours.

Koch's periodic reports were sent to Germany, and he was greeted on return as a national hero (at a time of heightened national feeling in Germany) for having beaten the supposedly superior British and French scientists to the discovery of the cause of cholera. Koch's success was greeted with skepticism outside Germany, and even within Germany it was not universally accepted, especially by Pettenkofer and his protégés. In Britain, in particular, Koch's work was dismissed as inconclusive by the medical community, and the noncontagiousness of cholera was reasserted with greater conviction. The British Surgeon General, Sir William Hunter, offered "his unqualified opinion that the disease was non-contagious, non-specific, and endemic in Egypt" (that is, not imported from British India). Hunter believed meteorological conditions caused cholera.[76]

Koch's finding remained controversial for the remainder of the century, but the controversy gradually receded. Koch's position was aided by the 1892 cholera epidemic of Hamburg. The German government sent Koch to investigate, and he found that the tides sometimes carried downstream polluted water of the Elbe River upstream of the water intake for the city, where 18,000 people caught cholera (in a city of about 1 million) and 8,200 died. The neighboring towns of Altona and Wandsbeck, which had different sources of water, had virtually no cases of cholera. Koch could not resist a slap at the miasmatists and localists, as Pettenkofer and his followers were called: "The cholera . . . found out with sharp precision . . . the frontier of the water supplies of the two cities. . . . Sky, sun, wind, rain, etc., were distributed with absolute equality on both sides of the frontier."[77] So increasingly the bacterial origins of cholera were accepted. The world was more ready for them—but still not without dissent—than it had been for Pacini's discovery in 1854.

During the thirty years following 1880, there was a revolution in what is now called bacteriology. The plague-causing bacillus was isolated by Alexandre Yersin in 1894 and rats were incriminated by 1903, but the intermediate vector of the flea, conjectured by Ogata in 1897, was not finally confirmed until 1907.[78] The Cuban doctor Carlos Finlay first suggested the possibility that insect vectors transmit yellow fever in 1881, but that was not finally demonstrated until the work of Walter Reed's Yellow Fever Commission in Havana in 1900. It was clearly established by volunteers' allowing themselves to be bitten that a particular mosquito, *Aëdes aëgypti*, which bred in urban areas in fresh water, transmitted the yellow fever virus from diseased to healthy persons. The disease could be controlled by eliminating the mosquito, especially by eliminating or covering pools of fresh water in urban areas. This discovery made possible, among other things, the construction of the Panama Canal in 1903–14, which DeLesseps had attempted and given up twenty years earlier because of the devastations of yellow fever.

Sir Ronald Ross made the first conclusive identification of an insect vector—for avian malaria—in 1898, for which he won the Nobel Prize in 1902.[79] The importance of insects as transmitters of disease is a matter of common knowledge now, and it is too easy, in hindsight, to find fault with the hesitation and delays and false starts that characterized the late nineteenth century. Why did it take nineteen years from Finlay's conjecture to Reed's proof, for instance, and another decade for wide acceptance of the new information? But there is a big difference between looking back at early pearls of wisdom and recognizing them at the time in the welter of conflicting hypotheses and evidence.

Modern knowledge about the environmental conditions required for all these diseases goes a long way toward explaining the mysteries of earlier years. For instance, the *Aëdes* mosquito does not bite at temperatures below 62 degrees Fahrenheit, which explains why yellow fever occurred only during warm months in the United States. Moreover, as Koch discovered, cholera bacteria cannot tolerate an acidic environment; thus many people who ingest the bacteria do not contract cholera because the bacteria are foiled in the acidic stomach before they reach the small intestine. Similarly, they die if dried out, hence a higher incidence near rivers and other bodies of water. Also, cholera bacteria can be carried and excreted by persons without apparent symptoms, as some delegates to the 1911 conference suspected, thus explaining the occasional examples of cholera appearing suddenly in a community without the arrival of a diseased person.

International Public Health since 1914

The permanent committee of the International Office of Public Hygiene (known as the OIHP for its name in French) did not meet between May 1914 and June 1919, during World War I. It met after the war in a period of great public consciousness in Europe about contagious diseases, since influenza killed an estimated 15 million people in the great epidemic of 1918–19 and nearly 2 million people in Poland and Russia contracted typhus in 1919. It was against this background, too, that the covenant of the League of Nations included a provision (Article 23) that members would "endeavor to take steps in matters of international concern for the prevention and control of disease." At British initiative an international health conference was held among the "big five"—France, Great Britain, Italy, Japan, and the United States—in April 1920 in London. This conference recommended the creation of a health section in the League of Nations, of which the OIHP should become a part. Before this recommendation could be carried out, however, the U.S. Senate failed to ratify the League of Nations treaty in March 1920 and the Wilson administration yielded to the Harding administration. The United States also took the view that no organization of which it was a member could be absorbed by the league. So during the interwar period three health organizations, including the Pan American Sanitary Organization, functioned at the international level.

The OIHP had already broadened its discussions beyond cholera, plague, and yellow fever before the war and had taken up leprosy, tuberculosis, typhoid, venereal diseases, and water purification. In the first meeting after the war the OIHP chairman expressed the view, with general assent, that international cooperation in health matters needed to be completely reoriented, away from quarantine, an obsolete scientific superstition, to "elimination of foci of infection at their points of origin, and this could be accomplished only by well-organized health services in all countries" and by extensive health education.[80] This suggestion was premature, but was later to take root and become the major orientation of the World Health Organization (WHO) after World War II. The OIHP continued its work on the traditional three epidemic diseases, including keeping the international conventions up to date with the latest scientific developments.

In the meantime, the health section of the League of Nations accepted a much broader charge, including malaria, cancer, nutrition, housing, medical education, and standardization of medical products. It also established contact directly with members of the biomedical scientific community (as distinguished from public health officials) for advice and research. The League health section also established the *Weekly Epidemiological Record*, which has been issued continuously since 1926, and the collection, standardization, and publication of international health statistics.

The Russian Revolution of 1917 led, after a civil war, to the creation of the Soviet Union, which was not immediately recognized by any other states and was not a member of the League of Nations. However, Russia had been an historic pathway for Asian diseases to Europe, and detailed knowledge about disease developments in the Soviet Union was highly desirable. The Russians cooperated through the artificial device of creating an "international committee," which met in Geneva on the occasion of league meetings of health officials, but had no formal connection with the league.

The Last Two International Sanitary Conferences

The thirteenth International Sanitary Conference was held in Paris (with preparation by the OIHP) in May–June 1926. It was attended by delegates from over fifty states, including the Soviet Union, roughly half from outside Europe. The main purpose of the conference was to update the 1912 convention. It was generally agreed that two of the three traditional scourges, cholera and yellow fever, had been effectively tamed, and that outside its endemic areas plague was confined to ports. Wide confidence was expressed (wrongly, as is now known) in the efficacy of an anticholera vaccine, and it was suggested that principal reliance could be placed on vaccination to contain cholera. As for yellow fever, the Brazilian scientist Carlos Chagas suggested that "it is a certain conclusion of present epidemiology that yellow fever is a disease near to disappearance, and that the measures that must still be included in the convention will soon become useless."[81] This judgment was also premature. But it was based on the remarkable success of the Rockefeller Foundation, in cooperation with governments, in clearing the urban areas of Latin America of yellow fever during 1917–23 by eliminating the *Aëdes aëgypti* mosquito from those areas.

There was considerable support for adding both influenza and smallpox to the list of epidemic diseases. But in the end the impracticality of quarantine measures against influenza kept it out; and smallpox was deemed to be universal in its presence, thus requiring no special international cooperation. The conference finally agreed that notification of first confirmed cases of cholera, plague, and yellow fever would be sent to the OIHP and, through it, to other countries; and notice of *epidemics* of smallpox and typhus would be sent. "Epidemic" was not defined, but usually means an unusual outbreak of a disease, so the number of cases required to make an epidemic depends on the normal incidence of the disease in the locality in question.

The continuing advance of technology created problems as well as helping to solve them. After 1929 the introduction of commercial transoceanic air service was only a question of time (transoceanic airmail service began in 1935 and the first transoceanic passenger service across the Pacific started in 1937). This opened a new and rapid channel by which disease might be spread, without the long ocean voyage during which a person exposed to disease before departure would normally develop symptoms. In 1933 an international convention was signed (without a conference) on the health treatment of airline crew, passengers, and cargo.

A fourteenth and final International Sanitary Conference was held in Paris in 1938 with the sole purpose and result of eliminating the Maritime Health and Quarantine Council of Egypt and passing its responsibilities to the Egyptian government. This council had been established in 1855 (with antecedents dating back to the cholera epidemic in 1831) to quarantine ships under the flags of the major European powers. Under the "capitulations" of the Ottoman Empire, Egypt could not legally do this without consular approval. The council had been put under international supervision at the International Sanitary Conference of 1892 and greatly strengthened in 1897, when it was also given responsibility for the health of the Suez Canal and the quarantine station at El Tor on the Sinai Peninsula. It was financed partly by the Egyptian government, but partly by health dues on pilgrims and ships using the Suez Canal, and it had the right to levy fines on ships that violated the international health regulations—perhaps the first example of a distinctly international legal offense with international sanctions.[82]

Creation of the World Health Organization

World War II disrupted international health work, although epidemiological reports continued to be received and sent out. The United Nations Relief and Rehabilitation Agency (UNRRA) carried out emergency health activities in war-torn areas after the war. In the meantime, the creation of a World Health Organization (WHO), absorbing what was left of the OIHP and the health section of the League of Nations, was approved in July 1946. It came into being in September 1948 with fifty-five members. WHO is formally governed by an annual World Health Assembly and between meetings by an executive board of twenty-four members who act in their individual capacity. They are selected by twenty-four member governments, which in turn are selected by the World Health Assembly. Each country has one vote in the assembly, regardless of financial contributions, which are related to the country's GNP. A permanent secretariat, with headquarters in Geneva and regional offices elsewhere in the world, carries out the day-to-day functions of WHO. WHO's constitution is wide in scope, encompassing positive health measures as well as defensive measures against disease, and permits WHO to do whatever its members want and are willing to pay for in the area of health, broadly defined.

The creation of WHO brought about several innovations. First, countries were assumed to have adopted internationally agreed health regulations unless they specifically opted out or expressed reservations. This practice avoided the lengthy ratification procedure that had previously attended International Sanitary Conventions and sometimes never occurred at all. This agreement was made possible by general acceptance of WHO's constitution. Second, WHO's secretariat could take the initiative in investigating health problems brought to their attention from whatever source. While their investigations require governmental consent, they do not have to await government initiative to address a possible problem. Third, as foreseen thirty years earlier, the emphasis on containment of contagious diseases shifted from quarantine to control or even eradication at the source.

In its early years WHO concentrated on three types of action. First, it continued earlier work on the standardization of diagnostic, prophylactic, and therapeutic substances and on medical research methods, so that health workers around the world would know exactly what reported substances were or what research had been done. One result is the *International Pharmacopoeia* of drugs and similar standards for biological materials, so that, for example, diabetics can be assured of the potency of insulin anywhere they travel. In addition, WHO promulgates the International Classification of Diseases, Inquiries, and Causes of Death so that national authorities operate from a common system.

Second, WHO has worked to build up the national institutional structure and qualified personnel to promote public health in member countries through extensive technical assistance, fellowships, and training programs both for health workers and for health educators.

Third, WHO mobilizes information and resources to control and combat serious diseases. This activity includes laboratory and field research on disease-causing creatures and the vectors that may carry them. Research is also carried out on vaccines, on therapeutic techniques, and on insecticides for attacking disease vectors with minimal side effects. WHO has launched large-scale eradication programs against malaria and smallpox and has inaugurated control programs for many other diseases, such as onchocerciasis (river blindness) in the Volta River basin. It has done extensive preventive work (for example, against tuberculosis with a vaccine), and therapeutic work (for example, against yaws with penicillin and leprosy with chemotherapy).

More recently, WHO has also broadened its attention to the poverty-nutrition-infection syndrome, worked on health organization and education at the village level, and addressed the risks to mothers and infants arising from unplanned fertility. In 1977 the World Health Assembly adopted its "Health for All by 2000" program, a broad-gauged, largely hortatory, effort to achieve a level of health by 2000 that would allow everyone to lead a socially and economically productive life. WHO plans to concentrate especially on the provision of safe water supplies during the 1990s—a global movement that recalls the nationwide work of Britain's General Board of Health in the 1850s. It has also inaugurated programs on noncommunicable diseases, such as heart problems and mental disorders, and has sponsored a cancer research center in Lyons, France.

Of course, most of these activities are undertaken by national public health authorities in the major countries. WHO helps serve as a clearinghouse for the useful information generated by these authorities and transmits it to countries that do not have highly developed medical research programs. Moreover, it can take on diseases, especially the tropical diseases, that are not high in the priorities of the public health systems in the wealthiest countries. And it can coordinate control programs that transcend national boundaries, as many do.

WHO maintains a telex system to provide up-to-date information on worldwide developments concerning the five epidemic diseases addressed by the International Sanitary Convention of 1926, as well as relapsing fever, influenza, paralytical poliomyelitis, and malaria. The provisions of the 1926 convention were revised in 1951 and again in 1969, when they were renamed international health regulations, and louse-borne typhus and relapsing fever were dropped as quarantinable diseases, leaving only cholera, plague, smallpox, and yellow fever. WHO's stated objective was to strengthen national health services to the point at which the international health regulations would become superfluous.

The traditional three scourges have receded greatly in importance and in the terror they can generate, but they have not disappeared completely as epidemic diseases. A weak (El Tor) variant of cholera broke out of Celebes (Indonesia), where it is endemic, in 1960 and spread to Iran, Iraq, Hong Kong, and Japan. It had receded by 1967, but remained in the Philippines, Vietnam, and Thailand. An outbreak of plague occurred in Ecuador and Peru in 1966, and it remains endemic throughout much of central Asia and in rodents in the western United States. There were early successes in apparently eliminating yellow fever from many Latin American countries, but in the 1960s it reappeared in Brazil, Panama, Mexico, and several other countries that thought they were rid of it. Moreover, the discovery that a variant called "jungle yellow fever" in West Africa can be carried by hosts other than the *Aëdes aëgypti* mosquito has thwarted early suggestions that yellow fever might be eradicated altogether. Indeed, an epidemic of yellow fever broke out in West Africa in late 1986.

In 1955 WHO launched a malaria eradication program. This was thought possible once the cheap, effective, and persistent insecticide DDT became available. Earlier programs had suggested that a determined effort could be successful. The Rockefeller Foundation, working with the Italian government, eliminated malaria from Sardinia in 1946–52. (During World War II the U.S. Army had described Sardinia as the third most malarial area in the world.) Malaria was also virtually eliminated from Mauritius by the British in 1948–52 and by WHO when it made a brief comeback in 1960. So a broader program was launched. By 1970 WHO could report that 39 percent of the 1.8 billion people who lived in malarial areas in 1952 were now free of malaria and had only to maintain careful watch; an additional 19 percent were in a consolidation phase, where malaria was still present but no longer endemic. Twenty percent more still had active antimalarial programs in operation, and 21 percent had no program.[83] Occasional setbacks have been due to incomplete programs, inadequate monitoring after the main phase of the program has been completed, and the emergence of some mosquitos that are resistant to DDT. New insecticides have had to be developed, partly to overcome this resistance and partly to avoid the longer-term deleterious effects now known to accompany the use of DDT. The main role of WHO in these programs has been to provide information, training, technical assistance, and coordination.

In the 1980s, AIDS was the epidemic disease attracting the most attention in the United States and Europe. By the end of 1988, 133,000 cases worldwide had been reported to WHO, but due to incomplete reporting WHO officials estimated that over 300,000 persons have the disease, and that 5 million to 10 million people carry the virus but have not yet developed the disease.[84]

Several factors led some poor countries to downplay the local prevalence of the disease in the 1980s: the high attention given to AIDS in the rich countries, to the relative exclusion of tropical diseases that (so far) are much more devastating in Africa; widespread assertions that AIDS originated in Africa; and the fact that detecting and dealing with AIDS is exceptionally expensive, hence difficult for poor countries. WHO is training local public health officials to identify AIDS and to educate people concerning its mode of propagation. WHO also transmits to public health authorities around the world information on constantly evolving scientific developments.[85]

The Eradication of Smallpox

The crowning achievement of international collaboration in public health is the eradication, in 1977, of smallpox as a naturally occurring disease.[86] Smallpox was formerly the scourge of mankind, causing disfiguration or death for much of the population. As noted earlier, it is estimated that in 1775, 95 percent of Europeans had contracted smallpox at some time, and one in seven died from it.[87] Smallpox, like other contagious diseases, often had profound political effects, such as when it devastated 3 million Aztecs and permitted the Spanish takeover of Mexico in the early sixteenth century. In the eighteenth century five monarchs succumbed to it. It ended the Stuart line in Britain and Louis XV's happy reign in France. Disfigurement sent many women of the Middle Ages into the nunneries. Deaths from smallpox are estimated to have overwhelmed those from plague, cholera, and war put together.[88]

Curiously, because smallpox was endemic and considered a normal part of life in Europe, it is less well documented historically than are some other diseases. Furthermore, it attracted less attention as an international issue and was not even required to be reported internationally until the 1926 sanitary convention. But there was a strong interest in preventing this dreadful disease, and as early as the 1720s inoculation with the pus of diseased persons was introduced from Turkey into Europe as a way to increase resistance to the disease. In 1796 Edward Jenner established that cowpox serum was a safer substitute with much the same effect.[89] Thus those who could afford to be vaccinated could increasingly escape smallpox altogether. Vaccination gradually spread throughout the nineteenth century, starting with the compulsory vaccination of Napoleon's army in 1806.[90]

Smallpox follows a distinctive course, which was well understood by the mid-twentieth century. Exposure is through direct inhalation of the virus from an infected person with known symptoms. It takes ten to twelve days for the disease to incubate, following which there is fever and a feeling of soreness, and then in three to four days the distinctive rash breaks out all over the body, predominantly on the face and limbs. Vaccination virtually ensures immunity, at least for some years. There is no known cure for the disease once it is contracted.

Extensive vaccination in the nineteenth and twentieth centuries greatly reduced the incidence of smallpox in Europe and America. In the United States there were still 102,000 cases in 1921, but the last case was recorded in 1949. Europe had 122,000 cases in 1921; this had declined to 281 cases by 1950. But there were nearly half a million cases in the Indonesian epidemic of 1949, and India suffered 230,000 deaths from smallpox in 1944, implying over 1 million cases. Moreover, these last two estimates are almost certainly substantially below the true figures.[91]

The great decline in incidence in the Americas led Fred Soper, director of the Pan American Health Organization, to propose in 1950 the eradication of smallpox from the Western hemisphere. Operationally, this was taken to mean vaccination of 80 percent of the population, which was thought to introduce a sufficient barrier to the transmission of smallpox that it would die out. The main locus of smallpox in the Americas at the time was Brazil, and a program was launched there.

In 1958 the Soviet Union, which had withdrawn from WHO in 1949 but rejoined in 1957, proposed to the World Health Assembly a global program to eradicate smallpox. One reason for this proposal was that the USSR was exposed to the reintroduction of smallpox from South Asia, one of the areas in which it was still endemic. The Soviet Union played a key role in the eradication program, providing most of the vaccine.[92]

WHO experts who studied the question found that such a program would be feasible, and in 1965 the World Health Assembly stated that eradication of smallpox was a major objective of WHO. The plan was to assist all countries where smallpox was endemic to vaccinate 80 percent of the population. But this represented a major task for public health authorities. Thoughtful observation by Dr. William Foege in Nigeria suggested that a better way was possible. With timely and accurate reporting on new cases of smallpox, the infected persons could be completely isolated and mass local vaccination of the village and others with whom the infected person might recently have been in contact could be undertaken. The aim was to break the chain of transmission of smallpox, which must go directly from an infected person to unvaccinated persons. Extensive training of public health auxiliaries was undertaken and rewards were offered for reports of symptoms that might be smallpox. The technique worked in country after country. The last cases of smallpox were recorded in Nepal, India, and Bangladesh in 1975, in Ethiopia in 1976, and in Kenya and Somalia in 1977. A subsequent two-year waiting and watching period was required before certification was given that the disease was eradicated from each country.

A major incentive for a smallpox eradication program was that the estimated costs of eradication could be more than recouped by savings on vaccination and quarantines against its spread. The total cost of the smallpox eradication program to WHO and other international donors came to $112 million, plus perhaps an additional $200 million spent by the national governments of the countries in which smallpox was still found. WHO estimates that this $312 million one-time expenditure saved at least $1 billion a year in terms of vaccination programs, care of infected persons, and quarantine if smallpox existed on the scale it did in the late 1960s.[93] Thus eradication of smallpox was not only an international public good in terms of the alleviation of suffering, but it also offered a handsome return on investment by reducing precautionary expenditures worldwide.

An interesting feature of smallpox is that, because it is transmitted by a virus, the understanding of its exact etiology is still extremely imperfect. The difference between the smallpox virus and the virus that is used in vaccination is not even clear.[94] Although detailed scientific understanding of smallpox is weak, the very good clinical and epidemiological knowledge of how the disease was transmitted, the incubation period, and the nature of its infectiousness proved sufficient to launch an effective program of eradication.

Animal Diseases

This paper has focused on international control of the spread of contagious diseases among humans. An analogous problem exists for contagious diseases among animals, particularly those that are useful to people. Some diseases, such as rabies and brucellosis, occur both in people and in domesticated animals and have been addressed by WHO. Those that affect economically important animals such as cattle and pigs have been addressed by the Food and Agriculture Organization (FAO), founded in 1945 with forty-two members. Over the years the FAO has made systematic attacks on rinderpest, African horse sickness, foot and mouth disease, and African swine fever. In the 1980s it has devoted major efforts to controlling the tsetse fly in Africa, which infects cattle with trypanosomiasis (and also people with sleeping sickness), and to controlling ticks, which infect cattle with East Coast fever, anaplasmosis, and a host of other diseases. The FAO provides mainly technical assistance, training and guidance materials, research, and coordination among countries; funds come from the countries where control programs are undertaken or from aid programs of the major aid donors.

An example of international cooperation is provided by the efforts to control rinderpest (cattle plague), a directly contagious viral disease with mortality rates up to 90 percent in newly infected regions. No cure is known, but vaccination provides effective immunization against the disease for five or six years. Rinderpest is believed to have been brought into Western Asia from China by Mongols in the first century A.D. Epizootics occurred from time to time thereafter in Europe and the Middle East. The most devastating one was in Africa in 1880–95, when 80–90 percent of the continent's cattle and wild ruminants are estimated to have died. Up until 1950, when vaccines became more widely used, some 2 million head of cattle in Africa, Asia, and part of Europe died of rinderpest every year. A major international control program was launched in Africa in 1962, and by 1976 the disease was confined to three West African countries. It was eliminated in Nigeria by 1972. A cost-benefit analysis put the internal rate of return of the rinderpest control programs (mostly mass vaccination and destruction of diseased cattle) at 47 percent.

Unfortunately there was a resurgence of the disease after 1979, and it spread eastward across Africa and northeastward into Egypt and the Middle East by the mid-1980s. The spread resulted partly from the breakdown of veterinary services in areas of political unrest and economic privation due to drought. Another international control effort was launched in 1982.[95]

African horse sickness was eliminated from the Middle East under an international program in 1959–63 and has not returned. Foot and mouth disease was virtually eliminated from Europe by 1953, and an eradication program for Latin America was launched in 1981. African swine fever has been eliminated from several Latin American countries.[96] International cooperation has therefore had considerable effect in controlling animal as well as human diseases.

Why Did International Health Cooperation Take So Long?

It took over seventy years from the first call for international cooperation in the containment of the spread of contagious disease in 1834 to 1907, when an international organization was first put in place to deal with the problem—and even that represented only the beginning. Why did it take so long to achieve international cooperation despite the widely shared objective of preventing the spread of virulent disease? It is now evident that it was due to conflicting views over how best to tackle the problem, over means-ends relationships. The ends were shared: to stop the spread of epidemic disease. But there were sharp disagreements over how best to do this. The means were costly, and their costs would have been borne unevenly by different countries. Each party understandably wanted to pay the lowest possible cost.

Costs were related to remedies, and remedies in turn were related to the causes of the diseases, about which disagreement continued for much of the century. The main intellectual disagreement was between miasmatists and contagionists, although there were many shadings between the extremes of these two views. Britain was the most vigorous official adherent of the miasmatic view. Throughout most of the century Britain insisted that cholera did not originate in India and was not transmitted by diseased persons. These views had some support from scientists in other countries and from some other governments from time to time; and some British scientists were strong supporters of the contagion hypothesis. The main official support for the contagionist view came from countries around the Mediterranean, which thought themselves to be most highly exposed to the initial importation of disease by ships from the Middle East and Asia.

All scientific parties to the debate were aware of the evidence, but the evidence was ambiguous and could be used to support conflicting theories. Epidemiology in the nineteenth century was much like economics in the twentieth century: a subject of intense public interest and concern, in which theories abounded but the scope for controlled experiments was limited. (Personally imbibing or injecting diseased cultures was more an act of bravado than scientific experiment.) These circumstances led to detailed observation of persons showing symptoms of the disease, especially in western Europe. These observations were partly guided by theory, but they were also designed to inform the observers about the nature of disease propagation through a process of induction. Without adequate statistical methodology, however, it was impossible to form firm, universally persuasive conclusions. So long as contention continued over the efficacy of different courses of action, it was similarly impossible to get agreement among countries on a common course of action.

Many countries supported the age-old technique of quarantining ships that were infected or under suspicion of being infected with disease. For Britain, however, with its profitable and rapidly growing merchant fleet that traveled increasingly on fixed timetables between Europe and Asia, the old quarantine practices represented an intolerable burden on trade and shipping. This view was shared by others with merchant interests. It is not surprising that the British embraced the theories that happened to be dominant in mid-century, which implied that quarantine was pointless for cholera and possibly also for plague. And yet when cholera or plague arrived in a country, it understandably struck terror into the local population and gave rise to calls for urgent action by the governments in question. Quarantining ships arriving from areas suspected of infection became a political necessity in the absence of compelling reasons to the contrary. But when the disease receded, the pressure for action declined and quarantine was relaxed.

Experience reinforced Britain's miasmatic position. Benthamite reformers, armed with "truth" and contemptuous of "old-fashioned" views about the propagation of disease, began to clean up Britain's cities and water supplies in the 1850s. The incidence of cholera in Britain declined rapidly, despite greatly increased shipping traffic between India and Britain. Could there have been more compelling evidence for the miasmatic—or at least anticontagionist—view of cholera?

If Britain's experience was so favorable, why was not Britain's behavior widely emulated elsewhere? To some extent it was, especially in New York and other American cities after the mid-1860s, in Prussia, and here and there in other parts of Europe. But the sanitation movement did not at once become universal. This was in part because few countries had just the blend of central authority and local autonomy that prevailed in Britain, which was especially suitable for introducing new ideas that required extensive local initiative and cooperation to execute successfully. But I suspect that the main reason was that cleaning up the cities and installing systems for supplying clean water and taking away sewage were very expensive. Most countries were unwilling to undertake the expense. The great sanitation movement in Britain of the 1850s bore strong similarities to the antipollution movement in the United States and Europe in the late 1960s and early 1970s. Both were spearheaded by relatively well-to-do reformers, who were offended aesthetically by the state of the environment as they found it. In both cases the reformers successfully urged large public expenditures (and public regulations of private activity) to improve the health of the poor. And in both cases the reformers' motivation went well beyond improving the health of the poor: to economic benefits from a healthy urban labor force in the nineteenth century and to aesthetic considerations in the twentieth century.

By the mid-nineteenth century Britain (and the United States) had much higher per capita incomes than most other countries. Around 1870, for instance, Britain had a per capita income of about $180 and the United States, about $170. In contrast, Germany had a per capita income of less than $80, Italy around $70, Sweden about $60, and European Russia under $50.[97] The governments of Britain, Germany, Japan, and the United States in those days collected and spent about 10 percent of GNP. France spent somewhat more.[98] These figures rose to the 15–20 percent range by 1900, except in the United States, where it remained about 10 percent of GNP. The countries with higher per capita incomes could obviously afford to spend more on local public goods such as water supplies and orderly sewage disposal. It has been estimated that Britain spent $400 million dollars over 1860–90 on public health measures.[99] This figure averages out at about one-quarter of 1 percent of GNP over this period. By 1902 local governments in the United States were spending $135 million for public health (excluding hospitals), water, and sanitation, or about three-quarters of 1 percent of GNP.[100] These were relatively large sums to spend on the strength of a hypothesis, and they would be proportionately greater in poorer countries for comparable coverage of their citizens. In the presence of conflicting hypotheses about the propagation of epidemic disease, poorer countries' cost-benefit calculations favored the contagion theory with its policy implication of quarantine rather than the miasmatic theory with its policy implication of provision of an extensive urban infrastructure. Quarantine could be loosened or tightened according to the prevalence of disease, and the costs would be borne largely by someone else. Ignorance permitted adoption of the hypothesis that best served each country's circumstances.

Late in the century ignorance was rapidly reduced by the modern subject of bacteriology, so the contention between major hypotheses gradually declined. The contagionists won the scientific battle, more or less, but the miasmatists were right about the practical course of action, at least as far as cholera and other water-borne diseases were concerned. Once the intellectual pieces fell into place, disagreement over what broadly needed to be done dropped sharply, and a framework of international cooperation became possible. The key components of this development were, first, the intellectual advances that with testing gradually became incontrovertible; second, the ability to reach pragmatic consensus around the new knowledge, even when disagreements on the detailed features of propagation remained; and third, the timely availability of information on new outbreaks of interest to all parties, which required an international channel of communication. Until the mid-twentieth century all of the actions were undertaken by national or local governments, not by international authority. But they were increasingly based on international information and were taken within an internationally agreed framework that in some cases put limits on national action—for example, quarantine provisions—and in other cases enjoined particular national action—for example, the obligatory provision of information to others, or the regulations regarding the elimination of rats on ships.

Lessons for Macroeconomic Cooperation

What lessons does the experience of international cooperation in public health contain for other forms of international cooperation, especially macroeconomic cooperation? There have been regular calls for better coordination of macroeconomic policies among the major industrialized countries for at least the past quarter century. Indeed, in some sense such calls can be traced back to the London Economic Conference of 1933, which was called in the depths of the Great Depression to achieve concerted action toward economic recovery. But what exactly does international cooperation mean? It is worth noting the many different forms of international cooperation that are possible.

There can be exchange of information; agreement on common concepts and standards; exchange of views on prospective national policy actions; agreement on rules that set boundaries to national behavior, but leave decisions at the national level; formally coordinated national policy actions; and joint action under common direction and (if appropriate) shared expenditure.

All these forms of cooperation can be observed in public health. Timely and reasonably accurate information is crucial in controlling the spread of infectious disease, and indeed that was the first agreed function of the International Office of Public Hygiene. Countries very quickly came to realize that interpretation of information required common standards of assessment and measurement (for example, the reporting week, or the symptoms that indicate a particular disease is present), and soon thereafter, common standards were extended to diagnostic and therapeutic pharmaceuticals. Indeed, the genesis of international public health cooperation was the lack of standardization of quarantine timing and procedures, and rules were laid down for local health authorities to minimize the social costs of quarantine. The OIHP also provided a conduit for exchanging information on actions proposed and taken following the outbreak of an infectious disease. Finally, there have been closely coordinated and joint actions under common direction and with shared expenditure on programs to control malaria and eradicate smallpox in the second half of the twentieth century, although disease eradication began earlier in limited areas under the stimulus of the Rockefeller Foundation.

Examples of Cooperation

Examples of all of these forms of cooperation can also be found in the macroeconomic arena. In the 1930s the League of Nations initiated a number of comparative studies of national economies, which suggested a strong need to standardize data concepts. The United Nations, the International Monetary Fund (IMF), and the Organization for Economic Cooperation and Development (OECD) have all done much useful technical work on standardizing the national accounts, the balance-of-payments accounts, and other economic statistics across countries.

Moreover, there have been a number of attempts to lay down guidelines, or even rules, to govern the behavior of national monetary authorities in the interests of a well-functioning international economic system. Among the early examples was the Genoa Conference sponsored by the League of Nations in 1922. This conference resulted in recommendations that governments call in gold from circulation, with the purpose of concentrating monetary gold in central banks, and issuing instead paper money for circulation; and instruct their central banks to hold some portion of their international reserves in the form of currencies convertible into gold rather than gold itself, that is, to hold sterling. These recommendations would break the formal symmetry of the gold standard, whereby gold transfer from one country to another led to monetary contraction in the country of export and monetary expansion in the country of import, although even before 1914 countries frequently took steps to offset the monetary effect of gold exportation or importation.[101] Under the Genoa recommendations, a "reserve loss" by Britain would not necessarily mean monetary contraction by Britain, since foreigners would hold their reserves in London in the form of sterling balances. So the system could be expected to perform differently from the classical gold standard with respect to macroeconomic policy. Formally, however, the effort was to coordinate reserve policies rather than monetary policies.

A more ambitious attempt at rulemaking was undertaken in 1944 at Bretton Woods. One objective of the Bretton Woods conference was to create an international system in which it was *not* necessary for nations to coordinate their macroeconomic policies. On the contrary, each country was to be left free to pursue its own social and economic objectives, but subject to certain international rules: currencies were to be convertible for current account transactions, and exchange rates were to be nearly fixed, although adjusted from time to time if necessary. In practice, the Bretton Woods system compelled some coordination of macroeconomic policies insofar as countries wanted to avoid having to alter their exchange rates. And of course once a country needed to go to the International Monetary Fund for financial support, IMF lending was made conditional on some changes in policy, usually involving the exchange rate and monetary and fiscal actions to support the new exchange rate.

Other codes of behavior have occasionally been agreed upon. Some involve firm commitments, such as the General Agreement on Tariffs and Trade (GATT); some involve pledges to general principles rather than firm commitments, such as the OECD code on foreign direct investment. Again, these codes limit the instruments of macroeco-

nomic policy, but they do not address direct coordination of macroeconomic policy.

A modest step toward coordination took place through the Organization for European Economic Cooperation (OEEC), which was set
up to help allocate Marshall Plan aid from the United States and continued through the 1950s. In 1961 it was transformed into the Organization for Economic Cooperation and Development (OECD), whose
Economic Policy Committee (EPC) was to discuss internationally, in
the words of Walter Heller at its inaugural meeting, "economic policy
in the making." In fact EPC discussions fell short of that, usually involving a first-hand report by responsible officials on the course of national policy after decisions had been made. Its role was thus infor-
mational. That was in general also true of the more restricted Working
Party Three of the EPC, where from time to time government actions
were criticized, diplomatically but unmistakably, but there was no attempt to coordinate actions.

Thus examples of all of the weaker forms of cooperation can also
be found in the macroeconomic arena. The calls for closer cooperation
in management of economies, though often vague, usually mean coordination of policies in amount and timing—or, what is hardly different, joint decisionmaking with respect to macroeconomic action.
There have been a few examples of that, but they have been relatively
rare.

In a widely publicized meeting at Checquers in Britain in 1967,
finance ministers from the major countries announced their intention
to achieve a general lowering of interest rates, which each country had
been keeping up for balance-of-payments reasons. Under the conditions prevailing in 1967, however, they were too high for the sake of
buoyant economic activity. It is unclear whether U.S. and German officials cleared this action ahead of time with their independent central
banks, but interest rates did indeed come down following the meeting.

In 1977 the United States attempted to achieve joint fiscal expansion with Japan and West Germany. Again the concern was with the
serious pause in world recovery from the 1975 economic slump. In the
presence of flexible exchange rates, economic expansion by a single
country was thought to lead to depreciation of its currency and a worsened short-run trade-off between inflation and employment. Joint action by the three major countries could avoid marked movements in
the exchange rates among their currencies and thus reduce the infla-

tionary effect of expansionary action in any one of them. The timing was off; the United States went ahead alone in 1977, with some of the predicted undesirable consequences. Japan and Germany were persuaded to act by the Bonn summit of July 1978, at which both agreed to fiscal expansion.[102] More recently, but less ambitiously, in September 1985 finance ministers from the five leading countries agreed that the dollar was too strong relative to the other currencies and pledged joint action to reduce its value.[103]

Difficulties of Coordination

It is perhaps useful to enumerate the reasons why coordination of macroeconomic policy has been so rare. Sometimes there has been disagreement over the objectives to be served, in particular on the balance to be struck between encouraging economic expansion and discouraging inflation. There has also been disagreement on the prognostication of future economic events, which obviously strongly influence what current actions should be taken. There has been continuing disagreement on means-ends relationships, on the effect of particular economic measures on the course of economic events. And there has been disagreement on how the costs of any particular desired outcome should be shared among the leading countries. (The term "costs" in this instance usually refers to the costs of politically controversial action, but sometimes also refers to the costs in terms of compromising national economic objectives.) Absence of leadership and lack of trust among nations can also inhibit close economic cooperation, as can misguided notions of national sovereignty.[104]

Disagreement over objectives was relatively unimportant when it came to preventing the spread of infectious disease. Before the 1840s, disease was sometimes welcomed for its role in "cleansing" society, but thereafter the objective of stopping the disease was universally shared. Once disease was reported, there was more disagreement over what to do about it. Here disagreement on means-ends relationships and disagreement on prognostication were closely linked, with miasmatists taking the view that diseases could not be imported and contagionists insisting that they were. Public dread of these diseases often led to calls for more action than the authorities thought was necessary. The decisive barrier to early cooperation was therefore ignorance over the nature (what might be called the "technology") of disease propagation. That in turn influenced both forecasts and perceptions with respect to burden sharing. Indeed, the costs of implied action may well have influenced preferences of governments among the contending technological hypotheses, although there is only inferential evidence for that. As I have shown, lack of trust and misguided notions of national sovereignty also played a role in inhibiting early cooperation among countries in the area of public health. Onerous restrictions on shipping created an incentive to conceal exposure to disease, and that in turn led to distrust of bills of health. Recall that the United States proposed in 1881 to require consular certification of health conditions in ports of embarkation, on the grounds that local reports about infectious disease and other medical conditions could not be fully trusted, and this proposal was rejected on the grounds that it represented an infringement of national sovereignty.

Interestingly enough, it was not necessary for international cooperation in public health to reach consensus on the exact etiological details of a given disease. A striking case is provided by smallpox, which was completely eradicated without exact knowledge of how the smallpox virus does its damage within the body. What was necessary was consensus on a reasonably accurate picture of how the disease moved from person to person so that an effective way could be found to interrupt the transmission.

Macroeconomics is more complicated than disease propagation. Objectives are shared at a very general level: virtually everyone desires high employment growth without inflation. Choices among the three components that are rolled together in this clause—high employment, growth, and inflation—are given different weight by different governments, by different political parties within countries, and even by the same government over time. Forecasts differ, often sharply, and governments are understandably reluctant to take politically controversial actions that are thought to be unnecessary or possibly even perverse in their effects on the basis of uncertain forecasts about prospective economic developments.

Disagreement over Economic Determinants

But I would conjecture that the major stumbling block to closer macroeconomic cooperation is sharp continuing disagreement on means-ends relationships, on the "technology" of macroeconomics and the influence of instruments of policy on national economies. These disagreements are now substantial. There is less consensus in the late 1980s than there was in the late 1960s, although there was much disagreement even then. There are at present several fundamental cleavages among economists concerning the determinants of overall economic activity in major national economies. Simplifying labels, such as "Keynesian" or "monetarist" or "new classicist," have been placed on the diverse schools of thought, just as theorists of epidemic disease were divided in the mid-nineteenth century into miasmatists and contagionists. But as among scientists in the nineteenth century, so also among economists in the twentieth century there are countless variants and refinements of each school. As a result, those near the borders of different schools of thought may be closer together in their views about how economies work—or how diseases are transmitted—than two individuals supposedly of the same school might be.

When it comes to recommendations for macroeconomic policy, the differences of view are quite profound. For instance, "Keynesians" typically hold that an increase in government expenditure (or a reduction in taxes), by stimulating demand, will increase the output of an economy unless its resources are already fully utilized, and this will occur even if the government finances the resulting budget deficit by floating securities on the capital market. On this view, the government budget might be used—if it is sufficiently flexible—to help stabilize total output and employment in the face of diverse disturbances that would otherwise result in loss of output and employment. Of course, the actions could be reversed (and in the view of most Keynesians should be) if private demand tends for whatever reason to outrun an economy's productive capacity, creating inflationary pressures.

The underlying assumption is questioned by some "monetarists," who argue that a rise in the budget deficit financed outside the banking system will simply drive up interest rates, which in turn will serve to reduce investment or increase private savings; or an increase in the deficit may appreciate the currency in a regime of floating exchange rates, which in turn will reduce exports and increase imports to the point at which any stimulus to demand and output from the budget deficit will be nullified. Hence active use of fiscal policy for stabilizing the economy is fruitless, because it cannot work.

Some Keynesians, under at least some circumstances, while not conceding the above point, would nonetheless be prepared to accompany stimulative fiscal action with some monetary expansion brought about by central bank financing of part of the government deficit. Monetarists, joined by new classicists, counter that monetary expansion cannot, in general, stimulate production, at least beyond the few months it takes for the public to understand what is happening. Rather, monetary expansion works, at least after a relatively short period, directly and proportionately on the price level. So monetary action, whether or not accompanied by fiscal action, cannot be used to stabilize the real output of an economy; what is worse, attempts to do so, because of long and variable lags, may actually destabilize an economy. In contrast, a necessary and sufficient condition for reducing the rate of inflation in an economy is to reduce the rate of growth of the money supply, somehow defined.

Put another way, monetarists believe that monetary expansion cannot reduce real interest rates for more than a short period, measured in months, whereas Keynesians believe it can; and some even appear to believe that monetary expansion can lower real (inflation-corrected) interest rates in the long run.

The new classicists usefully emphasize that economic agents— households and firms—will when possible be forward-looking in making their decisions. That is, they will be influenced by their expectations about future developments. But in the new classicists' formal work, which often leads to strong negative conclusions about the efficacy of macroeconomic policy, they assume that economic agents have information that they cannot possibly have about the structure of the economy and about future developments. And their after-the-fact interpretation of events can be perfectly validated simply by assuming that economic agents held expectations about upcoming events that led to behavior exactly as it was observed. In short, new classicists are able to invoke nonobserved variables to explain perfectly any event, after the fact. This scientifically unacceptable procedure can be remedied only by gathering direct information, insofar as possible, on what people believe will happen in the future, that is, by turning to the survey techniques of social psychology to gather information that is critical for understanding how the economy actually works—analogous to the important role that meticulous observation played in establishing the etiology of epidemic disease.

Differences of view about how economies work go beyond the differences identified above, involving the reliability of the relationship of consumption to disposable income, the extent to which labor can be involuntarily unemployed for a relatively long period, the speed with which markets for goods and services restore equilibrium following a disturbance, and whether people's expectations about the future are more usefully characterized by some extrapolation of their recent experience or by an assumption that they have complete knowledge of the future path of their national economy except for randomly distributed, unforeseeable disturbances. But these differences of view are alone sufficient to stymie cooperation among governments in the face of some known disturbance, since governments' economic advisers may disagree strongly about the most appropriate response.

For example, on several occasions from the late 1970s to the late 1980s the U.S. and various European governments urged the German authorities to stimulate their economy through fiscal or, more circumspectly, monetary action. These urgings evidently reflected something akin to what has been called the Keynesian view. German authorities resisted this advice, on grounds that no doubt are complex and among other things involve complicated interparty and intergovernmental relations within the Federal Republic (federal tax revenues are shared with the various German *Länder*, or states, for example). But at the level of macroeconomic analysis, many Germans argued that neither an increase in government spending nor a reduction in taxes would stimulate domestic demand, in part because both businesses and households would become so fearful of the resulting budget deficit that they would reduce their spending by more than the stimulus injected by the government. This view is given some theoretical support by new classicists. There sometimes was also a tendency, not consistent with the above position, for German authorities to argue that increased government spending, even when not accompanied by monetary expansion, would be inflationary. In contrast, it was argued or implied that increased exports, another major component of total demand, would not be inflationary.

Tangible representation of the diversity of views among economists is offered by a unique exercise performed at the Brookings Institution in 1987. Twelve macroeconomic models were calibrated to a standard base and set of projections and then were asked to indicate the effect on several economic variables of standardized changes in fiscal and monetary policy in the United States and other industrialized countries. These mostly large-scale models reflected a variety of macroeconomic perspectives, and not surprisingly they revealed a variety of results, with a range so wide that in many circumstances they would offer sharply conflicting advice to economic policymakers.[105]

Drawing on these models, and providing some plausible but not necessarily accurate structure as to national preferences, Frankel and

Rockett have shown that coordinated economic actions can actually leave the cooperating nations worse off if they are cooperating on the basis of models of the economy that deviate sufficiently from reality.[106] Of course, they may often improve their position, as they expect. But ignorance of the underlying reality can also result in consequential mistakes. If this is so, it is not surprising that disagreement over how economies work leads to hesitation when it comes to coordinated action.

So long as fundamental disagreements exist on means-ends relationships, close international cooperation in the sense of joint decisionmaking will not generally be possible. Of course this does not rule out an occasional but coincidental convergence of interests that permits joint action at a particular moment.

If this conjecture is correct, it sets an agenda for the economics profession. Economists should strive hard to reduce the areas of disagreement on the technology of macroeconomic relationships, and this inevitably will require close empirical (including institutional) observation and modeling of national economies and their interactions; it cannot be done through theoretical reasoning alone. It does not necessarily require establishing macroeconomics on a firm microeconomic foundation, any more than effective epidemiology required exact knowledge of how the microbic parasites function in the body. That might be necessary if there were a need to understand and predict macroeconomic behavior under *all* circumstances; but practical problems of policymaking usually arise in a much more limited domain. Macroeconomic behavior within that prevailing domain may often be understood sufficiently without firm microeconomic foundations, however desirable those may be. But it is likely to require much closer observation of how economies actually behave than professional economists—drawn as they are by professional norms to economic theory—are currently inclined to give.

The history of epidemiology offers many examples, such as Pettenkofer's ground water theory, of how a theory not only can persist despite little supporting evidence if pressed continually with sufficient vigor and creativeness in interpreting the evidence, but also can lead to suppression of alternative hypotheses that are correct. The collection of meticulous case histories of infected persons played a major role in building support for preventive measures; but so did the discovery of the importance of microbes and of intermediate insect vectors in transmitting them from person to person. So theoretical ideas and careful empirical observation reinforced one another; in the end, both were crucial to success in public health.

Notes

1. Institute for International Economics, "Promoting World Recovery: A Statement on Global Strategy," Special Report no. 1 (Washington, December 1982); and Helmut Schmidt, "Helmut Schmidt's Prescription: The World Economy at Stake," *The Economist*, February 1983, pp. 19–30.

2. Institute for International Economics, "Resolving the Global Economic Crisis: After Wall Street," Special Report no. 6 (Washington, December 1987).

3. Fernand Braudel, *Civilization and Capitalism, 15th–18th Century*, vol. 1: *The Structures of Everyday Life* (Harper and Row, 1981), p. 79.

4. Carlo M. Cipolla, *Fighting the Plague in Seventeenth-Century Italy* (University of Wisconsin Press, 1981), p. 100.

5. Daniel DeFoe, *A Journal of the Plague Year* (Baltimore, Md.: Penguin Books, 1966).

6. Cipolla, *Fighting the Plague*, p. 8.

7. DeFoe, *A Journal of the Plague Year*, p. 92.

8. Neville M. Goodman, *International Health Organizations and Their Work*, 2d ed. (London: Churchill Livingstone, 1971), p. 29.

9. Paul Cassar, *Medical History of Malta* (London: Wellcome Historical Medical Library, 1964), pp. 288, 295.

10. As recently as 1884 an Italian ship with 200 passengers left Genoa for Montevideo, Uruguay. Cholera broke out and the ship was refused entry either at Montevideo or at Rio de Janeiro. It returned to Italy to perform quarantine and the passengers were finally put in at Leghorn, seventy-eight miles from where they had started, after four months. Goodman, *International Health Organizations*, p. 35.

11. Geoffrey Marks and William K. Beatty, *Epidemics* (Charles Scribner's Sons, 1976), p. 193.

12. Marks and Beatty, *Epidemics*, pp. 201, 206.

13. Marks and Beatty, *Epidemics*, p. 195.

14. William H. McNeill, *Plagues and Peoples* (Garden City, N.Y.: Anchor Press/Doubleday, 1976), p. 261.

15. Norman Howard-Jones, *The Scientific Background of the International Sanitary Conferences, 1851–1938* (Geneva: World Health Organization, 1975), p. 11.

16. Howard-Jones, *Scientific Background*, pp. 15, 29.

17. McNeill, *Plagues and Peoples*, p. 275.

18. George Rosen, *A History of Public Health* (New York: MD Publications, 1958), p. 211.

19. Edwin Chadwick, *Report on an Inquiry into the Sanitary Condition of the Labouring Population of Great Britain*, quoted in Rosen, *History of Public Health*, p. 215.

20. Rosen, *History of Public Health*, p. 212.

21. Rosen, *History of Public Health*, p. 221.

22. Quoted in Rosen, *History of Public Health*, pp. 242–43.

23. See Rosen, *History of Public Health*, app. I.

24. *London Medical Gazette* (1851), quoted in Goodman, *International Health Organizations*, pp. 43–44.

25. Quoted in Howard-Jones, *Scientific Background*, pp. 13, 15.

26. For a summary, see Goodman, *International Health Organizations*, pp. 42–44.

27. Howard-Jones, *Scientific Background*, p. 22.

28. Folke Henschen, *The History and Geography of Diseases*, trans. Joan Tate (New York: Delacorte Press, 1967), p. 71.

29. Norbert Hirschhorn and William B. Greenough III, "Cholera," *Scientific American*, vol. 225 (August 1971), pp. 15–21.

30. August Hirsch, *Handbook of Geographical and Historical Pathology*, vol. 1, trans. Charles Creighton (London: New Sydenham Society, 1883), pp. 414–20.

31. See Charles E. Rosenberg, *The Cholera Years: The United States in 1832, 1849, 1866* (University of Chicago Press, 1962), pp. 202–11, esp. p. 209n, where he cites New York State Metropolitan Board of Health, *Annual Report, 1866*, p. 189. However, Hirsch, *Handbook of Geographical and Historical Pathology*, p. 420, reports approximately 1,200 cholera deaths in New York in 1866.

32. *Report to the International Sanitary Conference [of Constantinople in 1866] of a Commission from That Body, to Which Were Referred the Questions Relative to the Origin, Endemnicity, Transmissibility and Propagation of Asiatic Cholera*, trans. Samuel Abbot (Boston, Mass.: Alfred Mudge and Son, 1867). Much of the following discussion of cholera is found in this report.

33. John M. Woodworth, *The Cholera Epidemic of 1873 in the United States* (Government Printing Office, 1875), pp. 62–63.

34. Woodworth, *Cholera Epidemic of 1873*, pp. 13, 62.

35. Goodman, *International Health Organizations*, p. 60.

36. See Erwin H. Ackerknecht, "Anticontagionism between 1821 and 1867," *Bulletin of the History of Medicine*, vol. 22 (1948), p. 571 ff.

37. Henschen, *History and Geography of Diseases*, p. 37.

38. Rosen, *History of Public Health*, p. 249.

39. U.S. Congress, *Proceedings of the International Sanitary Conference* [of Washington in 1881] (GPO, 1881), p. 17.

40. Hirsch, *Handbook of Geographical and Historical Pathology*, pp. 373–74.

41. John L. Cabell, "The National Board of Health and the International Sanitary Conference of Washington," *Transactions of the American Medical Association* (1881), pp. 334–35.

42. Hirsch, *Handbook of Geographical and Historical Pathology*, pp. 373, 375 (italics in original).

43. U.S. Congress, *Proceedings*, p. 119.

44. For a summary, see Goodman, *International Health Organizations*, pp. 61–62.

45. Howard-Jones, *Scientific Background*, pp. 56–57.

46. Koch did not mention Pacini anywhere in his work, even though Pacini had continued to work and publish his views on cholera up until 1879. Pacini died in 1883, one year before Koch's work and twenty-nine years after his own identification of the same bacillus as the cause of cholera in 1854. Recognition came finally in 1965 when the cholera microbe was officially named *vibrio cholerae Pacini*.

47. Howard-Jones, *Scientific Background*, p. 55.

48. Local Government Board, *Reports and Papers on Cholera in England in 1893* (London: Eyre and Spottiswoode, 1894).

49. Quoted in Howard-Jones, *Scientific Background*, p. 64.

50. Local Government Board, *Reports and Papers on Cholera*.

51. Howard-Jones, *Scientific Background*, p. 70.

52. Howard-Jones, *Scientific Background*, p. 71.

53. Goodman, *International Health Organizations*, p. 68.

54. Marks and Beatty, *Epidemics*, p. 211.

55. Hirsch, *Handbook of Geographical and Historical Pathology*, pp. 504–05.

56. This view apparently developed around the dubious historical observation that plague first appeared in Egypt around 550 A.D. after the Egyptians, under Christian influence, dropped embalming in favor of burying.

57. Howard-Jones, *Scientific Background*, p. 79.

58. This bizarre communication illustrated the difficulties for international cooperation of a federal system of government, in which international commitments are made by the central government but executed by state or local governments. It also underlines the importance of direct communication among public health officials, rather than having to go through formal diplomatic channels.

59. Marks and Beatty, *Epidemics*, pp. 257–60.

60. Eduardo Liceaga, "Report Presented to the 12th International Sanitary Convention, Washington, D.C., 1905" (Mexico, 1905).

61. Goodman, *International Health Organizations*, p. 70.

62. Norman Howard-Jones, *The Pan American Health Organization: Origins and Evolution* (Geneva: World Health Organization, 1981), p. 7.

63. Howard-Jones, *Scientific Background*, p. 87.

64. Howard-Jones, *Scientific Background*, p. 25.

65. Rosenberg, *The Cholera Years*, p. 271.

66. Howard-Jones, *Scientific Background*, p. 17.

67. Howard-Jones, *Scientific Background*, pp. 19–20.

68. Arne Barkhuus, "The Dawn of International Cooperation in Medicine," *Ciba Symposia*, vol. 5 (October 1943), p. 1567.

69. Howard-Jones, *Scientific Background*, pp. 35–36.

70. Howard-Jones, *Scientific Background*, pp. 12, 53.

71. Quoted in Howard-Jones, *Scientific Background*, p. 29.

72. Farr wrote at a period when "scientific laws" were being discovered rap-

idly. These "laws" did not proceed from basic theory, but rather roughly and economically characterized empirical regularities. In short, they were simple mathematical formulas that seemed to fit the data well. In the case of Farr's elevation law for cholera, the formula was $C/C' = (e + 13)(e' + 13)$, where C and C' are the incidence of cholera in two districts whose mean elevations above the Thames River were e and e', respectively. See John M. Eyler, "William Farr on the Cholera: The Sanitarian's Disease Theory and the Statistician's Method," *Journal of the History of Medicine and Applied Sciences*, vol. 28 (April 1973), p. 89.

73. Hirsch, *Handbook of Geographical and Historical Pathology*, pp. 527, 535.

74. Hirsch, *Handbook of Geographical and Historical Pathology*, pp. 474, 481, 493 (italics in original).

75. Hirsch, *Handbook of Geographical and Historical Pathology*, pp. 369, 371, 373 (italics in original).

76. Howard-Jones, *Scientific Background*, p. 52.

77. Quoted in Norman Longmate, *King Cholera: The Biography of a Disease* (London: Hamish Hamilton, 1966), pp. 228–29.

78. As so often is the case, there were antecedents: in 1606, while with Hungarian troops, Tobias Cober noted the relationship of lice to the spread of typhus; it took 300 years to rediscover it. See Marks and Beatty, *Epidemics*, p. 263. Hirsch nowhere mentions lice in his discussion of typhus, and he considers it an "exquisitely contagious disease," which does not fit his strict use of the term "contagious," quoted above. See Hirsch, *Handbook of Geographical and Historical Pathology*, p. 591.

79. In 1893 Theobald Smith and Frederick Kilborne had shown that Texas cattle fever was carried by the cattle tick, but without the definitiveness of Ross's experiment.

80. Howard-Jones, *Scientific Background*, p. 93.

81. Quoted in Howard-Jones, *Scientific Background*, p. 97.

82. Goodman, *International Health Organizations*, p. 320.

83. Goodman, *International Health Organizations*, p. 250.

84. *Washington Post*, January 5, 1989, p. A5.

85. For a description of international cooperation, see Lincoln C. Chen, "The AIDS Pandemic: An Internationalist Approach to Disease Control," *Daedalus*, vol. 116 (Spring 1987), pp. 181–95.

86. Smallpox virus is still maintained in two laboratories. In 1978 two cases of smallpox occurred in Britain as a result of mishandling in a laboratory. See World Health Organization, *The Eradication of Smallpox* (Geneva, 1980), pp. 51, 105.

87. Braudel, *Civilization and Capitalism*, p. 79.

88. Henschen, *History and Geography of Diseases*, p. 140.

89. Jenner had noticed that dairymaids contracted smallpox much less often than the general population and inferred their immunity must have something to do with cows—a nice example of careful observation combined with inductive reasoning and systematic follow-through.

90. McNeill, *Plagues and Peoples*, p. 252.

91. World Health Organization, *Eradication of Smallpox*, p. 24, app. 1.

92. World Health Organization, *Eradication of Smallpox*, p. 108.

93. World Health Organization, *Eradication of Smallpox*, p. 64.

94. Donald A. Henderson, "The History of Smallpox Eradication," in Abraham M. Lilienfield, ed., *Times, Places, and Persons: Aspects of the History of Epidemiology* (Johns Hopkins University Press, 1980), p. 111.

95. Food and Agriculture Organization, *World Animal Review*, special issue: *Rinderpest* (1983).

96. Food and Agriculture Organization, *World Animal Review*, no. 56 (1985).

97. Calculated from B. R. Mitchell, *European Historical Statistics, 1750–1970* (Columbia University Press, 1976); U.S. Bureau of the Census, *Historical Statistics of the United States from Colonial Times to 1970*, vol. 1 (Government Printing Office, 1975), p. 224; and Simon Kuznets, "Quantitative Aspects of the Economic Growth of Nations," *Economic Development and Cultural Change*, vol. 5 (October 1956), pp. 5–94.

98. See W. W. Rostow, *Politics and the Stages of Growth* (London: Cambridge University Press, 1971), pp. 105–29.

99. Howard-Jones, *Scientific Background*, p. 64.

100. Bureau of the Census, *Historical Statistics of the United States from Colonial Times to 1970*, vol. 2 (GPO, 1975), p. 1134.

101. Arthur I. Bloomfield, *Monetary Policy under the International Gold Standard: 1880–1914* (Federal Reserve Bank of New York, 1959).

102. The bargain at the Bonn summit was more complicated and extended beyond macroeconomic issues. Britain and France pledged to go ahead with the multilateral trade negotiations, and the United States pledged to raise its oil prices to world levels, while Germany and Japan pledged fiscal expansion. For a detailed discussion of economic summitry, see Robert D. Putnam and Nicholas Bayne, *Hanging Together: Cooperation and Conflict in the Seven-Power Summits*, rev. ed. (Harvard University Press, 1987). For further information on the 1978 Bonn summit, see the paper by Putnam and Henning in this volume.

103. For a detailed account, see Yoichi Funabashi, *Managing the Dollar: From the Plaza to the Louvre* (Washington: Institute for International Economics, 1988).

104. See Richard N. Cooper, "Economic Interdependence and Coordination of Economic Policies," in Ronald W. Jones and Peter B. Kenen, eds., *Handbook of International Economics*, vol. 2 (Amsterdam: Elsevier Science Publishers, 1985), pp. 1195–1234.

105. See Richard N. Cooper, "U.S. Macroeconomic Policy, 1986–88: Are the Models Useful?" in Ralph C. Bryant and others, eds., *Empirical Macroeconomics for Interdependent Economies* (Brookings, 1988), pp. 255–66.

106. Jeffrey A. Frankel and Katharine E. Rockett, "International Macroeconomic Policy Coordination When Policymakers Do Not Agree on the True Model," *American Economic Review*, vol. 78 (June 1988), pp. 318–40.

Hegemonic Stability Theories of the International Monetary System

BARRY EICHENGREEN

A
N INTERNATIONAL MONETARY SYSTEM is a set of rules or conventions governing the economic policies of nations. From a narrowly national perspective, it is an unnatural state of affairs. Adherence to a common set of rules or conventions requires a certain harmonization of monetary and fiscal policies, even though the preferences and constraints influencing policy formulation diverge markedly across countries. Governments are expected to forswear policies that redistribute economic welfare from foreigners to domestic residents and to contribute voluntarily to providing the international public good of global monetary stability. In effect, they are expected to solve the defection problem that plagues cartels and—equivalently in this context—the free-rider problem hindering public good provision.[1] Since they are likely to succeed incompletely, the public good of international monetary stability tends to be underproduced. From this perspective, the paradox of international monetary affairs is not the difficulty of designing a stable international monetary system, but the fact that such systems have actually persisted for decades.

Specialists in international relations have offered the notion that dominance by one country—a hegemonic power—is needed to ensure the smooth functioning of an international regime.[2] The concentration of economic power is seen as a way of internalizing the externalities associated with systemic stability and of ensuring its adequate provision. The application of this "theory of hegemonic stability" to international monetary affairs is straightforward.[3] The maintenance of the Bretton Woods System for a quarter century is ascribed to the singular power of the United States in the postwar world, much as the persis-

An earlier version of this paper was prepared for the Centre for Economic Policy Research Conference on International Regimes and the Design of Macroeconomic Policy. I thank my conference discussant, Peter Kenen, as well as Dilip Abreu, Robert Gilpin, Joanne Gowa, Robert Keohane, Charles Kindleberger, and Kala Krishna for comments and discussion.

tence of the classical gold standard is ascribed to Britain's dominance
of international financial affairs in the second half of the nineteenth
century. "The monetary systems of the past were relatively stable when
a single currency dominated: sterling through most of the nineteenth
century, the dollar in the early postwar period."[4] By contrast, the instability of the interwar gold exchange standard is attributed to the absence of a hegemonic power, due to Britain's inability to play the dominant role and America's unwillingness to accept it.

The appeal of this notion lies in its resonance with the public good
and cartel analogies for international monetary affairs, through what
might be called the carrot and stick variants of hegemonic stability
theory. In the carrot variant, the hegemon, like a dominant firm in an
oligopolistic market, maintains the cohesion of the cartel by making
the equivalent of side payments to members of the fringe. In the stick
variant, the hegemon, like a dominant firm, deters defection from the
international monetary cartel by using its economic policies to
threaten retaliation against renegades. In strong versions of the theory
(what Snidal refers to as the benevolent strand of the theory), all participants are rendered better off by the intervention of the dominant
power. In weak versions (what Snidal refers to as the coercive strand of
the theory), either because systemic stability is not a purely public
good or because its costs are shunted onto smaller states, the benefits
of stability accrue disproportionately or even exclusively to the hegemon.[5]

Three problems bedevil attempts to apply hegemonic stability
theory to international monetary affairs. First is the ambiguity surrounding three concepts central to the theory; *hegemony*, the *power* the
hegemon is assumed to possess, and the *regime* whose stability is ostensibly enhanced by the exercise of hegemonic power. Rather than
adopting general definitions offered previously and devoting this paper
to their criticism, I adopt specialized definitions tailored to my concern
with the international monetary system. I employ the economist's definition of economic—or market—power: sufficient size in the relevent
market to influence prices and quantities.[6] I define a hegemon analo-
gously to a dominant firm: as a country whose market power, understood in this sense, significantly exceeds that of all rivals. Finally, I
avoid defining the concept of regime around which much debate has
revolved by posing the question narrowly: whether hegemony is conducive to the stability of the international monetary system (where the
system is defined as those explicit rules and procedures governing in-

ternational monetary affairs), rather than whether it is conducive to the stability of the international regime, however defined.[7]

The second problem plaguing attempts to apply hegemonic stability theory to international monetary affairs is ambiguity about the instruments with which the hegemon makes its influence felt. This is the distinction between what are characterized above as the carrot and stick variants of the theory. Does the hegemon alter its monetary, fiscal, or commercial policies to discipline countries that refuse to play by its rules, as "basic force" models of international relations would suggest?[8] Does it link international economic policy to other issue areas and impose military or diplomatic sanctions on uncooperative nations?[9] Or does it stabilize the system through the use of "positive sanctions," financing the public good of international monetary stability by acting as lender of last resort even when the probability of repayment is slim and forsaking beggar-thy-neighbor policies even when used to advantage by other countries?[10]

The third problem is ambiguity about the scope of hegemonic stability theories. In principle, such theories could be applied equally to the design, the operation, or the decline of the international monetary system.[11] Yet in practice, hegemonic stability theories may shed light on the success of efforts to design or reform the international monetary system but not on its day-to-day operation or eventual decline. Other combinations are equally plausible a priori. Only analysis of individual cases can throw light on the theory's range of applicability.

In this paper, I structure an analysis of hegemonic stability theories of the international monetary system around the dual problems of range of applicability and mode of implementation. I consider separately the genesis of international monetary systems, their operation in normal periods and times of crisis, and their disintegration. In each context, I draw evidence from three modern incarnations of the international monetary system: the classical gold standard, the interwar gold exchange standard, and Bretton Woods. These three episodes in the history of the international monetary system are typically thought to offer two examples of hegemonic stability—Britain before 1914, the United States after 1944—and one episode—the interwar years—destabilized by the absence of hegemony. I do not attempt to document Britain's dominance of international markets before 1914 or the dominance of the United States after 1944; I simply ask whether the market power they possessed was causally connected to the stability of the international monetary system.

The historical analysis indicates that the relationship between the market power of the leading economy and the stability of the international monetary system is considerably more complex than suggested by simple variants of hegemonic stability theory. While one cannot simply reject the hypothesis that on more than one occasion the stabilizing capacity of a dominant economic power has contributed to the smooth functioning of the international monetary system, neither can one reconcile much of the evidence, notably on the central role of international negotiation and collaboration even in periods of hegemonic dominance, with simple versions of the theory. Although both the appeal and limitations of hegemonic stability theories are apparent when one takes a static view of the international monetary system, those limitations are most evident when one considers the evolution of an international monetary system over time. An international monetary system whose smooth operation at one point is predicated on the dominance of one powerful country may in fact be dynamically unstable. Historical experience suggests that the hegemon's willingness to act in a stabilizing capacity at a single point tends to undermine its continued capacity to do so over time.

The notion that a concentration of economic power may be intrinsic to the smooth operation of the international monetary system, while intuitively appealing to political scientists for whom the concept of power is bread and butter, may seem to economists as strange as the ideas of the pareto optimality of free trade or the efficiency of perfect competition are to nearly everyone but economists.[12] The point of departure of this paper is necessarily different, therefore, from that which characterizes most work in economics, and requires of economists in the audience, like theater goers, a willing suspension of disbelief.

The Genesis of Monetary Systems and the Theory of Hegemonic Stability

My analysis begins with an examination of the genesis of three different monetary systems: the classical gold standard, the interwar gold exchange standard, and the Bretton Woods system.

The Classical Gold Standard

Of the three episodes considered here, the origins of the classical gold standard are the most difficult to assess, for in the nineteenth century there were no centralized discussions, like those in Genoa in 1922 or Bretton Woods in 1944, concerned with the design of the international monetary system.[13] There was general agreement that currencies should have a metallic basis and that payments imbalances should be settled by international shipments of specie. But there was no consensus about which precious metals should serve as the basis for money supplies or how free international specie movements should be.

Only Britain maintained a full-fledged gold standard for anything approaching the century preceding 1913. Although gold coins had circulated alongside silver since the fourteenth century, Britain had been on a de facto gold standard since 1717, when Sir Isaac Newton, as master of the mint, set too high a silver price of gold and drove full-bodied silver coins from circulation. In 1798 silver coinage was suspended, and after 1819 silver was no longer accepted to redeem paper currency. But for half a century following its official adoption of the gold standard in 1821, Britain essentially remained alone. Other countries that retained bimetallic standards were buffeted by alternating gold and silver discoveries. The United States and France, for example, were officially bimetallic, but their internal circulations were placed on a silver basis by growing Mexican and South American silver production in the early decades of the nineteenth century. The market price of silver was thus depressed relative to the mint price, which encouraged silver to be imported for coinage and gold to be shipped abroad where its price was higher. Then, starting in 1848, gold discoveries in Russia, Australia, and California depressed the market price of gold below the mint price, all but driving silver from circulation and placing bimetallic currencies on a gold basis. Finally, silver discoveries in Nevada and other mining territories starting in the 1870s dramatically inflated the silver price of gold and forced the bimetallic currencies back onto a silver basis.

The last of these disturbances led nearly all bimetallic countries to adopt the gold standard, starting with Germany in 1871.[14] Why, after taking no comparable action in response to previous disturbances, did countries respond to post-1870 fluctuations in the price of silver by abandoning bimetallism and adopting gold? What role, if any, did Britain, the hegemonic financial power, play in their decisions?

One reason for the decision to adopt gold was the desire to prevent the inflation that would result from continued silver convertibility and coinage. Hence the plausible explanation for the contrast between the 1870s and earlier years is the danger of exceptionally rapid inflation due to the magnitude of post-1870 silver discoveries. Between 1814 and 1870, the sterling price of silver, of which so much was written, remained within 2 percentage points of its 1814 value, alternatively driving gold or silver from circulation in bimetallic countries but fluctuating insufficiently to raise the specter of significant price level changes. Then between 1871 and 1881 the London price of silver fell by 15 percent, and by 1891 the cumulative fall had reached 25 percent.[15] Gold convertibility was the only alternative to continued silver coinage that was judged both respectable and viable.[16] The only significant resistance to the adoption of gold convertibility emanated from silver-mining regions and from agricultural areas like the American West, populated by proprietors of encumbered land who might benefit from inflation.

Seen from this perspective, the impetus for adopting the gold standard existed independently of Britain's rapid industrialization, dominance of international finance, and preeminence in trade. Still, the British example surely provided encouragement to follow the path ultimately chosen. The experience of the Latin Monetary Union impressed upon contemporaries the advantages of a common monetary standard in minimizing transactions costs.[17] The scope of that common standard would be greatest for countries that linked their currencies to sterling. The gold standard was also attractive to domestic interests concerned with promoting economic growth. Industrialization required foreign capital, and attracting foreign capital required monetary stability. For Britain, the principal source of foreign capital, monetary stability was measured in terms of sterling and best ensured by joining Britain on gold. Moreover, London's near monopoly of trade credit was of concern to other governments, which hoped that they might reduce their dependence on the London discount market by establishing gold parities and central banks. Aware that Britain monopolized trade in newly mined gold and was the home of the world's largest organized commodity markets, other governments hoped that by emulating Britain's gold standard and financial system they might secure a share of this business.

Britain's prominence in foreign commerce, overseas investment, and trade credit forcefully conditioned the evolution of the gold standard system mainly through central banks' practice of holding key currency balances abroad, especially in London. This practice probably would not have developed so quickly if foreign countries had not grown accustomed to transacting in the London market. It would probably not have become so widespread if there had not been such strong confidence in the stability and liquidity of sterling deposits. And such a large share of foreign deposits would not have gravitated to a single center if Britain had not possessed such a highly articulated set of financial markets.

But neither Britain's dominance of international transactions nor the desire to emulate Bank of England practice prevented countries from tailoring the gold standard to their own needs. Germany and France continued to allow large internal gold circulation, while other nations limited gold coin circulation to low levels. The central banks of France, Belgium, and Switzerland retained the right to redeem their notes in silver, and the French did not hesitate to charge a premium for gold.[18] The Reichsbank could at its option issue fiduciary notes upon the payment of a tax.[19] In no sense did British example or suggestion dictate the form of the monetary system.

The Interwar Gold Exchange Standard

The interwar gold exchange standard offers a radically different picture: on the one hand, there was no single dominant power like nineteenth century Britain or mid-twentieth century America; on the other, there were conscious efforts by rivals to shape the international monetary order to their national advantage.

Contemporary views of the design of the interwar monetary system were aired at a series of international meetings, the most important of which was the Genoa Economic and Financial Conference convened in April 1922.[20] Although the United States declined to send an official delegation to Genoa, proceedings there reflected the differing economic objectives of Britain and the United States. British officials were aware that the war had burdened domestic industry with adjustment problems, had disrupted trade, and had accentuated financial rivalry between London and New York. Their objectives were to prevent worldwide deflation (which was sure to exacerbate the problems of structural adjustment), to promote the expansion of international trade (to which the nation's prosperity was inextricably linked), and to recapture the financial business diverted to New York as a result of the war.[21] To prevent deflation, they advocated that countries economize on the use of gold by adopting the gold exchange standard along lines prac-

ticed by members of the British Empire. Presuming London to be a
reserve center, British officials hoped that these measures would restore the City to its traditional prominence in international finance.
Stable exchange rates would stimulate international trade, particularly
if the United States forgave its war debt claims, which would permit
reparations to be reduced and encourage creditor countries to extend
loans to Central Europe.

The United States, in contrast, was less dependent for its prosperity
on the rapid expansion of trade. It was less reliant on income from
financial and insurance services and perceived as less urgent the need
to encourage the deposit of foreign balances in New York. Influential
American officials, notably Benjamin Strong of the Federal Reserve
Bank of New York, opposed any extension of the gold exchange standard.[22] Above all, American officials were hesitant to participate in a
conference whose success appeared to hinge on unilateral concessions
regarding war debts.[23]

In the absence of an American delegation, Britain's proposals
formed the basis for the resolutions of the Financial Committee of the
Genoa Conference. These resolutions proposed the adoption of an international monetary convention formally empowering countries, "in
addition to any gold reserve held at home, [to] maintain in any other
participant country reserves of approved assets in the form of bank
balances, bills, short-term securities, or other suitable liquid resources."[24] Participating countries would fix their exchange rates
against one another, and any that failed to do so would lose the right
to hold the reserve balances of the others. The principal creditor nations were encouraged to take immediate steps to restore convertibility
in order to become "gold centers" where the bulk of foreign exchange
reserves would be held. Following earlier recommendations by the
Cunliffe committee, governments were urged to economize on gold by
eliminating gold coin from circulation and concentrating reserves at
central banks. Countries with significantly depreciated currencies
were urged to stabilize at current exchange rates rather than attempting to restore prewar parities through drastic deflation, which would
only delay stabilization.

To implement this convention, the Bank of England was instructed
to call an early meeting of central banks, including the Federal Reserve. But efforts to arrange this meeting, which bogged down in the
dispute over war debts and reparations, proved unavailing. Still, if the

official convention advocated by the Financial Committee failed to materialize, the Genoa resolutions were not without influence.[25] Many of the innovations suggested there were adopted by individual countries on a unilateral basis and comprised the distinguishing features differentiating the prewar and interwar monetary standards.[26]

The first effect of Genoa was to encourage the adoption of statutes permitting central banks to back notes and sight deposits with foreign exchange as well as gold. New regulations broadening the definition of eligible assets and specifying minimum proportions of total reserves to be held in gold were widely implemented in succeeding years. The second effect was to encourage the adoption of gold economy measures, including the withdrawal of gold coin from circulation and provision of bullion for export only by the authorities. The third effect was to provide subtle encouragement to countries experiencing ongoing inflation to stabilize at depreciated rates. Thus Genoa deserves partial credit for transforming the international monetary system from a gold to a gold exchange standard, from a gold coin to a gold bullion standard, and from a fixed-rate system to one in which central banks were vested with some discretion over the choice of parities.

Given its dominance of the proceedings at Genoa, Britain's imprint on the interwar gold exchange standard was as apparent as its influence over the structure of the prewar system. That British policymakers achieved this despite a pronounced decline in Britain's position in the world economy and the opposition of influential American officials suggests that planning and effort were substitutes, to some extent, for economic power.

The Bretton Woods System

Of the three cases considered here, U.S. dominance of the Bretton Woods negotiations is most clearly supportive of hegemonic stability theories about the genesis of the international monetary system. U.S. dominance of the postwar world economy is unmistakable.[27] Yet despite the trappings of hegemony and American dominance of the proceedings at Bretton Woods, a less influential power—Great Britain— was able to secure surprisingly extensive concessions in the design of the international monetary system.

American and British officials offered different plans for postwar monetary reconstruction both because they had different views of the problem of international economic adjustment and because they represented economies with different strengths and weaknesses. British officials were preoccupied by two weaknesses of their economic position. First was the specter of widespread unemployment. Between 1920 and 1938, unemployment in Britain had scarcely dipped below double-digit levels, and British policymakers feared its recurrence. Second was the problem of sterling balances. Britain had concentrated its wartime purchases within the sterling bloc and, because they were allies and sterling was a reserve currency, members of the bloc had accepted settlement in sterling, now held in London. Since these sterling balances were large relative to Britain's hard currency reserves, the mere possibility that they might be presented for conversion threatened plans for the restoration of convertibility.[28]

U.S. officials, in contrast, were confident that the competitive position of American industry was strong and were little concerned about the threat of unemployment. The concentration of gold reserves in the United States, combined with the economy's international creditor position, freed them from worry that speculative capital flows or foreign government policies might undermine the dollar's stability. U.S. concerns centered on the growth of preferential trading systems from which its exports were excluded, notably the sterling bloc.

The British view of international economic adjustment was dominated by concern about inadequate liquidity and asymmetrical adjustment. A central lesson drawn by British policymakers from the experience of the 1920s was the difficulty of operating an international monetary system in which liquidity or reserves were scarce. Given how slowly the global supply of monetary gold responded to fluctuations in its relative price and how sensitive its international distribution had proven to be to the economic policies of individual states, they considered it foolhardy to base the international monetary system on a reserve base composed exclusively of gold. Given the perceived inelasticity of global gold supplies, a gold-based system threatened to impart a deflationary bias to the world economy and to worsen unemployment. This preoccupation with unemployment due to external constraints was reinforced by another lesson drawn from the 1920s: the costs of asymmetries in the operation of the adjustment mechanism. If the experience of the 1920s was repeated, surplus countries, in response to external imbalances, would need only to sterilize reserve inflows, while deficit countries would be forced to initiate monetary contraction to prevent the depletion of reserves. Monetary contraction, according to Keynes, whose views heavily influenced those of the British delegation, facilitated adjustment by causing unemployment. To prevent unemployment, symmetry had to be restored to the adjustment mechanism through the incorporation of sanctions compelling surplus countries to revalue their currencies or stimulate demand.

From the American perspective, the principal lessons of interwar experience were not the costs of asymmetries and inadequate liquidity, but the instability of floating rates and the disruptive effects of exchange rate and trade protection. U.S. officials were concerned about ensuring order and stability in the foreign exchange market and preventing the development of preferential trading systems cultivated through expedients such as exchange control.

The Keynes and White plans, which formed each side's basis for negotiations, require only a brief summary.[29] Exchange control and the centralized provision of liquidity ("bancor") were two central elements of Keynes's plan for an international clearing union. Provision of bancor was designed to permit "the substitution of an expansionist, in place of a contractionist, pressure on world trade."[30] Exchange control would insulate pegged exchange rates from the sudden liquidation of short-term balances. Symmetry would be ensured by a charge on creditor balances held with the clearing bank.

The White plan acknowledged the validity of the British concern with liquidity, but was intended to prevent both inflation and deflation rather than to exert an expansionary influence. It limited the Stabilization Fund's total resources to $5 billion, compared with $26 billion under the Keynes plan. It was patterned on the principles of American bank lending, under which decisionmaking power rested ultimately with the bank; the Keynes plan resembled the British overdraft system, in which the overdraft was at the borrower's discretion.[31] The fundamental difference, however, was that the White plan limited the total U.S. obligation to its $2 billion contribution, while the Keynes plan limited the value of unrequited U.S. exports that might be financed by bancor to the total drawing rights of other countries ($23 billion).

It is typically argued that the Bretton Woods agreement reflected America's dominant position, presumably on the grounds that the International Monetary Fund charter specified quotas of $8.8 billion (closer to the White plan's $5 billion than to the Keynes plan's $26 billion) and a maximum U.S. obligation of $2.75 billion (much closer to $2 billion under the White plan than to $23 billion under the Keynes plan). Yet, relative to the implications of simple versions of hegemonic stability theory, a surprising number of British priorities were incorporated. One was the priority Britain attached to exchange rate flexibility. The United States initially had wished to invest the IMF with veto power over a country's decision to change its exchange rate. Subsequently it proposed that 80 percent of IMF members be required to approve any change in parity. But the Articles of Agreement permitted devaluation without fund objection when needed to eliminate fundamental disequilibrium. Lacking any definition of this term, there was scope for devaluation by countries other than the United States to reconcile internal and external balance. Only once did the fund treat an exchange rate change as unauthorized.[32] If countries hesitated to devalue, they did so as much for domestic reasons as for reasons related to the structure of the international monetary system.

Another British priority incorporated into the agreement was tolerance of exchange control. Originally, the White plan obliged members to abandon all exchange restrictions within six months of ceasing hostilities or joining the IMF, whichever came first. A subsequent U.S. proposal would have required a country to eliminate all exchange controls within a year of joining the fund. But Britain succeeded in incorporating into the Articles of Agreement a distinction between controls for capital transactions, which were permitted, from controls on current transactions, which were not. In practice, even nondiscriminatory exchange controls on current transactions were sometimes authorized under IMF Article VIII.[33] As a result of this compromise, the United States protected itself from efforts to divert sterling bloc trade toward the British market, while Britain protected itself from destabilization by overseas sterling balances.[34]

In comparison with these concessions, British efforts to restore symmetry to the international adjustment mechanism proved unavailing. With abandonment of the overdraft principle, the British embraced White's "scarce currency" proposal, under which the fund was empowered to ration its supply of a scarce currency and members were authorized to impose limitations on freedom of exchange operations in that currency. Thus a country running payments surpluses sufficiently large to threaten the fund's ability to supply its currency might face restrictions on foreign customers' ability to purchase its exports. But the scarce currency clause had been drafted by the United States not with the principle of symmetry in mind, but in order to deal with problems of immediate postwar adjustment—specifically, the prospective dollar shortage. With the development of the Marshall Plan, the dollar shortage never achieved the severity anticipated by the authors of the scarce currency clause, and the provision was never invoked.

If the "Joint Statement by Experts on the Establishment of an International Monetary Fund," made public in April 1944, bore the imprint of the U.S. delegation to Bretton Woods, to a surprising extent it also embodied important elements of the British negotiating position. It is curious from the perspective of hegemonic stability theory that a war-battered economy—Britain—heavily dependent on the dominant economic power—America—for capital goods, financial capital, and export markets was able to extract significant concessions in the design of the international monetary system.[35] Britain was ably represented in the negotiations. But even more important, the United States also required an international agreement and wished to secure it even while hostilities in Europe prevented enemy nations from taking part in negotiations and minimized the involvement of the allies on whose territory the war was fought. The United States therefore had little opportunity to play off countries against one another or to brand as renegades any that disputed the advisability of its design. As the Western world's second largest economy, Britain symbolized, if it did not actually represent, the other nations of the world and was able to advance their case more effectively than if they had attempted more actively to do so themselves.

What conclusions regarding the applicability of hegemonic stability theory to the genesis of international monetary systems follow from the evidence of these three cases? In the two clearest instances of hegemony—the United Kingdom in the second half of the nineteenth century and the United States following World War II—the leading economic power significantly influenced the form of the international monetary system, by example in the first instance and by negotiation in the second. But the evidence also underscores the fact that the hegemon has been incapable of dictating the form of the monetary system. In the first instance, British example did nothing to prevent significant modifications in the form of the gold standard adopted abroad. In the second, the exceptional dominance of the U.S. economy was unable to eliminate the need to compromise with other countries in the design of the monetary system.

The Operation of Monetary Systems and the
Theory of Hegemonic Stability

It is necessary to consider not only the genesis of monetary systems, but also how the theory of hegemonic stability applies to the operation of such systems. I consider adjustment, liquidity, and the lender-of-last-resort function in turn.

Adjustment

Adjustment under the classical gold standard has frequently been characterized in terms compatible with hegemonic stability theory. The gold standard is portrayed as a managed system whose preservation and smooth operation were ensured through its regulation by a hegemonic power, Great Britain, and its agent, the Bank of England. In the words of Cohen, "The classical gold standard *was* a sterling standard—a hegemonic regime—in the sense that Britain not only dominated the international monetary order, establishing and maintaining the prevailing rules of the game, but also gave monetary relations whatever degree of inherent stability they possessed."[36]

Before 1914, London was indisputably the world's leading financial center. A large proportion of world trade—60 percent by one estimate—was settled through payment in sterling bills, with London functioning as a clearinghouse for importers and exporters of other nations.[37] British discount houses bought bills from abroad, either directly or through the London agencies of foreign banks. Foreigners maintained balances in London to meet commitments on bills outstanding and to service British portfolio investments overseas. Foreign governments and central banks held deposits in London as interest-earning alternatives to gold reserves. Although the pound was not the only reserve currency of the pre-1914 era, sterling reserves matched the combined value of reserves denominated in other currencies. At the same time, Britain possessed perhaps £350 million of short-term capital overseas. Though it is unclear whether Britain was a net short-term debtor or creditor before the war, it is certain that a large volume of short-term funds was responsive to changes in domestic interest rates.[38]

Such changes in interest rates might be instigated by the Bank of England. By altering the rates at which it discounted for its customers and rediscounted for the discount houses, the bank could affect rates prevailing in the discount market.[39] But the effect of Bank rate was not limited to the bill market. While in part this reflected the exceptional integration characteristic of British financial markets, it was reinforced by institutionalization. In London, banks automatically fixed their deposit rates half a percentage point above Bank rate. Loan rates were similarly indexed to Bank rate but at a higher level. Though there were exceptions to these rules, changes in Bank rate were immediately reflected in a broad range of British interest rates.

An increase in Bank rate, by raising the general level of British interest rates, induced foreign investors to accumulate additional funds in London and to delay the repatriation or transfer of existing balances to other centers. British balances abroad were repatriated to earn the higher rate of return. Drawings of finance bills, which represented half of total bills in 1913, were similarly sensitive to changes in interest rates. Higher interest rates spread to the security market and delayed the flotation of new issues for overseas borrowers. In this way the Bank of England was able to insulate its gold reserve from disturbances in the external accounts.[40]

Because of the size of the London market and the Bank of England's leverage over the interest rates prevailing there, Bank rate seemed to have "a controlling influence on Britain's balance of payments, regardless of what other central banks were doing." When Bank rate was raised, Britain's external position strengthened even when *"other central banks raised or lowered their discount rates along with Bank rate, as they normally did."*[41] Hence the hegemonic center was rarely threatened by convertibility crises under the classical gold standard.

But why did the Bank of England's exceptional leverage not threaten convertibility abroad? The answer commonly offered is that Britain's unrivaled market power led to a de facto harmonization of national policies. As the report of the Macmillan committee characterized the prewar situation, Britain could "by the operation of her Bank Rate almost immediately adjust her reserve position. Other countries had, therefore, in the main to adjust their conditions to hers."[42] As Keynes wrote in the *Treatise on Money,* "During the latter half of the nineteenth century the influence of London on credit conditions throughout the world was so predominant that the Bank of England could almost have claimed to be the conductor of the international orchestra."[43]

Since fiscal harmonization requires no discussion in an era of balanced budgets, the stability of the classical gold standard can be explained by the desire and ability of central banks to harmonize their monetary policies in the interest of external balance. External balance, or maintaining gold reserves adequate to defend the established gold parity, was the foremost target of monetary policy in the period preceding World War I. In the absence of a coherent theory of unemployment, much less a consensus on its relation to monetary policy, there was relatively little pressure for central banks to accommodate domestic needs. External balance was not the sole target of policy, but when internal and external balance came into conflict, the latter took precedence.[44] Viewed from an international perspective, British leadership played a role in this process of harmonization insofar as the market power and prominence of the Bank of England served as a focal point for policy coordination.

But if the Bank of England could be sure of defeating its European counterparts when they engaged in a tug of war over short-term capital, mere harmonization of central bank policies, in the face of external disturbances, would have been insufficient to prevent convertibility crises on the Continent. The explanation for the absence of such crises would appear to be the greater market power of European countries compared with their non-European counterparts. Some observers have distinguished the market power of capital-exporting countries from the inability of capital importers to influence the direction of financial flows.[45] Others have suggested the existence of a hierarchical structure of financial markets: below the London market were the less active markets of Berlin, Paris, Vienna, Amsterdam, Brussels, Zurich, and New York, followed by the still less active markets of the Scandinavian countries, and finally the nascent markets of Latin America and other parts of the non-European world.[46] When Bank rate was raised in London, thus redistributing reserves to Britain from other regions, compensatory discount rate increases on the Continent drew funds from the non-European world or curtailed capital outflows. Developing countries, due to either the thinness of markets or the absence of relevant institutions, were unable to prevent these events. In times of crisis, therefore, convertibility was threatened primarily outside Europe and North America. If Britain and Europe managed the system, they did so "partly at the expense of its weakest members."[47]

Thus, insofar as hegemony played some role in the efficiency of the adjustment mechanism, it was not the British hegemony of which so much has been written but the collective hegemony of the European center relative to the non-European periphery. Not only does this case challenge the conception of the hegemon, therefore, but because the stability of the classical gold standard was enjoyed exclusively by the countries of the center, it supports only the weak form of hegemonic stability theory—that the benefits of stability accrued exclusively to the powerful.[48]

The relation between hegemonic power and the need for policy harmonization is equally relevant to the case of the interwar gold exchange standard. One interpretation of Nevin's argument that "the existence of more than one center . . . [led] to the existence of more than one policy" is that in the absence of a hegemon there was no focal point for policy, which interfered with efforts at coordination.[49] But more important than a declining ability to harmonize policies may have been a diminished desire to do so. Although the advent of explicit stabilization policy was not to occur until the 1930s and 1940s, during the 1920s central banks placed increasing weight on internal conditions when formulating monetary policy.[50] The rise of socialism and the example of the Bolshevik revolution in particular provided a counterweight to central bankers' instinctive wish to base policy solely on external conditions. External adjustment was rendered difficult by policymakers' increasing hesitancy to sacrifice other objectives on the altar of external balance. Britain's balance-of-payments problems, for example, cannot be attributed to "the existence of more than one policy" in the world economy without considering also a domestic unemployment problem that placed pressure on the Bank of England to resist restrictive measures that might strengthen the external accounts at the expense of industry and trade.

Under Bretton Woods, the problem of adjustment was exacerbated by the difficulty of using exchange rate changes to restore external balance. Hesitancy to change their exchange rates posed few problems for countries in surplus. However, those in deficit had to choose between aggravating unemployment and tolerating external deficits; the latter was infeasible in the long run and promoted an increase in the volume of short-term capital that moved in response to anticipations of devaluation. Although the IMF charter did not encourage devaluation, the hesitancy of deficit countries to employ this option is easier to ascribe to the governments' tendency to attach their prestige to the stability of established exchange rates than to U.S. hegemony, however defined. Where the singular role of the United States was important was in precluding a dollar devaluation. A possible solution to the problem of U.S. deficits, one that would not have threatened other countries' ability to accumulate reserves, was an increase in the dollar price of gold, that is, a dollar devaluation. It is sometimes argued that the United States was incapable of adjusting through exchange rate changes since other countries would have devalued in response to prevent any change in bilateral rates against the dollar. However, raising the dollar price of gold would have increased the dollar value of monetary gold, reducing the global excess demand for reserves and encouraging other countries to increase domestic demand and cut back on their balance-of-payments surpluses. But while a rise in the price of gold might have alleviated central banks' immediate dependence on dollars,[51] it would have done nothing to prevent the problem from recurring. It would also have promoted skepticism about the U.S. government's commitment to the new gold price, thereby encouraging other countries to increase their demands for gold and advancing the date of future difficulties.

Does this evidence on adjustment support hegemonic theories of international monetary stability? The contrast between the apparently smooth adjustment under the classical gold standard and Bretton Woods and the adjustment difficulties of the interwar years suggests that a dominant power's policies served as a fixed target that was easier to hit than a moving one. As in Luce and Raiffa's "battle of the sexes" game, what mattered was not so much the particular stance of monetary policy but that the leading players settled on the same stance.[52] The argument, advanced by Snidal in a similar context, is that a dominant player is best placed to signal the other players the nature of the most probable stance.[53] The effectiveness of the adjustment mechanism under the two regimes reflected not just British and American market power but also the existence of an international consensus on the objectives and formulation of monetary policy that permitted central bank policies to be harmonized. The essential role of Britain before 1914 and the United States after 1944 was not so much to force other countries to alter their policies as to provide a focal point for policy harmonization.

Liquidity

Under the classical gold standard, the principal source of liquidity was newly mined gold. It is hard to see how British dominance of international markets could have much influenced the changes in the world price level and mining technology upon which these supplies depended. As argued above, where Britain's prominence mattered was in facilitating the provision of supplementary liquidity in the form of sterling reserves, which grew at an accelerating rate starting in the 1890s. It is conceivable, therefore, that in the absence of British hegemony a reserve shortage would have developed and the classical gold standard would have exhibited a deflationary bias.

Liquidity was an issue of more concern under the interwar gold exchange standard. Between 1915 and 1925, prices rose worldwide due to the inflation associated with wartime finance and postwar reconstruction; these rising prices combined with economic growth to increase the transactions demand for money. Yet under a system of convertible currencies, world money supply was constrained by the availability of reserves. Statutory restrictions required central banks to back their money supplies with eligible reserves, while recent experience with inflation deterred politicians from liberalizing the statutes. The output of newly mined gold had been depressed since the beginning of World War I, and experts offered pessimistic forecasts of future supplies. Increasing the real value of world gold reserves by forcing a reduction in the world price level would only add to the difficulties of an already troubled world economy. Countries were encouraged, therefore, to stabilize on a gold exchange basis to prevent the development of a gold shortage.

There are difficulties with this explanation of interwar liquidity problems, which emphasizes a shortage of gold.[54] For one, the danger of a gold shortage's constraining the volume of transactions was alleviated by the all but complete withdrawal of gold coin from circulation during the war. As a result, the percentage of short-term liabilities of all central banks backed by gold was little different in 1928 from its level in 1913, while the volume of the liabilities backed by that gold stock was considerably increased. It is hard to see why a gold shortage, after having exhibited only weak effects in previous years, should have had such a dramatic impact starting in 1929. It is even less clear how the absence of a hegemon contributed to the purported gold shortage. The obvious linkages between hegemony and the provision of liquidity work in the wrong direction. The straightforward way of increasing the monetary value of reserves was a round of currency devaluation, which would revalue gold reserves and, by raising the real price of gold, increase the output of the mining industry. As demonstrated in 1931, when the pound's depreciation set off a round of competitive devaluations, sterling remained the linchpin of the international currency system; the only way a round of currency devaluation could have taken place, therefore, was if Britain had stabilized in 1925 at a lower level. But had her dominance of the international economy not eroded over the first quarter of the twentieth century, the political pressure on Britain to return to gold at the prewar parity would have increased rather than being reduced.[55] It seems unlikely, therefore, that a more successful maintenance of British hegemony, ceteris paribus, would have alleviated any gold shortage.

An alternative and more appealing explanation for interwar liquidity problems emphasizes mismanagement of gold reserves rather than their overall insufficiency. It blames France and the United States for absorbing disproportionate shares of global gold supplies and for imposing deflation on the rest of the world.[56] Between 1928 and 1932, French gold reserves rose from $1.25 billion to $3.26 billion of constant gold content, or from 13 to 28 percent of the world total. Meanwhile, the United States, which had released gold between 1924 and 1928, facilitating the reestablishment of convertibility in other countries, reversed its position and imported $1.49 billion of gold between 1928 and 1930. By the end of 1932 the United States and France together possessed nearly 63 percent of the world's central monetary gold. The British Macmillan committee attributed to this maldistribution of gold "a large measure of responsibility for the heavy fall in prices in recent years."[57]

The maldistribution of reserves can be understood by focusing on the systematic interaction of central banks. This approach builds on the literature that characterizes the interwar gold standard as a competitive struggle for gold between countries that viewed the size of their gold reserve as a measure of national prestige and as insurance against financial instability.[58] France and the United States in particular, but gold standard countries generally, repeatedly raised their discount rates relative to one another in efforts to attract gold from abroad. By leading to the accumulation of excess reserves, these restrictive policies exacerbated the problem of inadequate liquidity, but by offsetting one another they also failed to achieve their objective of attracting gold from abroad. As Keynes explained, "what helps each [central bank] is not a high Bank rate but a higher rate than the others. So that a raising of rates all round helps no one until, after an interregnum during which the economic activity of the whole world has been retarded, prices and wages have been forced to a lower level."[59]

The origins of this competitive struggle for gold are popularly attributed to the absence of a hegemon. The competing financial centers—London, Paris, and New York—worked at cross-purposes because, in contrast to the preceding period, no one central bank was sufficiently powerful to call the tune.[60] Before the war, the Bank of England had been sufficiently dominant to act as a leader, setting its discount rate with the reaction of other central banks in mind, while other central banks responded in the manner of a competitive fringe. By using this power to defend the gold parity of sterling despite the maintenance of slender reserves, the bank prevented the development of a competitive scramble for gold. But after World War I, with the United States unwilling to accept responsibility for leadership, no one central bank formulated its monetary policy with foreign reactions and global conditions in mind, and the noncooperative struggle for gold was the result.[61] In this interpretation of the interwar liquidity problem, hegemony—or, more precisely, its absence—plays a critical role.

In discussing the provision of liquidity under Bretton Woods, it is critical to distinguish the decade ending in 1958—when the convertibility of European currencies was restored and before U.S. dominance of international trade, foreign lending, and industrial production was unrivaled—from the decade that followed. In the first period, the most important source of incremental liquidity was dollar reserves. Between 1949 and 1958, when global reserves rose by 29 percent, less than one-third of the increment took the form of gold and one-fifteenth was in quotas at the IMF. The role of sterling as a reserve currency was limited almost exclusively to Commonwealth members and former British colonies that had traditionally held reserves in London and traded heavily with Britain. Consequently, the accumulation of dollar balances accounted for roughly half of incremental liquidity in the first decade of Bretton Woods.

In one sense, U.S. dominance of international markets facilitated the provision of liquidity. At the end of World War II, the United States had amassed 60 percent of the world's gold stock; at $35 an ounce, this was worth six times the value of the official dollar claims accumulated by foreign governments by 1949. There was little immediate question, given U.S. dominance of global gold reserves, of the stability of the gold price of the dollar and hence little hesitation to accumulate incremental liquidity in the form of dollar claims. But in another sense, U.S. international economic power in the immediate postwar years impeded the supply of liquidity to the world economy. Wartime destruction of industry in Europe and Japan left U.S. manufactured exports highly competitive in world markets and rendered Europe dependent on U.S. capital goods for industrial reconstruction. The persistent excess demand for U.S. goods tended to push the U.S. balance of payments into surplus, creating the famous "dollar shortage" of the immediate postwar years. While U.S. hegemony left other countries willing to hold dollar claims, it rendered them extremely difficult to obtain.

Various policies were initiated in response to the dollar shortage, including discrimination against dollar area exports, special incentives for European and Japanese exports to the United States, and a round of European currency devaluations starting in September 1949. Ultimately the solution took the form of two sharply contrasting actions by the hegemon: Marshall Plan grants of $11.6 billion between mid-1948 and mid-1952, and Korean War expenditures. Largely as a result of these two factors, U.S. trade surpluses shrank from $10.1 billion in 1947 to $2.6 billion in 1952; more important, U.S. government grants and private capital outflows exceeded the surplus on current account. By 1950 the U.S. balance of payments was in deficit and, after moving back into surplus in 1951–52, deficits returned to stay. Insofar as its singular economic power encouraged the United States to undertake both the Marshall Plan and the Korean War, hegemony played a significant role in both the form and adequacy of the liquidity provided in the first decade of Bretton Woods.

Between 1958 and 1969, global reserves grew more rapidly, by 51 percent, than they had in the first decade of Bretton Woods. Again, gold was a minor share of the increment, about one-twentieth, and IMF quotas were one-eighth. While foreign exchange reserves again provided roughly half, Eurodollars and other foreign currencies grew in importance: their contribution actually exceeded that of official claims on the United States.[62] In part these trends reflected rapid growth in Europe and Japan. More important, they reflected the fact that starting in 1965 the value of foreign government claims on the United States exceeded U.S. gold reserves. Prudence dictated that foreign governments diversify their reserve positions out of dollars.

The role of U.S. hegemony in the provision of liquidity during this second decade has been much debated. The growth of liquidity reflected both supply and demand pressures: both demands by other countries for additional reserves, which translated into balance-of-payments surpluses, and the capacity of the United States to consume more than it produced by running balance-of-payments deficits financed by the willingness of other countries to accumulate dollar reserves. The United States was criticized sharply, mainly by the French, for exporting inflation and for financing purchases of foreign companies and pursuit of the Vietnam War through the balance of payments.[63] Although these complaints cannot be dismissed, it is incorrect to conclude that the dollar's singular position in the Bretton Woods system permitted the United States to run whatever balance-of-payments deficit it wished.[64] Moreover, it is difficult to envisage an alternative scenario in which the U.S. balance of payments was zero but the world was not starved of liquidity. Owing to the sheer size of the American economy, new claims on the United States continued to exceed vastly the contribution of new claims on any other nation. Moreover, U.S. economic, military, and diplomatic influence did much to encourage if not compel other countries to maintain their holdings of dollar claims. Thus U.S. dominance of international markets played a critical role in resolving the liquidity crisis of the 1960s.[65]

The distinguishing feature of Bretton Woods is not that other countries continued to hold dollar reserves in the face of exchange rate uncertainty and economic growth abroad, for neither development has deterred them from holding dollars under the flexible exchange rate regime of the 1970s and 1980s. Rather, it is that they continued to hold dollar reserves in the face of a one-way bet resulting from dollar convertibility at a fixed price when the dollar price of gold seemed poised to rise. In part, the importance of American foreign investments and the size of the U.S. market for European exports caused other countries to hesitate before cashing in their chips. Yet foreign governments also saw dollar convertibility as essential to the defense of the gold-dollar system and viewed the fixed exchange rates of that system as an international public good worthy of defense. Not until 1965 did the French government decide to convert into gold some $300 million of its dollar holdings and subsequently to step up its monthly gold purchases from the United States. But when pressure on U.S. gold reserves mounted following the 1967 devaluation of sterling, other countries, including France, sold gold instead of capitalizing on the one-way bet. They joined the United States in the formation of a gold pool whose purpose was to sell a sufficient quantity of gold to defend the official price. Between sterling's devaluation in 1967 and closure of the gold market on March 15, 1968, the pool sold $3 billion of gold, of which U.S. sales were $2.2 billion. France purchased no gold in 1967 or 1968, presumably due in part to foreign pressure.[66] U.S. leverage undoubt-edly contributed to their decisions. But a plausible interpretation of these events is that foreign governments, rather than simply being coerced into support of the dollar by U.S. economic power, were willing to take limited steps to defend the international public good of a fixed exchange rate system defined in terms of the dollar price of gold.

What does this discussion imply for the role of hegemony in the provision of international liquidity? The strongest evidence for the im-portance of a hegemon is negative evidence from the interwar years, when the absence of a hegemon and the failure of competing financial centers to coordinate their policies effectively contributed greatly to the liquidity shortage. In other periods, when a dominant economic power was present, it is difficult to credit that power with sole responsibility for ensuring the adequate provision of liquidity. Under the gold stan-dard, the principal source of incremental liquidity was newly mined gold; Britain contributed to the provision of liquidity only insofar as its financial stature encouraged other countries to augment their specie holdings with sterling reserves. After World War II, U.S. economic power similarly rendered dollars a desirable form in which to acquire liquid reserves, but the same factors that made dollars desirable also rendered them difficult to obtain.

The Lender of Last Resort

If adjustment were always accomplished smoothly and liquidity were consistently adequate, there would be no need for an interna-tional lender of last resort to stabilize the international monetary sys-tem. Yet countries' capacity to adjust and the system's ability to provide liquidity may be inadequate to accommodate disturbances to confi-dence. Like domestic banking systems, an international financial sys-tem based on convertibility is vulnerable to problems of confidence that threaten to ignite speculative runs. Like depositors who rush to close their accounts upon receiving the news of a neighboring bank failure, exchange market participants, upon hearing of a convertibility crisis abroad, may rush to liquidate their foreign exchange balances because of incomplete information about the liabilities and intentions of particular governments. This analogy leads Charles Kindleberger, for example, to adopt from the domestic central banking literature the notion that a lender of last resort is needed to discount in times of crisis, provide countercyclical long-term lending, and maintain an open market for distress goods, and to suggest that, in the absence of a supranational institution, only a hegemonic power can carry out this international lender-of-last-resort function on the requisite scale.[67]

Of the episodes considered here, the early Bretton Woods era provides the clearest illustration of the benefits of an international lender of last resort. The large amount of credit provided Europe in the form of grants and long-term loans and the willingness of the United States to accept European and Japanese exports even when these had been promoted by the extension of special incentives illustrate two of the lender-of-last-resort functions identified by Kindleberger: countercyclical lending and provision of an open market for distress goods. Many histories of the Marshall Plan characterize it in terms consistent with the benevolent strand of hegemonic stability theory: the United States was mainly interested in European prosperity and stood to benefit only insofar as that prosperity promoted geopolitical stability. Revisionist histories have more in common with the coercive strand of hegemonic stability theory: they suggest that the United States used Marshall aid to exact concessions from Europe in the form of most-favored-nation status for Germany, IMF exchange rate oversight, and Swiss links with the Organization for European Economic Cooperation.[68] While it is certain that the European countries could not have moved so quickly to relax capital controls and quantitative trade restrictions without these forms of U.S. assistance, it is not clear how far the argument can be generalized. The Marshall Plan coincided with a very special era in the history of the international monetary system, in which convertibility outside the United States had not yet been restored. Hence there was little role for the central function of the lender of last resort: discounting freely when a convertibility crisis threatens.[69] When convertibility was threatened in the 1960s, rescue operations were mounted not by the United States but cooperatively by the Group of Ten.

Kindleberger has argued that the 1929–31 financial crisis might have been avoided by the intervention of an international lender of last resort. The unwillingness of Britain and the United States to engage in countercyclical long-term lending and to provide an open market for distress goods surely exacerbated convertibility crises in the non-European world. Both the curtailment of overseas lending and the imposition of restrictive trade policies contributed greatly to the balance-of-payments difficulties that led to the suspension of convertibility by primary producers as early as 1929.[70] Gold movements from the periphery to London and New York in 1930 heightened the problem and hastened its spread to Central Europe.

But it is not obvious that additional U.S. loans to Britain and other European countries attempting to fend off threats to convertibility would have succeeded in altering significantly the course of the 1931 financial crisis. Heading off the crisis would have required a successful defense of the pound sterling, whose depreciation was followed almost immediately by purposeful devaluation in some two dozen other countries. Britain did succeed in obtaining a substantial amount of short-term credit abroad in support of the pound, raising $650 million in New York and Paris after only minimal delay. Total short-term lending to countries under pressure amounted to approximately $1 billion, or roughly 10 percent of total international short-term indebtedness and 5 percent of world imports (more than the ratio of total IMF quotas to world imports in the mid-1970s).[71] It is noteworthy that these credits were obtained not from a dominant power but from a coalition of creditor countries.

Could additional short-term credits from an international lender of last resort have prevented Britain's suspension of convertibility? If the run on sterling reflected merely a temporary loss of confidence in the stability of fixed parities, then additional loans from an international lender of last resort—like central bank loans to temporarily illiquid banks—might have permitted the crisis to be surmounted. But if the loss of confidence had a basis in economic fundamentals, no amount of short-term lending would have done more than delay the crisis in the absence of measures to eliminate the underlying imbalance. The existence of an international lender of last resort could have affected the timing but not the fact of collapse.

The fundamental disequilibrium that undermined confidence in sterling is typically sought in the government budget. The argument is that by stimulating absorption, Britain's budget deficit, in conjunction with the collapse of foreign demand for British exports, weakened the balance of trade. Although the second Labour government fell in 1931 precisely because of its failure to agree on measures to reduce the size of the budget deficit, historians disagree over whether the budget contributed significantly to the balance-of-payments deficit.[72] The trade balance, after all, was only one component of the balance of payments. The effect on the balance of payments of shocks to the trade balance appears to have been small compared with the Bank of England's capacity to attract short-term capital. If this is correct and the 1931 financial crisis in Britain reflected mainly a temporary loss of confidence in sterling rather than a fundamental disequilibrium, then additional short-term loans from the United States or a group of creditor countries might have succeeded in tiding Britain over the crisis. But the loans required would have been extremely large by the standards of either the pre-1914 period of British hegemony or the post-1944 period of U.S. dominance.

The international lender-of-last-resort argument is more difficult to apply to the classical gold standard. Cohen asserts that the three lender-of-last-resort functions identified by Kindleberger—maintaining an open market, providing countercyclical foreign lending, and discounting freely in times of crisis—were practiced by Britain before 1913.[73] But, according to Moggridge, Kindleberger argues the opposite: that under the classical gold standard certain international crises, like that of 1873, were rendered severe by the absence of an international lender of last resort.[74] By my reading, Kindleberger's views are more circumspect. He examines whether international loans were solicited and whether their extension might have moderated the 1873 crisis. But he notes that in 1873, as in 1890 and 1907, the hegemonic monetary authority, the Bank of England, would have been the "borrower of last resort" rather than the lender. These facts might be reconciled with the theory of hegemonic stability if the lender, Paris, is elevated to the status of a hegemonic financial center—a possibility to which Kindleberger is led by his analysis of late nineteenth century financial crises. But elevating Paris to parity with London would do much to undermine the view of the classical gold standard that attributes its durability to management by a single financial center.

What does this historical analysis of the lender-of-last-resort function imply for the validity of hegemonic theories of international monetary stability? It confirms that there have been instances, notably the aftermath of World War II, when the economic power of the leading country so greatly surpassed that of all rivals that it succeeded in ensuring the system's stability in times of crisis by discounting freely, providing countercyclical lending, and maintaining an open market. It suggests, at the same time, that such instances are rare. For a leading economic power to effectively act as lender of last resort, not only must its market power exceed that of all rivals, but it must do so by a very substantial margin. British economic power in the 1870s and U.S. economic power in the 1960s were inadequate in this regard, and other economic powers—France in the first instance, the Group of Ten in the second—were needed to cooperate in providing lender-of-last-resort facilities.

The Dynamics of Hegemonic Decline

Might an international monetary system that depends for its smooth operation on the dominance of a hegemonic power be dynamically unstable? There are two channels through which dynamic instability might operate: the system itself might evolve in directions that attenuate the hegemon's stabilizing capacity; or the system might remain the same, but its operation might influence relative rates of economic growth in such a way as to progressively reduce the economic power and, by implication, the stabilizing capacity of the hegemon.[75]

The hypothesis that the Bretton Woods System was dynamically unstable was mooted by Robert Triffin as early as 1947.[76] Triffin focused on what he saw as inevitable changes in the composition of reserves, arguing that the system's viability hinged on the willingness of foreign governments to accumulate dollars, which depended in turn on confidence in the maintenance of dollar convertibility. Although gold dominated the dollar as a source of international liquidity (in 1958 the value of gold reserves was four times the value of dollar reserves when all countries were considered, two times when the United States was excluded), dollars were the main source of liquidity on the margin. Yet the willingness of foreign governments to accumulate dollars at the required pace and hence the stability of the gold-dollar system were predicated on America's commitment and capacity to maintain the convertibility of dollars into gold at $35 an ounce. The threat to its ability to do so was that, under a system in which reserves could take the form of either dollars or gold (a scarce natural resource whose supply was insufficiently elastic to keep pace with the demand for liquidity), the share of dollars in total reserves could only increase. An ever-growing volume of foreign dollar liabilities was based on a fixed or even shrinking U.S. gold reserve. Thus the very structure of Bretton Woods—specifically, the monetary role for gold—progressively undermined the hegemon's capacity to ensure the system's smooth operation through the provision of adequate liquidity.[77]

Dynamic instability also could have operated through the effect of the international monetary system on the relative rates of growth of the U.S. and foreign economies. If the dollar was systematically overvalued for a significant portion of the Bretton Woods era, this could have reduced the competitiveness of U.S. exports and stimulated foreign penetration of U.S. markets. If the dollar was overvalued due to some combination of European devaluations at the beginning of the 1950s, subsequent devaluations by developing countries, and the inability of the United States to respond to competitive difficulties by altering its exchange rate, how might this have depressed the relative rate of growth of the U.S. economy, leading to hegemonic decline? One can think of two arguments: one that proceeds along Heckscher-Ohlin lines, another that draws on dynamic theories of international trade.

The Heckscher-Ohlin hypothesis builds on the observation that the United States was relatively abundant in human and physical capital. Since, under Heckscher-Ohlin assumptions, U.S. exports were capital intensive, any measure that depressed exports would have reduced its rate of return. Reducing the rate of return would have discouraged investment, depressing the rate of economic growth and accelerating the U.S. economy's relative decline.

The dynamic trade theory hypothesis builds on the existence of learning curves in the production of traded goods. If production costs fall with cumulative output and the benefits of learning are external to the firm but internal to domestic industry, then exchange rate overvaluation, by depressing the competitiveness of exports, will inhibit their production and reduce the benefits of learning.[78] If overvaluation is sufficiently large and persistent, it will shift comparative advantage in production to foreign competitors. The weakness of this hypothesis is that it is predicated on the unsubstantiated assumption that learning effects are more important in the production of traded goods than nontraded goods. Its strength lies in the extent to which it conforms with informal characterizations of recent trends.

Precisely the same arguments have been applied to the downfall of the interwar gold exchange standard. The interwar system, which depended for liquidity on gold, dollars, and sterling, was if anything even more susceptible than its post–World War II analog to destabilization by the operation of Gresham's law. As noted above, the legacy of the Genoa conference encouraged central banks to accumulate foreign exchange. Promoting the use of exchange reserves while attempting to maintain gold convertibility threatened the system's stability for the same reasons as under Bretton Woods. But because foreign exchange reserves were not then concentrated in a single currency to the same extent as after World War II, it was even easier under the interwar system for central banks to liquidate foreign balances in response to any event that undermined confidence in sterling or the dollar. Instead of initiating the relatively costly and complex process of acquiring gold from foreign monetary authorities in the face of at least moral suasion to refrain, central banks needed only to swap one reserve currency for the other on the open market. Gresham's law operated even more powerfully when gold coexisted with two reserve currencies than with one.[79]

This instability manifested itself when the 1931 financial crisis, by undermining faith in sterling convertibility, induced a large-scale shift out of London balances. Once Britain was forced to devalue, faith in the stability of the other major reserve currency was shaken, and speculative pressure shifted to the dollar. The National Bank of Belgium, which had lost 25 percent of the value of its sterling reserve as a result of Britain's devaluation, moved to liquidate its dollar balances. The Eastern European countries, including Poland, Czechoslovakia, and Bulgaria, then liquidated their deposits in New York. Between the end of 1930 and the end of 1931, the share of foreign exchange in the reserve portfolios of twenty-three European countries fell from 35 to 19 percent, signaling the demise of the exchange portion of the gold exchange standard.

The argument that structuring the international monetary system around a reserve asset provided by the leading economic power led eventually to that country's loss of preeminence has been applied even more frequently to Britain after World War I than to the United States after World War II. Because the gold exchange standard created a foreign demand for sterling balances, Britain was able to run larger trade balance deficits than would have been permitted otherwise. In a sense, Britain's reserve currency status was one of the factors that facilitated the restoration of sterling's prewar parity. Despite an enormous literature predicated on the view that the pound was overvalued at $4.86, there remains skepticism that the extent of overvaluation was great or the effect on the macroeconomy was significant.[80] While it is not possible to resolve this debate here, the point relevant to the theory of hegemonic stability is that evidence of reserve currency overvaluation is as substantial in the earlier period, when hegemony was threatened, as in the later period, when it was triumphant.

Of the three monetary systems considered here, the classical gold standard is the most difficult to analyze in terms of the dynamics of hegemonic decline. It might be argued that the pound was overvalued for at least a decade before 1913 and that Britain's failure to devalue resulted in sluggish growth, which accelerated the economy's hegemonic decline.[81] The competitive difficulties of older British industries, notably iron and steel, and the decelerating rate of economic growth in the first decade of the twentieth century are consistent with this view.[82] The deceleration in the rate of British economic growth has been ascribed to both a decline in productivity growth and a fall in the rate of domestic capital formation.[83] This fall in the rate of domestic capital formation, especially after 1900, reflected not a decline in British savings rates but a surge of foreign investment. Thus, if Britain's hegemonic position in the international economy is to have caused its relative decline, this hegemony would have had to be responsible for the country's exceptionally high propensity to export capital. The volume of British capital exports in the decades preceding World War I has been attributed, alternatively, to the spread of industrialization and associated investment opportunities to other countries and continents and to imperfections in the structure of British capital markets that resulted in a bias toward investment overseas.[84] It is impossible to resolve this debate here. But the version of the market imperfections argument that attributes the London capital market's lack of interest in domestic investment to Britain's relatively early and labor-intensive form of industrialization implies that the same factors responsible for Britain's mid-nineteenth century hegemony (the industrial revolution occurred there first) may also have been responsible for the capital market biases that accelerated its hegemonic decline.

Although the classical gold standard experienced a number of serious disruptions, such as the 1907 panic when a financial crisis threatened to undermine its European core, the prewar system survived these disturbances intact. Eventually, however, the same forces that led to the downfall of the interwar gold exchange standard would have undermined the stability of the prewar system.[85] As the rate of economic growth continued to outstrip the rate of growth of gold (the supply of which was limited by the availability of ore), countries would have grown increasingly dependent on foreign exchange reserves as a source of incremental liquidity. As in the 1960s, growing reliance on exchange reserves in the face of relatively inelastic gold supplies would have eventually proven incompatible with the reserve center's ability to maintain gold convertibility.

De Cecco argues that the situation was already beginning to unravel in the first decade of the twentieth century—that the Boer War sig-

naled the end of the long peace of the nineteenth century, thereby
undermining the willingness of potential belligerents to hold their reserves as deposits in foreign countries. "In the years following the Boer
War, the international monetary system once more showed a distinct
tendency towards becoming a pure gold standard. . . ."[86] More important for our purposes, he suggests that the system was destabilized by
the growth of U.S. economic power relative to that of Great Britain.
Given the experimental nature of U.S. Treasury efforts to accommodate seasonal variations in money demand, the United States relied
heavily on gold imports whenever economic conditions required an
increase in money supply, notably during harvest and planting sea-
sons.[87] When the demand for money increased, the United States imported gold, mainly from the Bank of England, which was charged
with pegging the sterling price of gold on the London market with a
gold reserve of only £30 million. As the American economy grew, both
its average demand for gold from London and that demand's seasonal
fluctuation increased relative to the Bank of England's primary reserve
and its capacity to attract supplementary funds from other centers. To
rephrase de Cecco's argument in terms of hegemonic stability theory,
the growth of the United States relative to that of Britain undermined
Britain's capacity to stabilize international financial markets: specifically, its ability to serve simultaneously as the world's only free gold
market, providing however much gold was required by other countries,
and to maintain the stability of sterling, the reference point for the
global system of fixed exchange rates. In a sense, de Cecco sees indi-
cations of the interwar stalemate—a Britain incapable of stabilizing
the international system and a United States unwilling to do so—
emerging in the first decade of the twentieth century. From this perspective, the process of hegemonic decline that culminated in the international monetary difficulties of the interwar years was at most accelerated by World War I. Even before the war, the processes that led
to the downfall of established monetary arrangements were already
under way.

Conclusion

Much of the international relations literature concerned with prospects for international monetary reform can be read as a search for an
alternative to hegemony as a basis for international monetary stability.

Great play is given to the contrast between earlier periods of hegemonic dominance, notably 1890–1914 and 1945–71, and the nature of the task presently confronting aspiring architects of international monetary institutions in an increasingly multipolar world. In this paper I suggest that hegemonic stability theories are helpful for understanding the relatively smooth operation of the classical gold standard and the early Bretton Woods system, as well as some of the difficulties of the interwar years. At the same time, much of the evidence is difficult to reconcile with the hegemonic stability view. Even when individual countries occupied positions of exceptional prominence in the world economy and that prominence was reflected in the form and functioning of the international monetary system, that system was still fundamentally predicated on international collaboration. Keohane's notion of "hegemonic cooperation"—that cooperation is required for systemic stability even in periods of hegemonic dominance, although the presence of a hegemon may encourage cooperative behavior—seems directly applicable to international monetary relations. The importance of collaboration is equally apparent in the design of the international monetary system, its operation under normal circumstances, and the management of crises. Despite the usefulness of hegemonic stability theory when applied to short periods and well-defined aspects of international monetary relations, the international monetary system has always been "after hegemony" in the sense that more than a dominant economic power was required to ensure the provision and maintenance of international monetary stability. Moreover, it was precisely when important economic power most forcefully conditioned the form of the international system that the potential for instability, in a dynamic sense, was greatest. Above all, historical experience demonstrates the speed and pervasiveness of changes in national economic power; since hegemony is transitory, so must be any international monetary system that takes hegemony as its basis. Given the costs of international monetary reform, it would seem unwise to predicate a new system on such a transient basis.

Notes

1. See Mancur Olson, Jr., and Richard Zeckhauser, "An Economic Theory of Alliances," *Review of Economics and Statistics*, vol. 48 (August 1966), pp. 266–79.

2. I refer to this as "the theory of hegemonic stability," a phrase coined by Robert O. Keohane, "The Theory of Hegemonic Stability and Changes in International Economic Regimes, 1967–1977," in Ole R. Holsti, Randolph M. Siverson, and Alexander L. George, eds., *Change in the International System* (Westview, 1980), pp. 131–62. In Keohane's words, the theory of hegemonic stability posits that "hegemonic structures of power, dominated by a single country, are most conducive to the development of strong international regimes whose rules are relatively precise and well obeyed" (p. 132). See Robert Gilpin, *U.S. Power and the Multinational Corporation: The Political Economy of Foreign Direct Investment* (Basic Books, 1975); Stephen D. Krasner, "State Power and the Structure of International Trade," *World Politics*, vol. 28 (April 1976), pp. 317–47; Peter F. Cowhey and Edward Long, "Testing Theories of Regime Change: Hegemonic Decline or Surplus Capacity?" *International Organization*, vol. 37 (Spring 1983), pp. 157–88; Joanne Gowa, "Hegemons, IOs, and Markets: The Case of the Substitution Account," *International Organization*, vol. 38 (Autumn 1984), pp. 661–83; Charles Lipson, "The Transformation of Trade: The Sources and Effects of Regime Changes," *International Organization*, vol. 36 (Spring 1982), pp. 417–56; Duncan Snidal, "The Limits of Hegemonic Stability Theory," *International Organization*, vol. 39 (Autumn 1985), pp. 579–614; Arthur A. Stein, "The Hegemon's Dilemma: Great Britain, the United States, and the International Economic Order," *International Organization*, vol. 38 (Spring 1984), pp. 355–86; and Beth V. Yarbrough and Robert M. Yarbrough, "Free Trade, Hegemony, and the Theory of Agency," *Kyklos*, vol. 38, no. 3 (1985), pp. 348–64.

3. Attempts to test the applicability of hegemonic stability theory have considered international trade policy. See Krasner, "State Power and the Structure of International Trade"; John A. C. Conybeare, "Tariff Protection in Developed and Developing Countries: A Cross-Sectional and Longitudinal Analysis," *International Organization*, vol. 37 (Summer 1983), pp. 441–67; Fred Lawson, "Hegemony and the Structure of International Trade Reassessed: A View from Arabia," *International Organization*, vol. 37 (Spring 1983), pp. 317–37; Timothy J. McKeown, "Hegemonic Stability Theory and 19th Century Tariff Levels in Europe," *International Organization*, vol. 37 (Winter 1983), pp. 73–91; and David A. Lake, *Power, Protection and Free Trade: International Sources of U.S. Commercial Strategy, 1887–1939* (Cornell University Press, 1988). Attempts to do such testing also have considered international investment. See, for example, Gilpin, *U.S. Power and the Multinational Corporation*. For attempts to test applicability to international monetary arrangements, see Robert O. Keohane, "Inflation and the Decline of American Power," in Raymond E. Lombra and Willard E. Witte, eds., *Political Economy of International and Domestic Monetary Relations* (Iowa State University Press, 1982), pp. 7–24; John S. Odell, "Bretton Woods and International Political Disintegration: Implications for Monetary Diplomacy," in ibid., pp. 39–58; and Kenneth A. Oye, "The Sterling-Dollar-Franc Triangle: Monetary Diplomacy 1929–1937," in Kenneth A. Oye, ed., *Cooperation under Anarchy* (Princeton University Press, 1986), pp. 173–99. Finally, such attempts have also considered international administration of world oil prices. See Keohane, "The

Theory of Hegemonic Stability," and Robert O. Keohane, *After Hegemony: Cooperation and Discord in the World Political Economy* (Princeton University Press, 1984). The theory's popularity was stimulated by Charles Kindleberger's argument, following William Adams Brown, that the international financial system and macroeconomic environment of the interwar years were destabilized by lack of leadership by a dominant economic power willing to provide the public good of international monetary stability by acting as international lender of last resort. See Charles P. Kindleberger, *The World in Depression, 1929–1939* (University of California, 1973); and William Adams Brown, Jr., *The International Gold Standard Reinterpreted, 1914–1934*, 2 vols. (New York: National Bureau of Economic Research, 1940).

4. C. Fred Bergsten, *Toward a New International Economic Order: Selected Papers of C. Fred Bergsten, 1972–1974* (Lexington Books, 1975), p. 31.

5. See Snidal, "Limits of Hegemonic Stability Theory," pp. 581–82.

6. Alternatives to this definition are offered by Jeffrey Hart, "Three Approaches to the Measurement of Power in International Relations," *International Organization*, vol. 30 (Spring 1976), pp. 289–305.

7. The concept of regime was introduced into the international relations literature by John Gerard Ruggie, "International Responses to Technology: Concepts and Trends," *International Organization*, vol. 29 (Summer 1975), pp. 557–83. For critical analyses of its uses, see Oran R. Young, "International Regimes: Problems of Concept Formation," *World Politics*, vol. 32 (April 1980), pp. 331–56; and Susan Strange, "Still an Extraordinary Power: America's Role in a Global Monetary System," in Lombra and Witte, eds., *Political Economy of International and Domestic Monetary Relations*, pp. 73–93. Keohane, "The Theory of Hegemonic Stability," p. 132, defines a regime as "the norms, rules, and procedures that guide the behavior of states and other important actors." Since my method of analysis does not hinge on a particular definition of the international monetary regime, it is compatible with a range of alternative definitions. I prefer to distinguish between the monetary system, which is made up of a set of explicit rules and procedures (pegging rules, intervention strategies, IMF statutes governing reserve availability, for example), and the international monetary regime as a broader framework that incorporates the explicit rules constituting the system but embeds them within a set of implicit understandings about how economic policymakers will behave (promises to coordinate macroeconomic policies or to provide loans in times of convertibility crisis, for example). Thus, while the compass of the international monetary system is limited to matters that impinge directly on monetary affairs, the international monetary regime may involve issues that impinge indirectly, such as trade policy or diplomatic action. In effect, I am distinguishing between the monetary "system" and "regime" in the same way that the monetary "system" and "order" were distinguished by Robert A. Mundell, "The Future of the International Financial System," in A. L. K. Acheson, J. F. Chant, and M. F. J. Prachowny, eds., *Bretton Woods Revisited* (University of Toronto Press, 1972), pp. 91–104.

8. See James March, "The Power of Power," in David Easton, ed., *Varieties of Political Theory* (Prentice-Hall, 1966), pp. 39–70.

9. For discussions of issue linkage, see Richard N. Cooper, "Trade Policy Is Foreign Policy," *Foreign Policy*, no. 9 (Winter 1972–73), pp. 18–36; and Ernst B. Haas, "Why Collaborate? Issue-Linkage and International Regimes," *World Politics*, vol. 32 (April 1980), pp. 357–405.

10. See Kindleberger, *The World in Depression*, p. 28; and Keohane, "The Theory of Hegemonic Stability," p. 136.

11. For example, Kindleberger, *The World in Depression*, is primarily concerned with the role of hegemony in ensuring the smooth operation of an extant system, while Gilpin, *U.S. Power and the Multinational Corporation*, and Krasner, "State Power and the Structure of International Trade," focus instead on the role of hegemony in system design and formation. Similar distinctions are emphasized by Stein, "The Hegemon's Dilemma."

12. In *U.S. Power and the Multinational Corporation*, p. 5, Gilpin's characterization is a bit strong: "Economists do not really believe in power; political scientists, for their part, do not really believe in markets."

13. A limited parallel is the International Monetary Conference of 1881, which brought together the members of the Latin Monetary Union, discussed below. Another candidate is the conference that resulted from the U.S. Bland-Allison Act of 1878, which instructed the president to invite members of the Latin Monetary Union and other European countries to a conference intended to result in mutual adoption of a bimetallic system based on a common ratio of silver to gold. See A. Barton Hepburn, *A History of Currency in the United States*, rev. ed. (Macmillan, 1924).

14. Although German politicians had previously perceived the country's silver standard as beneficial to the development of its Eastern European trade, by 1870 most of that region had suspended convertibility. Germany used the proceeds of the indemnity received as victor in the Franco-Prussian War to purchase gold on the world market, thereby contributing to the ongoing rise in its price. Silver inflation led to the suspension of silver coinage and convertibility by Holland, Denmark, Norway, Sweden, France, and the countries of the Latin Monetary Union (Belgium, Switzerland, Italy, and Greece), making gold the basis for the monetary standard in every European country except those that retained inconvertible paper. In 1879 the United States ended the greenback period, and Russia and Japan restored gold convertibility. While neither Italy nor the Hapsburg monarchy adopted formal convertibility, from the turn of the century both pegged their currencies to gold. Further details may be found in Barry Eichengreen, ed., *The Gold Standard in Theory and History* (London: Methuen, 1985).

15. See Marcello de Cecco, *The International Gold Standard: Money and Empire*, 2d ed. (London: Frances Pinter, 1984), p. 239.

16. A third option, maintaining bimetallism but raising the relative price of gold, had been discredited by the difficulties of the Latin Monetary Union and evoked little enthusiasm when advocated by the United States at the international conference convened under the provisions of the Bland-Allison Act of 1878. Contemporaries recognized that international cooperation was necessary for the successful functioning of a bimetallic system. The more countries that participated in a bimetallic system, the greater the probability that their

common mint ratio would dominate the market ratio. But of the major countries, only the United States and Italy favored immediate adoption of a global bimetallic standard. While France, Holland, and Austria also favored bimetallism, they viewed its immediate implementation on a global basis as impractical. Germany, Belgium, and the Scandinavian states favored immediate adoption of the gold standard, Germany so strongly that it boycotted the conference. The record of conference proceedings is found in *International Monetary Conferences Held in Paris, in August 1878*, Senate Executive Doc. 58, 45 Cong. 3 sess. (Government Printing Office, 1879). Also see Henry B. Russell, *International Monetary Conferences* (Harper and Brothers, 1898).

17. In 1850 Belgium and Swiss silver coins were new and full-bodied, in contrast to French coins, which had lost up to 8 percent of their silver content through wear. Hence French coins were exported to Belgium and Switzerland, while Belgium coins were exported to Germany and the Netherlands. In 1862 Italy adopted a bimetallic standard, but the country's silver coins were only 0.835 percent pure and hence ended up being shipped to France. The confusion that resulted convinced the countries involved to adopt a common standard that entailed the French parity of 15½ ounces of silver per ounce of gold and silver coins that were 0.835 percent pure. See Henry Parker Willis, *A History of The Latin Monetary Union: A Study of International Monetary Action* (University of Chicago Press, 1901).

18. Harry D. White, *The French International Accounts, 1880–1913* (Harvard University Press, 1933), pp. 182–200.

19. Arthur I. Bloomfield, *Monetary Policy under the International Gold Standard: 1880–1914* (Federal Reserve Bank of New York, 1959), pp. 13–15.

20. These are reviewed by Dean E. Traynor, *International Monetary and Financial Conferences in the Interwar Period* (Catholic University of America Press, 1949).

21. A more politically oriented assessment of policymakers' objectives is provided by Frank Costigliola, *Awkward Dominion: American Political, Economic, and Cultural Relations with Europe, 1919–1933* (Cornell University Press, 1984).

22. For further discussion of Strong and the American position, see Stephen V. O. Clarke, "The Reconstruction of the International Monetary System: The Attempts of 1922 and 1933," *Princeton Studies in International Finance*, no. 33 (Princeton University, Department of Economics, November 1973).

23. Frank Costigliola, "Anglo-American Financial Rivalry in the 1920s," *Journal of Economic History*, vol. 37 (December 1977), pp. 911–34; and Traynor, *International Monetary and Financial Conferences*, p. 72.

24. For the text of the resolution and related correspondence, see United Kingdom, *International Economic Conference, Genoa, Papers Presented to Parliament by Command of His Majesty, April-May 1922*, Cmd. 1667 (London: His Majesty's Stationery Office, 1922).

25. Details are provided in Barry Eichengreen, "International Policy Coordination in Historical Perspective: A View from the Interwar Years," in Willem H. Buiter and Richard C. Marston, eds., *International Economic Policy Coordination* (Cambridge University Press, 1985), pp. 151–52.

26. The significance of the Genoa resolutions is discussed at greater length in Barry Eichengreen, "The Gold-Exchange Standard and the Great Depression," in *Elusive Stability: Essays in the History of International Finance, 1919–1939* (Cambridge University Press, forthcoming), chap. 10.

27. In the immediate post–World War II period, the United States produced a majority of the global industrial output of the capital goods and equipment needed for economic reconstruction abroad. It was the largest holder of gold and the major creditor on long-term capital account. Observers anticipated that its creditor position would strengthen yet further as the United States continued to finance deficit spending for European reconstruction. Such observations lead Keohane to conclude that the extent of American predominance after World War II was unprecedented, unmatched even by Britain before World War I (*After Hegemony*, pp. 36–37).

28. See R. S. Sayers, *Financial Policy, 1939–1945* (London: Her Majesty's Stationery Office and Longmans, Green, 1956), pp. 438–40; and Alec Cairncross and Barry Eichengreen, *Sterling in Decline: The Devaluations of 1931, 1949 and 1967* (Oxford: Basil Blackwell, 1983), chap. 4.

29. See, in particular, J. Keith Horsefield, ed., *The International Monetary Fund, 1945–1965: Twenty Years of International Monetary Cooperation*, 3 vols. (International Monetary Fund, 1969); and Richard N. Gardner, *Sterling-Dollar Diplomacy: The Origins and Prospects of Our International Economic Order* (McGraw-Hall, 1969).

30. Horsefield, *International Monetary Fund*, vol. 3, p. 26.

31. See, for example, Benjamin J. Cohen, "Balance-of-Payments Financing: Evolution of a Regime," in Stephen D. Krasner, ed., *International Regimes* (Cornell University Press, 1983), pp. 315–36.

32. Kenneth W. Dam, *The Rules of the Game: Reform and Evolution in the International Monetary System* (University of Chicago Press, 1982), p. 92.

33. Brian Tew, *The Evolution of the International Monetary System, 1945–88*, 4th ed. (London: Hutchinson, 1988), p. 99.

34. Fund procedures also represented a compromise between the British preference for free access to fund resources and the American preference for conditionality. The Articles of Agreement flatly stated that a country "shall be entitled" to buy currency from the IMF providing only that currency is needed for purposes consistent with the fund agreement. Initially it was unclear whether the fund had legal authority to make borrowing subject to conditions. But in 1948 the IMF's Board of Executive Directors asserted its right to limit access to fund reserves if the member was using its resources in a manner contrary to the purposes of the organization and to make that access subject to conditions. The conditionality that evolved treated access to successive credit tranches in different ways. While attempts to borrow in the gold tranche would receive "the overwhelming benefit of any doubt," access to higher tranches would be subject to increasingly stringent conditions. Horsefield, *International Monetary Fund*, vol. 3, p. 230.

35. This portrayal of Bretton Woods as neither an American triumph nor a defeat is at variance with characterizations of it as a construct of the American hegemon. But it is not inconsistent with the view that, as a compromise be-

tween the Keynes and White plans, it "contained less of the Keynes and more of the White plans." Sidney E. Rolfe, *Gold and World Power: The Dollar, the Pound, and the Plans for Reform* (Harper and Row, 1966), p. 78.

36. Benjamin J. Cohen, *Organizing the World's Money: The Political Economy of International Monetary Relations* (Basic Books, 1977), p. 81 (italics in original).

37. David Williams, "The Evolution of the Sterling System" in C. R. Whittlesey and J. S. G. Wilson, *Essays in Money and Banking in Honour of R. S. Sayers* (Oxford: Clarendon Press, 1968), p. 268.

38. Peter H. Lindert, "Key Currencies and Gold 1900–1913," *Princeton Studies in International Finance*, no. 24 (Princeton University, Department of Economics, August 1969), pp. 56–57.

39. Of course, the bank might have to intervene with purchases or sales of bills and bonds to render its rate effective. R. S. Sayers, *Bank of England Operations, 1890–1914* (London: P. S. King and Son, 1936), chap. 2.

40. This brief account draws on Donald E. Moggridge, *British Monetary Policy, 1924–1931: The Norman Conquest of $4.86* (Cambridge University Press, 1972), pp. 8–9.

41. Harold van B. Cleveland, "The International Monetary System in the Interwar Period," in Benjamin M. Rowland, ed., *Balance of Power or Hegemony: The Interwar Monetary System* (New York University Press, 1976), p. 17 (italics in original).

42. Committee on Finance and Industry, *Report* (London: HMSO, 1931), p. 125.

43. John Maynard Keynes, *A Treatise on Money*, vol. 2: *The Applied Theory of Money* (London: Macmillan, 1930), pp. 306–07. Evidence to this effect is presented by Barry Eichengreen, "Conducting the International Orchestra: Bank of England Leadership under the Classical Gold Standard," *Journal of International Money and Finance*, vol. 6 (March 1987), pp. 5–29. Regression results reported there reveal that, while the Bank of England's discount rate was responsive to changes in French and German rates, the influence of the Bank of England rate over foreign rates was stronger and more systematic.

44. As R. S. Sayers, *Central Banking after Bagehot* (Oxford: Clarendon Press, 1957), p. 61, described the British case, while the Bank of England was "a little sensitive to the state of trade," in deciding whether to change the bank rate it "looked almost exclusively at the size of its reserve." An extensive literature analyzes the extent to which central banks of the classical gold standard era adhered to the rules of the game, which dictated that they should adjust their policies in order to bring about external balance. In the classic study, Bloomfield (*Monetary Policy under the International Gold Standard*) revealed that external considerations were by no means the sole determinant of monetary policies before 1913. But if central banks were in fact responsive to internal considerations, this raises the question of how they managed to defend their gold standard parities. A more recent study emphasizes the distinction between short-run and long-run policy responses and concludes that in the short run the Bank of England may have hesitated to take the steps needed to restore external balance and neutralize gold outflows, but in the long run the

goal of maintaining the gold standard dominated, leading the bank to reverse its initial sterilization of gold flows to ensure that external balance would be restored. See John Pippenger, "Bank of England Operations, 1893–1913," in Michael D. Bordo and Anna J. Schwartz, eds., *A Retrospective on the Classical Gold Standard, 1821–1931* (University of Chicago Press, 1984), pp. 203–22.

45. See A. G. Ford, *The Gold Standard, 1880–1914: Britain and Argentina* (Oxford: Clarendon Press, 1962); and Robert Triffin, "The Myth and Realities of the So-called Gold Standard," in Eichengreen, ed., *Gold Standard in Theory and History*, pp. 121–40.

46. See, for example, Benjamin Cohen, *The Future of Sterling as an International Currency* (London: Macmillan, 1971).

47. Fred Hirsch, *Money International* (London: Allen Lane Penguin Press, 1967), p. 28.

48. As I indicated at the beginning of this paper, I define the strong form of hegemonic stability theory as the benefits of stability accruing to both the hegemon and other countries and the weak form as benefits accruing only to the hegemon. It is tempting to suggest a parallel between this "collective hegemony of the center countries" and the argument by Joanne Gowa, which she attributes to Keohane and Snidal, that even in the absence of a hegemon the public good of collective stability might still be provided so long as the number of countries is sufficiently small for them to solve the free-rider problem. See Gowa, "Hegemons, IOs, and Markets." But the case considered here differs in that instability, rather than being eliminated, is shifted onto countries that are not members of the hegemonic cartel.

49. Edward Nevin, *The Mechanism of Cheap Money: A Study of British Monetary Policy, 1931–1939* (Cardiff: University of Wales Press, 1955), p. 12.

50. On the United States, see Elmus R. Wicker, *Federal Reserve Monetary Policy, 1917–1933* (Random House, 1966). On the United Kingdom, see Barry Eichengreen, Mark W. Watson, and Richard S. Grossman, "Bank Rate Policy under the Interwar Gold Standard: A Dynamic Probit Model," *Economic Journal*, vol. 95 (September 1985), pp. 725–45. A general discussion of the growing conflict between the needs of internal and external balance is provided by J. W. Beyen, *Money in a Maelstrom* (Macmillan, 1949), chap. 2.

51. This was advocated by, among others, Milton Gilbert, "The Gold-Dollar System: Conditions of Equilibrium and the Price of Gold," in Eichengreen, ed., *Gold Standard in Theory and History*, pp. 229–49; and Roy Harrod, "Triple the Dollar Price of Gold," reprinted in Gerald M. Meier, *Problems of a World Monetary Order*, 2d ed. (New York: Oxford University Press, 1982), pp. 107–08.

52. See R. Duncan Luce and Howard Raiffa, *Games and Decisions: Introduction and Critical Survey* (Wiley, 1957).

53. This problem is referred to as a "coordination game," by Duncan Snidal, "Coordination versus Prisoners' Dilemma: Implications for International Cooperation and Regimes," *American Political Science Review*, vol. 79 (December 1985), pp. 923–42.

54. The leading exponent of the gold shortage explanation was Gustav Cassel. For a summary of his views, see Gustav Cassel, *The Crisis in the World's*

Monetary System (Oxford: Clarendon Press, 1932); and for a critical perspective, Charles O. Hardy, *Is There Enough Gold?* (Brookings, 1936). The argument here draws on Eichengreen, "The Gold-Exchange Standard and the Great Depression."

55. The most compelling argument for returning to gold cited the importance of the prewar parity for the maintenance of Britain's position in international transactions—specifically, its importance for maintaining London's preeminent position in international finance. See Donald E. Moggridge, *The Return to Gold, 1925: The Formulation of Economic Policy and Its Critics* (Cambridge University Press, 1969).

56. Gold inflows into France can be attributed to stabilization of the franc at an undervalued rate in 1926 in conjunction with statutory limitations that prevented the Banque de France from expanding the domestic credit component of the money supply through open market operations. Inflows into the United States can be attributed to the misguided policies of the Federal Reserve: initially, its failure to moderate the Wall Street boom responsible for curtailing U.S. foreign investment and for inducing capital inflows into the United States; and subsequently, its failure to prevent the contraction of the money supply, which created an excess demand for money that could be met only by gold inflows. On French policy, see Barry Eichengreen, "The Bank of France and the Sterilization of Gold, 1926–1932," *Explorations in Economic History*, vol. 23 (January 1986), pp. 56–84. On the controversy over U.S. policy, see Milton Friedman and Anna Jacobson Schwartz, *A Monetary History of the United States, 1867–1960* (Princeton University Press, 1963); and Wicker, *Federal Reserve Monetary Policy, 1917–1933*.

57. Committee on Finance and Industry, *Report.*

58. See Barry Eichengreen, "Central Bank Cooperation under the Interwar Gold Standard," *Explorations in Economic History*, vol. 21 (January 1984), pp. 64–87; and Eichengreen, "International Policy Coordination in Historical Perspective."

59. John Maynard Keynes, "Is There Enough Gold? The League of Nations Inquiry," in Donald Moggridge, ed., *The Collected Writings of John Maynard Keynes: Activities 1922–1929: The Return to Gold and Industrial Policy*, pt. 2 (Cambridge University Press, 1981), pp. 775–80.

60. Jacob Viner, "International Aspects of the Gold Standard," in Quincy Wright, ed., *Gold and Monetary Stabilization* (University of Chicago Press, 1932), p. 28; and A. D. Gayer, *Monetary Policy and Economic Stabilization: A Study of the Gold Standard* (London: Black, 1937), p. 29.

61. As one Bank of England official put it, "Such leadership as we possessed has certainly been affected by the position which America has gained." Macmillan Committee evidence of Sir Ernest Harvey, reprinted in Richard S. Sayers, *The Bank of England, 1891–1944*, appendixes (Cambridge University Press, 1976), p. 206.

62. Statistics are drawn from IMF publications, notably the *Annual Reports.*

63. The evidence typically invoked is that the Johnson administration financed the Vietnam War without a tax increase until 1968, and that except for 1969 monetary policy was expansionary over much of the period.

64. The size of the deficit, if not its existence, served as a significant constraint on policy. For example, when the dollar price of gold on the London market rose above the U.S. Treasury's selling price in 1960, inducing foreign monetary authorities to purchase substantial amounts of U.S. gold, the Eisenhower administration responded by reducing the number of military dependents abroad, cutting back foreign Defense Department procurement, and tying U.S. development assistance to American exports. Restrictions on capital outflows, including the interest equalization tax, the voluntary foreign credit restraint programs, and the foreign direct investment program, were imposed from 1963. As Tew, *The Evolution of the International Monetary System, 1945–88*, put it, U.S. authorities "were not conspicuously less ready than those of other deficit countries to adopt measures to prevent [the deficit] getting worse" (p. 71).

65. The most notable instance of the use of U.S. power—clearly an illustration of the stick variant of hegemonic stability theory—was in 1967 when Germany explicitly agreed to forgo any future conversions of dollars in U.S. gold in response to American threats to reduce troop levels in Europe. See Bergsten, *Toward a New International Economic Order*, chap. 4.

66. The world was reminded of the difficulties posed by the free-rider problem confronting efforts to supply a public good when Algeria purchased $150 million of gold from the United States in 1967, "presumably at French instigation." Robert Solomon, *The International Monetary System, 1945–1976: An Insider's View* (Harper and Row, 1977), p. 115.

67. See Kindleberger, *The World in Depression;* and Kindleberger, *Manias, Panics, and Crashes: A History of Financial Crises* (Basic Books, 1978).

68. See the discussion in Alan S. Milward, *The Reconstruction of Western Europe, 1945–51* (University of California Press, 1984), pp. 113–25.

69. The notable exception to this generalization is the abortive attempt to restore sterling convertibility in 1947, which was taken at the hegemon's insistence and failed in part because the United States was unwilling to supply the funds needed to defend sterling. See Cairncross and Eichengreen, *Sterling in Decline*, chap. 4; and Milward, *The Reconstruction of Western Europe*, chap. 1.

70. The links between foreign lending, foreign trade, and currency convertibility in this period are analyzed by Barry Eichengreen and Richard Portes, "The Anatomy of Financial Crises," in Richard Portes and Alexander K. Swoboda, eds., *Threats to International Financial Stability* (Cambridge University Press, 1987), pp. 10–58.

71. These calculations are drawn from Donald E. Moggridge, "Financial Crises and Lenders of Last Resort: Policy in the Crisis of 1920 and 1929," *Journal of European Economic History*, vol. 10 (1981), p. 66.

72. Moggridge, "The 1931 Financial Crisis," argues yes, while Cairncross and Eichengreen, *Sterling in Decline*, argue no, largely on the basis of econometric simulations.

73. Cohen, *Organizing the World's Money*, pp. 81–82.

74. Moggridge, "Financial Crises and Lenders of Last Resort," p. 49, citing Kindleberger, *Manias, Panics, and Crashes*, p. 188.

75. After writing this section, I discovered its resemblance, both in general

and in its particular emphasis on the role of foreign investment, to Gilpin, *U.S. Power and the Multinational Corporation.*

76. See Robert Triffin, "National Central Banking and the International Economy," *Postwar Economic Studies,* vol. 7 (Washington, D.C.: Board of Governors of the Federal Reserve System, 1947), pp. 46–81; Robert Triffin, *Gold and the Dollar Crisis: The Future of Convertibility* (Yale University Press, 1960); and Peter B. Kenen, *British Monetary Policy and the Balance of Payments, 1951–1957,* Harvard Economic Studies, vol. 66 (Harvard University Press, 1960).

77. See Triffin, *Gold and the Dollar Crisis.* For a conventional view, see Donald MacDougall, "The Dollar Problem: A Reappraisal," *Essays in International Finance,* no. 35 (Princeton University, Department of Economics, November 1960). Ironically, it was the hegemonic power—the United States—that had insisted on retaining a monetary role for gold at Bretton Woods. The British would have preferred to free themselves from dependence on yellow metal, so long as the clearing union rather than the United States regulated the creation of reserves. But the United States was suspicious that the clearing union might be an engine of inflation and would hesitate to demonetize gold just when it had accumulated a majority of world stocks. Given U.S. opposition to British plans for the large-scale creation of liquidity by the clearing union, the British had to settle for restraints on U.S. ability to unilaterally determine global liquidity in the form of a monetary role for gold.

78. See Paul Krugman, "The Narrow Moving Band, the Dutch Disease, and the Competitive Consequences of Mrs. Thatcher: Notes on Trade in the Presence of Dynamic Scale Economies," *Journal of Development Economics,* vol. 27 (October 1987), pp. 41–55; and Krugman, "Market Access and International Competition in High Technology: A Simulation Exercise," Massachusetts Institute of Technology, Department of Economics, 1985.

79. The same argument is advanced by Bergsten, *Toward a New International Economic Order,* chap. 4, although he suggests that the existence of a well-defined institutional framework can minimize this source of instability.

80. See John Maynard Keynes, "Is Sterling Over-Valued?" in Moggridge, ed., *Collected Writings of John Maynard Keynes: Activities, 1922–1929: The Return to Gold and Industrial Policy,* pt. 1, pp. 349–54. See also John Maynard Keynes, *The Economic Consequences of Sterling Parity* (Harcourt-Brace, 1925). A reassessment of Keynes's evidence is in Moggridge, *The Return to Gold, 1925.*

81. See R. C. O. Matthews, C. H. Feinstein, and J. C. Odling-Smee, *British Economic Growth, 1856–1973* (Stanford University Press, 1982), pp. 455, 526. N. F. R. Crafts, following James Foreman-Peck, suggests that learning by doing and its associated externalities were particularly important in the new traded-goods industries of the turn of the century, such as motor cars, implying that the dynamic effects emphasized by new trade theory may have also come into play. See N. F. R. Crafts, *British Economic Growth during the Industrial Revolution* (Oxford: Clarendon Press, 1985); and James S. Foreman-Peck, "Tariff Protection and Economies of Scale: The British Motor Industry before 1939," *Oxford Economic Papers,* vol. 31 (July 1979), pp. 237–57.

82. Donald N. McCloskey, "Did Victorian Britain Fail?" *Economic History Review*, vol. 23 (December 1970), table 2, pinpoints the deceleration in the rate of British economic growth as taking place in the first decade of the twentieth century. The traditional view of the British climacteric is also criticized by D. J. Coppock, "The Climacteric of the 1890's: A Critical Note," *The Manchester School of Economic and Social Studies*, vol. 24 (January 1956), pp. 1–31, but subsequently defended by W. P. Kennedy, "Foreign Investment, Trade and Growth in the United Kingdom, 1870–1913," *Explorations in Economic History*, vol. 11 (Summer 1974), pp. 415–44.

83. See Matthews and others, *British Economic Growth*, table 8.1, p. 222.

84. For the traditional view that emphasizes capital market imperfections, see the Committee on Finance and Industry, *Report;* Charles P. Kindleberger, *Economic Growth in France and Britain, 1851–1950* (Harvard University Press, 1964); or David S. Landes, *The Unbound Prometheus: Technological Change and Industrial Development in Western Europe from 1750 to the Present* (Cambridge University Press, 1969). The revisionist view is represented by McCloskey, "Did Victorian Britain Fail?"

85. In Charles Kindleberger's words, "The problem posed by Gresham's Law exists not only on the gold-exchange standard, but on the gold standard itself." Charles P. Kindleberger, *Power and Money: The Economics of International Politics and the Politics of International Economics* (Basic Books, 1970), p. 213. See also James D. Hamilton, "Role of the International Gold Standard in Propagating the Great Depression," *Contemporary Policy Issues*, vol. 6 (April 1988), pp. 67–89.

86. De Cecco, *The International Gold Standard*, p. 125.

87. At the beginning of the century, Treasury Secretary Leslie M. Shaw began managing public deposits in such a way as to provide some seasonal elasticity of money supply but these early efforts were modest and experimental. On the seasonality of U.S. money demand, see Barry Eichengreen, "Currency and Credit in the Gilded Age," in Gary Saxonhouse and Gavin Wright, eds., *Technique, Spirit and Form in the Making of the Modern Economies: Essays in Honor of William N. Parker* (Greenwich, Conn.: JAI Press, 1984), pp. 87–114.

Index